Dorothy Richardson

A BIOGRAPHY

GLORIA G. FROMM

UNIVERSITY OF ILLINOIS PRESS
Urbana, Chicago, London

PUBLICATION OF THIS WORK WAS SUPPORTED IN PART
BY A GRANT FROM THE ANDREW W. MELLON FOUNDATION

LIBRARY OF CONGRESS CATALOGING IN PUBLICATION DATA

Fromm, Gloria G., 1931–
  Dorothy Richardson.

  Bibliography: p.
  Includes index.
  1. Richardson, Dorothy Miller, 1873–1957.
2. Novelists, English—20th century—Biography.
I. Title.
PR6035.I34Z68   823'.9'12 [B]   77-8455
ISBN 0-252-00631-3

Dorothy Richardson

FOR NORAH AND EDWARD
OF ROSE COTTAGE, TREVONE

Contents

Part Four
1938–57

Illustrations

Preface

WITH the early "chapters" of *Pilgrimage,* which began to appear in 1915, Dorothy Richardson sounded a new note in fiction and as a result earned for herself both renown and notoriety. Her novel attracted attention at once, because in it its original readers heard the distinctive voice of modernism that was heard as well, in different keys and modes, in the work of James Joyce, D. H. Lawrence, Virginia Woolf, and Marcel Proust. Yet *Pilgrimage* also had an uncompromisingly single—and feminine—point of view that became more familiar and more exasperating as time passed.

There is no escaping the fact that even though most readers of fiction in the twenties and thirties knew who Miriam Henderson was, many found her exceedingly hard to take. With a penchant for observing nuance and detail that was admittedly Proustian, she nonetheless seemed critical of everything and everyone, of women as well as of men, of idol-worship as well as of idol-smashing; and all this made her anomalous, if not bewildering. To complicate matters more, it was difficult to tell just how much of the author was embodied in Dorothy Richardson's late-Victorian and Edwardian heroine. Was the presentation of her ironic or not? Was the point of view in fact as limited as it seemed? Had Dorothy Richardson's narrative method exhausted itself even before the novel was finished, or would a grand design emerge at last?

By 1938, on the eve of World War II, when a supposedly complete *Pilgrimage* was published in an omnibus edition of four volumes, none of the questions the novel had raised had been answered, but the world that had greeted it was not the same, and the spirit of the thirties dwelled in books other than Dorothy Richardson's. Expressing a minority view, the distinguished poet and translator Horace Gregory chose this moment to praise *Pilgrimage* as precisely the kind of balanced work he thought the world needed just then. In his review of the omnibus edition, Gregory described Dorothy Richardson's novel as a rarity in English prose, "a true and humanistic comedy." It did not seem like fiction to him, so he could not think of Dorothy Richardson's heroine in the way one thought of characters such as Moll Flanders and Mr. Micawber, or Leopold Bloom for that matter. But he was also unwilling to assume that Dorothy Richardson and her heroine were interchangeable, even though they obviously shared many of the opinions expressed in *Pilgrimage*. Rejecting the simple solution of autobiography, Gregory said he liked to think of Miriam Henderson as a moral realist, a critic of life, indeed "as a seeing eye, awake on a long journey."

At the time he wrote his essay, virtually nothing was known of Dorothy Richardson except her work. No one even knew her age. There was certainly none of the documentary evidence needed to argue (if one wished to do so) the autobiographical nature of *Pilgrimage*, though it had always been suspected. But Horace Gregory (who had met Dorothy Richardson in 1934) chose to treat *Pilgrimage* as its author seemed to wish, as a work independent of her personal existence. I say "seemed to wish" because it was she who consistently refused to supply even the barest facts about herself, and who in 1933 had said there was "little to tell" of her. Yet at the very same time, her close friend J. D. Beresford was also quoted as saying that *Pilgrimage* was "the story of her life." Sensing the complex character of this large book that he knew was not yet finished (though few other people realized it), Horace Gregory related *Pilgrimage* to the realistic tradition in literature rather than to "stream of consciousness" fiction or the real life of Dorothy Richardson, but he also suggested that it would always be a difficult work to place.

The years that followed proved how right he was. Dorothy Richardson remained a shadowy figure, with little more known about her than the date and place of her birth, which she revealed grudgingly in a series of letters written during 1950–51. By then her novel had faded from view, largely because in an era devoted to definition it seemed amorphous and hard to define—except to those who saw it as a quaint period-novel belonging to another age altogether. It emerged again, however, in the pages of Leon Edel's study of the psychological novel, first published in 1955, and it has not been lost sight of since as one of the most original works of our time. Nonetheless, when Dorothy Richardson died in 1957 and the facts of her life gradually became available, the conception of *Pilgrimage* began to change. It entered a new phase.

In 1963 I published an essay in *PMLA* that was the first account of Dorothy Richardson's life. It showed that *Pilgrimage* was indeed an autobiographical novel and that any portrait of Dorothy Richardson (as she herself insisted) must take its fundamental lines from her own novel, because it was here that she felt she had fully revealed herself. She had once said that the usual facts about a writer are "secondary" to his work, that "we should meet him first in his achievements." Since we find among her own achievements a more consciously drawn self-portrait than is commonly to be found, it would seem that in Dorothy Richardson's case at least, the critic and the biographer must truly join forces. As I saw it then, one of the principal tasks of her biographer would be to examine the facts of her life in conjunction with the fictional shape they took, in an effort to determine the role that imagination played in *Pilgrimage* and through that determination get at the art of this novel. Another task would be to ascertain the relationship between the continuing life of Dorothy Richardson and the novel written over such a long period of time. But it also seemed to me that for such a large undertaking a great deal more needed to be known about Dorothy Richardson's life than was available at the time.

The materials I used for my essay were the letters and miscellaneous papers gathered after Miss Richardson's death by her literary executrix, the late Rose Isserlis Odle (Mrs. Odle died in October 1972). Some of them had been left by Miss Richardson, others had been sought out by Mrs. Odle, and together they now constitute the Dorothy Richardson Papers housed in the Beinecke Library of Yale University. These papers were invaluable, especially for the clues they furnished to primary historical sources: county registers and directories, relatives, and friends. (Dorothy Richardson was as chary of hard facts in most of her letters as she had been in her rare public utterances.) But they were only the nucleus, the core if you will, of a full biography.* A sizable body of additional material

---

*They were the basis of Horace Gregory's new essay (in which he took autobiography into account), published in 1967 along with the American reissue of the four-volume edition; and they were used most recently for the book brought out by John Rosenberg to mark the centenary of Dorothy Richardson's birth.

(described in the headnote to sources at the back of this book) was accumulating at the New York Public Library, the University of Texas at Austin, Rice University at Houston, Princeton University, and the British Museum, as well as in private hands. Though I did not know all of this when Mrs. Odle asked me in 1964 to undertake a biography, I was already aware of the various kinds of research I would have to conduct on my own. I knew I would have to try to reconstruct a long, rather complicated life carried on for the most part in out-of-the-way places, that I would have to try to separate fact from memory (by checking the data as often as I could) and inconclusive evidence or record from the indisputable, and that above all I would have to try to separate the living person of Dorothy Richardson from the character she had created. In the extent to which I have met these challenges lies the value of this book.

I doubt that I would have ventured such a book if I had not known from the start that I could count on help and support from Dorothy Richardson's friends and relatives. I have already indicated the nature of my debt to Rose Odle. I should like to record here my appreciation of her friendship and of all the help she gave me during the years in which I gathered material. I owe an equally special debt to Dorothy Richardson's younger sister, the late Jessie Abbot Hale (who died in San Antonio, Texas, in June 1962). Mrs. Hale provided me with information about the novelist's childhood and adolescence that no one else was able to provide, and she gave me access to all the letters from her sister in her possession. Dorothy Richardson's nephew, Mr. Phillip Batchelor, kindly answered as many questions as he could; and her nephew, the late Mr. Francis Odle, her literary executor until his untimely death in October 1975, was always helpful and hospitable. I should like to express here my great sadness at his passing, and to thank his wife for offering, despite her bereavement, to help facilitate the publication of this book.

This book is dedicated to two of Dorothy Richardson's friends (and mine), Norah and Edward Hickey, whose knowledge of her life in Cornwall during its last fifteen years and of Cornwall itself they have painstakingly passed on to me. My debt to them is incalculable; and I owe nearly as much to Miss Pauline Marrian, Mr. P. Beaumont Wadsworth, Miss Evelyn Morrison, and the late Miss Lina Symons of Hillside for their long and vivid memories. To

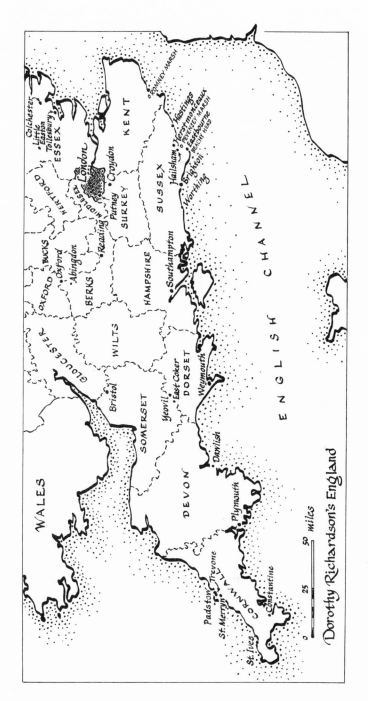

Dorothy Richardson's England

Marjorie Watts (the daughter of Mrs. C. A. Dawson-Scott, the novelist and founder of the P.E.N. Club), for her inexhaustible store of information about Cornwall and things English, I wish to express my deep gratitude in this formal way. I want to thank Joan George (the daughter of Dorothy Richardson's friend and informal oculist, Dr. A. S. Cobbledick) and her husband Graham for their unfailing help and encouragement. I should like also to express my thanks to Mr. and Mrs. John Beecham, the owners of Zansizzey, for providing me with the opportunity to live for a time in what was Dorothy Richardson's home during the Second World War.

In 1967, a few years before her death, Mrs. Beatrice Beresford, the widow of J. D. Beresford, provided me with invaluable information, again that no one else could have provided, about the close association she and her husband had with Dorothy Richardson during the period of the beginnings of *Pilgrimage*. Mr. Guy Rayne Savage generously allowed me to examine the mass of materials left by his father, the late Henry Savage, including twenty-four diary notebooks and an unpublished memoir titled "Promenade Picaresque." Miss Mary Mitchell-Smith, the executrix of the painter Adrian Allinson, kindly showed me the materials left in her possession. Among these were his autobiography and the painting and sketches he had made of Dorothy Richardson and Alan Odle. She has also kindly granted permission for the reproduction of some of the artwork in this volume. Mr. Harold Mortlake, bookseller and collector, allowed me to examine the various drawings and miscellaneous papers of Alan Odle in his possession. The late Mr. John H. Thompson, former publisher of the magazine *Signatures,* was good enough to provide me with a photographed copy of the manuscript of *Dawn's Left Hand,* which he owned, and with photographed copies of Dorothy Richardson's letters to him. The late Mr. Richard Church generously provided me with copies of letters to him from Dorothy Richardson (and others), and gave me the benefit of his personal recollections. Dr. W. R. Trotter gave me a copy of Dorothy Richardson's letter to his father, which is one of his own most prized possessions.

The Reverend Malcolm M. Thomson of East Coker, Somerset, spent an entire afternoon helping me search through the church records for information about Dorothy Richardson's mother's family, and gave me the benefit as well of his knowledge of the history of the village. Miss Evelyn Rant of Abingdon (granddaughter of

Mr. George Rant, who bought the Richardson business) was kind enough to share with me her knowledge of the Richardson family in Abingdon and environs. Mrs. Olive Caudwell made known to me the Baptist ties of the Richardson family.

Mrs. Felicia Tombs (whose husband had entered into partnership with Mr. Rant in the final period of the business) permitted me to examine the historical records in her possession having to do with the business, and to reproduce here the watercolor sketch she owns of the original structure in Ock Street, Abingdon. When I was in Abingdon in 1965, that somewhat modernized structure was in the process of being dismantled, and various items had already been removed, among which was a photograph of the founder, Dorothy Richardson's grandfather, which had always hung on the wall. Mrs. Tombs retrieved the photograph for me still in its frame, and behind it I discovered yet another, of the entire Richardson clan. The latter is reproduced in this volume with Mrs. Tombs's permission.

I must also thank the ministers of the various Abingdon churches for the light they helped to shed on the affiliations of the Richardson family, and Mr. Peter Walne, M.A., formerly County Archivist of Berkshire, for tracing the background and movements of the Richardson family.

I wish to thank Miss A. L. Reeve, Assistant Archivist of the London County Record Office, for the information she supplied me about the school Dorothy Richardson attended in Putney, which Miss Reeve's aunts and cousin happened also to have attended.

Dr. Herbert Mundhenke of the Stadtarchiv, Hanover, helped me to search through the various directories of the city, and gave me valuable information about the city as it was in the 1890s.

Mr. Anthony West was kind enough to share with me his memories of Dorothy Richardson and his view of her relationship with his father. For this I am very grateful to him.

The kindness, patience, and assistance of the people in the villages and hamlets surrounding Padstow, who remembered Dorothy Richardson and her husband with such astonishing vividness, can only be recorded in this inadequate way; but I wish to express here my deep appreciation of the friendliness and courtesy they showed to a "foreigner" in their midst. For the kinds of help too various to specify, I want to thank the late Major Edgar Andrew and Mrs. Andrew, Mrs. Ruth Bennett, Mrs. Stanley Bennett, Mrs. H. Brewer, Mr. Maurice Buckingham, Mrs. Gregor, the Higman family,

Mr. Jack Ingry, Mrs. Mildred Ingry, Mr. and Mrs. John Keatt, Mrs. Gwen Kennedy, the late Mr. Max Lindley, Mrs. Mabel Parsons, Mrs. E. A. Shirvell, Miss Jane S. Tearle, the late Mr. Freathy Tippett and Mrs. Tippett, Mr. and Mrs. Ernie Trenouth. For different kinds of assistance, again too varied to specify, I should like to thank the late Dr. Bertrand Allinson, Mrs. Natalie Bushee, Miss Babette Deutsch, Mr. Jonathan Farley, Miss Muriel Fudge, Mrs. Diana Hopkinson, Mr. Billy Morrison, Mrs. Maxwell Robertson.

Through the years, I have had the help, support, and encouragement of both individual scholars and scholarly institutions. I should like to thank the Yale University Library and its staff, in particular Miss Marjorie G. Wynne, Research Librarian, who did everything she could to facilitate my study of the Dorothy Richardson Papers; the Academic Center Library of the University of Texas at Austin, in particular Mrs. Mary M. Hirth, Librarian; the Fondren Library of Rice University, in particular Mrs. Jane Clark, Librarian; the Henry W. and Albert A. Berg Collection of the New York Public Library and its staff, in particular the late Dr. John D. Gordan and Dr. Lola Szladitz; the staff of the Princeton University Library; and the staff of the British Museum.

For their individual help as gentlemen and scholars, and for their continued interest in Dorothy Richardson, I wish to acknowledge my very great indebtedness to the late Professor Norman Holmes Pearson of Yale University, Professor Leon Edel of the University of Hawaii, Professor Joseph Prescott of Wayne State University, and Mr. Horace Gregory.

I should like also to thank my former colleagues at Brooklyn College of the City University of New York for their sustaining confidence in me during the years of our association, in particular Professors Karl Beckson, Margaret Ganz (and her husband, Arthur F. Ganz of City College), Jules Gelernt, Vincent Quinn, and not least the late Richard H. Barker, biographer of Proust.

I am grateful to my present colleagues in the English Department of the University of Illinois at Chicago Circle for their interest and patience, to the University for the sabbatical leave which enabled me to put the finishing touches on this book, and to Rita Zelewsky of the University of Illinois Press for her meticulous editing.

I wish to thank the American Philosophical Society, the American Council of Learned Societies, and the City University of New

York for their financial assistance in the form of grants which allowed me to conduct some of the research needed for this book.

My final acknowledgments are most personal: to Leon and Roberta Edel; Miltiades Zaphiropoulos; and my husband, Harold Fromm, who read the manuscript of this book with a perfect blend of love and care.

G. G. F.

Part One
1873-1915

Prologue

ABINGDON, where the river Ock joins with the Thames, is an old market town in the northern part of the southern county of Berkshire. Dorothy Richardson was born there, on May 17, 1873, the third daughter of a man who seemed to want, more than anything else, to have a son and to be a gentleman. But when Dorothy was seventeen months old, still another girl made her disappointing appearance. Her father was not entirely inconsolable, for by then he had satisfied his second great wish. His own father, who had built up a flourishing business in wines and provisions over a period of more than forty years, died in January 1874. Charles was his only son and the principal heir. He inherited the shop and house on Ock Street in which he had been raised, three branches of the business in nearby villages (Blewbury, Marcham, Steventon), a freehold in Abingdon's Stert Street (which gave him the right to vote), and £8,000. Charles lost no time. Four months after Thomas Richardson was buried in the sizable vault he had made sure was ready for him, befitting a proud and prosperous tradesman, his son unburdened himself of a hateful heritage. He sold everything: the buildings, the fixtures, the fittings, all the utensils, all the horses (including Punch the chestnut, Flower the gray mare, and Tommy the nag), and all the carts and vans. The man who bought all this for £5,000 felt a sense of achievement and good fortune. He could not have been happier than the tall, angular, light-haired, immaculately dressed Charles Richardson, who felt positively triumphant: he had washed his hands entirely clean of trade.

He had already rejected his family's Nonconformism. While *they* attended Dissenting services, Charles took his wife and daughters to Abingdon's elegant parish church, St. Helen's. It was not for God, however, that he came to St. Helen's but for pleasure, which his father and mother frowned upon. St. Helen's was incomparably

3

situated, nearly on the bank of the river Ock at the point where it met the Thames. The wharf was Abingdon's promenade. Every Sunday, as the white swans of St. Helen's glided by, Abingdon society aired itself; and Charles Richardson was there—to see and to be seen, with his delicate, diminutive dark-haired wife and their two eldest daughters, who were told, when they asked their father a question about God, to take note of the graceful spire, the sweet bells, the medieval painted ceiling of their church. And if they persisted with the earnestness of Victorian girls who heard their grandmother always inveighing against frivolity, he mocked them—as he mocked chapelgoers; people ignorant of science and the arts; and, once a decent interval had passed, those engaged in trade.

Charles Richardson carried himself with ease—and determination—as a member of the gentry. He had retained the Stert Street freehold in order to be able to vote, and he collected rent for the Ock Street premises. Even before his emancipation, he had removed his family from the vicinity of the business. From a house on Marcham Road (a continuation of Ock Street) in which his first two daughters were born, Charles had shifted his residence by the time Dorothy arrived to a newly fashionable area called Albert Park. The park had recently been commemorated to the late Prince Consort, and around it had sprung up a crescent of homes. Charles rented one of these, a large white-stoned house with a walled garden, which Dorothy would remember as the scene and source of her first experiences. Her father settled down here, once he was completely free, to a life of leisure.

He joined the British Association for the Advancement of Science. He went often to nearby Oxford to attend lectures and meetings. (Sometimes he took his children there, for the sake of the architecture and the stained-glass windows.) And he invited dons to his home and entertained them lavishly. His wine cellar was superb, his table epicurean, his conversation acerbic. In politics, in music, and in art, he had impeccably conservative tastes, and he sneered at the slightest departure from tradition. No one could accuse him of vulgarity—or of radicalism, which amounted in his eyes to the same thing. In a few years he would quite properly hate Gladstone, make fun of all modern music (except Wagner and Chopin), and when he joined a London club (it had to be, alas, the Junior Constitutional, because in spite of everything he was irrevocably the son of a

Dorothy Richardson's grandfather, Thomas Richardson, c. 1860s.

tradesman), he would act as guardian of its moral tone. He was to find, one day, a copy of the first issue of W. T. Stead's *Review of Reviews* on a table in his club. The very name of the social reformer enraged Charles Richardson, and the sight of a magazine actually produced by him was more than Charles could bear. With a pair of tongs from the club hearth, he lifted the *Review of Reviews* and dropped it into the fire.

His daughter Dorothy never forgot this episode as it was described to the family by its indignant head, who happened to be just then, in 1890, on the verge of bankruptcy. Charles's gentlemanly life had been fated to last little more than sixteen years. For his daughter, though, it would go on and on—in memory, in longing, in anger—as an irrecoverable but also contaminated paradise.

CHAPTER ONE

Alternations

IN July 1866, when Charles Richardson was thirty years old and still a grocer, he married a Somerset girl named Mary Miller Taylor, who was twenty-three. She was one of twenty-two children in a family that lived in East Coker, a tiny village of thatched roofs and red-cheeked West country folk. Though her ancestors may have been yeomen (as her daughter Dorothy would be fond of claiming), her father was a manufacturer, and the family was not Anglican by tradition. As a matter of fact, on a June day in 1859, five young Taylors were received together into the Established Church in what seems to have been a communal baptism. Sixteen-year-old Mary was one of them, along with four older sisters and brothers, none of them older than twenty-five. In all likelihood, they wanted to be able to take part in the social life of East Coker, which would not have been possible except through the church. In any case, seven years later Mary's Anglicanism would prove to be a source of satisfaction to the man she married, who instantly removed her from East Coker's provinciality.

It was not in the least a source of satisfaction to him that his wife had grown up in a large, loosely run, informal family. He expected her to be organized and disciplined in the management of his household, and she, quite naturally, wanted to please her handsome husband. She coveted his praise, for she felt that besides beauty he had infinite knowledge and immense authority. At the same time, however, she liked to be carefree and impulsive, and she thought life ought to be *jolly*. Charles saw clearly that he would have to direct his wife's attention to the important things of her new life. He established the rules of the household, set into motion the elaborate rituals that would govern nearly every aspect of Richardson family life, and expected his wife to maintain them religiously. If the light-hearted Mary began to feel smothered after a while, she kept it

7

to herself—and instead gradually went mad with the sense of her own worthlessness.

1

Whatever was to come, the married life of Charles and Mary Richardson began ideally. Little more than a year after they had settled into the house on Marcham Road, their first child, Frances Kate, was born, and sixteen months later, in December 1868, their second, Alice Mary. Charles had high hopes that the third would be the boy he wanted. After five years, not only did *Dorothy* arrive, but her birth was a difficult one. To help Mary regain her strength, Charles hired an undernurse to care for the baby, in addition to the governess he had intended to bring in for the older girls. By then they were living in the large Albert Park house, and a governess was *de rigueur*. The nurse, however, seemed to have been a mistake. She took a peculiar delight in startling her infant charge with sudden noises and movements, but it was months before the older girls, who noticed the strange things she did, were able to express what they saw to their mother. By that time, the baby's fear was pretty well fixed. Until her eighth year, Dorothy suffered a kind of nervous seizure at sudden loud noises; and throughout her life she trembled at the sound of thunder, shrank from loud-voiced people, and considered herself a hopeless coward.

It might well have been her father who first introduced the notion of cowardice. At some point or other, after his fourth daughter was born in October 1874, he took to referring to his third as his son. Years later, Dorothy herself suggested that he had fallen into this habit because of the supposedly boyish willfulness and unmanageability she exhibited. She seemed proud of these traits, perhaps because she thought her father esteemed them. If this was how she read him, she might also have seen him expressing contempt for timidity.

In most other respects, childhood in Abingdon was virtually idyllic. Dorothy and her younger sister Jessie romped at home while the older girls attended one of Abingdon's privately run schools for girls—a "seminary for young ladies" theirs was called. But each summer the entire family traveled to Dawlish, on the south Devon coast, for a yearly holiday. All the children understood, in due course, that going to Dawlish conferred distinction upon them—a distinction that like all the others, such as eating only meat roasted on a jack and never having the tea loaf on the table, they owed to their father. No one else's father took his family as far as Dawlish for the summer.

It was indeed advanced of him. Though Dawlish had become fashionable in the early years of the century (Jane Austen had had one of her characters evince surprise that anybody could live anywhere in Devon except near Dawlish), it was not until the middle of the century that the railroad made the resort accessible. Even then it was a distant place (about 130 miles from Abingdon), and most people in the 1870s would not have dreamed of traveling that many miles and that many hours—especially with children and boxes—for pleasure. But Charles Richardson had uncommon dreams, and he was used to acting them out. Dawlish, moreover, was exquisitely beautiful, with red cliffs, shingled beaches, caves, and tunnels that to a child amounted to Paradise—a seaside paradise Dorothy would remember as the gift of her father, the English gentleman whose bearing was perfect not only "by nature" but also "by the grace of an almost religious cultivation."

If Dawlish was the far-off summer paradise, Abingdon was close at hand for the rest of the year. The walled garden of the Albert Park house contrasted in Dorothy's young mind with the sea of Dawlish that "stretched outwards forever." Home and holiday, garden and sea, the finite and the infinite: this was the pattern of her earliest conscious years. She never forgot that in the Abingdon garden, among the flowers and the bees and the sunlight, the sense that she existed first began; and for the rest of her life, whenever she was in a garden she felt the irresistible urge to celebrate existence—by dancing a jig.

The child in Abingdon, who did not know the meaning of celebration, was learning what it meant to *be*—"in the child's way of direct apprehension," as Dorothy later put it, without intermediary, without order, without anyone classifying and spoiling things. She would always prize, above any other, the knowledge gained in this way; and when she went to school at the age of five, nothing was supportable except being taught how to read. She rejected nearly everything else. As early as that, she had a deep suspicion of facts—fostered, though not consciously, she said, by her mother, who seemed to have thought of them as mainly destructive.

Dorothy's sympathies lay with her fun-loving mother, but her mother's helplessness was not appealing. One of the earliest conclusions Dorothy drew from the evidence of her own senses was that in a state of dependence there could be no paradise, there could only be hell—such as her mother endured. The older she grew and the more aware she became of the nature of her mother's suffering, the more she resented her father's cruelty and yet more closely identified with him. To a child, the power he seemed to have, the complete independence, the unlimited capacity for self-gratification could not have been anything but eminently desirable, so that, even though the sense of his power did not last very long, the circuit of feelings established here would scarcely ever vary.

After all, her father's judgments and her father's tastes always prevailed. Indeed they are manifest in her own memories of Abingdon, which include, for example, St. Helen's, the church her father had praised so highly, remembered by Dorothy as a thing of beauty with a sweet-sounding name and without a trace of religious piety. They also include a number of visits to certain "chapel" relations, and these are remembered as one of the unpleasant obligations of superiors to inferiors. Dorothy described such a visit in a story written when she was seventy-two.

She had been a child of seven and her sister Jessie was not quite six when the two girls were sent alone to Blewbury, eleven miles from Abingdon, to stay for a few days in a household that would have disconcerted almost any child. It was composed of two great-aunts (their grandfather's sister, who was over eighty and totally blind, and his brother's wife, who was seventy-six), a crippled spinster aunt of thirty-five who ran a school in the village, and two rather odd bachelor uncles. Not surprisingly, the children felt they had to protect themselves from all the strange and ugly things around them.

The strongest weapon they had was their father and the incontestable superiority of his way of seeing and doing everything. They proceeded to note, without a shred of mercy, all the shortcomings of the Blewbury household: the meat was not roasted, the loaf of bread sat in full view on the table; there was no cake for tea and no grace before meals; it was forbidden to play in the garden on Sunday; and instead of their father's graceful violin there was, in a storeroom, with bulging sacks lying about, an old crooked harmonium on which one of their uncles played hymns "out of tune and out of time." According to Dorothy, it was her sister Jessie who could not refrain from pronouncing every defect on the spot, as she kicked

The Richardson clan, c. 1873. The infant is Dorothy Richardson.

Jessie under the table. It must have required great forbearance on the part of their aunts and uncles not to have kicked *both* of them.

2

Dorothy was eight when life in Abingdon came to an abrupt end. Charles Richardson moved his family to the Channel coast, to Worthing in Sussex, where they remained for two years in a furnished house on Victoria Road. Dorothy remembered the move as necessitated by her mother's ill-health. Her younger sister's memory was that it had been made for the sake of economy. Whatever the reason (and perhaps both memories were accurate), Dorothy saw Worthing, ever after, as a blot on her childhood. She complained about the "hired house with alien furniture" (though the Albert Park house had also been rented), about the Sussex sea as inferior to south Devon's, about the school in Worthing that was large and competitive and tried to *force* instruction upon her, about the new church they went to with the ugly name of St. Botolph. It was a word, she said, that "touche[d] the mind like the edge of an inflated balloon," and it led her one day to refuse to go through the door. (She saw this, through adult eyes, as the first real assertion of her mind.) But she did not utter a word of complaint against her father, having apparently absolved him of the responsibility for Worthing.

In a sense he may be said to have absolved himself, for in the spring of 1883, just before Easter, he moved the family again, and restored with interest everything they had lost. He set them down in the London suburb of Putney, in a three-story red-brick house on Northumberland Avenue that to his daughters seemed magnificent. Years later, Dorothy would reverently describe the day of their arrival. They turned in from a wide roadway that was lined with pollarded limes, she said, and drove up to the house between blooming "maytrees." Then they swept round past a lawn encircled with flowering shrubs, to pull up in front of a deep porch. Here, she said, was "continuous enchantment," a future "bathed in gold," and indeed a "lost eternity" retrieved.

The house on Northumberland Avenue was frankly luxurious. It was brilliantly furnished and stocked, fully staffed with servants, and supervised down to the smallest detail by the great magician who had waved his wand and made it all appear. Not even the most trusted maid could touch a bottle of wine in Charles Richardson's cellar. On dinner-party days, he alone "tenderly" carried the choicest of his store upstairs. On other days he would serve the *vin ordinaire* from his "cellaret" in the dining-room sideboard. And in the breakfast-room sideboard—"for emergencies, including spells of frost," as Dorothy remembered—he kept decanters of spirits, each with a silver label hung by a chain round its neck. Dorothy remembered all these as religiously as her father had arranged them. After sixty years she would claim she could still see his "sacred bottle of green Chartreuse warming itself on the pale-blue-tile hearth in front of the polished brass bars of the drawing-room fire." Nor did she ever forget the other enormous fire, the one that always burned—even in the stifling heat of summer—to roast their meat. And, of course, there were the heavy trays the servants carried up the stone stairs, trays filled with hot plates, dish cover, huge joint, everything the meticulous master required.

Everything indeed was just as it should have been in the home of a gentleman. The Richardson girls grew up with all the privileges of a cultivated family life and a wealthy (some thought it a vulgar) suburb. Their father soon established a fixed pattern of "musical evenings" for a select group of friends, who added their various stringed instruments to his own violin. The music included Bach, of course, and, as the only moderns he accepted, Chopin and Wagner. His older daughters managed to prevail upon him, and he allowed some sentimental ballads and even a bit of light instrumental music as well; but he absolutely refused to admit either popular songs or dance music. These, in addition to Gilbert and Sullivan, were relegated to the schoolroom. Occasionally he took the girls to concerts in London, and every Sunday, as he was proud to point out, they had the music of the service in their new, splendid All Saints' Church on Putney Lower Common. Dorothy approved of both the music and the church without a single qualification. She loved its "opulent" name and looked forward all through the week to the litany intoned by old Mr. Booker and to the organ playing by young Harry Dansey. Putney was truly a magical place.

The perfection of the house on Northumberland Avenue could not be marred even by a governess. This one had been hired for Dorothy and Jessie. The younger girls were much less serious than their sisters had been at the same age, and they were not kind to her. Dorothy remembered a "bugled bonnet" and herself sliding under the schoolroom table. She had wanted no part, she claimed, of the "female education" the governess offered; there was little knowledge in it, and nothing of value. The governess was released after a year, and Dorothy and Jessie were sent to school.

They went to Miss Harriet Rebecca Sandell's "ladies' school," which was attended by "the daughters of gentlefolk." This institution, located in Southborough House (soon to be designated No. 17, Putney Hill), somewhat later came to be known as "South West London College for Girls." It was a mile and a half away, along the Upper Richmond Road from Northumberland Avenue. Here it was that Dorothy received the only formal education she would ever esteem.

The curricula at the school were, in general, standard for the period. Dorothy studied English history with the Head, who was a disciple of Ruskin. Her aged literature master was a friend of Browning. (The presence of Swinburne in their very midst, at "The Pines" in Putney, went unregarded.) The teacher of Shakespeare, Dorothy recalled, required as many "learned annotations" committed to memory as lines of a play. Her French master took for granted that his students had learned their weekly page of rules, and he spoke at large to them, gently told or read them stories, and dictated French prose. German was taught by a fräulein of Junker birth and convictions, who had a hot temper. Her classes consisted of a series of emotional scenes. Dorothy also studied scripture, science, mathematics, and pianoforte. She objected only to geography, because it seemed to her "unrelated to anything else on earth," so she was placed instead in a newly introduced class in logic and psychology, a class she attended with delight twice a week. Learning how to detect faulty reasoning, she would claim, gave her as much pleasure at this stage of her life as did the acquisition of a latchkey later on; psychology, however, made her uneasy.

The subject that suited her best and in which she excelled was pianoforte. The instructor, Herr Froude, began to pay particular attention to this blonde-haired girl who wore thick *pince-nez* and had large hands that rendered the music of Chopin surprisingly well. Herr Froude took to featuring her in the annual school concerts. She could always be counted upon to perform proficiently and never betray nervousness, for she was used to playing to an audience at home, under her father's direction. The music master's praise led her to thoughts of a career on the concert stage, but she dreamed quite as often of the theater: she was an excellent mimic, much appreciated by her younger sister and the servants, who applauded her dramatic performances in the basement. Even as a teenager, she could imitate virtually every speech sound she heard.

Yet not even Dorothy took her gifts seriously. All the Richardson girls understood that the future for them lay in marriage and the domestic life. Meanwhile they were free to enjoy themselves and to join in the social and sporting activities suited to the daughters of a gentleman. Their father properly provided croquet for them on the front lawn; and in the back garden, on the sunken lawn, he had the gardener chalk a regulation-size tennis court. At this the older—and soon the younger—girls learned to play "a good hard game," and in due course they were all elected to the local club. Dorothy remembered that at one point she, as the youngest member, was treated so indulgently that she even won a tournament or two.

She was proud of the mobility she and her sisters attained in spite of the clothes they were forced to wear. In the 1880s, a young lady played tennis in a tilted straw hat, a long skirt worn over several petticoats, a petersham waistband with a silver clasp, and—as a relic of the bustle—a cushion tied round the waist "to make the skirt set." These were "deadly garments" indeed.

Every girl must have suffered some variation of the agony Dorothy watched her sister Kate endure on the courts one day. She and her partner were playing a dramatic game with the secretary of the club and his wife. Half of the club members had lined up to watch. Midway through the match, as Kate was racing along the back line to position herself should her partner miss the ball, the string of her bustle broke, depositing the little cushion covered in red Turkey twill on the green lawn. She had felt it go, but in that split second before her eyes turned down to see, the nearest female in the line of spectators had pounced on it and had run off to the ladies' room. Not a soul in the crowd snickered. Dorothy thought the silence was the "awfullest measure of the disaster."

Nevertheless, like everyone they knew, the Richardson girls not only played tennis in these perilous garments, they also rowed and sculled and punted on the Thames in the spring, skated in the winter, and as time went on began to cycle as well. Indeed, it was the new sport of cycling that brought some of the late-Victorian girls a breath of release. Those who had the courage could substitute knickers for one of the petticoats. But only "the brazen few" took advantage of the freedom, and they were considered by "the virtuous many'' (including the Richardsons) to have lowered themselves nearly to the level of "the utterly abandoned"—the girls, mostly in America, who sported bloomers. Virtue, however, was soon rewarded. Those who had refused knickers could accept, without the faintest blush, the divided skirts that came next.

So Dorothy would remember herself as perfectly ordinary in a typical suburban world. She was short-tempered and brusque at home, even with Jessie, but among her peers she was a little less pugnacious. She arrived at the age of sixteen with only two serious concerns: her mother's "fluctuating health," as she put it, and "the problem of free-will." Otherwise her thoughts were centered on the tall and handsome son of a neighboring family, on an approaching dance, or on the annual tennis tournament. On occasion, to be sure, the unexpected might occur, such as the purchase of the house next door by a family that owned a shop in Putney. The Richardson girls, who had been instructed by their father long before not to recognize tradespeople in the street, shared his sense of outrage. What were they to do now, with tradespeople actually living next door? But before the problem could be solved, a genuine crisis arose.

Dorothy and Jessie began to notice signs of change. Their older sisters looked troubled, not to speak of their mother, and their father gave fewer and fewer dinner parties. He continued to go into London nearly every day. (As they understood it, he went to the Stock Exchange to keep an eye on his investments and to confer with his broker, to drop in at the Junior Constitutional, or to stop off for a game at the chess club.) But he began coming home for the evening instead of staying in town for the theater or a concert. He still attended all the lectures and meetings of the Association, but he gave up the outings and the trips. In 1888, when Dorothy was fifteen, he had gone with the Association to America. That trip might well have been his last fling. During the two years that followed, the signs of trouble grew more and more pronounced, until finally, in 1890, during Dorothy's last term at school, they were impossible to ignore. Nearly all the servants were gone, and the four Richardson girls conferred gravely. But what, in 1890, could a mere young female do?

In private Dorothy looked through the work advertisements in the *Times*. She found one that seemed plausible and answered it without telling even Jessie what she had done. The advertisement called for a pupil-teacher in a school in Prussian Hanover (now a part of

Watercolor sketch of the Richardson business establishment at 58 Ock Street, Abingdon.

northern Germany). Dorothy thought that, if she were expected to study as well as teach, her youth would act in her favor. She had reasoned cogently; she was offered the job. She mailed off her letter of acceptance at once. Only then did she make her announcement to the family. No one was pleased, least of all her father, but under the circumstances there was nothing anyone could say or do—as Dorothy had known. Having gotten her way, she set about preparing to leave her home and family. She was seventeen and a half, five feet four inches tall, and full-figured, with long, light, curled hair and very fair skin. She wanted, above everything, to direct her own life.

3

When Dorothy arrived in Hanover early in 1891, the city had not yet lost its medieval look. Though it was gradually being commercialized, there were still the curious brick buildings, the peaked, red-roofed houses, the projecting stories that had given such character and charm to the ancient town. Indeed, Dorothy promptly fell in love with this old Germany. She was probably unaware that the country surrounding Hanover—heath, mountain, and river, woods and valleys—was very much like the Berkshire of her earliest days. Even Hanover itself, with its ancient past everywhere in evidence, was like the old and many-layered Abingdon, with the remains of its Saxon abbey in its midst. Both, too, were river towns. Hanover (or Hanovere), situated on the Leine, was said to have been named for its high banks (*hohen Ufer*). Abingdon had grown up on the single bank of the river Ock. And curiously enough, as if the starting point of her life could have been either Abingdon or Hanover, twenty years later Dorothy would choose to begin her autobiographical novel with the German experience instead of the English.

Now, in 1891, she came to a school that stood on a quiet, tree-shaded street several minutes and turnings from both the railroad station and the center of town. The houses here on Meterstrasse were close together, narrow and high-windowed, with the quaint Hanoverian gabled roofs. No. 13 was the "Lehrenstalt and Erzie-hungsanft" run by Fräulein Lily Pabst, who had been engaged in the business of education for some years. Back in 1876 she had run a boardinghouse and school "*für Töchter höh Stände,*" in partnership with one of her two sisters. The following year Lily alone was directing an "institute" in Meterstrasse, her sister another in Prin-zenstrasse, and the third sister had a boardinghouse elsewhere. But during the few years before Lily Pabst hired Dorothy, she had been settled at No. 13 Meterstrasse, managing what she liked to refer to as her *"fröhlichen Bienenkorb."* Dorothy spent six months in Lily's beehive, by no means certain that she was always one of the happy bees.

Supposedly Dorothy, in helping to finish the daughters of gen-tlemen, was being gently finished herself. But she found group life new and intimidating. Moreover, in her own family she had gotten used to having her own way. Lily Pabst seems to have been used to this, too, with the result that she and Dorothy clashed. Whether they clashed in the competitive—and erotic—way Dorothy would have it happen in *Pointed Roofs* is not known. The evidence indicates no more than a surprisingly short stay. Dorothy went home at the end of the summer, having achieved virtually nothing from a practical point of view. She never made it clear whether she left voluntarily, at Lily Pabst's request, or by mutual agreement. In any case, it was clear, when Dorothy returned to Putney, that what she *had* achieved was independence. She could not remain at home.

She found the situation there much the same. In spite of her father's shrunken field of activity, he was as magisterial as ever. Her mother trembled sometimes, but for the most part she was quiet. And though the air in Northumberland Avenue reeked of failure, everyone pretended not to notice. Kate, the eldest girl, was actually in charge. It was she who ran the skeleton household, leaning in turn on the older man she had recently met and planned to marry. The second daughter, Richie, had already left to take a position (which she did not want). She was living, unhappily, in the opulent Wiltshire home of a very rich family, where she served as governess. Jessie, the youngest girl, had just finished school and had engaged herself to a wealthy young man. So when Dorothy returned home from Hanover, it was to find things both unchanged and radically different.

She herself had had a taste of experience, and it lured her on. By October she left Northumberland Avenue again for another teaching position, this one in a school in North London. It was run by spinster sisters named Ayre, who called their school Edgeworth House, after the Irish novelist. It served as Dorothy's home for a year and a half. Though she spent her holidays in Putney (expecting

19

each one to be the last), her real life lay in the school in Finsbury Park where, despite the green common directly across the road, one's eyes met mostly grey and the air was always sooty. North London was a grim and dreary place. Dorothy felt drained by it, exhausted by the little girls who came every day with their overwhelming need for personal attention, and as if this were not enough, she found herself subtly drawn to one of the Ayre sisters, who was astonished at the skepticism, the utter lack of faith of so young a girl. Miss Ayre's appeal was emotional, and Dorothy knew it might turn into tyranny.

Teaching itself made her throat ache and her head throb. It left her with no energy for anything else at the end of the day. She felt confined, if not trapped. When two of her pupils (sisters), who were clearly from a more elegant environment than the other girls, made overtures of friendship to her, she responded—cautiously at first, but with curiosity and a vague hope that somehow they would offer her relief. They invited her to their home for tea, and when that was successful asked her to spend a weekend with them. The weekends and the friendship went on for years, and the girls became the Broom sisters of *Pilgrimage,* playing in fiction the same restorative role.

They had rescued Dorothy not only from Edgeworth House but from home as well. Going to Putney meant simply another kind of pain. Her father managed to cling to solvency, by a hair, until 1893. At the end of this year, his broker died suddenly, and the whole flimsy edifice collapsed. Charles Richardson was declared a bankrupt, and a public auction took place, which Dorothy did not attend. The family move was also accomplished without her. It was Kate who arranged it, with the help of her fiancé, Arthur Batchelor. He had been living with his business partner in a small house in Chiswick. As it happened, his partner had recently absconded with funds, and Batchelor decided to move into lodgings. He turned over the house, rent-free, to the Richardson family. It would be a temporary residence for them, he thought, giving Charles Richardson a chance to collect himself. Besides, Batchelor hoped to be married to Kate almost immediately. The wedding did not take place, however, until the following April, and when it did, he and Kate settled nearby in Bedford Park, so Kate could continue to watch over her increasingly unstable mother. Her father was no less arrogant than he had ever been.

Fräulein Lily Pabst's "institute" at No. 13 Meterstrasse, Hanover, the setting of *Pointed Roofs*.

Dorothy stayed away as much as possible. She had left Edgeworth House before Kate's marriage to try out a position as governess. It had seemed to her that, as sad as her sister Richie was in her situation, it would be less painful than teaching in a place like Edgeworth House. Dorothy was hired by an upper-class suburban family, but she lived with them for only a short time during 1895. In June, two months after Kate was married, Jessie and her young man, Jack Hale, had an elaborate wedding. Dorothy was a bridesmaid, and all the Richardsons made every effort to enjoy the sumptuous affair. But it was difficult to ignore the fact that Mary Richardson was very ill. Her mental state was obviously deteriorating. She needed close attention. By the fall, it became apparent that something had to be done. Once before, she had been helped by a month of rest at the seaside, at Hastings in Sussex, with a Richardson cousin she liked. Now both of her sons-in-law felt that a second trip might help her again. They offered to provide the funds if Dorothy would go with her.

Lodgings were rented at 11 Devonshire Terrace in Hastings, and Dorothy and her mother arrived there late in November. The sea was rough, the air somewhat cool, but after a few days Dorothy thought her mother looked better. She did not leave her alone for a moment. There was always something her mother needed done for her or something she wanted to try to express. At night Mary Richardson found it hard to sleep. Dorothy heard her moans and tried to reassure her: she was not stupid, she was not sinful, she was not eternally damned. Dorothy wanted desperately to convince her mother of all this, but Mary Richardson had accumulated nearly thirty years of evidence to the contrary. And precisely because her husband would have found it incontrovertible proof of her stupidity that she believed in her damnation, she was absolutely certain of both. In the face of such certainty, Dorothy herself wanted to cry out in loathing and anguish. Instead, she went out one morning, to escape. It was Saturday, November 30. Hastings was quiet, the season long over. Dorothy wandered about for an hour or so, hoping to still the pounding in her head and erase from her mind's eye the image of self-loathing that was her mother's entire being, hoping she would not herself go mad. When she got back to Devonshire Terrace, her mother was dead. Somehow she had laid her hands upon a kitchen knife and cut her throat with it. She was fifty-two years old; Dorothy was twenty-two.

CHAPTER TWO

London and H. G. Wells

"... to have the freedom of London was a life in itself."

—*Deadlock*, p. 106

THE coroner's inquest was held on December 2, 1895, and the suicide was registered the next day, listing Mary as the wife of Charles—"gentleman of no occupation." The body was brought back to Chiswick for burial, and the Richardsons tried to pull themselves together. Kate took in her father (for life, as it turned out), and Jessie her two unmarried sisters. But Richie would soon go back to Wiltshire as governess, while Dorothy had no idea what she was going to do. For the time being, more than enough had happened, and no one wanted to be alone. Christmas came and went, a thoroughly grim affair. Not even the cheerful Jessie could puncture the gloom. It was she nonetheless who in January convinced Dorothy they could accept an invitation to dine with one of her young husband's friends, she who dismissed Dorothy's sense of guilt, and she who quite simply placed the blame on their father's shoulders.

More than willing to transfer the guilt, Dorothy allowed her younger sister to take charge. Jessie, who was efficiently running a large house in Grove Park and already expected a child, had never believed there was the slightest virtue in being miserable. She was determined now to root out Dorothy's morbidity; and as it happened, Dorothy wanted most of all at this particular time to be taken care of by someone who was sane. She did not even object to the entire family conferring about a job for her—and finding one in London. The son of old friends of the Richardsons had set himself up in the city as a dental surgeon. Approached in his West End surgery, Harry Badcock said he needed an assistant/receptionist/secretary. The salary would be £1 a week, enough to live on frugally. Dorothy could find a room in London without any trouble, and Harry promised to look out for her. But his assurance alarmed Kate, who wondered whether they might be throwing Dorothy to the wolves. Even the fearless Jessie began to doubt their wisdom, and it occurred to her that since she was about to have her baby, Dorothy might as well stay on with her and Jack a while longer. The more concern her sisters felt, the stronger was Dorothy's resolve to get to London.

Yet she herself had secret fears, and on the eve of her departure for London she almost gave it up. She had gone down to Wiltshire to stay with Richie for a few days at the invitation of the Harris family. They were fond of their governess, and thinking she was still brooding over her mother's death, they hoped a visit from one of her sisters might cheer her up. In the end it did more for Dorothy. She had never been to Wiltshire, had never seen the Downs or Bath or Bristol. Besides, the Harris home, called Chilvester Lodge and lying just outside of Calne, not far from Salisbury Plain, was quite luxurious. The Harrises treated Dorothy as though, like Richie, she were part of the family. Richie knew most of their friends; and Dorothy, introduced to some of them, thus met some of Calne society. She even played at a concert in the Town Hall (and remembered years later being asked by the organist's wife if the light elegant French piece she had played was by Wagner). The visit was something of a triumph for her. She was flattered and courted. A wealthy old lady of Calne wanted her to stay with her, and promised that in time she would marry her off to an excellent man of her (the lady's) choice. Dorothy did not have great difficulty refusing, though for a brief moment she felt tempted by the exquisite ease of life in this world. But she had entered into a "pact," she said, with Harry Badcock and Harley Street and London.

1

In 1896, when Dorothy Richardson arrived in London, it was a veritable palimpsest, with layers (or ages) superimposed one upon the other. Through the streets of the city, horse-trams and horse-buses still jingled and plocked as they had in the days of Charles Dickens, but the mechanized future was clearly on its way. The first motorcar exhibit had already been held in London, and a thirty-year-old law was about to be repealed: no longer would a man with a red flag have to attend a mechanically propelled vehicle, and no longer would such a vehicle be limited to the speed of two miles an hour in the towns. Along with the motorcar, moreover, the railway was making great strides, and Londoners could now travel farther from the city for their holidays than they had ever dreamed. Some of the adventurous type whose incomes were rising and who had never gone beyond Brighton or Blackpool began to think of venturing as far as Cornwall. Others were lured to comparably exotic places by the wiles of the new art of advertising, which came in with the popular press that itself was born, one might say, just as Dorothy arrived in London. The first number of the *Daily Mail* had appeared in May 1896.

By the time Dorothy arrived, still another mode of travel had established itself: the low-wheeled bicycle that young Willie Ashenden in Maugham's *Cakes and Ale* would have so much difficulty learning how to ride. Willie was a character not yet conceived in 1896, but in Dorothy's early London days H. G. Wells had sent an equally young draper's assistant on a bicycling adventure in the pages of *Wheels of Chance;* and Wells's Hoopdriver, exploring the English countryside with his pack and his dreams, had fast become a prototype. He had imitators of both sexes, for not only were men and women scouring the countryside together, but women were bicycling alone, in their slightly shorter and fewer skirts (or in the less and less daring knickers) and with their growing sense of freedom. In another ten years, the war of the suffragettes would titillate—and enrage—a large segment of London, not to speak of the entire country and the world.

The suffragettes lay hidden in Dorothy's future, and so did the Fabian Society. Not long before, the Society had charged a big London match firm, Bryant and May, with practicing "white slavery" on the 1,400 girls whom they employed and grossly underpaid. The girls had risen up to protest their enslavement, and London watched the struggle with interest and surprise. The striking girls actually won, and they succeeded in getting not only higher wages but a union as well. When the city had recovered from the matchgirls, the dockworkers went on strike and virtually cut London off for a month. (This was the strike which the eighty-two-year-old Cardinal Manning helped to arbitrate, and in the end he tried to persuade the victorious workers not to press too hard.)

Understandable as the dockworkers' strike was from several points of view, London was mostly baffled by the attempt to blow up the Greenwich Observatory only a few years later. This seemed the height of madness to nearly everyone, yet it served to point up the presence of an infinite variety of revolutionaries and anarchists in London. Such was the face that Joseph Conrad put on the bombing, which he used in his novel *The Secret Agent,* set in the London of the nineties that Dorothy Richardson would describe years later as composed of "secret societies" that above all she had wanted to penetrate. Conrad, however, saw anarchism as one of the "plague-spots" of Europe, and a London filled with radical socialists and anarchists (as it had been since the seventies and eighties) was for him "a monstrous town." But what horrified Conrad was for some of the English, including Dorothy Richardson, more in the nature of challenge and spectacle, providing color and excitement and seeming quite harmless in itself, a view that no doubt intensified Conrad's horror. This was certainly the view that in the very year of the Greenwich bombing lay behind the remark in the *Contemporary Review* about the "anarchist prince" himself, Peter Kropotkin, as "England's most distinguished refugee." It was true that by then the prince had become retiring and scholarly, so respectable as to be invited to address a conference of the Teachers' Guild. But that did not render him safe to someone like Conrad, who saw in Kropotkin's *kind*—in fact in the horde of London's hospitably received aliens and refugees—the most serious threat to European society.

Nonetheless, while Conrad brooded and suffered and Dorothy Richardson felt the challenge of new worlds to conquer, the refugees came throughout the nineties. They crowded into certain areas of the city, the Germans and French gravitating to the West End, the Eastern European Jews remaining together in the East End, where they had disembarked. Some of them, however, ventured to go their own way, like a young Russian Jew named Benjamin Grad, who took a room in a house on the fringe of Bloomsbury, at No. 7, Endsleigh Street, and promptly made friends with a young, blonde, curious girl who seemed to him so thoroughly English that he thought he could learn all about the country—and the language— from her. She agreed to give him English lessons and to roam through the city with him. But as he grew to know her better, it was their talks rather than the sights of London that mattered most to him. She had a formidable way of seeming so certain of the truth of what she said that one hesitated to contradict her. But Benjamin Grad had his own brand of authoritativeness, his pride in being male, and he had had a thorough education, so that intellectual combat was a joy. At the same time, he was fascinated by English blondness, which is to say that he gradually fell in love with his young teacher, who had, he thought, so very English a name and manner. He himself was dark and foreign-looking, and he had (as Miss Richardson never tired of pointing out) a number of questionable—that is, non-English—habits. She liked him anyway, for one reason, because he listened to her.

2

By the time Benjamin Grad appeared at the Bloomsbury house where Dorothy Richardson lived, and joined his fate to hers, she had decided that overcrowded and even threatening as London might be, it was also incomparable. It offered everything, even a refuge from itself, which was how she saw the area in which she had chosen to live: the "oasis" of Bloomsbury, northeast of the British Museum. To her it seemed to offer a peace that was deeper than any you could find elsewhere, one quiet square following almost at once upon another, the interspaces seeming nearly as quiet as the squares themselves. Whatever sound you heard from distant tumultuous thoroughfares became in the squares but a murmur from far away. Even when she wandered to the "narrow, crowded, disreputable lane of the Euston Road," or to the "thronged corridor of Oxford Street," or into the "din of Tottenham Court Road," she felt behind her the peace of Bloomsbury stretching serenely backward, square beyond square.

Even the buildings of Bloomsbury, though many of them had already been turned into boarding or rooming houses, stood as tall, quiet tokens of an earlier splendor. "Society" had moved westward, but left its houses, "acre upon acre of cool grey stone... thick-walled [and] spacious," many of them with gardens and all of them looking out on the trees in the squares. The breath of those trees reached up to the most stifling attics of the boardinghouses, reached up as far as the attic room of No. 7, Endsleigh Street, where Dorothy herself lived.

But it was at night that Bloomsbury was at its best. The silence of the streets might often be broken by a whistle for a cab and then by the "jingle-jingle, plock-plock of [the] hansom," but these were not interruptions; they were evocative; they were incidents; and they left one free to attend to the clusters of trees and the moist evening-breath they gave off. It was a breath of the forest in the midst of the artificial air of London, and it grew richer as the evening aged.

By day, on the other hand, Bloomsbury was the home of museums, of the Slade School, of hospitals, colleges, medical schools—the home, in a word, of students, though there were some who preferred to call it "the mecca of the aesthetes" even in the days before the Omega Workshops. But it was still too early for groups or circles or movements when Dorothy first began to walk through Bloomsbury every weekday morning, absorbing the sights, the sounds, the smells of all the squares. She walked four or five miles to Harley Street each day and the same distance back in the evening, moving from one distinct world to another, from the "mecca of the aesthetes," if you will, to the mecca of physicians and surgeons that Harley and Wimpole Streets had been for an age.

No. 140, Harley Street was a stone's throw from Regent's Park, one of the eighteenth-century town houses once occupied by personages such as the Duke of Wellington. Gradually these five-story private houses had been broken up into doctors' offices, though many of the upper floors are even now private residences still (at least they were in 1969). They were highly civilized houses, with good moldings, thick doors, and wide staircases. The consulting-rooms, though always rather dark, had a magnificence that would become more and more seedy, but in Dorothy's time there was scarcely a trace of decay. She spent all day in the house, having both her lunch and her tea within doors. It was a typical establishment, occupied, when Dorothy first came, by three surgeon dentists who lived on the upper floors. The eldest, Charles Baly, had been in residence since 1876; he had a wife and son. John Henry Badcock, who had hired Dorothy and was still a bachelor, had joined Baly in 1889. In 1895, Baly's son Peyton had also begun to practice. Dorothy was taken into this dental family when she arrived the following year.

Though she served both the Balys and Badcock (as attendant when they needed her, but mainly as a secretary and receptionist), it was Harry Badcock she always thought of as her employer. He had wide interests, some of which (music and the theater) she already shared, but some about which (art, for example) she knew nothing; and Badcock was a devotee, with a special interest in the Orient. He took her with him occasionally to meetings of the Japan Society, and reported in great detail what went on at the meetings she did not attend. He liked to describe everything: all his encounters and all his impressions; how poised and serene the Chinese ambassador had been; how infinitely superior the East was to the nervous West, all of this while Dorothy was busy replenishing the supplies in his surgery. He was a very serious young man, somewhat dogmatic, and ambitious, becoming during the next ten years a well-known figure in his field. He invented an expansion plate that bore his name. He read papers before the British Dental Association and the Orthodontics Society. At one of the International Dental congresses, he presided over the Orthodontic group. His secretary could not help but admire him, and sometimes she even thought of him romantically, but in her own expanding life he was probably the most conventional person she knew.

3

At the start of Dorothy Richardson's life in London, no one could have predicted that after a decade of the city, she would turn into a writer. It would have seemed, then, a magical transformation. Many years later, she herself remembered that at a garden party in the golden days of her Putney youth, a palmist had told her she ought to begin writing at once. Perhaps there lay behind this memory the obscure sense that for what had happened to her, magic was the only explanation possible.

Yet all of us know something of the kind of magic performed by people and places experienced at exactly the right moment in psychological time. Which is to say, in the modified spirit of Taine, that the milieu of London at the end of one century and the beginning of another made certain singular and potent combinations possible in the life of a girl named Dorothy Richardson: learned Russian Jews, anarchists, freethinkers, vegetarians, Cambridge philosophers, Anglican bishops, mystics, Quakers, scientists, writers; all of these and more worked their special effects, mixed with each other, and entered the lifestream of a girl one would scarcely have noticed on a London street.

There was nothing remarkable about either her appearance or her behavior. Benjamin Grad was drawn to her for the very reason she went unnoticed by nearly everyone else. She looked typically English and behaved as typically: she had come to live in a huge, opaque metropolis, and one of the first things she did was to try to find out whether anyone she had ever known was there. She found a cousin (though, in all fairness, he turned up on his own), then a schoolmate (Maude Beaton, from the fifth and sixth forms at Miss Sandell's school, who actually lived now in a room much like hers near Endsleigh Street), and then another schoolmate (Amy Catherine Robbins, who used to be known as Perky when she and Dorothy had walked together along the Upper Richmond Road in Putney). There would be others in due course, such as Mabel Heath, the girl she had met down in Wiltshire, who appeared in London with an interesting German roommate named Ellie (or Johnny) Schleussner, but for the moment she felt secure enough. Her cousin Arthur French (who was studying at the London School of Mines) took her boating on the Thames, to tea sometimes, and occasionally to Cambridge (where his brother Charles taught mathematics). Amy Catherine Robbins, who was married now, invited Dorothy to meet her husband at their home in Worcester Park in Surrey. They had been married only a short time. He had been her science instructor at London University, but recently he had begun to publish books. Dorothy did not recognize his name (H. G. Wells).

Mildly intrigued by her old friend's note, Dorothy went down to Worcester Park one Saturday afternoon (she usually spent the mornings in Harley Street) to find her friend's husband not at all what she had expected. In the first place, he looked like a perfectly ordinary man, short and slender, fair-haired, with a slightly straggling moustache. He would pass, she thought at once, for a grocer's assistant. But then she noticed his eyes (they were gray-blue, with strikingly dark rings around them), and she heard his voice (it was husky, yet frail as well, and even thin, which made it extraordinarily effective somehow). After that, she began to realize how often he mimicked someone, how quickly his mind worked, how little she really knew about anything, and how vulnerable she therefore was. In spite of which Dorothy went down to Worcester Park again, and again, and again. Nor did she go down for the sake of her old friend, who was no longer Amy or Catherine, or Perky for that matter, but someone her husband had christened Jane; it was Jane's husband who fascinated Dorothy.

Wells was thirty when Dorothy met him in 1896, the year after he had published *The Time Machine*. Its success quite astonished him, though it was just what he wanted—to be "something in the world," as he himself put it at the time, "after all the years of trying and disappointment," not to speak of the inauspiciousness of the very beginning of his life. He had been born in Bromley, Kent, to a poor inept couple (themselves the children of an innkeeper and a gardener) who struggled under the weight of a hopelessly unprofitable china shop they should not have taken on and had had no part in naming Atlas House. In its window stood a figure of the Titan, an image that wove itself into the mind of their third son. During nearly the whole of his adult life, Wells would speak as if he carried the world on his shoulders. But when he was the child known as Bertie, Atlas House bore down on him as much as on his parents. For a boy of his class (the "upper-servant tenant class," he called it), with uncertain health to boot, there were few avenues of escape. Indeed, it scarcely occurred to his mother that he would wish to flee, though his father understood the impulse perfectly. It was she who arranged her boys' futures by her own narrow lights, and she who apprenticed him at fourteen, like the others, to a draper. Instead of learning the trade, he read books and eventually slipped from the grasp of that dark world by winning a "free studentship" at the Normal School of Science in London. But the scientific career, which Wells would always claim he had wanted more than anything else, was in like fashion to elude him. Almost at the same time that he failed as a student, Wells collapsed with a damaged kidney and a seemingly tubercular lung. He was then twenty-one years old, stood five feet five inches tall, and weighed slightly more than 100 pounds. On a spring afternoon in the country, where he was trying to recuperate, Wells convinced himself that he had "died enough." He would say years later in his autobiography, "I stopped dying then and there, and in spite of moments of some provocation, I have never died since."

He would also say that as "compensation" for the loss of a career in science, he had barged into journalism—and thence into literature. He had set about healing his wounded ego, he claimed, by persuading himself he was "a remarkable wit and potential writer." By the time Dorothy met him, he had succeeded in persuading others as well: W. E. Henley, for example, editor of the *National Observer*, who thought Wells's talent was "unique"; Harry Cust, editor of the *Pall Mall Gazette*, who took everything Wells sent him and kept asking for more; and Frank Harris of the prestigious *Saturday Review*, who at first (when he was editing the *Fortnightly*) made fun of Wells's unorthodox notions about time and then (when he acquired the new magazine) allowed him to become one of its chief contributors. Added to this, Wells had already published two volumes of short fiction and two longer pieces (*The Time Machine* and

31

The Wonderful Visit). He was at work on a full-length novel (*Love and Mr. Lewisham*), witty, realistic, rueful, about a young man very much like himself whose ambition to be a scientist is thwarted. Before finishing *Lewisham*, though, Wells brought out a story with so different a theme and tone that it might have been someone else who wrote it. The story was *The Island of Dr. Moreau*, in which Wells saw science, not as the golden apple Mr. Lewisham lost because he fell in love and got married and had to support a wife and child (all of which made him happy as well), but as a threat to the entire human race. Here Wells chose to view man as essentially animal—not reasonable, not moral, indeed perpetually in conflict with his reason and his moral sense—and if his scientific mind were allowed to develop freely, the result, as Wells conceived it, would be disaster. The animal would win out, Wells maintained, in spite of the theoretical assumption on the part of science that the intellect would prevail instead. So Moreau's scientific experiments produce nothing more than a tormented brute; and Moreau himself is a far cry from the sweet whimsical Lewisham who had given in to his body's need. At the same time one can see them as reverse sides of the same coin, which Wells would flip again and again. During the same year in which *The Island of Dr. Moreau* was published, his *The Wheels of Chance* appeared. This little book was about the dreamy, bicycling draper's assistant who was first cousin to Lewisham—and to Bertie Wells.

The man Dorothy Richardson met this very year, who had become "H. G." to everyone, was the puzzling and complex personality showing its various sides in the books he wrote. She read the books as they poured out, and she observed him at home on Saturday afternoons in the midst of increasing numbers of guests. George Gissing might have been there on occasion, inclined to explosive laughter, and Grant Allen, with his earnest manner and emancipated views of women. Frank Harris sometimes put in an appearance, leading Wells to say afterward that "in talk, [Harris] went over [him] like a steam roller and flattened [him] out completely." Curiously enough, this was exactly what Dorothy felt Wells himself did to her. He was impatient and satirical when she failed to grasp his point or when she disagreed with it. His scorn, expressed in a Cockney voice (that tended to squeak if he tried to project it), accompanied by his flailing arms, and without a trace of her father's studied elegance, was just as devastating as Charles Richardson's

32

had been. But Dorothy did not fall silent for long. She talked back to Wells and won his admiration.

These were the days she would remember long after as spent in her freezing attic room on Endsleigh Street, when what mattered most was "the dawn in [her] mind of a new idea." She was reading not only the books Wells wrote but also the books he and his friends talked about and her own friend Benjamin Grad argued from. She liked to bring Wells a new book or a new idea. When she read Kidd's *Social Evolution,* she carried down to Surrey a view quite opposed, she knew, to Wells's scientific socialism; and as she had expected, he made fun of her naive mind. But she held out against him, and he responded to her own sharpness and wit. She could even hear a "little creak in his voice" when he knew he was about to be entertained. Dorothy stored things up for him—oddities she observed, uncommon people she met, phrases that occurred to her. She had all of London in which to gather the material that would amuse Wells and bring to his eyes a gleam of respect.

She was at large in the vast city on most evenings and weekends. Wells was amazed at how much she saw and did despite the long hours in Harley Street; and she had only thirteen shillings left each week from the salary of £1 that Badcock paid her (the attic room cost seven shillings). Wells often warned her of the perils of poor feeding and harped on his own thin and undernourished body, which he had hated since puberty and which was only just beginning to fill out because he could finally afford to eat all he wanted. In fact, the wispy young man of the early and mid-nineties was rapidly thickening. He grew increasingly assertive as well, as his confidence—and his income—steadily rose. His favorite remark to Dorothy, however, was that the world was a world and not a charitable institution; he himself was working hard for his money and his fame.

Yet he also knew that his writing vein would be rich. He published seven books between 1897 and 1900 (among them *The Invisible Man* and *The War of the Worlds*) and during this time also worked on the longer *Love and Mr. Lewisham,* the first novel he was taking conscious pains with. He hoped it would win him critical esteem. In like fashion, he thought he should live in a house that suited his rising fortunes. He moved from Surrey into neighboring Kent, where he decided to have a house built for him on a site he chose between Folkestone and Sandgate, overlooking the Strait of Dover. He put in sunken lawns and a central garden, and called it Spade House. Even before settling down in it late in 1900, he made a new beginning in his work with a book entitled *Anticipations*. It was the turn of the century, after all; and Wells was brimming with plans for the world.

Even though he continued to fear that man's intellect and his inhumanity might flourish at the same rate, Wells was determined on progress. He thought he knew not only what sort of progress it should be but also how to bring it about. In the sociological books he now began to produce (*Anticipations, Mankind in the Making*), there were platforms for improvement of the world. Essentially Wells believed that by exercising "intelligence and good will" mankind could find its way out of the morass of wasted life. He himself had found his own way out of the wasteland of life as a draper. If everyone's mind were free and enlightened like his, then everyone would work as he did for the betterment of man. Thus Wells could not help translating into universal terms his own experience and his own ambition. What was necessary to his own personal health and happiness he assumed was necessary to everyone's. And what was "plain" to him should be "plain to everyone." This was the kind of conviction that gradually hardened in Wells and ultimately alienated other people from him.

Until then, in pamphlets, in lectures, in conversation, as well as in his novels and sociological books, Wells caught and held the attention of a good part of the world. In person, moreover, he was brash and clever and sensual. To his joy, women liked him. Many of them, including Dorothy Richardson, thought him the most attractive man they knew. She, in particular, watched him gathering power into his hands as though it were rosebuds strewn in his path and he had only to bend down and scoop them up. It might have seemed curious: he had none of the dignity or the elegance or the grace of her tall gentlemanly father. Wells was awkward and clumsy—a "typical Cockney," he called himself, who grabbed what he could, revered nothing, felt inferior to no one, and pronounced all this pontifically. But Dorothy saw him as successful and independent, filled with more vitality than her father would have thought it proper ever to express.

Indeed, her father, who was in Bedford Park with Kate at the time, clung to all the forms of power with none of its substance. He virtually ruled Kate's household and depended on the charity of his son-in-law. Dorothy sent him half a crown with some regularity and went less and less to Bedford Park. But neither could she go to Jessie as the century turned, for in that household, too, was an image of failure. Jessie's husband had made his own unwise investments, and after trying without success to run a boardinghouse on the coast of Sussex, he and Jessie and their little girl left England for the continent of America. Though none of them knew this, they were never to return. Dorothy and her younger sister never saw each other again.

So it was that her family circle shrank. She herself withdrew more and more from the unpleasantness it contained, and the life apart that was opening up and growing around her in London became the only one she had. Her only home was the one she made for herself in the attic room on Endsleigh Street. From here, while the nineteenth century ran its course, Dorothy Richardson, at twenty-five, twenty-six, and twenty-seven years of age, sallied forth each day into a city and world whose boundaries expanded endlessly. The Prince of Wales opened an electrified Tuppenny Tube from the Bank to Shepherd's Bush, a Boer War was fought, an African continent began to emerge. And Dorothy seemed bent on illustrating the unproven axiom that everything either attracts or contains its opposite: she savored the freedom of London and also went down to Spade House as often as she could to visit the domineering if not tyrannical H. G. Wells. With Wells she could carry on the special game of the Richardson family: she could watch him luxuriate in success; she could love, admire, and challenge him; and she could wait for the fall that, in line with all her experience thus far, would have to come.

CHAPTER THREE

An Affair of the Will

TO KEEP AN EYE on Wells was nearly a full-time occupation, for not only did the books and articles continue to flow, but he carried on debates, entered into quarrels, and in due time caused a generous number of scandals as well. Until the scandals caught the public eye, no sign of a fall was visible so far as Dorothy could tell, and there was little concerning him that escaped her attention.

He was always somewhere in her mind, always somehow prodding her, with his eyes, his voice, his mimicking tones. Everything she did apart from him, all the other people she met and the places she went to, circled back inevitably to him. She would spend weekends at Cambridge and make fun of pretentious dons for the amusement of the irreverent H. G. She could not help agreeing, however, with the Cambridge metaphysician McTaggart when he lectured that the real nature of the world could not be explained by science, and she challenged Wells to refute him. But she also described him vividly, to H. G.'s delight, as an ungainly and helpless-looking child, and she imitated to perfection the way he seemed to be speaking in a strangely empty world.

How different it was to hear the handsome Basil Wilberforce preach. On some Sundays she would join her friends Mab Heath and Johnny Schleussner on their weekly pilgrimage to Westminster, and she provided Wells with detailed accounts of the famous sermons. One of them was entirely devoted to the evolution of the Mohammedan Abdul Baha, regarded by Wilberforce as the first full meeting of East and West. In others he would preach for Total Abstinence, or against Vivisection, or in praise of "One Universal Omnipotent Parent-Source": the Mother-Father Spirit of the universe. Dorothy reported what a vibrating voice he had, and how his audience thrilled to his beauty. Wells might shrug an indifferent shoulder, but he thought Dorothy was growing up at a remarkably rapid rate, and he often told her so. She liked hearing him say this and wanted him to go on saying it. But she began to notice with increasing alarm that Wells, in an instant, by an ironic or contemptuous word, could spoil the person she was trying to describe or the feeling she wanted to express. It was one thing when she herself mimicked Benjamin Grad's accent or manner and quite another when Wells made fun of him, laughing at his dependence upon her, at his anarchist friends, or at the Russian writers (such as Andreyev) he introduced her to, whom Wells considered inferior. The trouble was she could not always tell what his response would be. Sometimes certain of his scorn, she would get praise instead, or sanction, or amused interest. It was maddening.

Maddening or not, there was no one for close to ten years who mattered the way Wells did. The vital center of her life was this young insatiable man on his blazing upward path who claimed he was interested in *her*. Grateful for the listening ear he seemed to offer, she wrote him long, passionate, disputatious letters which he barely deigned to answer. But the few words he sent in return were more than enough, for the letters she felt free to write were the thing. They allowed her to spill out her thoughts and opinions, to weigh the value of one idea against another, and to argue the merits of feeling this way instead of that. (Years later, in rereading these letters, she would be astonished at their total lack of inhibition). Even though it was now true that more and more often when she saw Wells he made her anxious, or angry, or speechless, she could not give him up. After one of these occasions, he might again be especially warm, loving, and full of charm. He would tell her how clever she was, what a marvelous ear she had. With an ear (and an eye) like hers, she ought to write: sketches, stories, a novel. "Mmmm," she might say, and go on watching H. G.

These were the days, the early years of the new century, when Dorothy roamed through London with Grad and his unconventional friends, and two sons were born to the Wellses. The world was paying Wells homage (in money and growing fame), yet he felt restless and discontented. It was now that he began to speak out boldly, insisting he could cure the ills of the world and describing such a mission as tailored to an outsider such as he. Shaw was another, Wells would say, both of them without a "predetermined" role to play and without a class whose traditions they had to choose to uphold or betray. As such a classless man, Wells claimed he felt perfectly free, and in no time at all he had numerous fights on his hands, nearly as many as he seemed to wish.

He carried on intense little wars which Dorothy Richardson observed as intensely from within and without. One of them was with the Fabians, another with the feminists, but both were for the same reason: neither the Fabians nor the feminists were doing what Wells thought they should do. The largest and most serious war was with the entire world, and Wells waged it as a prophet and dictator, predicting the future of the world and the human race and decreeing both preventive measures and instant remedies. But these decrees were for himself as well, for the problems of the world were his own writ large. He was trying to understand—and satisfy—his own insatiable and determined self.

During the next few quarrelsome years of his life, Dorothy moved in and out of it, unsure at first of what she herself wanted and then as determined as he. Although she witnessed and absorbed everything that happened to him during the whole of this sensitive time, of most importance for Dorothy were the course of Wells's quarrel with the Fabians and his crusade for free love, because these involved her most directly. When his association with individual Fabians began early in the century, Dorothy took to attending the large meetings of the Society that were open to everyone and at which public lectures were usually delivered. She especially liked to listen to the clever and witty Shaw, who would turn out to be Wells's prime adversary in the fight with the Fabians.

By the time Wells formally joined the Society in 1903, Dorothy had a good idea what sort of fight it would be, though it did not take place until 1906, when he was able to muster his restless wandering energies. From the start, she knew Wells was prodding the Fabians in the way so familiar to her, claiming over and over that they were neither active nor vigorous enough. Since they were supposed to be "reconstructing society," Wells pressed them to get on with that task. He had no patience whatever with the method of Fabius, with waiting for the right moment and then striking hard. He insisted that Fabius never had struck hard and told the Fabians that neither would they unless they followed his advice. He firmly believed they had only to decide they were capable of great things and they would surely accomplish them, which the secretary of the Society heard quite simply as a call to megalomania.

But Beatrice and Sidney Webb, Graham Wallas, and Shaw, all of them founders of the Fabians, reserved their judgment. They had sought out Wells as a young social thinker whom they wanted on their side, having read *Anticipations* when it was published in 1901; and they felt then that they could strengthen the Society, which had by now become a middle-aged group (though the founders were known as the "Old Gang"), with a vigorous newcomer like Wells. They would not even have minded if Wells gained power, so long as he used it to lead them, by which they meant serving the Fabian cause. But it was never to be clear to anyone, least of all to Wells himself, how much he was genuinely willing to "serve" *any* cause. The very tone of his behavior fluctuated: earnest and sober one day, arrogant and malicious the next. He alternated between respect for Shaw and the Webbs and contempt for the entire Fabian lot as a pack of old ladies.

Dorothy followed his alternations, laughed at his witty gibes, and considered the difficult question of his motives. Both she and the Old Gang tried to fathom this mercurial man, and with him they all played the same game of cat and mouse. Knowing Wells thought the Fabians old-fashioned and "prissy," and eager to prove her own modernity, Dorothy went to a meeting of young women who had gathered to talk about motherhood and the state, women much like Dorothy herself, labeled by one sociologist as poor-law girls, who lived on small incomes barely above the poverty line but happy and independent nonetheless. On this occasion they were trying to decide how desirable it would actually be to choose a suitable male, produce an infant, and earn the support of the state. Wells apparently sanctioned such a scheme. He believed in producing the best children for the good of both the race and society; and he kept insisting that a woman with a child should be economically free of a man, that it was better for the state than for the biological father to support the education and upbringing of the young. But while Dorothy agreed with Wells in principle, she was not as certain of his practice. Though he usually preached freedom, he was also revealing a decidedly tyrannical streak. As the secretary of the Fabians would later put it, Wells found it hard to believe that anyone could "honestly differ from him."

The game with the Fabians that Dorothy watched intently (because it paralleled her own) did not take a serious turn until 1905.

Meanwhile, she was also involved with Benjamin Grad's revolutionary and anarchist friends, spending evenings in East End rooms with everybody, as she put it, "monologuing to the universe." But in contrast with her lasting assent to socialism, her anarchist sympathies were short-lived. They were a point of view to try on, whose failure was hastened by Wells himself when he one day remarked to her that the only kind of anarchist she could ever be was the Tory kind. He showed an equal contempt for her taste in writers. Andreyev, to whom Grad had introduced her, was in vogue among European intellectuals at the turn of the century, for he had caught the mood and tone of a twilight civilization: doubting, bewildered, reluctant to risk even the hint of an answer. Grad, who was fond of Andreyev's work, had translated a few of his stories into French, and he hoped Dorothy would turn them into English as a way of improving her French. Diffident at first, Dorothy put the task off, but when she finally made a stab at it, the whole process struck her as intricate and challenging. She showed the stories to Wells, who was unimpressed. He cared little for the problems of translation and less for the mood of Andreyev. No solutions? Nonsense. Wells himself was working them out. This tragic Russian, he said, had the weakness of most intellectuals, who spent their time on the form of questions while the world went to rack and ruin. What was Dorothy doing with him?

Wells's irritation with Andreyev was a mild version of his uneasy affair with art, which unlike the Fabian Society did not respond to the tactics of a self-styled *enfant terrible*. In the face of someone like Henry James, for instance, patient, dedicated, civilized, Wells was bound to feel (when he allowed himself, that is) like a street urchin—or at best like a housekeeper's son. James, however, was interested in Wells and urged him to develop his gifts in the direction of art. As flattered as Wells was by the attention of so esteemed a personage as James, he did not have the patience for art (he scarcely had the patience for people). Ultimately James infuriated Wells, perhaps because for the older man compromise was unthinkable, while for the younger it was fast becoming a mode of life; and one assumes that long before Wells's crude attack on James in *Boon* in 1915, he had taken to speaking of him in private as a tiresome and inflated bore. Dorothy would have heard him speak thus in Kent, only a short distance away, as it were, from the Master's home in

Dorothy Richardson, 1917.

Rye. But she had also read *The Ambassadors* soon after it came out in 1903 and had found it the least boring novel ever written.

There is no record that she argued with Wells about James, yet her judgments were increasingly at variance with his the more strident he became. When he called her a fool, by which he usually meant she was neglecting the concrete—and scientific—facts of life for vague inner states of being, she felt angry as well as hurt. By this time in her life, hardly anyone but Wells would have called her a fool. Most of the people who met her during these early Edwardian years saw a poised and slim young woman who looked a youthful thirty and seemed remarkably well-informed. Grad's Russian friends thought her wonderfully droll and keen. They hoped she would marry him at last. His vegetarian friends, the Daniels, who were also "simple-lifers," were more interested in the Tolstoy Society and the ideas of Henry George than in the marriage of Dorothy and Grad. In fact, the four of them became ardent single-taxers and spent long evenings in the Daniels' suburban Brentwood home arguing about land and meat and the virtues of brown bread. But through it all Dorothy kept refusing to marry Grad.

Though he does not seem to have known it, the marriage Grad wanted so much had scarcely a chance of coming about. Dorothy felt more English all the time, and she saw Grad as increasingly foreign instead of rich and compellingly strange, as he had been when he first appeared in Endsleigh Street. Behind him as a Jew were centuries of an entirely different culture and experience: she would never feel that she knew him. There were disturbing signs, as well, of an all too familiar attitude toward women in Benjamin Grad. It was not the contempt her father had expressed openly but rather an underlying belief in the superiority of the man, with the woman more or less (depending on the individual case) a slave to him. She may have been overly sensitive, but it was also clear that though Grad seemed to love her, what he wanted most of all was a wife who would bear him a son. That was a wish Dorothy also knew something about, and it gave her pause. Finally, the matter of Grad's psychological state cannot be underestimated. He had suffered a breakdown at the age of twenty and had spent a year in an asylum in Basel before coming to England. Dorothy's memories of her mother's instability were far too vivid to suppress.

Ignorant of these correspondences, Grad hoped he could persuade her to marry him, and Dorothy kept putting him off. She seemed unable to either marry him or let him go. Later on, in a similar situation, when Wells began to suggest that they be lovers, Dorothy would again find herself advancing and retreating in stages. But even before this she shied away from decisions. For example, in 1903, when H. G. Wells officially joined the Fabians, Dorothy was still living in Endsleigh Street, but with much less satisfaction than at first. The house had been turned into a boardinghouse by Mrs. Baker, the landlady, because she thought that would be more profitable than simply renting rooms. Dorothy had been filled with dismay when she learned of the prospective change, and Mrs. Baker tried to reassure her. If Dorothy wished, she could go on just as before, paying only for her room, with not the slightest obligation about meals. What Mrs. Baker had not understood was Dorothy's fear of losing her privacy in a house where meals would be served and people would be visible and audible, hovering about to be met on the stairs and expecting to be spoken to. If she could not reach her room without encountering someone (or fearing the possibility), it was no longer the refuge she had always prized. But, incapable of deciding to move, she stayed on for another year and a half, until her own game of cat and mouse with Wells took its serious turn, at about the same time, in fact, as the one with the Fabians.

Before then, to offset the loss of privacy at Endsleigh Street, Dorothy joined the local women's club as a nonresident. It would provide her with a refuge whenever she wished to escape from the house for an evening, allow her to entertain her friends, and even permit her to put up her sister Richie when she came to town. The club was called the Arachne, the name of the weaver in the Greek myth who was turned into a spider for her boldness with the gods. When Dorothy joined the club, she could not have dreamed that the myth behind the name would play an actual part in her life, that a modern web was about to be spun about her. With no thought of either webs or spiders, Dorothy made a few casual friends at the club (one of whom happened to be named Miss Moffat) and carried on her life much as before.

But by this time—1904—she had caught the restless mood of Wells and felt at loose ends, aimless and discontented. She was becoming bored with the nature of her work in Harley Street, for though she realized there were duller places than a dental surgery, eight years of it seemed more than enough. In the surgery at Harley Street she took to complaining languidly, first about Mrs. Baker's

boardinghouse, then about the limitations of life itself. Harry Badcock, who still felt responsible for her, listened attentively. He
noted how pale she seemed and the listless way she was moving.
Perhaps he guessed that she was not telling him what troubled her
most, but he would not have pried; instead, he would have uttered a
few words of caution in his sensible, brotherly tones. She was no
doubt skimping on meals again and not getting nearly enough sleep.
What she needed was a holiday.

Why not go off, he said, for a fortnight of rest. Dorothy demurred. Harry brought it up again and again. He had got it into his head
that change was the answer to Dorothy's unexpressed problem. She
told him at last she had no money for that. But when Harry replied
that he would gladly pay for the trip, Dorothy decided to go to
Switzerland, where H. G. and his wife Jane had gone two years
before. The following year Wells had gone again, on a walking tour
with a fellow Fabian. Dorothy's own plan was to get as far away as
she could, and at the end of 1904 she went to the Bernese Oberland,
which turned out to be just what she had wanted—a magic world
beyond the reach of the real one. After fourteen glorious days and
nights, Dorothy felt that she had a clearer view than ever of the
world to which she returned; in fact, she felt ready to make decisions at last.

By now she had been in London nearly ten years. In May 1905
she would be thirty-two, quite old enough to take a lover, and if
H. G. wanted an affair, she would not resist. But it would be an affair
stemming less from sexual passion than from a half-admiring love
and a clash of wills, and it would serve in effect as the end of the
erotic side of their relationship. At the moment, it apparently required a change of scene, for still another decision Dorothy made
was to move out of Mrs. Baker's house at last. The move itself was
less mysterious than the manner in which she made it. For reasons
that remain obscure, she agreed to share a room with a woman she
had met at the Arachne and had seen perhaps twice in all: Miss
Moffat.

They set themselves up, in the early summer of 1905, not very far
from Endsleigh Street and the club, in Woburn Walk. Dorothy
would one day describe it as a Bloomsbury backwater and a "ter-
rifying" place to live. The walk was a narrow passage ("a flagged
alley") that led to Flaxman Terrace and was nearly under the
shadow of St. Pancras Church in Upper Woburn Place. The church

faced the square known as Endsleigh Gardens, below the Euston Road which there ran east and west. Dorothy and her new friend had a large room in Woburn Buildings (as they were then called), narrow, closely packed, four-storied houses that, in spite of their general decrepitude, retained something of an ancient dignity. Though the ground floors had been turned into shops, the main rooms above them had high painted ceilings, faded by now but still touched with their former splendor.

The room Dorothy shared with Miss Moffat was above the shop of a stonemason. Across the court, above the shop of a cobbler, lived the poet Yeats. His room, as it turned out, was directly opposite theirs. They saw him standing at the window on hot summer nights, with his curtains drawn aside to let in the "parched air" and the thin light of the alley's "narrow sky." But besides that dubiously romantic image, the summer nights gave off the smells and noise of squalor. The alley was poor, and some of the people who lived there were loud and bitter. Dorothy discovered soon enough that she had left Endsleigh Street only to hear, on certain nights well into the morning hours, the quarrels of crude lovers and crowded families.

There, living as she was in rather close quarters with a prim and staid young woman, her choice of a roommate proved to be equally unwise. The soul of conventionality, Miss Moffat was wary of anything approaching flamboyance, and poets in the style of Yeats seemed to her to be dangerous beings. It is hard to believe that Dorothy knew nothing of this beforehand, and one suspects that she was trying to balance her affair with Wells on the invisible scale of the unconscious. She did not keep the liaison a secret from Miss Moffat, and if what she wanted was disapproval, she got it from day to day. There were no lectures on morality (Dorothy was too old and formidable for that), but rather a constant (and soundless) clucking of the moral tongue. She stayed on, despite the unpleasant circumstances. The winter came, residents of Woburn Walk shut their windows, and the domestic quarrels grew faint. But by this time the squabble of H. G. and the Fabians had moved into high gear.

2

Just when Dorothy and Miss Moffat settled themselves in Woburn Walk, Wells had begun to see that with a concerted effort and the help of a sympathetic element within the Society he might be able to gain the control he wanted. He opened the new year—1906—by delivering to the Society one of his most memorable tracts, *This Misery of Boots*. It was a brilliant satire of English society and a rousing call to the socialists to remedy abuses at last. In February he threw down the real gauntlet and delivered a manifesto entitled *The Faults of the Fabian*. He also managed without objection to establish a committee that was charged to consider how the scope, influence, income, and activity of the Fabians could be increased; and he was given his own way in the choice of its members. The Old Gang observed with great interest this clear bid on Wells's part, though in the secretary's unfriendly opinion the committee was already run entirely by Wells and the real issue at large was absolute power. As Pease bluntly put it: "Was the Society to be controlled by those who had made it, or was it to be handed over to Mr. Wells?" Though Shaw and the Webbs felt less strongly than Edward Pease, they were nonetheless wary of Wells. So when he tried to push through a quick draft of his committee proposals before he left on a visit to the United States in March, they blocked him. And when he came back in the spring, they delayed the matter until the fall, aware—as everyone was by then—that Wells was counting on a pitched battle.

As Dorothy already understood it, if the Fabians had turned themselves over to Wells without a struggle, he would no doubt have lost interest in them. But they hesitated and temporized and moved with great caution, making the impatient Wells more and more eager to fight. In July 1906, Beatrice Webb spent a day at Spade House and noted how confident, if not conceited and testy, Wells was. He had had a remarkably successful tour through Chicago and Boston and New York, which had been capped by a stroll in the White House garden and a long talk with Theodore Roosevelt. A man to whom presidents listened could scarcely remain very modest; and the book that came out of the visit was loud and bold. It would appear in the fall, entitled *The Future in America,* with a dedication unnoticed then and since: "To D.M.R." (Dorothy would use the initials, after this, as her signature.) But Wells's war with the Fabians (like his affair with Dorothy) was a quiet, if not genteel affair, and by Christmas he had lost. He had tried unsuccessfully to detach the Executive Committee (which ran the Society) from the Old Gang, and the ranks had finally closed against him. Though he had failed in his bid for power, Wells did not resign from the Society at once;

indeed, no one wanted him to. It was clear nevertheless that the defeat rankled and that, consciously or not, he would find a way to even the score. The crusade for free love, which he now proceeded to launch in earnest, must have offered the first opportunity to do this.

The subject was not a new one for Wells: he had already made unsettling remarks about sex. In *Anticipations,* the book that had first attracted the Fabians to him, Wells had brought up, though somewhat obliquely, the subject of "endowed motherhood." Beatrice Webb—as well as Dorothy—had not missed the point, but Wells had done little more with it for several years. Then in 1905 he had published *A Modern Utopia* and made clear what he thought about marriage. It need be binding, he felt, only when children were involved; and with methods of birth control then available, children could be entirely a matter of choice. All other relationships seemed to Wells private affairs, of no concern whatever to the state. It was unmistakably an attack on conventional marriage, but most people focused instead on the curious "Order of the Samurai" Wells had drawn up in the book, and on his plans for improving the world. It was not quite so easy to ignore certain aspects of *In the Days of the Comet,* a book he published during the summer of 1906. In this scientific-socialist romance, a comet passes close to Earth and lets off a mysterious gas with unusual properties. When human beings breathe this gas, their attitudes are completely transformed: socialism prevails, and sexual relationships are freed from all the old inhibitions.

Beatrice Webb, along with many others, understood this freedom in sexual relationships as promiscuity, a concept known by the more familiar name of free love; and the high-minded Beatrice Webb, for one, thought the idea socially destructive as well as perturbing to the individual mind. She firmly believed sexual relationships of the sort Wells seemed to be advocating would interfere with intellectual activity; and she hoped that for Wells free love was one of the ideas he enjoyed throwing out just to see what reception it got. He was "gambling" with the idea, she suggested, in the reckless way her husband, among others, could not endure. To Sidney Webb, a man like Wells, who seemed to treat ideas in such a totally irresponsible way, could not be trusted. His wife felt that for the sake of "collectivism," as well as for Wells's own sake, one should try not to dislike him. But her attitude was bound to change as Wells's recklessness increased and his private life became more and more public. She would finally decide that Wells, instead of merely gambling with the idea of free love, which was bad enough, was actually using it to justify his own increasingly complicated and unconventional personal life.

For the time being his affair with Dorothy was discreet enough even for Beatrice Webb, who probably did not know of it. Dorothy herself was not interested in publicity. In 1906 she had begun to write reviews for her friend Charles Daniel's newly launched monthly called, at first, *Crank: An Unconventional Magazine,* and it was inevitable that among the books she reviewed would be Wells's. As though needing a deep breath first, however, she tackled four other books before any of his, and then in her review of the *Comet* she revealed (if one happened to have the key) that her relationship with Wells had already taken a turn for the worse. She ignored the aspect of the book which had to do with free love and chose to concentrate instead on the evidence it had to offer of Wells's future as a writer. In a tone that hovered between respect and condescension, Dorothy voiced the hope that Wells would someday produce the great work of art she was sure he was capable of producing. He needed, of course, to shake himself free of certain "limitations" first. One of them had to do with his portrayal of women. They were nearly all "one specimen," she said, "carried away from some biological museum of his student days, dressed up in varying trappings, with different shades of hair and proportions of freckles, with neatly tabulated instincts and one vague smile between them all." These were scarcely the words of a pleased, much less adoring mistress.

Years later, in his autobiography, Wells gave an account of his personal life during this period that sheds a certain light on Dorothy's evident dissatisfaction with him and the incompleteness of their relationship. Wells claimed that he and his wife had reached an agreement that left him free to have what he called "*passades.*" The word was used by the French to mean, as Wells saw it, "a stroke of mutual attraction" that might happen to any two people and was distinguished, as such, from "a real love affair." According to Wells, he was "in theory" to have *passades,* but he later discovered, as he goes on to explain, how spurious was the distinction he thought he had made. Originally, it would seem, he had managed to convince both himself and his wife that people with "an excess of sexual energy and imagination" (he was one of them, but his wife was not) would be much healthier if they found each other out and "assuaged" each other. Everything else, meaning the marriage of both persons and their family life, would remain exactly the same. But by the time Wells wrote his autobiography, he had come to realize that "nothing does remain as it was before," that as a matter of fact "two worlds are altered every time a man and woman associate." Dorothy was perfectly aware of this, as was Beatrice Webb; but Wells had a different point of view when his sexual adventures were gradually becoming the talk—if not the scandal— of London and the Fabian Society. While arguing with Dorothy and the feminists, who seemed to him bent on minimizing sex, he became involved successively with two young daughters of Fabians. One of them in due course bore him a child (a few months after her marriage to someone else). Wells saw nothing in any of this to be contrite or modest about. Indeed, the more he was attacked the less modest he became, and he even went so far as to boast that the girl had continued their intimacy after her marriage.

When he made this boast in July 1909, his notoriety had nearly reached its peak. He had already resigned from the Fabians, and people like Beatrice Webb who had been disposed to bear with him had given him up. His crudeness and his adolescence had overwhelmed them. But more was to come. Later that year Wells published a novel entitled *Ann Veronica* which was clearly about his own personal life: the heroine was the girl about to bear his child, and he himself was the married man she had knowingly enticed. The storm that had been gathering over Wells's head broke at last: Wells was wicked and dangerous; his book was "poisonous"; it taught that there was no such thing as a woman's honor, that chastity and self-restraint were delusions, and that the promptings of "lust" should be obeyed instead of resisted. He was denounced everywhere, in the correspondence columns of the *Spectator,* as well as from the church pulpits. A Watch Committee was set up with full support of the Girls' Friendly Society and the Mothers' Union. An informal group of librarians, those connected with the circulating libraries, formed their own Watch Committee to censor all novels published before they were circulated, in the hope that nothing like *Ann Veronica* would ever get through again to pollute the "moral standards of [English] home life."

Wells had no public defenders. He had gone too far for his time. Writing novels suggesting that women had just as much right as men to all the sexual experience they wanted (in or out of marriage) was

49

one thing, and shocking enough to a number of souls. It was quite another when the characters were drawn transparently from his own extramarital life. Some of his friends sympathized in private; none spoke up in public, though a letter from Edmund Gosse appeared in the *Times,* condemning the role of the lending libraries as censors and warning that in just this way a book like Darwin's *Origin of Species* could be missed. The librarians replied that they were only planning to censor fiction.

Thus, Wells was driven to defend himself, and he put on his most aggressive style to do so. "My personal unpopularity," he remarked to a friend, "is immense but amusing, and people listen with blanched faces to the tale of my vices, and go and buy my books." The "tale" had largely to do with *Ann Veronica* and the two young daughters of Fabians (Rosamund Bland and Amber Reeves) that Wells had supposedly seduced. It was they about whom people heard and talked. But scarcely anyone knew anything about the quiet affair he had had with his wife's schoolfriend Dorothy Richardson, whose name after all meant nothing, who was the daughter of no one special, and who provided none of the stuff of melodrama. Indeed, that was probably the last thing in the world she wanted. Besides, by the time of *Ann Veronica* in 1909, she had settled into a lifelong friendship with Wells, which bore little trace of their low-keyed sexual encounters.

3

Dorothy's first review for Charles Daniel's unconventional magazine had appeared in August 1906. She was then enduring a second summer in Woburn Walk and was seeking more than occasional relief in evenings at the club or in services at St. Pancras Church. On one of these occasions (either at the church or in the club), a new young resident of the Arachne approached her. Veronica Leslie-Jones was her name, and she had just turned twenty-one in July. Dorothy was struck at once by a combination of bright-eyed youth and elegance. Veronica was quite beautiful, with a fresh-looking, delicate face that was also full of passionate intensity. She would insist years later that Dorothy had been equally striking, and indeed that no one but she knew how "pretty," with her golden hair and skin, Dorothy was. The point seems to be, as Dorothy gradually saw, that Veronica's affections had fastened themselves upon her, that she saw Dorothy as somehow belonging to her. In the weeks and months to come, as though the Greek legend had sprung into new being, a web such as spiders spin—fragile but incredibly tenacious—began to be woven around Dorothy. If she knew what was happening, she did not seriously resist: Veronica was irresistible.

But Veronica did not attach herself exclusively to Dorothy. She had come to London (against the wishes of her large, wealthy, indulgent family) to study dramatic art. It was in the drama of actual human relationships, however, that she most wanted to play a part. She had already had an affair with a married man, whom she had met on a family holiday. She told Dorothy all about this and about the older man she now loved, whose name was Philip. Dorothy, in turn, introduced her to Benjamin Grad, whom Veronica thought she should marry at once because he was so beautiful; and she brought Veronica to Woburn Walk to meet Miss Moffat, who in no time at all had learned all about her. She thought Veronica needed moral guidance, which in her opinion Dorothy was quite unfit to provide. She was an innocent, helpless, beautiful girl, Miss Moffat felt, and the natural prey of a dissipated, desperate old man. Dorothy and Veronica smiled.

The "helpless" Veronica had just joined the Women's Suffrage Movement, the new militant "suffragettes" (as the *Daily Mail* had dubbed them) who hurled stones and smashed windows. She threw herself wholeheartedly into the fray. She believed in the struggle, revered Mrs. Pankhurst, and approved of the risks that demonstrating women had begun to take. She thought it quite right that one should pay a price for everything, and in due course was proudly led off to the women's prison in Holloway, where indignities such as forced feeding reportedly took place. By this time Dorothy had known her for several months, and she was aware of how complex and various were Veronica's needs. Dorothy went to Holloway to see her because they were friends, but she had little sympathy for sacrifices of this kind. She agreed that some things cost a lot and one had to be prepared to pay; but in Dorothy's mind it was not true that the law which governed this operated inflexibly. One did not have to *seek out* the price one was supposed to pay. It seemed to Dorothy that this was what Veronica was bent on doing. Whether Dorothy realized it or not, there was no difference for her exacting friend between price and punishment.

51

Before Holloway, in the earliest days of their ambiguous relationship, Dorothy was dazzled by the charm and affection of Veronica. It was a whirlwind courtship that Veronica conducted, and Dorothy scarcely had time to breathe. Under Veronica's influence, she gave up the room in Woburn Walk and moved back to Endsleigh Street, where Veronica herself was living. There, at odds with her family and low in funds, she had offered herself to Mrs. Baker as domestic help in the late summer holidays. She stayed on at Endsleigh Street for nearly nine months, until April 1907 and her brief interment in Holloway. After that, in her unpredictable way, she went to Woburn Walk, to live in the slum which Dorothy had left only a few months before. But wherever Veronica's room happened to be, she felt that her real place was at the center of the life of the person she loved. And Dorothy, after years of emotional privacy, after years dominated by her own image of Wells, suddenly found herself invaded. Now she herself was the object that Wells had been for her—indeed, that Wells no longer was.

The truth of all this dawned slowly in the course of a climactic year. Veronica had come into Dorothy's life when she was in the midst of her affair with Wells and at the time when she was reviewing books for Charles Daniel. Strangely enough, reviewing for Daniel and the vibrant, insistent girl had one common effect: they weakened her attachment to Wells. While Veronica was taking hold of her emotionally, Dorothy was breaking free of Wells in a series of reviews and essays that one can read secondarily as a dialogue with him. All the books she reviewed and the essays she began to write in January 1907 were linked to Wells, either through his visit to America or through socialism. Though she actually reviewed only two of his own books, his name cropped up here and there, sometimes favorably, sometimes not. She disliked Sinclair's *The Jungle,* for instance, and criticized its negative and bitter mood, remarking that she preferred Mr. Wells's use of fiction for "Socialist propaganda," even though she did not always agree with the lines along which he claimed things would be modified.

Even more than his name, Wells's ideas were scattered through her writing. She took positions recognizably influenced by him and even chose books to review that either directly or indirectly reflected his stand on certain controversial issues. She chose one book, for example, that argued for the abolition of the House of Lords (Wells would have liked the monarchy itself abolished), another that described a utopian society as conceived by a Frenchman (published about the same time as Wells's *A Modern Utopia*). She defended "endowed motherhood," argued that socialism was "primarily a state of mind" (as Wells himself kept saying), but went on to insist that the "main business" of socialism was to propagate this state of mind (which Wells would not have agreed with, believing as he did in programs of action). Nor would he have gone along with her firmly expressed belief that "personal matters [were] quite outside the Socialist purview." By that she meant such matters as the relations of the sexes, but also food and drink and the immortality of the soul. Though Wells thought the state should by no means meddle with sex, he was showing signs of the not quite consistent belief that advanced thinkers such as he knew what was best in everything. His Samurai in *A Modern Utopia* had been benevolent dictators who aimed at improving the race, in part through a strict sexual code. When *A Modern Utopia* first came out in 1905, Wells and Dorothy had not yet been lovers. Now, more than a year later, it was clear that she had thought a number of things through.

For one thing, she had decided that the writer was not a being apart from the man, that the only way to regard a book was as "a psychological study of the author." She made this remark in a review published in June 1907. Only a few months before, in February, she had reviewed the book dedicated to her, *The Future in America,* in a way that amounted even then to a quiet declaration of independence. Wells, in describing what America seemed to him to be like in 1906 and what he thought it might become in the future, had drawn an analogy between the will of a nation and the will of a man. In his view, the fate of each rested ultimately on the "quality and quantity of its will." Dorothy singled out this point in her discussion of the book. She apparently agreed that will and greatness go hand in hand, and she agreed also with Wells's premise that without "purpose or design" not even will is enough. This line of Wells's reasoning was familiar to her. In one form or another he had been saying this for years: one had to know what one wanted, and one needed a plan of action to get it. It did not matter who you were: the world, a country, a group such as the Fabian Society, or an individual person. He had probably told her, over and over again, that people who were not able to decide such things for themselves should allow those who *were* able to take over. And in his own treatment of her she would have seen that he drew a thin line indeed between those who were truly incompetent and those who differed from him.

By the time she reviewed *The Future in America,* she had learned that unless one pitted one's own will against his, one's own personal life—or destiny—would be controlled by the benevolent H. G. She appeared to be deciding, once and for all, that whatever the world might think of Wells (and it had more than one opinion even then), to her he was a tyrant. She would not let him run her life, not even if she bore him a child.

Early in 1907, a child had been a definite possibility. As the spring approached, Dorothy was sure she was pregnant, and she was less inclined than ever to be dominated by anyone. Wells was brimming with plans for the *accouchement* (as he would be again with Amber Reeves). They were plans that to Dorothy's mind meant dependence, in spite of Wells's supposedly enlightened views about the freedom of a woman and a child. She felt hemmed in. The boundless world of ten years before, when she had come to London and met Wells and fallen under the spell of both, now seemed a cage inside which the suffragettes demonstrated and Veronica went to Holloway. Dorothy moved from scene to scene, from Wells to Benjamin Grad to Veronica, each scene rising in emotional pitch to a crescendo reached one climactic evening in June when Veronica came to Dorothy in anguish and shock to tell her that her lover Philip had died suddenly.

Veronica stayed with Dorothy through that night; and in trying to comfort her, Dorothy grasped the full extent of her extravagant feelings: Veronica was convinced not merely that there was a special sympathy between her and Dorothy, but that they were two halves of a single whole. Dorothy understood at last that Veronica wanted to share her life, to experience *everything* in common. But Dorothy wanted her own life. Was she working herself free of Wells only to give herself up to Veronica? Yet she did not want to give up Veronica entirely, as she had not wished to give up Benjamin Grad. With the force of an electrical shock, the thought came into Dorothy's mind that if Veronica were to marry Benjamin Grad, she could keep them both and at the same time be left to herself. It seemed so perfect an idea that she blurted it out to Veronica, who did not resist. Dorothy said nothing, then or afterward, of Benjamin's youthful breakdown.

By late August, with something like the unclear yet not inscrutable sequence of a dream, Veronica and Benjamin were engaged, and Dorothy also freed herself from Wells—but at great cost to her own mental stability. Sometime during the early summer, if not before, she had miscarried and gone into the country to recover, knowing that her old life in London was finally over. It was time at last to leave the incomparable city, if only she could bring herself to do so; it was time indeed to make the grand effort: to find out, after all these years and such a narrow escape, who she had actually become.

CHAPTER FOUR

Downs and Alps

IN August 1907, when Veronica and Benjamin decided to marry, Dorothy was not in London. She was still feeling ill and tired and had taken leave from Harley Street to spend several weeks in Sussex, in the tiny coastal village of Pevensey which Grad had recommended. From here she sent Charles Daniel a small essay that appeared in his September issue. It struck a rather personal note.

She had fled London, she wrote, without any books, so she could not send along her September review as the editor asked. She might have had a book posted to her, she admitted; but that could be done the following month, she decided, when she expected to be "conscious once more of opinions and points of view." At the moment she wanted to say something that had come to her in the midst of "whirling sea-mews," as she sat watching the harbor, with the outline of the Downs in the near distance. Strangely enough, the scene before her had conjured up the image of a "high and airless" lecture hall in London. She remembered the lecture itself, and especially the recurrent phrase—heard then for the first time—that had become a fixed idea in the background of her thought: the indestructibility of matter. It was one of those fixed and unquestioned ideas to which the youth of Europe was still, she felt, "ruthlessly" exposed. And only now, when her own youth was very nearly over, could she bring herself at last to ask what that colorless little man in the London lecture hall had actually meant and what right he had had to afflict her "restless and helpless brain" with the "destructive formula" which had haunted her ever since. Sitting there on the edge of the sea, watching the tide come up, and knowing that soon the water would be beating, beating, beating at the little spit of land, she saw the futility—and the humor—of this particular fixed idea, if not of all fixed ideas.

One cannot help but see the essay from Sussex as continuing her declaration of independence from tyrannical ideas and possessive people, from Veronica and Grad and Wells. But at the same time, as she would show in the two reviews which came from her after this, she felt uneasy about the marriage. She returned to London in October, to attend the wedding ceremony, and left again almost at once. She was going to Switzerland for the winter, to recover there from the lingering effects of her miscarriage and the entire year. But she was composed enough to write a pair of final reviews, which appeared in the November and December issues of Daniel's magazine when she was already abroad. The books she chose are of some interest. One book, by a fellow reviewer, was entitled *Love: Sacred and Profane;* the other was a study of Nietzsche by A. R. Orage, the dynamic Socialist editor of the *New Age* (to which Wells and Shaw, among others, contributed). Dorothy thought Orage was far too enthusiastic about Nietzsche's "thundering and lightening [*sic*]" to do the philosopher any real service. Indeed, she felt, it did him harm by confirming the popular association of him with the Superman. What English readers unacquainted with Nietzsche's work should have, in her opinion, was as much direct quotation as possible, so that they might begin to discover him to be, not the "decadent monster" they had been led to believe him, but rather the "luminous and tender" man he was. Only such a man, she suggested, could have said, "All that is done for love is done beyond good and evil," and "If a man would no longer think himself wicked he would cease to be so." And she went on to agree with the gentle insistence of Nietzsche himself that "the secret of a joyful life is to live dangerously." This she understood to mean making no terms moment by moment and allowing no other motive but love for doing anything.

These were some of her thoughts at the time of Veronica's marriage to Benjamin Grad, a marriage Veronica claimed she had entered into for the love of Dorothy. The children of the marriage would be Dorothy's as well, she said; they would share them. Dorothy assented to this and knew that the Grads were a permanent part of her life. But she also sensed that Veronica would never be satisfied with Dorothy's feelings for her, that they would never be passionate enough, and that Dorothy would be accused again and again of coldness and selfishness. She felt nonetheless that her life

57

was freer than it had been for years and that a closed door had opened—if only she could bring herself to walk through. In any case, she had decided to celebrate her new freedom in Switzerland, in French-speaking Vaud this time instead of the Oberland.

She settled into a Château d'Oex pension, which was run by Miss Laurence Taylor. Near Montreux (which was probably the chief resort of French Switzerland), Château d'Oex stood in an open green valley, with pine woods and rocks on either hand. Six thousand feet above it, accessible by car-lift from La Bray, towered the Gummfluh mountain. Just outside Château d'Oex, in the little village called La Rossinière, was Le Grand Châlet, where Victor Hugo was supposed to have written *Les Miserables*. A short distance to the north, in the direction of Fribourg, lay the hamlet of Gruyères, famed for its strawberries and cream, its black-and-white cows, its cheese with the tiny holes (or better still, none at all), its stern gray castle, and on the left side of the approach to the castle gates a sixteenth-century house, decorated with gargoyles and clowns' heads, that had once been the residence of Chalamala, jester to the Duke of Gruyères. Dorothy made the "pilgrimage" to Gruyères twice during her stay in Château d'Oex and took the winding path up to the castle. She stood on the terrace looking down on the "great black shadow" of one of the Fribourg Alps, and in the distance rose "an oberland of clustering giants." It was a scene that made one want to write or paint.

Eventually Dorothy sketched in words one of her visits to Gruyères and another to a tiny mountain church for an organ concert by a native son of the village. She wrote, too, of the "moving witchery" of champion skiers, and of the fierce north wind, *la bise,* that filled the winter skies of Switzerland with snow clouds. In Château d'Oex Dorothy began to write in a new vein. The pension apparently had other guests who were interested in literature, and one of them received copies of the *Saturday Review* while there. He lent them to Dorothy. It was still a prestigious weekly, with Max Beerbohm and Arthur Symons among the regular contributors, and reviews of James, Shaw, and Wells that were of consistently high quality. Miscellaneous articles appeared as well, many of them written by a man named George Dewar, who often described natural scenes. Those by Dewar struck Dorothy as poor catalogs of things taken for granted instead of actually experienced. She thought Dewar's manner was like that of a museum curator who handed out information to the people he was conducting from item to item. In protest, on a winter's night while still in Château d'Oex, she herself wrote one of these miscellaneous articles (which came to be known as "middles") and sent it to the *Saturday Review* the next morning, neglecting to include a return address and nearly forgetting the whole thing.

When this piece, which she had called "A Sussex Auction," appeared the following June, Dorothy was already back in England. Upon her return in the spring of 1908, she had fallen ill at once with influenza, and her sister Kate, who was then living in Long Ditton, Surrey, took her in. During her recuperation Dorothy formally resigned from the Harley Street position and decided that where she most wanted to be, as one might have guessed from her article, was in Sussex.

2

The lure of Sussex lay in the land itself, the marshes and downs, the line of coast with the loftiest headland in southern England, and the charming bays, points, and coves. It combined the garden and the sea she had loved as a child. But still another attraction of a different sort showed through the piece she had written at Château d'Oex. In that piece she described the progress of a farm auction in Sussex and the way in which two Quaker brothers had bought a chain harrow.

The brothers were drawn from life. They belonged to the Penrose family, who ran a flourishing fruit farm in Windmill Hill, inland from Pevensey Bay, near Hailsham and Herstmonceaux. She had met the family through Benjamin Grad and had seen something of them the previous year, during her stay in Pevensey. In the family were three brothers—Arthur, James, and Jehn—a sister, and an old but still vigorous mother. Dorothy arranged to live with them on the farm in the vague position of someone neither well nor ill but somewhat unsure of herself. They seemed to understand that she was recovering from a mild nervous disorder, which she herself came to realize only gradually amounted to a virtual breakdown.

In her anomalous role Dorothy picked strawberries, thinned grapes, and often went with Jehn to Eastbourne, where they "hawked" their wares. Such a trip would occupy an entire day, and Dorothy seemed to find it an experience that never palled. It began in the early hours of the morning, when a sleepy old brown horse set out across the Pevensey marshes pulling a rickety farm cart stacked high with fruit and vegetables. By the time they reached the first Martello, it was the lunch hour, and they devoured their huge farm sandwiches. Then they continued on into the "hinterland" of Eastbourne. In the afternoon, while Jehn continued hawking, Dorothy would sit on the pier taking in the light over the waters. Sometimes she wandered on to Beachy Head to contemplate its vast height. In the evening she always walked back through Eastbourne to the inn called (like so many other inns in England) The Rising Sun. There she was supposed to wait for Jehn, who never failed to appear at eight o'clock sharp. Until nine they sat quietly over cocoa and cakes. Then they started back on the "long long glow-worm-lit drive" to Windmill Hill, where they arrived at midnight. Dorothy liked the trip best in the late autumn, when the marsh cattle were like "hippos, humping up out of a sea of mist."

As a matter of fact, Dorothy liked everything about this part of Sussex, in all seasons; and in a series of sketches for the *Saturday Review* she paid tribute to the beauties of the cycle of the year and of life in the villages and on the farms of Sussex. Sometimes she would give the impression of actually writing from the Penrose farm itself. Always her descriptions were those of an "insider." By then she had caught the rhythms of both Sussex and Windmill Hill, which is not surprising since she lived there the better part of three years, supporting herself largely, it seems, by writing for the *Saturday Review* and reading manuscripts for Wells.

These are veiled years she spent in Sussex. A brief note to Wells on his "pinnacle in London" in 1910 is all that survives of whatever correspondence she carried on then. There might have been a romantic episode with one of the Penrose brothers, but Dorothy's chief concern seems to have been, in plain terms, to pull herself together. To do this she needed a refuge from the world, and everything she wrote about Sussex indicates that it served that purpose ideally. The sketches strike the same note over and over in slightly different ways: the note of security and enclosure out of reach of "the stirring world" she had left behind. Stillness, shelter, serenity, warmth: these are the recurrent words Dorothy used. She joined in the quiet life of the farm and the villages and went with the family on Sundays to the little meetinghouse at Gardner Street, the village next to Herstmonceaux. Once, when she happened to be in London at the time of the Yearly Meeting, she attended that event, which was regarded as the peak of the Quaker year.

What seemed to attract her most to the Quakers attracted her also to Sussex—their way of life, their way of being, and the serenity she thought these gave them. Hints of her feelings about them are in the piece "A Sussex Auction" written at Château d'Oex. In that piece she described the Quaker brothers as quiet and gentle but also authoritative. They had come to Sussex knowing exactly what they wanted to buy, and they had waited patiently for the bidding to begin, untouched by the inflamed and excited air of the farm auction that was inevitably a social event as well. Men were drinking gin, and girls were flirting, but the two Friends remained sober and determined. They were "less involved" than the others, Dorothy wrote, "less easily stimulated," and because they were more detached, they were also more observant. She admired the combination.

In the book she eventually wrote about the Quakers, their appeal for her is more directly stated. They had an affirmative attitude to life, they believed in "the possibility here and now of complete freedom from sin," and they recognized the "spiritual identity" of a woman. The "inner light," they felt, was universal; women were not "an appendage to be controlled, guided, and managed by man." But perhaps most important of all, the Quakers seemed to Dorothy to be searching always for the "center of being" where one might remain, remote and impersonal, and yet "see freshly all the time." This was where she had sensed the Penrose brothers were; this was where she herself wanted to be; and in the process of finding her way, she evolved a technique for art.

The technique can be traced through the sketches she continued to write for the *Saturday Review* until the middle of 1912. In them she tried to be both participant and observer, to achieve a form of distance that paradoxically made for closeness. She wanted to implicate her reader by conveying a sense of immediacy, a sense of the experience taking place in the present, and she wanted also to be the agent of transmission. Which means that from the start her creative impulse was autobiographical: to write of what one knows, as the person who knows, at the moment of knowing.

Another striking characteristic of these sketches is the part that memory (or the past) played in them. Almost as if to test the power of her momory, she began writing about Vaud only toward the end of her stay in Sussex (that is, three years after she had been there), and then, when she had left Sussex, writing about Sussex again. One of these later Sussex sketches, "Strawberries," has a special significance in this regard. It begins in London as Dorothy walks through a windy, hot, dusty street to the graystone house where she lives in an attic room. In her room the air is even more lifeless than in the street below, but there at least the sun no longer stings. Then from the street the sound of a "long cry"—English stra-a-w-berries!—which "pierces like an arrow to the heart of memory," is carried up to her. What follows is a re-creation of Sussex in strawberry time, and this becomes the new, even more vivid and sensuous present of the sketch. The point being made is that the past has a greater reality than the present, but it is a past that becomes the present with all its immediacy and is superior to the actual (and here rather dusty) moment in time.

3

"Strawberries" appeared in June 1912, when Dorothy's writing as well as her life had taken another sharp new turn. She had begun to think about if not actually to write a novel, she had left Sussex and the Penroses, and she had no particular residence. Most of the time, during the few years after she left the farm in 1911, she stayed with friends, usually with her new friends, novelist Jack Beresford and his wife Beatrice. It was he who now had more to do with the shape of Dorothy's life than anyone else.

She had met him through her friend Ellie (or Johnny) Schleussner, and though they were virtually the same age (Jack's birthday was in March, Dorothy's in May), she felt at once that he was older than she and that she could lean on him and be taken care of. Whether it was his face (which some described as the face of a "seeker") or his lameness (he had been crippled since childhood from a form of infantile paralysis) or his interests in theosophy and the occult, the fact remains that something about Beresford caused her to depend upon him like a child. In his presence she felt all her burdens instantly removed. But this did not mean they had a harmonious relationship. As a matter of fact, it was an acrimonious and abusive one, with Dorothy challenging his judgments all the time and making him feel, as he himself put it, "small and undistinguished." Indeed, they often stood opposite one another and hurled insults. Whatever else she may have gained from the Quakers, Dorothy had not acquired their traditionally gentle manner. But neither she nor Jack took these scenes seriously. Jack looked upon Dorothy as a difficult and powerful personality who somehow compelled both patience and admiration (his wife Trissie, however, was not so sure as he was of Dorothy's special gifts). For her part, Dorothy saw Jack as "mildly intellectual," someone who liked to collect systems of thought, but she respected him for the way in which he supported himself and his wife entirely by writing.

Dorothy spent weeks (if not months) at a time with the Beresfords. They introduced her to Cornwall as the economical place for struggling writers to live. She went to stay with them in St. Ives, a small fishing village a few miles from Penzance on the north coast (where Virginia Woolf as a Stephen child used to stay), and felt she was rediscovering the Dawlish sea of her childhood in a rougher and wilder form. The Cornish coast, especially the northern side, had none of the softness of south Devon, and the narrow tapering peninsula of Cornwall thrust out for some eighty aggressive miles into the Atlantic. Nevertheless it was the same splendid sea she had loved as a child.

Once again she felt the sense of adventure that her family had felt going down to Dawlish, for the far reaches of the West country were still relatively free of holiday-makers. In St. Ives a motorcar had scarcely been seen yet, and a pony-and-jingle was regarded as the luxurious mode of transportation. Of the two, Dorothy and the Beresfords preferred a donkey-and-jingle as "more leisurely and temperamental." The shaggy donkey that pulled the jingle could usually be persuaded, after a while, to go on. The real disadvantage was that a person with long legs had no alternative but to telescope himself, and even persons of normal size were so near the ground, Dorothy said, that "foxgloves on the wall-tops became exotic trees against the sky-line."

Dorothy spent the spring of 1912 in St. Ives. The Beresfords had rented a bungalow "with its knees on the rocks," Dorothy said, and the three of them roamed about together. For three weeks in May a nearby bungalow was occupied by a young man named Hugh Walpole with whom they immediately made friends. Though only twenty-eight, he had already published four novels. The most recent, *The Prelude to Adventure,* was getting good reviews and was selling better than the others. So with every reason to believe his great dream of being a successful novelist might actually come true, he was a happy genial young man on holiday. He and Dorothy and the Beresfords climbed to clifftops under the brilliant Cornish sky, talking all the while, and they continued to talk through most of the evenings of Hugh's stay. Dorothy liked his "pleasantly booming baritone voice" and the way he seemed to bring both warmth and the world with him when he entered a room. He was also someone who always had to be enthusiastic about something. One of his current enthusiasms was Wagner, and Dorothy's ear caught the strains of familiar motifs sounding from his bungalow. In due course, Hugh turned out to be what he then seemed in the process of becoming: a thoroughly popular and successful writer, an unquenchable storyteller. Though the youngest of the three, he would be the most successful by far.

Dorothy and Jack were already thirty-nine. She had published no books yet. Just the year before, Jack had brought out the first novel of a trilogy, *Jacob Stahl,* a story such as Wells (whom Jack admired) might have told; but there were no signs in its reception that he could expect anything more than the smallest rewards. (He was never to get any big ones.) Nonetheless he had been supporting himself entirely by writing, largely for the *Westminster Gazette,* an evening paper with literary interests. He wrote articles and reviews for the *Gazette,* but like Walpole it was largely fiction he wanted to produce. One of the things he admired about Dorothy was the diversity of her writing and the use she had been making of all her actual experiences: in Sussex and Switzerland, among Quakers and socialists and even vegetarians. She had begun to write articles for dental magazines, mostly the *Dental Record,* the organ—if not the spokesman—of the profession in England. One article, entitled "Women in Dentistry," had already appeared; a second, "Diet and Teeth," would come out in August 1912.

But that spring in St. Ives Dorothy was principally occupied with a book that was still only in her mind's eye. It would probably be a novel, since that was what the editors of the *Saturday Review* had been urging her to write. Jack thought she should attempt it. So did Wells, though she sometimes felt he was also discouraging her. In any case, she had already made several false starts and was coming to realize how much she did not want to write a novel in the manner of the day—in the socially realistic vein of Wells or Arnold Bennett or John Galsworthy. It was a different matter for Jack Beresford, who inclined that way naturally. He shared their belief that they were engaged in truthfully representing reality. But Dorothy believed this less and less. It seemed to her that nearly everything she considered important was being left out of novels. They had a realistic frame, and more or less lifelike characters placed in situations that exemplified the various kinds of problems facing the man of the day. There were moral, social, economic, political, and sexual problems; and they were solved—or not—by reason, courage, defiance (of convention), or luck. Where in all this, Dorothy wanted to know, was life itself?

It was one thing to criticize other people's novels and quite another to write one's own. By the end of the summer of 1912, Dorothy had gotten no further than she had been in the spring at St. Ives. She was still without a clear conception of the book she wanted to write, but she had the sense that certain conditions would help her. She needed above all to be alone, anywhere outside of London. Cornwall would be perfect, as Jack Beresford saw too; and he offered her the occupancy of a house he had just rented near the harbor of Padstow, farther up the coast from St. Ives. He and Trissie left Dorothy there in October, and the months that followed took their place in her memory as one of those magical moments in time that can never be duplicated.

4

The house Jack had rented for £12 a year was of mottled Cornish stone that looked, as it usually does, both ancient and indestructible. It was in a tiny farm hamlet, Trehemborne, with the small village of St. Merryn on one side and Porthcothan Bay on the other. A cottage was next door, Trehemborne Farm was across the road, and Kirketh Farm was up the road. The house belonged to Kirketh Farm, but it had once, not very long before, been a Bible Christian chapel. The Bible Christian sect, an offshoot of Wesleyanism, had a number of followers in the Padstow area, though not enough to rescue the chapel from mounting debts and to save it from the bank. The bank sold it to Farmer Geach, who thought he could make of it a decent cottage into which he and his wife would one day retire. Until then, they would rent it out. The first tenants after the conversion were two maiden sisters; the second were the Beresfords and Dorothy Richardson.

65

Dorothy always spoke of it as the converted chapel, and she claimed it was haunted. Somebody, she said, would stir sauce in a pan in the kitchen when she was upstairs, and every night at nine a thud would sound below the floor, at intervals, moving nearer and nearer until it got to the middle of the floor and stopped. The ghost did not disconcert her in the least, she said; in fact, it "enchanted" her. She thought it the perfect accompaniment to solitude, and her solitude was very nearly complete. She saw no one except the woman next door who cleaned for her once a week, brought her supplies, and occasionally cooked a chicken. She read no newspapers and no books. It was as if "the world had dropped away" but, at the same time, as if everything had taken on a "terrific intensity," and she was alive in a way she had never been before.

As she sat here in this purely Cornish setting with a mass of discarded drafts and plans about her, two things that had been rather vague and yet were always connected became absolutely clear. The first was that she had to write a novel about what she knew, and her own life was all she felt she could claim to know. The second was that her heroine—who had been central in her mind from the start and whom she saw now was no one but herself—was not enough, for she also saw that it was impossible to go on "telling" about her. There had to be another way; what was it? Then, in her own complete isolation, she understood at last that when this heroine of hers, this girl named Miriam, had appeared in her mind's eye, she, too, was alone. No one else was "*there* to *describe* her." With this realization that Miriam must seem to speak for herself and to meet experience directly, the method of her novel came into being: the developing consciousness of her heroine would be all there was. Early in 1913, after months of intense absorption, she finished a novel entitled *Pointed Roofs,* which she knew was only the first part of a whole already conceived as *Pilgrimage.*

Such was Dorothy's recollection, in later years, of the genesis of her novel. Her testimony in *Pilgrimage,* as well as the novel itself, suggests that more than this took place in Cornwall. First, the experience seems to have been an integration of an older lesson she had learned some ten years earlier when reading Henry James's *The Ambassadors.* She had understood his use of point of view and had called it the "first completely satisfying way of writing a novel." She combined the lesson of Henry James with the lesson of Quaker life: an impersonal narrative, like "discovery about oneself," could be highly personal as well; it could have both an objective existence and a subjective identity.

Second, as her novel would demonstrate, she was already convinced that the sensibility—or consciousness—of her youthful heroine had an intrinsic value and interest. So she would not argue, she would not explain, she would not justify; rather, she would present that sensibility in more and more detail. All of this meant that, besides recording such detail for its own sake, *Pilgrimage* was to be a historical document, an analysis of the self and a disciplined confession.

CHAPTER FIVE

"An Original Book"

DOROTHY went to London with the manuscript of *Pointed Roofs* in the early part of 1913. She took a room in St. John's Wood, the residential district of the borough of St. Marylebone that was then the artists' quarter. She showed Jack Beresford her novel, indicating that she knew it needed some revision. Jack returned it gingerly: he thought it an interesting experiment so far, he said, and now it was time to "let something happen." Dorothy thought quite enough had happened already. She made revisions and sent the manuscript to a publisher. It came back with an apologetic note from the publisher's reader, who was not sure what the book was about. She discarded the note and for the time being stored the manuscript in a trunk.

1

She had begun her novel in medias res, as it were, with her seventeenth year and the experience of Hanover, the first of her life that she had brought about by acting independently. But in its re-creation it is more an experience of the senses than of the mind. One can see in the manuscript of *Pointed Roofs* (the first draft and the revisions) that she virtually relived the stay in Hanover, that she had almost total recall. One can see also that she considered at least some of the problems of autobiography, those having to do, for example, with names. She changed the family name to Henderson, her older sister Richie to Eve, and her younger sister Jessie to Harriett. Her eldest sister appeared to give her trouble. Throughout the original manuscript as well as its various revisions, she called Kate by her actual first name (Frances), which Kate never used. But the name did not satisfy her, and at the last moment she must have changed it to Sarah, which occurs in the printed text but nowhere in the manuscript. The name of her birthplace was also troublesome. She alternated between Babingdon and Babington, finally settling on the latter. Yet without any hesitation she moved their big house in Putney to Barnes, one of the adjoining suburbs along the Thames. She gave the Henderson family the Richardson background in trade, but she made them all Wesleyan Methodists (when the evidence seems to be that a good many of them were Baptists). One can see perfectly well in all of this that Dorothy meant to throw little more than a thin veil over reality. But the veil was positively invisible when she took her heroine to Hanover in the third chapter and lost herself completely in the past. Not until midway through the first draft did it occur to her that the German names she had been using were the original ones and that she ought to make some changes, if only to protect herself.

This she now apparently began to do. Fräulein Lily Pabst turned into Lily Pfaff. The house on Meterstrasse was moved first to Gartenstrasse, then finally to Waldstrasse. Some of the girls' names, like Lily's, were changed only in part, perhaps as much for aesthetic reasons as any other. The sound of Ulrica Hesse in place of Erica would seem to have dictated the change; so, too, the change from Meta Weldertz to Minna Blum and from Emma Rauchheld to Emma Bergmann. She left unaltered the name of the music master and the famous confectioner of Hanover to whom generations of schoolgirls joyously went to enjoy *Schokolade*. The Konditorei Kreipe and the marble-topped tables at which the girls sat survived both world wars, but the view from the windows has never been of the wide and colorful Georgstrasse as it was in *Pointed Roofs*. The Konditorei Kreipe seems always to have stood at Bahnhofstrasse 12, where the outlook is much more prosaic. But Dorothy remembered, without flaw, the quaint and peaked little town of Hildesheim where the girls walked from Hanover. She remembered it down to the nestled look it had when she stood on the bridge near the railroad station, and she called the town Hoddenheim. In the matter of names and certain kinds of physical detail, one can see her being artful here, arbitrary there, and sometimes inventive. The manuscript also shows, when it is compared with the printed text, that Dorothy first recorded, in their raw state and as she experienced them again, the inchoate feelings of the seventeen-year-old girl. Then, in the act of revision, she gave form to these feelings without refining (or falsifying) them. Several scenes in the novel bear witness to the process. Two of them are worth noting here.

Most readers of *Pointed Roofs* will remember the scene between the young and innocent Miriam and the middle-aged Pastor (whose name is always Lahmann). In both the original and the final version of this scene, Miriam comes bounding into the room, clutching the music she plans to play and filled with the joy of having been asked by one of the little pupils, the wealthy Minna Blum, to stay with her in the luxuriant south of Pomerania. Lahmann, mildly aroused by the sight of the fair-haired, bright-cheeked, happy Miriam, begins a low-toned flirtation that throws her quite off balance. Veering between curiosity and a vague apprehensiveness, she can only recover her self by getting angry. Agreeing with Lahmann that she is indeed "vairy ambitious," though she is rightly puzzled by the remark, she then recoils from his own expressed ambition for "a little land, well-tilled" and "a little wife, well-willed."

Before Miriam can show Lahmann that she does not even "recognize such a thing as 'a well-willed wife,'" he has gone on, smoothly and sympathetically, to ask why she wears glasses. She hammers out, "I have a severe myopic astigmatism," but her response does not produce the desired effect. Lahmann is by no means cowed. Instead he asks to see her glasses, and Miriam, cowed, takes them off. Without them, half of her already limited youthful vision is gone, and it would seem that at this point in the manuscript, since the handwriting takes on a radically different appearance, Dorothy must have removed her own glasses and finished writing the scene under the same handicap as her heroine. Both of them are looking at the same time at the blurred image of Lahmann as *he* gazes into the "lame eyes" of the "poor child," and remarks how "vairy, vairy blonde" she must have been as a child.

The original scene ends almost immediately after this, with the words of the middle-aged (and also unmarried) Fräulein Pfaff, "Na guten Tag, Herr Pastor," sounding from the door. In the published novel, three additional paragraphs round out this scene by characterizing for the reader the woman whose nature the girl can only sense. Fräulein Pfaff is given "speechless waiting eyes," and Pastor Lahmann is made to examine his fingernails. Miriam does not understand the significance of this silent drama and its sexual overtones, but she registers it, unconsciously absorbing the charged air, thereby broadening her own narrow view for the reader.

Another scene near the end of the novel also reveals how Dorothy was learning to manipulate—and expand—the limited point of view

Facsimile of a page from the manuscript of *Pointed Roofs*. Courtesy of the Beinecke Rare Book and Manuscript Library of Yale University.

of a seventeen-year-old. Miriam is lying in bed one night brooding about a talk with the Fräulein, who seems to think (or so Miriam believes) that her "manner" as a pupil-teacher might be improved. Convinced that she will have to return to England because of this (and because of a money problem as well), she holds a conversation in her mind with her sister Eve, to explain her position. She cannot "grimace," she tells Eve, as she interprets the manner Fräulein Pfaff wants her to adopt with her pupils. But the venture—coming out to Hanover—was not all in vain, she wants Eve to understand. The cost of keeping her at home during the past five months would have been more than her passage to and from Hanover. At this point, both her reason and her composure break down. Her mind is a seeming jumble of images and half-formed ideas that reflect her extreme youth but also her unchildish perception that one is helpless in a universe that seems to require so much strength merely to exist.

In the manuscript these passages were revised with a view to confirming their internal order. Despite the feverish quality of Miriam's thoughts, they proceed by the logic of association to form an emotional pattern. Miriam's mother, for example, did not appear in the original version. Dorothy added her, having Miriam hear her voice telling her not to "go deeply into everything" and wishing she were strong so that she could tell Miriam how to "enjoy life." The frail and sad Mrs. Henderson is meant to contrast with her laughing contemptuous father. And Miriam is meant to be seen admiring her father, loving her mother, and feeling guilty about both these feelings. She ought not to admire the man who had brought the family to the edge of ruin; and mixed with her love for her mother is the knowledge that her mother is aware that her daughter knows she (Mrs. Henderson) is not clever. The guilt that a child feels (and Miriam is no more than a child here) is often disproportionate for a sin that seems great and yet remains vague, though it also seems certain to bring down a heavy punishment. Miriam imagines she will be punished by Apollyon, who will claim her and one day come in flames, beating his wings. No one would succor her if she were fully known in all her sinfulness, no one except her eldest sister, who "would rush in without saying anything, with a red face and bang down a plate of melon."

Miriam emerges from *Pointed Roofs,* finally, as someone whose growing sense of self is her most valuable possession. Though still expressed largely in physical terms (feeling the strength of her hands, which are like "umbrellas," and the strong movements of her limbs), its frame of reference has already begun to expand. The novel ends with Miriam tacitly opposing her own matter-of-fact tight-lipped Englishness to Fräulein Pfaff's strong-willed German sentimentality. But Fräulein Pfaff also says she thinks that she and Miriam have much in common, at which Miriam freezes, and Dorothy has made her point about her heroine: the conflict between her and Fräulein has not necessarily been a conflict of opposites.

One would suppose this to be equally her point about herself. The evidence suggests it, down to the very last page, on which Dorothy has an "enormous" bell ring at the station platform, and Miriam (as the sensitive Dorothy would have done) puts her hands to her ears. But *Pointed Roofs* is only secondarily about herself as a historical person. She chose to tell the story of her own life because this was all she felt she could claim to *know;* and she wanted to tell this story, not only because it had for her an extraordinarily vivid and sensuous reality, but also because it seemed to her emblematic. Every girl, she thought, who had been born, as she had been, into a late-Victorian world inhospitable if not hostile to women would have to struggle as she did for selfhood. The struggle was the story worth telling, as before her George Eliot and Charlotte Brontë had also believed.

There are connections between Miriam Henderson and George Eliot's Dorothea Brooke or Gwendolyn Harleth, who were not docile and who fought against the roles assigned to them. There is probably an even stronger link between Dorothy Richardson's heroine and Charlotte Brontë's characters, the abrasive Lucy Snowe in particular, who has to make her own way in the world and is determined to do it as uncompromisingly as she can. But Lucy Snowe and Jane Eyre have a strong covert sexuality that is absent from Miriam Henderson. So that even though Fräulein Pfaff and Pastor Lahmann might be said to correspond to Madame Beck and Paul Emanuel in *Villette,* there is nothing in Dorothy Richardson's novel like the possibility of a sexual relationship between two adults that hovers tantalizingly over Charlotte Brontë's. Miriam is too young for that in *Pointed Roofs,* but the decisive element is not age. Miriam's passions will never be strongly sexual in nature. Neither were Dorothy Richardson's. They were bound up instead with forging a literary identity for herself, which turned out to be the equally passionate occupation of her contemporaries, Proust and Joyce, as well, and which may well prove to be the link that most significantly connects the three.

As it happened, however, Dorothy Richardson employed a new mode of narration to give her emblematic tale the actuality she wanted it to have for the reader. It would come to be called "stream of consciousness," a label she would dislike, but it would also account in large measure for the attention *Pointed Roofs* was to get. No one except the author's family and close friends would pay the slightest attention to the autobiographical nature of the book, for the simple reason that it had no relevance whatsoever. *Pointed Roofs* was read and reviewed as a novel mainly because Dorothy Richardson had succeeded in presenting herself as though she were someone else.

2

During 1913, while the manuscript of *Pointed Roofs* remained stored away, Dorothy was engaged in very different kinds of writing. Besides continuing to produce essays on dentistry (one appeared in the *Dental Record* of October), she arranged with her friend Charles Daniel to translate three texts from French and German. She was also working on her book about the Quakers, and she had contracted to put together an anthology from the works of the founder of the Quaker sect, George Fox. One of her sketches appeared in a July issue of the *Saturday Review,* and two book reviews were published in *Plain Talk*. She also found time for a brief holiday in Rottingdean (near Brighton on the south coast), a visit with Kate in Long Ditton, and with the Wellses in their relatively new Essex home (they had moved to Dunmow in 1910). Although she knew of Wells's latest involvement with young Rebecca West, she kept her opinions to herself, eager to lead her own life as a professional writer beyond the range of his increasingly tangled affairs.

Now, instead of the little magazines, *Ye Crank* and *The Open Road,* for which Dorothy had written her first essays and reviews, Charles Daniel was publishing another magazine called *The Healthy Life*. He had also begun to put out a companion series of Healthy Life booklets. Dorothy agreed to translate two works by a Frenchman named Paul Carton, which would be volumes seven and eleven in the series. They were entitled *Some Popular Foodstuffs Exposed* and *Consumption Doomed,* and both were variations on Dr. Carton's main theme: if man continued to consume meat, alcohol, and manufactured sugar, he would eventually die of tuberculosis, cancer, and insanity. Daniel and his wife, both of them vegetarians for years, were in total accord with Carton. Dorothy, in her translator's preface, seemed to be expressing a somewhat cautious agreement.

She said she agreed with Carton's emphasis on "choice and construction in place of inertia and acceptance" as regards the food we eat. Apparently she assented, as well, to his argument that man is not carnivorous by nature but is, rather, "frugivorous like his cousins the anthropoid apes." But in her preface to *Consumption Doomed,* she positively applauded his discovery that, among his own patients at least, the neglected condition of their livers and stomachs was far more serious than that of their lungs.

The third book she translated for Daniel was from the German of Professor Dr. Gustav Krüger: *Man's Best Food.* Krüger contributed his own preface, in which he repeated his central argument that to abstain from eating meat was to deliver man from "evil passions and diseases" and to set "the animal world free from its worst foe." Within the book he offered several amusing reasons for not eating meat. One was that it gave women "the most filthy and detestable work to do in the kitchen": they themselves often had to kill small animals or fowl or fish. This was bad enough, Krüger thought; but what about eels and crabs? he asked. Could anyone watch a woman skinning live eels or boiling live crabs and "kiss the hand which [did] such things?"

However thoroughly Dorothy may or may not have endorsed the views of men like Krüger and Carton, she did believe in the superiority of brown bread over white and eggs and nuts over meat. She often had a meal in one of the vegetarian restaurants of London, in Eustace Miles, for example. Here one evening she began a conversation unknowingly with Josiah Wedgwood, the radical M.P., whose book *The Road to Freedom* (written with his wife) she had reviewed in July. They struck up a friendship which seems to have waxed and waned during the next few years. Wedgwood and his wife separated during this time, and there may well have been talk between him and Dorothy about marriage, but it does not seem to have been very serious. Years later he remembered her as the person

75

who had introduced him to the subject of Zionism, a cause he would strongly support. She herself was neutral about it. Her mind was engaged elsewhere.

She had turned forty in the spring of 1913, an age no one can ignore, not even someone as young-looking and trim as she, who might also be said to have before her a new career if not a new life. That she did not ignore the imposing age she had reached can be seen in the work with which she inaugurated the decade of her forties. With *Pointed Roofs* she had gone back to recover her own young self when it had just begun to wonder about the nature of sin and to feel such things as guilt. With the book about George Fox she had gone into the life of a man she admired, a man who had wrestled with himself and had triumphed. He had founded a sect and earned a place in the history of the world. But he had also understood the primacy of the "single human soul" and had known that to love another human being one must "first love himself." Dorothy thought that in this he had grasped a fundamental truth that she herself had been struggling to live by. She saw him as standing for both freedom and love in a way that she assented to, and for intuition as she herself viewed it: the direct means by which one possessed reality and was possessed by reality. He was "a mystical genius," but also a strong-willed English individualist, a man of sturdy practical sense who knew how to organize and get things done and who knew, above all, how to build a unified life for himself. Dorothy identified with George Fox and with what he had achieved. But, as *Pointed Roofs* shows, she was drawn at the same time to a contemporary of Fox, the gnarled and struggling John Bunyan, for whom the odds were heavy, the stakes high, and sin lurked everywhere. Bunyan's journey infuses the whole of Dorothy Richardson's *Pilgrimage*. But Fox's life inspired her.

3

When *The Quakers Past and Present* appeared in February 1914, Dorothy was in Cornwall with the Beresfords. They had given up the converted chapel and were renting a wide rambling farmhouse, with five bedrooms facing the sea, just above Porthcothan Bay. Dorothy stayed here with them until the middle of April; then she went to spend the rest of the month alone, six miles away, in the village of Trevone. She planned to be back in London by May for the publication of *Gleanings from the Work of George Fox*.

The village of Trevone was one of her recent discoveries. Less than two miles from Padstow and the harbor, it was a quiet, gentle little place that spread and rose on winding lanes from its own cliff-topped bay. A walk on the cliffs would take one around to Harlyn Bay. From there one could get to Constantine Bay and St. Merryn and, probably, if one put one's ingenuity to work, to nearly all the bays, coves, and beaches in the Padstow area. Dorothy did not know this, but Padstow was to *be* Cornwall for her for the rest of her life. At the moment, it simply offered cheap lodgings for a brief holiday.

In May, when she got back to London, it seemed no different than it had been when she had left it. She had the same room in St. John's Wood (though it had begun to seem less desirable, for the house was somehow noisier) and went about her business with all the confidence in the world. But at the beginning of August, in the midst of an extraordinarily beautiful English summer, the world fell to bits. War was declared, and Londoners walked the streets feeling half-dazed. Dorothy remained in the city through December. In spite of the war that had come as such a shock to everyone, she believed in the future, in her own future as well as the world's. She took the resistance to Germany as a matter of course. One simply had to protest, she wrote, "against the desire for regimentation and domination of anything whatsoever" and, if necessary, to take arms. One also assumed the resistance would be successful.

In January 1915 Dorothy went to Cornwall to stay for another three months with the Beresfords in Porthcothan House. They were eager for news of London. There in Cornwall the war seemed remote, and Dorothy gave them a detailed report, describing the dazed city and the numbers of uniformed young men to be seen everywhere. She also told them she had met their friend Barbara Low (a psychoanalyst), who "raved" to her about D. H. Lawrence's new book (*The Rainbow*) to be published later in the year; she had read half of it in manuscript. According to Miss Low, Dorothy said, it was "a work of genius." Lawrence's publisher happened to be Gerald Duckworth, whose chief reader-editor, Edward Garnett, was a friend of Jack Beresford's. It now occurred to Jack that Dorothy ought to send her novel (which he had read again) to Duckworth.

As they expected, Garnett was the reader of *Pointed Roofs*. It did not take him long to reach a decision. The novel seemed to him an example of "feminine impressionism" and worthy of publication.

Duckworth accepted his recommendation, the date of publication was set for September, and Beresford was to write an introduction. Garnett counseled Beresford about the introduction, and Beresford counseled Garnett about Dorothy. "Be patient with her," he wrote, "I know it will be difficult, but think of my patience in having her here for three months, and not once quarrelling with her." Dorothy had gone to Trevone again in April 1915, this time to stay until June; and from here she carried on a correspondence with Edward Garnett for which he needed all the patience he could command.

Garnett did not know (and apparently the Beresfords, who did, were not divulging it) that Dorothy's father had died at the end of March. He was seventy-nine; and she had told Trissie and Jack that his death of old age was "a blessing" to everyone. No doubt it was, but it might also have made her especially difficult for Garnett to deal with. Very much a gentleman and thoroughly professional, he expected Dorothy to place her trust in him (as he knew she could, and as he might well have thought Jack Beresford had advised her she could) and leave the business end of the affair to him. He was understandably put out by her first communication. He had sent her the memorandum of agreement with Gerald Duckworth, but since the precise terms had not yet been decided upon, a blank space had been left, to be filled in at a later date. Dorothy had proceeded to fill in the blank space with the terms she thought would be most suitable. Garnett was surprised, to say the least. He wrote back to try to explain the realities of the publishing world.

From the cottage in Trevone, where she had gone for the spring, Dorothy now offered her own explanation, speaking of herself throughout the long letter in the third person. When the memorandum arrived in the mail, she said, and she "discovered that nearly everything had been left for her to fill in—she declared to the world at large that 'they must be the most perfect dears' and proceeded to fill in to the best of her ability" the appropriate terms. For presuming to do this, Garnett had seen fit to chastise her, and in defense of herself she cited her "life-long experience of office work." Then, in a careful and minute script, she argued for the logic of her own terms. First of all, she said, "An agreement is an agreement and if set out at all, cannot be set out too inclusively." Second, she went on, "the better the relationship between the parties, the wiser is a detailed and anticipatory inclusivness. These things have long been

78

articles of faith with her." There followed a rather cautiously expressed regret. She had hoped for an arrangement with Duckworth that would include the unwritten volumes of *Pilgrimage* and would help her to produce them without the strain of journalism. But Duckworth's terms, as Garnett had outlined them (to replace her own), covered only *Pointed Roofs,* and they were the terms that prevailed.

Despite its unpromising beginning, her relationship with Edward Garnett became easier and in time even cordial once they had reached something like an understanding about procedures and authority. Things had already improved when *Pointed Roofs* appeared, for a difficulty that arose at the very last moment was settled amicably. Dorothy wanted her novel to be entitled *Pilgrimage,* with *Pointed Roofs* as the sub-title, part one of the whole; this was how the first page was printed. Then, before the book was tied and bound, someone discovered that *Pilgrimage* was the title of another novel and could not be used as Dorothy wished, and the problem was resolved by changing the wording on the cover and title page to read "Pointed Roofs" only, with a note stubbed onto the title page explaining the discrepancy between this and the first page.

Pointed Roofs was an unassuming book in blue boards, with a plain dove-gray dust jacket that was wordless except for the title and the author's name. Curiously enough, Beresford's introduction (though it occupied four pages) seemed almost as wordless. Most of it was couched in figurative terms, as if no other would serve to describe such a novel, but the result is probably more an impression of tentativeness than Beresford intended. He began the introduction by saying that he had read the novel three times, in its three different "dresses"—manuscript, typescript, and print—and that each time he had seen it differently. In manuscript it looked objective, in typescript subjective, and in print neither one nor the other but instead "a new form in fiction," "a new attitude towards fiction" that could only be described metaphorically. Dorothy Richardson, he thought, was the first novelist to have taken what he called "the final plunge"; she had "gone head under and become a very part of the human element she . . . described." He was trying, in this way, to explain the method of the novel.

The first reviewer of *Pointed Roofs* put it another way: "The book somehow reads as if the reader did not exist." He meant by this that "no allusion [was] explained or incoherence apologized for," that in other words the reader was left entirely to his own devices. But he, for one, had not found this troubling. Nor had he found the novel in the least bit obscure. On the contrary, the whole seemed to him "clear with a clarity as keen as the gables of the charming 'pointed roofs' "—and all the more remarkable in consequence. Dorothy could not have asked for a better first notice (it came from the Sunday *Observer*).

The second appeared in the *Saturday Review*—where just a year before her very last "middle" had been published—and could not have been more hostile. Even the originality conceded to the book was presented as a dubious virtue, bordering indeed on the pathological. The reviewer saw evidence everywhere in *Pointed Roofs* of an "unsound mind" and a "sick imagination." Instead of a plot or a "love motive," he found "pages upon pages of foolish or fevered fantasies." He was repelled by the heroine's "self-absorption," "egoistic consciousness," "atrabilious eyes," all of which for him added up to little more than extreme mental disorder.

As a matter of fact, the *Saturday Review* had not been receptive lately to much fiction at all, whether traditional or experimental. Its chief complaint seemed to be the inability of modern authors to "efface" themselves and be "healthy." Lawrence was too visible in *Sons and Lovers*. Mr. Wells was said to have "an abiding faith in Mr. Wells." May Sinclair told "sordid" tales. Joyce's *Dubliners* left a "trail of morbidity"; it was "diseased art, and poison[ed] the springs of one's thoughts." It was not surprising that Dorothy Richardson's seventeen-year-old heroine should have struck the *Saturday Review* as a "misanthropic" and far less appealing descendant of Marie Bashkirtseff, "the youthful Russian neuropath of the late 'eighties" whose *Journal* had once been very popular.

The truth is that *Pointed Roofs* disconcerted many of its early readers. They were misled by the simple and straightforward manner of the opening pages into thinking it a traditional as well as feminine novel. But they soon discovered there were none of the usual threads of information to hold and to follow. Not until page 74, for example, did the heroine reveal that she was only seventeen; and if she had not been self-conscious about her age as she tried to teach English to four German girls, they would not have learned it even then. They also discovered that, in spite of the girlish heroine and her inevitably feminine outlook, the attitude toward women expressed in the novel was hostile. It should not have taken a discerning reader long to perceive that Dorothy Richardson's Miriam resented women, resented their smiles of knowledge and their "funny confidence," and indeed shared her own father's general dislike of women. Most fittingly, it was he who had escorted Miriam into Germany, into the "Fatherland," where, however, she would have humiliating encounters with Hanover men.

Germany would come to represent a crushingly "masculine culture" to which she had come unprepared, so that her loathing for women would be matched by a loathing for the men of the fatherland who defeated her at every turn. Her climactic defeat would be suffered at the hands of Pastor Lahmann and Fräulein Pfaff, the man and the woman who seemed to young Miriam the agents of denial—refusing her the individuality she wanted. For Lahmann she was little more than the potential "well-willed wife"; for Lily Pfaff she was the sexual rival. Miriam vehemently rejected these roles, both of which, she thought, stemmed from a flaunted power conferred by sexual experience. At the same time, in her extreme and inexperienced youth, attracted as she also was to a particular kind of passive female beauty, she was still only vaguely aware of what she was rejecting, with the result that there were signs of ambivalence in her. They did not mean—as certain readers were bound to feel—that she really longed for what she professed to loathe, except in the sense that all of us sometimes yearn for what we would probably have as a matter of course if we were other than ourselves. Which means, perhaps, that most of us sometimes covet the experience of being someone else.

Dorothy Richardson found the way to be someone else and herself at the same time. Curiously enough, so did two other writers, James Joyce in *A Portrait of the Artist as a Young Man* and Marcel Proust in *Du Côté de Chez Swann,* novels published almost simultaneously with *Pointed Roofs*. All three were at once autobiographical and subjective novels. All were about people who markedly resembled their creators, and all were preoccupied if not obsessed with the consciousness of their central characters. It was as if, independent of each other, these three writers had reached the same point on the evolutionary scale of the novel at the same moment and by the same route: the route of the importunate and willful self, the self determined moreover to create its own image which would then replace

81

the actual ordinary person of the writer. (It would be Proust and Dorothy Richardson especially who insisted on the ordinariness of the writer's daily self, and Joyce who demonstrated it dramatically.)

The novels did not at first strike their readers as linked, for, to begin with, they were read by separate groups of people. Proust's novel was not translated into English for some years, and Joyce's seemed unlike anything else. The opening lilting words of *Portrait,* with the convergent tones of adult and child, "Once upon a time and a very good time it was there was a moocow coming down along the road," were new and strange. *Pointed Roofs* began flatly by comparison, with the simple statement of a modest action: "Miriam left the gaslit hall and went slowly upstairs." The words are prosaic alongside the poetic rhythm of the first line of Proust: *"Longtemps, je me suis couché de bonne heure."* Nevertheless these three beginnings—one matter-of-fact, the other poetical, the third fabulous—compounded a like image of unhurrying time. Time in these novels had no boundaries; it was the limitless time of the mind, of memory, which can not only venture everywhere and range through the past as though in the present, but can also retrieve the past and give it shape as well as permanence.

So despite its traditional outward appearance, *Pointed Roofs* (as some of its puzzled early readers gradually learned) was new in the way that *Portrait* and *Swann* were new. Within a few years it became a commonplace of book reviewing and literary criticism to link the names and works of Proust, Joyce, and Dorothy Richardson, and to argue laboriously the merits of each.

Part Two
1915-28

CHAPTER SIX

The Artist

WHEN *Pointed Roofs* appeared in September 1915, Dorothy had been in London since June. She was already at work on the second volume of *Pilgrimage,* but having failed to persuade her publisher that the stresses and strains of journalism would harm her novel-writing, she arranged with the *Dental Record* (which by then had printed six of her articles) to produce an unsigned monthly column. It would begin with the November issue and would be called "Comments by a Layman." She was to go on writing this column as much for pleasure as for additional income, it would seem, until June 1919.

She must have been perfectly free to write whatever she wished, so long as it was drawn into some relation to dentistry. Her subjects ranged widely (and sometimes two or three subjects would be considered in a single column). Though many of her subjects were culled from magazines she read, they reflected her own particular interests. In *Everybody's Magazine,* for example, she found a piece about an American doctor's discovery that he could anesthetize pain (such as toothache) with a firm pressure on certain other spots in the nose, mouth, throat, and tongue. The "Layman" did not think any of this very new or revolutionary; as she saw it, this was simply a matter of consciousness being drawn from one "zone" to another. In the East, she said, men had long ago learned to master their bodily functions at will and to induce a local anesthesia while retaining full mental consciousness.

This was one of her timeless subjects. But with a war going on, London preparing for air raids, and bright young men leaving in droves for France, Dorothy also considered war-related dental topics. Month after month she wrote about traveling dental ambulances, about the necessity of caring for the teeth as well as the limbs of soldiers, about the only army in Europe with an efficient dental service being (ironically) Germany's. If she wished, she could even have been editor of the *Dental Record*. But she refused the offer, claiming that not even the dire shortage of men could induce her to take on anything so "specialist" in nature. Besides, she was preoccupied with the second volume of *Pilgrimage* (which was scheduled to come out in July 1916) and with someone she had recently met.

1

During the summer of 1915, Dorothy was feeling more dissatisfied than ever with her room in St. John's Wood, so she seriously began to look about for another. A friend told her of a vacancy in a house not far away on Queen's Terrace, and she went there to inquire. Queen's Terrace facing out to Marlborough Road was a semicircle of Regency houses long neglected by their owners. Even so, the tall windows, lofty rooms, and molded ceilings remained and were ideal for studios of sculptors and painters. Nos. 29 and 32 had virtually no other class of occupant save in the attic rooms, and it was the attic room at No. 32 that Dorothy had learned was available for 7s. 6d. a week. She questioned the landlady closely and learned that most of the artist tenants did not live in the house (though they were all respectable anyway). At the moment only one was a lodger (in a studio-bedroom on the second floor), a gentleman named "Mr. h'Odle" who rarely spoke to anyone. He was very polite, Dorothy was assured, but also very shy, and if he occasionally happened to eat breakfast in the basement room at the same time as she, she could be sure he would not speak to her. But most of the time he ate breakfast, if he ate it at all, at a much later than customary hour. The landlady was so convincing about the privacy a lodger would have in her house that Dorothy took the room.

For weeks there was no sign of the artist-gentleman. Then, amid great excitement, came news that royalty—the king and queen and their young daughter—would appear in Queen's Terrace for a dedication ceremony. Dorothy's landlady came to tell her that the best view of the royal trio could be had from Mr. Odle's second-floor front window, and she suggested that, since he was not at home as usual, they ought to go in and watch. At first Dorothy objected to the intrusion on his privacy; then she allowed herself to be led through the door of Mr. Odle's rooms. The moment she entered, her eyes were caught by a large drawing so wild and intense that she nearly lost her footing. Obviously Mr. Odle was not very shy or polite as an artist.

Dorothy did not meet Allan Odle in person until some time after this. One morning, just as she was finishing her breakfast, an extraordinary figure, unmistakably the creator of the drawing, glided into a chair opposite her and proceeded to eat his meal in silence. She sat on, observing him with some wonder. He wore an ancient-looking black velvet coat that hung loosely on a tall, emaciated form. His face was long and thin and pale—paler than pale against the dark, glowing brown of his eyes. His long pale hair was swathed about his head, leaving visible a pair of pointed ears which made him look like a faun—but a faun not entirely at home even in St. John's Wood. His hands were unforgettable: long, tapered fingers with nails none too clean that extended like stilettos. And yet, bizarre as his appearance was, the total effect was not entirely unpleasant. His manner was dignified, even elegant. He moved his hands with the utmost grace. There was intelligence in his eyes, and when he spoke at last, though the voice had a slightly harsh quality, it was low and deferential. The landlady had been perfectly right to describe him as a gentleman. He was, nonetheless, very odd. To Dorothy's surprise he continued to appear at breakfast, and they fell into the habit of talking.

She learned that until recently he would just be getting home when she sat down to breakfast, but the war had forced a change in his habits. The Café Royal, where for years he had been spending a good part of his nights, had suddenly begun to close at 10:30. Some of his companions simply went elsewhere earlier than usual (to an Armenian coffeehouse in Soho or to the Eiffel Tower restaurant in Percy Street), but Allan Odle came home instead—to begin appearing in the mornings for breakfast and then, it was clear, for talk. Their conversation at first was entirely about literature, which he discussed with an "eighteenth-century formality" that she said she liked. He had read virtually everything, or so it seemed, including *Pointed Roofs,* and this impressed her most of all. By then it had been out a few months, but Mr. Odle said it had been talked of in the Café Royal at once.

She noted the pride and reverence with which he spoke of the famous café. Her own knowledge of it was limited, though like most Londoners she had walked past it on Regent Street innumera-

ble times, vaguely aware that behind its imposing and gilded front a
frenetic crowd would gather night after night. Since the 1880s and
the era of Wilde and Whistler, it had become one of the landmarks
of London. In the eyes of some admirers, it was the closest London
would ever get to the Latin Quarter of Paris. In any case it could
always be counted on for a lively if not sensational feature story.
One such story had appeared, in fact, this past summer of 1915 in
the magazine *Colour:* "The Café Royal in War Time." Dorothy
had not seen it, but Allan Odle was *in* it—as one of the curiosities of
the café.

According to the writer in *Colour,* the Café Royal attracted and
tolerated an amazingly mixed clientele. All the arts and professions,
as well as the races, religions, and hobbies, were represented. There
cranks, idealists, lords, and reformers all mingled in "a true intellectual democracy." Most of the mingling (and fun) began about
nine o'clock in the evening in the Domino Room downstairs, where
the nightly spectacle took shape between gilded walls and under a
"painted and pagan ceiling." But not until midnight did the smoke,
voices, clatter of silver, and jingle of coins reach a peak. Then the
Domino Room, with its huge ornamental pillars and the Café Royal
emblem everywhere, became a pageant of color and a bedlam of
sound: a splash of blues and reds and greens, daubs of white and
black, mixed with the khaki of British soldiers and the bright uni-
forms of Belgian officers. The café emblem—an "N" decorated
with an imperial laurel wreath and capped with an imperial
crown—so the story went, had been designed by the Bonapartist
son-in-law of the unwitting café owner, who was himself a staunch
Royalist. The mirrors that in his innocence he had had installed
reflected everything: the ubiquitous emblem, the panels of
mythological figures, the decorative art in styles from Louis XIV to
Louis Phillipe, and the groups of café patrons seated democratically
among it all.

Since the earliest days of the café, there seemed to have been
distinguishable groups. Often they had centered about a key
figure—a Wilde or Whistler or Beardsley, a Frank Harris or Ronald
Firbank. In 1915, when Allan Odle had been sitting in the Domino
Room nearly every night for six years, several groups could be
made out, though not all of them had a star. The central figure of
one was the draftsman Augustus John, of another the sculptor Jacob
Epstein, of a third the futurist Wyndham Lewis. But there were

other groups too: Post-Impressionist, Colourist, Waterist, Cubist, and of course Literary. The head of the Literary group appeared to be the poet Henry Savage, who was editor of a magazine called *The Gypsy*. Allan Odle was its art editor, and according to the writer in *Colour*, he usually sat with Savage "in profound, sphinx-like slumber, knowingly or unknowingly coming to life when a good friend arrive[d] whom he wish[ed] to greet."

The friend who arrived might have been T. W. H. Crosland, the Yorkshire poet and pamphleteer, whose polemical book *Lovely Woman* had raised a storm of protest when it was published in 1903. He had chosen to take a rather controversial stand in the days of the suffrage movement—that Woman, as he put it, had got "out of hand to an almost irremediable extent." As might be expected, the book ultimately sold more that 100,000 copies. But Crosland never seemed to have any money. It was said that he often approached a newcomer to the Domino Room, large and white-faced in his perennial frock coat, to shake him by the hand and present him with his black-edged visiting card. On the card was a three-line inscription:

T. W. H. CROSLAND
JOBBING POET
FUNERALS ATTENDED

Another of Odle's friends was Townley Searle, a man almost as diversely employed as Crosland and certainly as eccentric. For a time he kept a large bear chained to a post in the middle of his basement room in lower Regent Street. It went mad during a zeppelin raid and had to be destroyed, but by then (1917) Searle was in Ireland, where he had gone to escape conscription after the Military Service Act was passed. Oddly enough, a friend of his in Hampstead had agreed to keep the bear for him during his absence, so it was in Hampstead that the bear met his unfortunate end. Searle was also fond of rare books (he dealt in them and even published a few), of Oriental food (he wrote a Chinese cookbook), of Gilbert and Sullivan (he produced a bibliography of the works of Sir William S. Gilbert), and of gypsies. After the war he came back to London with a young gypsy wife (who eventually drank herself to death).

Some time before the war, he and Crosland, with Allan Odle and Henry Savage, had formed the Gipsy Club, out of which a few years later came the magazine. In 1913, though, Searle had apparently been responsible for the printing of a somewhat fanciful list of the members of the club. One of the people on the list was H. G. Wells, who did not take kindly to usage of this sort. He wrote Searle a short and bellicose note, objecting to being named as a member of "the infernal little Gipsy Club" and also accusing Searle of having "started a particularly annoying lie" about him. He threatened to take legal action if necessary. Searle was probably glad to have the note (and might well have counted on getting it), since he was prone to sell just about anything he could find. Long after this, Henry Savage was to claim that Searle had even taken and sold some of the letters in the correspondence files of *The Gypsy*.

Before the war and during its first year or so, the quartet of friends—Savage, Searle, Crosland, and Odle—could often be found on the first floor of the old Apple Market, off Piccadilly Circus, where they had tumbledown offices. They were thus not very far from the Café Royal or, for that matter, from Soho. But Allan Odle always preferred the Café Royal and its potent absinthe, which was his favorite drink. Only special people could lure him away. One of these was his younger brother Vincent, whom he visited on Sunday evenings, usually bringing with him two bottles of stout. Another was Madame de Verley, who customarily provided food, drink, and entertainment in her painter's studio for many of the artists of London.

Ivy de Verley, the wealthy widow of a Jamaican planter, lived in South Kensington. At her salon Allan Odle was perhaps the most loyal guest. The side-whiskered Adrian Allinson came often too; and occasionally the handsome Mark Gertler appeared, as did the young poet Claude Houghton (Oldfield), whose portrait served as a cover illustration for an issue of *Colour*. Another portrait reproduced in *Colour* was that painted of Allan Odle by Madame de Verley. In it she recorded the black scarf and jacket he usually wore, the brilliant dark eyes and swathed hair, the long, needlelike fingers—one of them crooked against his temple—and his pointed ears. She saw him, it would seem, as a somewhat sinister faun.

Henry Savage agreed that there was something of an animal in the rapid, gliding way Odle walked, but not of a faun. The strongest impression Savage had of Allan's appearance was that he looked cadaverous—almost like a ghoul wearing a dilapidated bowler hat. He insisted, as a matter of fact, that Allan Odle had once been stopped by a terrified policeman as he walked home through St.

Portrait of Allan Odle by Ivy de Verley.

John's Wood Cemetery carrying a human skull. The skull had been lent to him by his friend John Flanagan, who ran a shop in which he often displayed Allan's drawings and sometimes sold one for him. Flanagan, like Savage, understood that it was Allan Odle's work one took seriously, not the way he looked. And though Savage was not sure, Crosland for one believed Odle had the mark of genius.

By the time Dorothy Richardson met him, his art had begun to attract the attention of critics. The first issue of *The Gypsy,* which appeared in May 1915, contained more of his work than had ever been reproduced before. (A tiny edition of Wilde's *The Sphinx,* which he had illustrated five years earlier, went almost unnoticed.) *The Gypsy* itself made a small splash, coming out as it did in the midst of the war, declaring in its foreword that Art was "of more importance than the fate of nations." But the principal artist of *The Gypsy* was the star. He had not only designed the cover, the title page, the foreword, and the page decorations, he had also contributed two full-scale illustrations—one to Lesage's novel *Le Diable Boiteux,* the other to Balzac's *La Comédie Humaine.*

In fact, the magazine was saturated with Allan Odle. With every stroke of the pen, he revealed that though he subscribed to the view of art expressed in the foreword (which he had no doubt helped to write) and was not concerned with the fate of nations, he was positively obsessed with the fate of mankind. As he saw them, human beings had little to hope for in the face of their own cruelty, vanity, and grossness. Everywhere in his drawings—in the corners, coming out of the decorations and the mouths of his figures, from heads and cauldrons—people were shown leering at themselves and at one another. The first impression one has of an Odle drawing—as Dorothy Richardson must have had the afternoon she stepped into his room—is of bestiality. Ugliness and violence leap out at the viewer. But by degrees, as one moves through the hectic scene, the first impression gives way to an understanding of an absolutely controlled and literary nightmare. For in addition to being "a master of the pen line" (as one reviewer put it), Odle was a writer in graphics and a rigid, uncompromising, moral judge of his own unconscious.

The review of *The Gypsy* that appeared in the *Observer* described him as an artist of "unquestionable genius." The reviewer thought he was playing the part in *The Gypsy* that Beardsley had played in *The Savoy.* (If *The Gypsy* had continued to publish, this might have proved to be true.) The comparison with Beardsley had to be made, given their equally strange appearance and art, but the similarity did not run deep. Beardsley was at heart an ironist with a brilliant sense of life as decorative fantasy. Allan Odle was a satirist with an eye fixed unblinkingly on man. In Beardsley's designs the details are often *things* mockingly conceived and executed; in Odle's they are nearly always human (or inhuman) figures. In later years Odle would freely admit that Beardsley had influenced his early drawings, but he claimed Hogarth was much more important, as to a lesser degree were Daumier and Blake.

He was to say that Hogarth had taught him all he knew about the "manipulation of crowds." It is probably safe to add that the Café Royal had also contributed to his education and that when it began to fade from his life—at the time of the war and his meeting with Dorothy Richardson—he had already learned quite enough from it and needed to move on. By then he had also drunk more than enough of the deadly pre-war absinthe, so it might be said that in several ironical ways the war saved his life. Though he was only twenty-six when the war began, he would not have survived much longer in the basement den of the Café Royal. One had only to observe him for a short time to gather that survival meant nothing at all to him, that he would not lift a finger in his own material behalf. Dorothy Richardson saw this almost at once, and she found it confirmed as little by little she learned of his physical circumstances and history.

2

The birth of Allan Odle on January 12, 1888, in Deptford, Kent, was registered on February 15 in the name of William Elsden Odle. Some time afterward, however, his father entered a change of name for him to Allan Elsden Odle. Nearly thirty years later Allan himself would alter the spelling of his name and become Alan for all intents and purposes. He would marry as Alan and thereafter sign all his drawings and letters as Alan, but when he died more than thirty years after that, his widow would scrupulously register his death in the name of Allan.

His father, Samuel Odle, who originally came from a small town near Northampton, was a bank clerk. He was tall in stature, practical-minded, and austere. His wife Fannie, who came from

Hertfordshire, was partly Welsh. She was small and delicate, with a taste for music and a whimsical turn of mind. Three sons were born to them: first Sidney, then Allan, and finally Edwin. As Samuel Odle rose in the bank from clerk to manager and moved his family first to Richmond and then to Sittingbourne, his boys grew up into frail young men, distant, puzzling, and sensitive. They cared only for art: Sidney for music, Allan for painting, Edwin (who preferred his middle name, Vincent) for literature. Such passionate devotion to art was not respectable in the eyes of the bank-manager father. Nonetheless he allowed himself to be persuaded that it would not be an utter scandal for Allan to attend the Sidney Cooper School of Art in Canterbury.

It was another matter, however, when Allan wanted to live in London and continue his studies at the St. John's Wood Art School. But Samuel Odle argued against it in vain. His son had a single aim in life; there was no contending with him. At last he agreed to an allowance for Allan, in return for which he required a weekly letter. The letter always arrived, sometimes without postage, and often without words, showing instead a thoroughly naked figure stretching out its hand. Surprisingly, the bank manager never stopped the allowance, even when Allan finished formal studies and settled down in the Café Royal, or when his mother died and his father remarried.

The trouble was that Allan spent nearly all the money he got on art supplies and in the Café Royal. He had little left for food or clothing. His ulster became antiquated, his velvet coat grew shabby, and his shoes wore thin. When Dorothy Richardson met him, he had an alarming cough. She did not need to have translated *Consumption Doomed* to suspect him of being tubercular, nor could she have known then that in just ten years his brother Sidney would die of the disease. After a while she began to talk to Allan about food and nourishment and to disparage the kipper he insisted upon eating for breakfast. He heard her out with exquisite attention—and went on eating kippers. She was undaunted, and with good reason. He did not so much *prefer* the food he ate as grow used to having it, and apparently he had been eating kippers for years. One had only to get him accustomed to something else, which Dorothy thought might be accomplished in time.

Meanwhile, one could do any number of things for this odd young man who was such a curious blend of bohemian and gentleman, so courteous and deferential, but usually unwashed and unsparing in his contempt for the mass of people who knew nothing about art. Everyone who was not actively engaged in some form of art he thought negligible. Dorothy disagreed, but she might just as well have tried to argue with her own father about tradesmen. Allan Odle disliked women, but as *Pointed Roofs* had shown, Dorothy shared this with him as she had shared it with her father. Except in matters of the mind, he was yielding and pliant, that is to say, indifferent. But he was touchingly grateful when someone was kind to him, and he could not get over finding in his bedroom an oil stove that Dorothy one day bought for him and put there while he was out.

She gave him the stove during the winter of 1916–17 when he coughed excessively and began to complain of neuralgia. They had known each other for about a year before he at last revealed her existence to his brother Vincent. Vincent and his wife Rose lifted their eyebrows when he began to sprinkle their conversations with the name "Miss Richardson." He told them that she was the author of two much discussed novels, that she looked at him disapprovingly while he ate his breakfast kipper, and that she had put an oil stove in his room that warmed it miraculously. But he did not tell them that she was urging him to see a doctor.

In spite of the solicitude of Miss Richardson, Allan Odle's health worsened through the winter. Yet he would not admit to being ill and counted on feeling better automatically in the spring. But when spring came, neither the neuralgia nor the cough went away. Dorothy, who had scarcely been out of London for months, was planning to spend a month in Cornwall with the Beresfords. She was nearly finished with the third volume of *Pilgrimage* and expected it to appear in the fall. The bulk of the manuscript had been mailed to Duckworth in March, and at the end of May she mailed what she thought was the concluding chapter of *Honeycomb*. She counted on leaving for Cornwall in a few weeks with the first set of proofs, but before she could get away Allan Odle gave her the surprising if not ludicrous news that he was being conscripted into the army. He had been notified to report on the third of July, when Dorothy had planned to be out of London. Now she decided on an earlier return.

Something of a crisis developed in Cornwall. It began with Gerald Duckworth telling her he thought *Honeycomb* needed another chapter, that the one she had sent did not really conclude the novel. Jack Beresford felt the same way. Dorothy resisted at first.

Then she had to admit that her own "inner conviction" substantiated their feeling. The trouble was that she did not know whether she could write the chapter, which would have to deal with the suicide of her heroine's mother, and she needed time to find out. She would not be able to get back to London by July 3 after all.

Allan Odle was writing her regularly. His messages, politely addressed to Miss Richardson, were sent on block-lettered scrolls, designed in all their borders with macabre figures and scenes. He said he did not like eating breakfast without her, and he had not been to Mudie's even once for books since she had left. He had gone to Regent Street though, in the middle of the day, to look for the shop window she had asked him to find. She had remembered it as displaying glass; this was how she had put it into *Honeycomb,* but was her memory accurate? The shop, alas, seemed no longer to exist. Allan Odle had to report "failure," which "upset" him so much, he said, that he had been driven to "consume green absinthe in [the] cerulear fastnesses of Verrey's" for two hours. He also reported such bits of London gossip as that Lord Alfred Douglas had "brought an injunction against George Moore for BLASPHEMY."

In another letter, written on June 29, he told her of the air raid he had heard quite distinctly as he lay on his bed fully clothed, reading the concluding chapters of *Pride and Prejudice* and smoking "to excess." A day or so afterward, he had ridden through the bombed area and found it "horrible, but full of the strange poetry of devastation," with "long lines of shattered houses, looking in the dusk like rows of blackened and decayed teeth...." Henry Savage, he reported, had been "strolling serenely" down the street when the raid began, and a bomb had exploded near him, blowing off his hat and killing two people a few yards away. *He* was "quite unhurt and his tranquillity remain[ed] unruffled." But the story had frightened Allan Odle, and the things he wanted to tell her about Jane Austen would have to wait until she returned; he was not up to literary discussion at the moment. He would send her a card, however, as soon as he knew the "verdict" on Tuesday.

Meanwhile Dorothy left Cornwall with the Beresfords to stay at the rambling old Tudor house in Winslow they had recently begun to let. From here she wrote to "Mr. Odle," advising him to "take reasonable care" of himself and hoping he did not feel he *had* to write to her. She said she could read the state of his mind in his drawings, meaning perhaps that it was not necessary for him to use

Drawing by Allan Odle to illustrate *Le Diable Boiteux*, a novel by Alain- René Lesage.

words to communicate with her. The state of her own mind is not so easily read. She had felt very tired—she told him—as though she had been "flung into an unknown sea." But now that she had "gasped," she was feeling better and could "look round." Most of what she said bore a certain relation to her novel and the difficult chapter about her mother, which she knew would be anguish to write. But not everything made this kind of sense, though Allan Odle might have thought it did. She was undeniably in the throes of remembering the days and nights in Hastings that more than twenty years earlier had led to her mother's grisly suicide.

At the same time, Allan Odle's letters must have made abundantly if not shockingly clear to her the state of their relationship (which could not have been entirely unknown to her, just as the opinion about *Honeycomb* could not have been a total surprise), and she "gasped" for breath. It was evident that Allan Odle had bound himself to her. What did *she* feel, at the age of forty-four, immersed as she was in a series of novels that were re-creating her youth and might even bring her distinction some day? It would seem, as she looked round, that she could not help but feel, above everything, a great tenderness for the innocent, gifted, unearthly young man who was no doubt destined never to grow old.

He sent her a detailed account of the events of July 3. He had actually passed the first physical examination and had been ordered to join the West Surreys regiment the following morning. Then for some reason the officer giving this order had looked up at him, remarked that he looked ill, and told him to go before the medical board at once. There two doctors examined him thoroughly. They were amazed, Allan said, that he had been passed, and they pronounced him tubercular. Six hours later he got a formal discharge, together with half a crown (one day's army pay) and an odd penny, which Allan presumed had been thrown in for luck.

He had spent most of this time among the dubious conscripts— Group C3, it was, that "looked like the sweepings of a casualty ward." Goiters, bandaged eyes, and maimed limbs were everywhere, and one man had had an epileptic fit in the dressing room. The scene might have come out of one of his own drawings, but it had obviously made him sick. His concluding remark was that the only complete exempts that day had been the epileptic and himself. He warned her in a postscript that she would find him "with cropped hair, looking like a scared rabbit." He was scared indeed, and he decided he had better consult a specialist.

Meanwhile, though Dorothy had finally set off for London, she stopped along the way at Harrow—to be alone, she said, and "break the back" of the new final chapter. Allan's next letter reached her there. He had inconclusive findings to report. Although the doctor was quite convinced something was wrong somewhere, the X rays failed to show any definite lesion in either lung. Allan thought this encouraging, but the doctor was doubtful and wanted to see him again. In the meantime he suggested a number of what Allan labeled "expensive cures" and told him to "feed well and do absolutely *nothing*—preferably in the country." For all this advice, Allan complained, the fee had been large, and to meet current expenses he had undersold two of his "best" drawings. But what about *her?* He was "very worried." If she felt tired and out of sorts in the country, she would not be able to cope with the heat of London. Did she have "plenty of books"?

She replied from Harrow that his letter had "cheered" her, but there was not a book she could think of at the moment that she wanted to read. She went on to ask very carefully whether he did not think that if the specialist confirmed his first opinion "it might be worth while to go away—for a while." She knew a lot of people, she said, who had become "permanently well." And all he really wanted, she felt sure, was "rest and inactivity and if not exactly feeding up, at least regular feeding." It would not, in his case, be anything like "giving in and sitting down to be ill." And when he "came out," she teased, he would be "a fat pink millionaire." Didn't that "tempt" him? Evidently it did not.

Toward the end of July, she returned to Queen's Terrace and sent off the new final chapter of *Honeycomb*. A month later, on August 29, 1917, she married Alan Odle at the registry office of St. Marylebone. He was twenty-nine; she was forty-four, although she entered her age as thirty-seven. She did this, it would seem, more to please herself than for any other reason. She must have known even as early as this that Alan Odle had no interest at all in such mundane matters as a woman's age; yet she was to make a point of keeping her actual age from him throughout their married life, as though she felt obliged to do so. It was, indeed, the first of a series of self-imposed—and ritualistic—obligations.

CHAPTER SEVEN

The New Life

WITH the publication of *Honeycomb* in October 1917, two months after her marriage, Dorothy brought to a close the fictional account of her pre-London life. In the next volume, which was already entitled *The Tunnel,* she would draw upon her early days in nineteenth-century gaslit London, when the scandal of Oscar Wilde still reverberated but a young girl was not supposed to recognize his name. Toward the end of *Honeycomb,* Dorothy had had Miriam overhear all the excited whisperings about that man who wrote plays and who had the "woodland springtime name" she could not remember. No one would tell her what he had done. In private she decided it could not be either murder or divorce. Murder would have been openly discussed, and a divorce case dropped out "abstractedly" in a "little shocked sentence" with the subject then changed at once. So it was worse than these. What on earth could it be? She simply had to ask, but in the face of the self-conscious response she got (without an answer) that made her own cheeks flush with shame, her mind cried out in anger. "Don't tell me... don't mention it, you don't know yourself what it is. Nobody knows what anything is."

This was the girl who not long afterward sat in a house in Brighton where her mother lay dead and tried to convince herself she had not been responsible, had not been neglectful, had not turned her back on a suffering human being. For if she had, then here was real sin (not the secret unnameable kind that adults keep to themselves) and she would really be in hell, where in the words of Bunyan "the worm of a guilty conscience never dies." Thus had Dorothy Richardson brought the childhood of her heroine to an end in the same way her own had ended on a November morning in 1895, at the very moment in 1917 when yet another stage of her life was drawing to a close.

The three novels she had now published, though they were parts of the large whole conceived as *Pilgrimage,* can be seen as forming in themselves a prelude, a preliminary series of small journeys, in each case involving a "passage into new experience." The most literal—and distant—journey was to Hanover in the first novel, *Pointed Roofs.* The second novel, *Backwater,* takes Miriam to a North London school, where she—as Dorothy did before her— holds a post as resident teacher. (The Finsbury Park of Dorothy's past becomes Banbury Park in the novel; Edgeworth House is trans- lated to Wordsworth; and the Ayre sisters become the Pernes.) But again the most significant setting of the book is in the mind of the central character, and the meaning of the novel resides in the texture of that mind as it expresses itself in images. The images that pre- dominate in *Backwater* are of hunger and death, for in that novel Dorothy was telling the story of her months in "ugly and shabby" North London, a struggle for survival worthy of comparison with the desperate sojourn of Robinson Crusoe, who is even explicitly named, but also linked no doubt with the strange spectral presence of Alan Odle.

In Miriam's case, the struggle is against both physical and emo- tional odds. The school is a dark, airless enclosure. The view from behind the heavy venetian blind on the schoolroom window is of a tiny garden "lying in deep shadow." The predominant sound in her ears is the "harsh" North London accent. She constantly feels the "cold grey" atmosphere. The vision of two of her pupils dressed always in black, mourning for their dead father, is unrelieved. Miriam's throat perpetually aches, her strength ebbs, she sees death in every face around her. Even a newcomer, the young pupil-teacher from Ireland, brings with her the sole ambition to play Chopin's "Funeral March."

Miriam tries to create diversification for herself. She discovers the domestic novels of Rosa Nouchette Carey, the society stories of Mrs. Hungerford, and the "grown-up," exciting, red-bound vol- umes of Ouida. Half of her nights are spent reading in an almost drugged state. Her days are filled with hunger: for food, for light, for beauty. She clings to her consoling original view of the Perne sisters, who run the school, as genteel, of an old-fashioned quality that has survived despite their need to support themselves (but the girls are still the "gels" on their North London tongues). Then one of the sisters begins to take an interest in Miriam's disrespectful attitude toward formal religion, and the concern threatens to become an "emotional tyranny." She feels herself drawn to this gentle, middle-aged woman, recognizes the danger of it, and struggles for independence. Gradually the way she must go makes itself known: out of North London by whatever means possible and then perhaps into the kind of position her sister has, as governess in a large, luxurious home. Such would be the setting of *Honeycomb;* and Miriam would become disillusioned.

Despite the opinion of some of its reviewers that *Backwater* was an "obscure" book, Dorothy Richardson's second novel had the simplicity and the innocence of its heroine's eighteen- and nineteen-year-old mind. But the method continued to throw readers off, especially since the place and experience in *Backwater* are more confined within Miriam than they were in *Pointed Roofs.* She is no longer quite so passive a receptor of impressions as in Hanover, whereby the reader could gain his own direct sensuous experience of Germany. Her uncomprehending encounters with adult human beings näively reported there were immediately translatable. One could easily grasp the significance of Lily Pfaff's ruling against pairs of girls walking or talking together and of her testiness where Pastor Lahmann was concerned. His attentions to Miriam were fairly obvious, in themselves and for the effect they would have upon Lily. The reader came into possession of more information than Miriam was aware she gave. It was perhaps for this reason that *Pointed Roofs* struck J. D. Beresford at first as one of the most objective novels he had ever read.

In *Backwater* and in each succeeding part of *Pilgrimage,* however, Miriam grows increasingly aware of her consciousness. Information is sometimes unrecorded, not only as in *Pointed Roofs* because Miriam's vision is physically obstructed, but also because the nature of what she sees is more apparent to her and frequently unpalatable. As a result, she often assimilates something without articulating it and suppresses a feeling without registering it, yet she thinks and acts accordingly. Eventually we learn of the assimilations and suppressions, either by a process of deduction or from Miriam herself. The situation of the reader, however, is by degrees reversed after *Pointed Roofs.* Whereas there we understood, for the most part, what Miriam herself did not understand, in the later books she will at times perceive and evaluate first, recording instead of primary data her sense of her sense of the fact. The data we receive sooner or later has been refined and filtered. It comes to us when we are already aware of the essential point: the cast of Miriam's consciousness. It is a consciousness, moreover, growing subtler all the time, though in *Backwater* (and *Honeycomb* as well) one would still characterize both the point of view and the experience as youthful.

In *Honeycomb* the twenty-year-old Miriam spends three trial months as a governess in the rich country home of Felix Corrie, Q.C. She leaves not only because of her mother's illness but also because she decides that the center of life in society (which had always seemed eminently desirable) was like a honeycomb, full of holes and partitions. What is also made clear, though Miriam is unaware of it, is that she has not been a personal success among the Corries. Her dissatisfaction with them stems as much from a sense of humiliation as from a perception of their inadequacies. At first, in a characteristically juvenile mode, she thought Felix Corrie admired her intelligence, indeed that he was secretly aware of her superiority to his wife, whom Miriam thought a silly and frivolous woman. But then, during a conversation at dinner, she suddenly sees how small and unenlightened he really is. There are guests present, and with them Corrie is carrying on a discussion of a current legal case. Miriam confidently contributes to the talk. Her first comment is received with good-humored respect. When she goes on to refine and extend, Corrie turns away. Miriam, angered and humiliated, glances at him now to find that he has "slightly hollow temples," a "small skull," and a generally mean appearance about the head. She condemns him as unable to "look at anything from the point of view of life as a whole." He is a lawyer thinking in "propositions," incapable of understanding any "real *movements* of thought." In his restricted opinion, she had gone too far back seeking a cause. But Miriam insists on the freedom to range: "of course you can go back, and round and up and everywhere."

Obviously, in her criticism of Felix Corrie and his class, there is a good deal that can be considered just; there is also a good deal that can only be considered obnoxious. Young and inexperienced as she is, she nonetheless has a high opinion of herself and respects her own judgment. The mixture of callowness and intelligence that by all accounts Dorothy Richardson herself had displayed in her youth is rendered by her now with scrupulous care. An attentive reader should not be taken in for one moment: Miriam is not being presented without irony, despite the fact that technically speaking she

103

presents herself. What complicates the situation is the undeniable presence of ideas that are rightly assumed to be the author's as well. Miriam arrives, in *Honeycomb,* at some of the same conclusions Dorothy Richardson had reached in her early book reviews; she even expands and clarifies them. She does not read books for the story, Miriam says, "but as a psychological study of the author." The people within a book do not emerge for her; the author himself does, and an absolute knowledge of everything about him. He is "there in every word." The book itself becomes, thus, a person "more real than actual people" and nearer to her. In life, on the contrary, all was "scrappy and mixed up."

These are interesting remarks in light of the autobiographical content of Dorothy Richardson's own books. She seems to be saying here that every book reveals the author more than anything or anybody else, and that it does not matter whether the substance of the book is fact or fiction. In other words, to describe a particular book as autobiographical would be superfluous if not tautological. At the same time, Dorothy Richardson was fully aware that in her own case the factual nature of most of her material created certain problems. It was one thing to put into her novels such relatively obscure people as Lily Pabst of Hanover or the Ayre sisters of Finsbury Park but quite another to put in someone as familiar to the world-at-large as H. G. Wells; and in the chronology of her life he was about to appear in the novel following *Honeycomb.* Evidently she was thinking about this while writing *Honeycomb.* We know it from one of the books she has Miriam read: W. H. Mallock's *A Human Document.*

Mallock's book is the story of two young people: a man who had been a promising poet in his youth and now stands on the threshold of a brilliant diplomatic career, and a beautiful married woman who is supposedly the grown-up counterpart of Marie Bashkirtseff. The book records their growing love for each other and the resultant sacrifice on the part of the man not only of his career but also of his family estate so that he would have both the leisure and the means to remain always near her. For Miriam it is another romance that she reads late into the night, and she decides that the author has deliberately made it into a tragedy.

But for Dorothy Richardson, Mallock's long introduction would have been the center of interest. In it he claimed to have been given a manuscript that was part journal, part letter, and part narrative (but none of it fiction) for the purpose of shaping it into a novel. He felt obliged, nonetheless, to raise with the owner of the manuscript the question of the delicacy and intimacy of the relationship it revealed. The owner, who had known the two principals, claimed that nothing whatever needed to be altered except the names and places. This in her opinion would provide a sufficient "veil." She went on to explain that no one connected with the principals had so much as suspected their relationship, so that even those who had taken "unconscious part in it" would not recognize themselves in an account of the affair. Even if the author herself had published the story, she maintained, her own friends would not have penetrated her secret.

Though Mallock was simply providing a realistic "frame" for his romantic novel, the quasi-theory he offered would prove to be a sound one when put into practice by Dorothy Richardson. She was to give Wells a fictional name and discover, as Mallock's lady had insisted, that no one guessed his identity because there was no reason to connect the author of *Pilgrimage* with H. G. Wells or, for that matter, with her heroine Miriam Henderson. Amusingly enough, Wells had more trouble with this sort of thing than she. He liked to use the first-person narrative in his novels and found himself taken again and again for his principal character, no matter how much he objected to such "vulgarity." It would seem that most people tended to read as fiction what purported to *be* fiction, so long as it was not narrated in the first person. But when the narrative was indeed in the first person, no amount of protesting would persuade most people that it was *not* fact.

2

During 1917, the year in which *Honeycomb* was published, a novel by Frank Swinnerton, entitled *Nocturne,* also appeared. Its American edition had a preface by H. G. Wells. In the course of his prefatory remarks, Wells likened Swinnerton to Dorothy Richardson, an English writer who, he said, had "probably carried impressionism in fiction to its furthest limits." He went on to describe her heroine as a "mirror" rather than a "mentality," going about "over her facts like those insects that run over water sustained by surface tension." Her "percepts," he claimed, never became "concepts." And he confessed finally that, writing as he did "at the extremest distance possible from such work," he found it "altogether too much" for him—unless it was more accurate to say it was "altogether too little." Though he had some grudging words of praise for Swinnerton, it was clear that Wells saw both of them as purely ornamental—and useless.

Dorothy Richardson might not have seen this preface, but she would have known what Wells thought of her novels anyway. She was also aware of his penchant for saying things dictated by his mood of the moment, a mood that was often irascible, or by the streak of nastiness in him. Cruel words about Henry James in *Boon* and, before that, the satiric fictional portrait of Sidney and Beatrice Webb in the novel *The New Macchiavelli* had come from this Wells. Dorothy herself was in another novel, *The Passionate Friends,* published in 1913. It contained a minor character named Stella Summersley Satchel who bore a certain resemblance to Dorothy Miller Richardson. Miss Satchel, a "moral guarantor" hired as companion to a beautiful woman, was "blonde, erect, huffy-mannered." She "marche[d] like the British Infantry but on a vegetarian 'basis.'" She was "business-like," with "a stumpy nose" and pince-nez, and was interested in etymology. She had no "charm" at all. At that point Wells could scarcely have realized that in a few years Dorothy Richardson would begin to draw a full-scale portrait of him in fiction. By the time of his preface to *Nocturne,* however, he would have known that, given the aubiographical nature of the first three volumes of *Pilgrimage,* his turn was bound to come sooner or later.

It came, of course, in *The Tunnel,* which Dorothy had begun to write almost as soon as *Honeycomb* was finished, just before her marriage. She would not have the new novel ready for publication, however, until late in 1918, and by the time it appeared in February 1919, she was well on the way to being one of the most talked-about novelists of the day. Her books were appearing in America under the imprint of Alfred Knopf and were attracting attention in the magazines devoted especially to the new and original. The young Randolph Bourne (only a few months before his untimely death) reviewed *Honeycomb* in the *Dial* of May 1918. He called it an "imagist novel," marveled at its "precision," and felt that it contained the "essence of quivering youth." A month earlier, in April, the novelist May Sinclair had attached the label "stream of consciousness" (borrowing the phrase from William James) to Dorothy Richardson's books. In an essay devoted to *Pointed Roofs, Backwa-*

106

ter, and *Honeycomb,* which appeared in the *Little Review* (a shorter version appeared simultaneously in the *Egoist*), Miss Sinclair claimed not only that the real subject of these novels was the stream of consciousness of their heroine, but that this was the important subject of the modern novel. A few months later, in July, the youthful poet Babette Deutsch described in her own delicate tones how impressive she thought Dorothy Richardson's achievement already was, and how certain passages in the novels reminded her of T. S. Eliot "in the sensitiveness of their rhythms." She thought the books were wonderfully real in spite of their setting in the far-off nineties of England and their remoteness from the war, in spite moreover of Miriam's immaturity and the uneventfulness of the narrative. It seemed to her that precisely because so much of what took place was by most standards trivial, one began to feel about it the way one felt about "certain curious intense personal memories" that could mean little to anybody else but had their own "marked tempo" and their own precious reality.

Babette Deutsch was probably the first to try to explain a reaction to *Pilgrimage* that became familiar over the years, especially among poets, who shared its method of realizing an emotion not by analysis but rather, as she put it, by "inducing its systole and diastole." It was the poets also who tended to agree with Randolph Bourne that the "short installments" were exactly right, whereas the inveterate readers of novels were more inclined to grumble. Some of them did not like having to wait for the next volume, others objected to not knowing when they were to reach the end of the "story," and a few thought it had gone on long enough as it was. As a matter of fact, the reviewer of *Honeycomb* in the *Times Literary Supplement* took the liberty of announcing that the "fourth and final volume, *The Tunnel,* [was] in preparation." It is unlikely that Dorothy Richardson herself knew when the end would come, or that she even thought consciously about it. A new life was just beginning for her. It had a great deal of promise, but it was also full of practical problems.

3

When they married in 1917, neither Dorothy nor Alan had anything that could reasonably be called an income. (Veronica and Benjamin

Grad had even supplied Dorothy with a wedding band.) Occasionally Alan sold a drawing, but he existed mostly on the allowance from his father. Dorothy had had advances from Duckworth for both *Backwater* and *Honeycomb*. As it turned out, the royalty payments due to her for *Backwater* had been less than the advance, so she actually owed Duckworth a small sum. She knew moreover even before *Honeycomb* appeared that she could expect nothing further from it; she would feel fortunate if her debt to Duckworth were not increased. She owed money, as well, to Curtis Brown, the agent who mediated with Duckworth and made the arrangements with Knopf in America. To publish *Pointed Roofs* and *Backwater,* Knopf had purchased a small number of sheets from Duckworth (although in 1919 he would manufacture a new edition of the first two volumes and print *Honeycomb* as well), and she knew there was little to hope for in the way of American profits. Under the circumstances, the only sensible thing she could think of doing was to ask Duckworth for a £15 advance on *The Tunnel*. Two days after her marriage, she wrote to Curtis Brown to tell him this.

By October, however, it was clear that the Odles would not have enough money to get through the following year. Dorothy would have to ask Duckworth for still another advance. But at the last moment she decided to ask instead for what she called "a regular living wage," to be paid "for the present" on the royalties that might accrue in the future. Duckworth agreed. Dorothy reported the agreement to Curtis Brown from a little cottage in Eastcote, Middlesex, where she and Alan were staying through the month.

They had spent the few days immediately following their wedding in Pinner; then they had gone back to London to inform Alan's brother Vincent of their marriage. (To protect his allowance, Alan thought his father should not be told.) Afterward they went to the cottage in Eastcote, a quiet Elizabethan village they had discovered while at Pinner, which was just a few miles away. From here Dorothy carried on her correspondence with Curtis Brown and Duckworth and worked out something of a plan for living in the years to come. Given the state of Alan's health, she had in mind spending as much time as possible in Cornwall, where the climate in winter was relatively mild and the accommodations were inexpensive during all seasons except summer. In any case, it seemed clear to her that Alan would not survive many more winters in London, but also that she could not say this to him. It was her understanding that Alan had such a fear and a horror of illness that one dared not even mention the matter.

Cornwall did not materialize until February, however. They spent the month of November at Bushey in Hertfordshire, December with her sister Kate in Surrey, but January in London. By then Alan seemed to feel he had had the equivalent of a world tour, though if Dorothy wanted to leave London again, he saw no reason why—having already been there—they should not return to Middlesex. Dorothy understood that going to Middlesex could easily become one of Alan's habits. There were even more of these habits than she had realized. His daily life consisted of a series of rules so rigidly observed that his punctilious father would have been more than gratified if only the hub of the wheel had been a Bank instead of Art. Alan always worked during certain hours and read (sometimes the same thing over and over) during others. Yet, as fixed as his habits were, he formed new ones and dropped old ones with a rapidity that astonished his wife. For example, he stopped drinking alcohol entirely, without any comment at all. He ate his meals according to the schedule Dorothy established, as though he had been doing just that for years. And now he was ready to go to Middlesex in the way he had gone to the Café Royal. Dorothy barely succeeded in substituting Cornwall.

One of her friends, Mrs. Dawson-Scott, a poet and novelist who had a passion for Cornwall and wrote novels about it, offered Dorothy for the month of February the cottage where she herself had been staying. It was in Constantine Bay, one of the rougher and more windswept bays near Padstow, craggy and stark. The land of Constantine (except around the large farm which dominated the bay) was mostly uncultivated. Thorns, brambles, and spire-grass made up the landscape. There were few cottages other than those belonging to the farm. One of these—at the end of a lane diagonal to the top of the hill which led down into the bay—belonged to Mr. Ben Old, who ran the general store in Constantine. This was the cottage Mrs. Dawson-Scott had rented. It was called Levorna and had been built of the traditional gray Cornish stone in the first half of the nineteenth century. Standing at the edge of an immense wild field, through which one could walk to the hamlet of Trehemborne, it looked like a section of rock carved by the careful hand of nature. Alongside the cottage were pigsties, no longer in use but redolent of their former life. From a rain pump came pure water for cooking and drinking, and a rainwater tank provided for baths and washing up. Sloping to the rear was a Cornish "linhay" or lean-to: the back kitchen, which was a kind of scullery.

There was no question about it, Levorna was a piece of pure Cornwall for Alan Odle to taste. He came to the West country in February and made his judgment. He saw at once that it was a draftsman's country: a crooked coastline, ragged crumbling cliffs against a moving sky, and tops of spare trees sloped by the wind into neat declivity. He decided to stay.

.   .   .

Since Levorna was available to them for only a month, Dorothy had made other arrangements for the period from March to June. A woman named Mrs. Pope, who lived in Trevone, had agreed to lodge them through the spring. Like Mrs. Pope, many of the residents of Cornwall took in boarders throughout the year. During the holiday season, beginning as early as Easter, some of them actually moved out of their homes entirely (or into smaller living quarters that were attached) in order to rent their cottages to whole families. Trevone happened to be full of such possibilities. Very near to Mrs. Pope's Trevone Cottage, for example, was Bloomfield, owned by Mrs. Bennett, who was also willing to take Dorothy and Alan as boarders, and she did so whenever Mrs. Pope was ill. Then only a few yards down the road was Rose Cottage, owned by two sisters named Ponder who could move into adjoining rooms if they wished, or even to one of their other cottages. It was their Rose Cottage that Dorothy had already arranged to rent for the coming autumn. She was planning to spend the summer in London in Alan's Queen's Terrace rooms (which they had decided to keep), to find a tenant for the winter, and to come to Cornwall again in October.

Such a pattern seemed eminently suitable, and she hoped to be able to establish it. Alan would be kept out of London during the cold raw months; they would keep house cheaply themselves during the fall and winter; and in the spring they would board with everything done for them, leaving them free to work uninterruptedly or, if they wished, to take a holiday. During this first spring, Alan took a long look around, exploring the coves and bays and cliffs of Padstow. He had his first experience, too, of Padstow's annual, age-old May Day celebration.

110

The Hobby Horse on May Day at Padstow.

Called Hobby Horse Day, it was (and still is) a survival of pagan and early Christian times, when the fertile season of summer was ushered in with the dance of a grotesquely shaped and painted Horse. On May Day morning a tense, eager crowd waits outside the Golden Lion pub in Padstow for the Horse to emerge. He comes out, always at the same time, in a resplendent black, hooped skirt held up inside by two Padstow men, and begins his dance through flower- and flag-lined streets. He weaves and dips, flinging his long tail, sounding his horse-head snappers. His conical mask painted red, black, and white sways with him. The crowd follows behind his retinue of youths and maidens dressed in white, singing the song of May. When they reach the tall, delicately colored May Pole set up in Broad Street, the Horse and the young singers circle about it, and the crowd watches intently as the ritual unfolds.

On May Day in 1918 Alan and Dorothy Odle walked into Padstow from deserted Trevone. For a while they followed the Hobby Horse and the surging crowd; then they ferried across the Camel River to Rock, the village on the eastern bank. Here they wandered over the dunes and on and on, quite willingly lost, until they reached Polzeath several miles away. But when they got back to Rock, the last ferry had already gone. Between them, they did not have enough money to stay the night at the little Rock hotel; neither did they have the energy to tramp the eight miles to the Wadebridge railroad station. They stood on the empty quay, and for some strange reason they could not themselves fathom they began to shout in vain. There was nobody to hear them. They would have to spend the night in a large hollow they spied out on the dune, partly sheltered by overhanging moss-grown sand. Just as they resigned themselves to the dune, they caught sight of a small boat coming across the water. Renewing their shouts, they watched the boat move toward them and land. It discharged a wild-looking skeletal being, with fierce red hair and gold earrings, who said he had seen them from the top of a cliff. The "knight-errant," as Dorothy dubbed him, could scarcely be persuaded to accept their combined store of coin.

As accustomed as the Cornish obviously were to the colorful and outlandish, the villagers of Trevone and Padstow, of Constantine, St. Merryn, and Harlyn very soon grew used to the sight of Alan Odle. He would stride up Trevone's steep hill as if it were level, or along the cliffs, swinging his stick, sometimes carrying gloves, and always looking up at the sharp or misty skyline. When he met someone, he lifted his battered bowler hat (later a trilby) three inches from his head in a swift, elaborate gesture, but he rarely stopped to talk. The observant villagers soon made out that of the two of them only Mrs. Odle would chat when she came into the shop or the post office, or if they greeted her as she walked with her head always down. It did not take them long to learn that she wrote books on oddly assorted shapes and sizes of paper, which could not be touched even to clean, and that he was just what he looked like: an artist. He worked every day at the table nearest the window, which he would rather one did not even approach. As foreigners (meaning everybody save the Cornish), they were more bearable than most, though what *Alan* thought of the Cornish he did not say. But by June, Cornwall itself had assumed for him the stature and permanence of a work of art. Now it was clear that he would not agree to leave except to go to London.

CHAPTER EIGHT

The Edge of Fame

DURING the summer of 1918, there was talk here and there of the strange new work by James Joyce appearing in installments in the *Little Review*. It had begun in the March issue (the April issue would contain May Sinclair's essay on the novels of Dorothy Richardson) and seemed thus far to be stirring up comment largely because of its pungent vocabulary. Even the *Little Review*'s foreign editor, Ezra Pound, admitted to deleting twenty lines from the manuscript of the fourth installment. But he had done this, he said, for good reason, and explained himself to Joyce. Joyce did not in the least disgust him, he claimed, as did, for example, someone like H. G. Wells.

Dorothy and Alan Odle heard some of the talk about *Ulysses* as they spent most of their summer working, she on *The Tunnel,* volume four of *Pilgrimage,* and he on his drawings. He had amassed a stack of illustrations for *Gulliver's Travels* and wanted to show them along with other samples of work he had done to date. By the end of the summer, it seemed fairly certain that the Bruton Galleries, managed by Robert Boss, would hold the exhibition. But the showing was likely to take place in January and February, which meant a winter in London.

They went to Cornwall and Rose Cottage in October and stayed only through December. Both were so busy they scarcely registered the Armistice in November or even the "primitive" condition of the cottage—that is, until they returned to it the following autumn. This time they were not in it long enough to realize what an entire winter there might involve. For the moment, Rose Cottage seemed very desirable at a rent of five shillings a week, and they looked forward to being in it again. Indeed, during the "demented" months of January and February 1919, Alan's show, and the bout with influenza that followed, the troublesome oil lamps of Rose Cottage and the cooking stove in the coal fireplace would have seemed utterly delightful. Furthermore, in the midst of the show, in February, *The Tunnel* was published and reviews of it began to appear almost at once. They were by no means entirely favorable, but there was no question in any of them of the importance of Dorothy Richardson's serial novel. She herself could not ignore the fact that within her grasp was a sizable measure of fame.

1

Dorothy reported in one of her letters that Alan Odle's drawings were praised in reviews of the exhibition as representing "the perfect meeting of literature and art." He himself was described, she said, as England's "most distinguished draughtsman since Beardsley." But very few people bought anything. One who did was H. G. Wells, who hung his Odle drawing above his writing desk. As the years passed, it became, he said, more and more suited to his own temper.

Alan Odle's wife thought that something more than a sale even to Wells should take place as a result of the exhibition. She happened to say this one day to a friend who knew Edward Garnett. Dorothy's friend immediately suggested him as just the person to persuade the publisher John Lane that Alan Odle ought to illustrate an edition of Rabelais or one of the books of Balzac. Dorothy wrote a letter to Garnett in which she carefully avoided any reference to Alan Odle as her husband, speaking instead of this "very dear friend" of hers who was art editor of *The Gypsy* and had just had his first exhibition. As she expected, Garnett wrote back to ask whether he could see Alan Odle's work even though the exhibition was over, and she directed him to the Bruton Galleries, where the drawings were still stacked and in their frames. Several days later, Garnett wrote again, this time advising Alan to take a few of his drawings in person to the office of the publisher. But John Lane was not interested. No one seemed interested, and Alan decided he would have a better chance with an American rather than a French writer. He settled on Poe and began to illustrate the *Masque of the Red Death*. The work went very much against the grain, for Poe's brand of horror did not suit Alan Odle at all: it was too *personal* for him, but he kept at it until something better came along.

Eventually Garnett thought of the cool and mocking Voltaire, who seemed to him a counterbalancing influence that might be of value in the heady atmosphere of postwar England, and Alan Odle seemed to him a perfect illustrator for *Candide*. Garnett had the idea of an entirely new translation as well, done by Dorothy Richardson. Alan agreed to his part at once. Dorothy mulled over hers. She began to read *Candide,* said she was delighted with it, but finally decided she did not want to translate it. She told Garnett that she was not entirely at home in satire, that she did not have firm enough opinions. She could be, she said, "anything or nothing, by turns." If Garnett smiled at this description of herself, there is no record of it. As far as we know, he was his usual gentlemanly self. He bowed to her decision and helped Alan get a commission from George Routledge and Sons to illustrate *Candide*.

The edition did not appear until 1922; but when Alan began work on the drawings in 1920, a bust of Voltaire made its appearance in Queen's Terrace and became a permanent part of the Odle sitting room. It surveyed the scene as if about to spin a moral tale whose hero could only be Alan the artist. For he was indeed a character out of Voltaire, in his undulating trousers and velvet coat, jeering at mankind in the mass and bowing politely to everyone he met, contemptuous of organized religion, yet as devout in service as a monk in a cloistered cell, except that in his eyes the only godly pursuit was the practice of art.

In the face of such devotion as his, one had to feel a certain awe. As he sat at work, bent over a table placed as close to the window as possible, his silhouette resembled that of a monk of the Middle Ages illuminating a holy text. Though *Candide* did not exactly qualify as scripture, Alan treated it as if it were just that. He revered Voltaire (or Françoise-Marie Arouet), who himself had been a curious mixture, seeking pleasure and deriding it at one and the same time. The combination of irreverence and piety in Alan Odle might have been conceived by Voltaire.

As it was, scenes and characters Voltaire *had* created came to visual life through the pen of Alan Odle. He preferred scenes that took place in teeming cities, and his favorite characters were the naïve young man himself, the battered and eternally smiling Pangloss, and the unsaintly daughter of Pope Urban X. In one of his most brilliant illustrations Candide is lying ill in a crowded room in Paris after his return from El Dorado, having brought with him the great wealth that was attracting the French as moths are drawn to a flame. In one corner of the room, a beautiful young woman is rifling the wardrobe chest, one of its drawers closed upon a single disembodied hand that looks both limp and voracious. In another corner a priest is holding out a cross, while behind his back and down his cassock a grinning, bald-headed imp is pouring a bucket of slops. Candide himself lies in the four-poster bed, seeming to breathe his last. Beside him stands the doctor, with one hand checking the patient's pulse, the other held up, a raised forefinger informing everybody that the happy moment of expiration is nigh.

Alan Odle apparently saw little in the nature of man that was not worthy of scorn. The illustrations to *Candide* are filled with evidence of this, and the actual world in which he lived provided at least some of the raw material. The progress of the *Little Review*, for example, which both he and his wife followed for various reasons, had the makings of an Odle drawing. The cast of characters, as usual, was large. The standard innocents were Margaret Anderson and Jane Heap, who thought that they would render a service to the literary world by publishing "experimental" prose rather than the critical essays they had at first emphasized in their magazine. Indeed, in the case of *Ulysses*, Miss Anderson felt she would never again publish anything so beautiful. But as it turned out, the New York Post Office took more interest in the *Little Review* serialization of *Ulysses* than did the literary world, and three times it confiscated an issue. One can imagine the men of the mails as Alan Odle might have drawn them: self-righteously and pruriently searching the magazine for obscene matter from which to protect the public. He would no doubt have drawn the public themselves as leering satyrs, far more obscene than the offending passages written by Joyce.

Soon after the confiscation of the second issue, in the spring of 1919, Dorothy Richardson was drawn into the fray. She, too, was an experimental writer, and Margaret Anderson, who had been following reviews of *The Tunnel,* decided that her "Magazine of the Arts Making No Compromise With the Public Taste" ought to do more than publish an essay about Miss Richardson's novels: it ought to publish one of the novels. Dorothy was in the midst of writing the fifth volume, entitled *Interim.* She had enough of it finished, however, for a serialization to begin almost at once in the *Little Review.* But did she want it to? Apart from its sensational aspects, what was the reputation of the *Little Review?* Neither she nor Alan really knew. Perhaps Curtis Brown or Alfred Knopf could tell her. She wrote to both of them. Curtis Brown was distinctly unenthusiastic,

117

and Knopf thought the "literary level" of the *Little Review* was low. In spite of their opinions, she went ahead and agreed to serialization of *Interim*. It seemed to her, thinking the matter over, that one could not say anything worse about the *Little Review* than that its material was "often deliberately outré." At the same time, two of its current contributors were Ford Madox Hueffer and James Joyce. They were justification enough for her.

So in June 1919 Dorothy Richardson's *Interim* joined *Ulysses* in the pages of the *Little Review,* and when in January 1920 the post office seized yet another issue, an installment of the relatively modest fifth volume of *Pilgrimage* was suppressed along with part of the Cyclops episode of *Ulysses*. No one thought it the least bit ironic that the author of *Pilgrimage* should be involved in an action directed against a work that was allegedly obscene, although some of her own readers thought that at times she too touched upon the seamier side of things. One of them, Lady Desborough, even reproved her for it. She granted that in Dorothy Richardson's books the "nauseas of life" were admitted much less than in those of most young writers—James Joyce, for instance; but did not Miss Richardson feel that the details of the dentist's room in *The Tunnel* were "almost *too* nasty?" Lady Desborough went on to say that she would be "quite ready to face" all this if it were "inevitable as in *Ghosts*" or "if it led from or on to anything," but really dear Miss Richardson, "does it?" she asked.

Whether or not Dorothy Richardson managed to soothe Lady Desborough's ruffled sensibilities, in the very pages of the *Little Review* a dogmatic argument went on about the literary-aesthetic as well as the moral-aesthetic side of contemporary prose. In the issue of September 1919, John Rodker compared Dorothy Richardson with Joyce and decided that Joyce was superior because anyone who had "a sufficiently sympathetic and cultured brain" could follow him and be moved by him, whereas Dorothy Richardson was "too intellectually subtle." On another page of the same issue, the poet William Carlos Williams chose to compare Richardson and Joyce as writers who had "form" with another pair, D. H. Lawrence and Richard Aldington, who Williams thought were guilty of "indecent exposure." He went on to say he knew as well as anyone that Joyce was "lewd and in the street" and Richardson "charming and in a girl's bedroom." But these were not things that mattered; it was vision that mattered. Joyce and Richardson had vision; Lawrence and Aldington did not.

Besides discussions such as these, the *Little Review* was also carrying a novel by May Sinclair entitled *Mary Olivier,* which most people agreed had been written under the influence of Dorothy Richardson. Its heroine (like Dorothy Richardson's) was engaged in wresting from a confining heritage the emotional and intellectual freedom she craved, and the inner development of this heroine was traced from infancy to middle age. Some people thought Miss Sinclair had tried to put too much into a single-volume novel. Dorothy Richardson, after all, had already written five volumes, and her heroine was still only twenty-five. She herself would have agreed with this criticism of May Sinclair, for in response to a young friend who told her he was considering such a fictional treatment of his own life, she described the plan as "vast," even in his particular case, where "babyhood" was not so very far off.

Equally under Dorothy Richardson's influence—in the opinion of some, that is—were Miss Romer Wilson and Mrs. C. A. Dawson-Scott. As a matter of fact, the influence on Mrs. Dawson-Scott was considered almost pernicious—by Dorothy Richardson's own American publisher. Knopf had been approached by William Heinemann, the English publisher of Mrs. Dawson-Scott, about an American edition of one of her novels. Knopf said he liked the book but felt certain changes needed to be made. Some of these had to do with punctuation, or rather the absence of it, which Knopf laid at the door of Dorothy Richardson and her "more or less notorious novels." He claimed that Mrs. Dawson-Scott was "suffering from an extreme case of Richardsonitis," that she had gone through her manuscript and with "unflagging pertinacity kicked out every punctuation she came across and stuck in its place a trio or quartette of periods."

In describing Dorothy Richardson's novels as "more or less notorious," Knopf was probably right. By the time of *The Tunnel* and *Interim,* Dorothy Richardson's novels were widely—and to some extent unfavorably—known. According to at least one reviewer of *Interim,* they had also received an "excessive amount of praise," which in his opinion had not "done her any good." If, however, the praise was excessive, so was the blame. The novels seemed to provoke extreme reactions, and it was inevitable that the fame of such books should be mixed with notoriety. They had an original and distinctive character and could therefore be made fun of, as Henry James's novels had been not long before. Someone said of *The Tunnel,* for example, that it was the "longest bore on earth.'' The heroine of all the novels was often described as ''wasp-ish'' or ''bitter'' or ''conceited.'' And Dorothy Richardson herself might be labeled, directly or otherwise, as something of an ''old maid.'' But even in the great exasperation, for instance, on the part of an ''elderly male reviewer'' (self-styled) who was proud that he had learned to delight in Mr. Conrad, one could hear tones of respect. Yet another reviewer said the novels making up *Pilgrimage* were ''the real expression of a real personality.'' And they were a dominant part of the literary scene. The names Richardson and Joyce (and soon Proust as well) occurred constantly together, quite naturally (said an essayist in the *English Review*) by the ''associa-tion of ideas.''

2

Among the signs of a writer's growing reputation are letters from admirers. During the summer of 1919, while the *Little Review* made its uncertain way across the Atlantic and Dorothy Richardson hag-gled with Curtis Brown and Knopf about her minuscule royalties, there came to Queen's Terrace a letter she felt compelled to answer almost at once. It was signed Owen Nugent and was unmistakably from someone who was young. The letter spoke of personal literary ambitions and excited readings of modern writers—Lawrence and Joyce and Dorothy Richardson. It asked questions about her and her work and even ventured to entreat a photograph. But it asked all this so ingenuously that she was charmed.

Without being sure whether Owen Nugent was male or female, she wrote back, responding to the youth, innocence, and sincerity the letter breathed. She gave advice, as she had been asked to do, but advised against listening to advice. Write ''from yourself,'' she said, without holding back. About her own work, she claimed that when *Pointed Roofs* was published, she had read none of the mod-erns and had read very little of them since. But she recognized in James Joyce someone who used the same method as she, though more beautifully (in the strict sense) and perhaps ''to a wider end'' (of this, however, she was not sure). And she had no photograph of herself to supply. Her letter was both warm and reserved in equal measure.

Owen Nugent turned out to be a young man of twenty-five, older than she had expected, and was really named Percy Beaumont

Percy Beaumont (Owen) Wadsworth, 1918.

Wadsworth. He decided that Dorothy Richardson had been receptive enough for him to write again. This time he told her more about himself and enclosed a few of his own manuscripts. He described how he had come to London from Lancashire in the north with but the rudiments of an education, not only to seek his fortune, but also to satisfy his curiosity about those who appeared to have found theirs. At the moment he was working as a clerk in the Burlington Arcade in Piccadilly and was educating himself. Dorothy Richardson invited him to Queen's Terrace and found him as delightful in person as he was in his letters. He chattered incessantly, had an endless fund of observations that he turned into witty stories, and was all admiring eyes.

He was writing about himself as someone named Bernard. Dorothy read the chapters he gave her and commented on them in considerable detail. She grew more and more fond of the "Boy," as she liked to address the slight, wiry, affectionate Wadsworth, who was Owen only to the more precious of his friends. He was not in the least averse to mothering, for he had never had any; and it would have been difficult, if he liked you, to pay him too much attention. When he decided in the fall that the Burlington Arcade was an absolutely dead end and he would go off to India for the experience of it, Dorothy (who knew little about India, though she got an occasional letter from a Richardson relation who had gone there years before) told him what kind of clothes he ought to take with him and the sort of food he ought not to eat there. Owen did not mind this at all. She was always telling him, too, that he need not worry, that youth would pass, that beyond its "palsy & paralysis" were "the gay green slopes, the stars & sunlight, the dreams & dancing of old age."

By the time Owen actually left in the winter of 1919, a friendship between him and the Odles had been firmly established, yet he knew hardly anything about them. Dorothy seemed to him always secure and unruffled, dispensing her wisdom and her affection in a deep, soothing voice which sounded "golden" in his ears. Alan seemed always the same, slighly bemused sometimes, but never preoccupied or remote. Owen saw them both, from the point of view of suffering youth, as perfectly contented beings. He had no idea that they, too, had money problems. Dorothy would not have let him know this so early in their friendship, but neither would it have occurred to him to wonder about the shabbiness of their Queen's

Terrace rooms. As a matter of fact, at the same time that she was writing cheerful notes to Owen, inviting him to Queen's Terrace and instructing him to rattle the flap of the letterbox twice because their knocker had rusted off, she was also penning gloom-filled, threatening letters to Curtis Brown about the state of her affairs.

Her debt to Duckworth seemed to be growing larger rather than smaller. The American editions of her books brought in virtually nothing. She had an agreement with Knopf, during this summer of 1919, for an advance of £5 on the appearance of *The Tunnel* and a royalty of 10 percent on the first four volumes he was then about to publish. He had offered her a 15 percent royalty on the fifth volume, *Interim,* but Dorothy decided she would rather have a bigger advance. As she explained to Curtis Brown at the end of July, she needed £10 before September and did not want to earn it by doing "hack work." Her eyes were badly strained. She wanted a holiday. £10 would give it to her. Knopf gave her nearly £15 and promised an equal sum when 500 copies had been sold. After that her royalty would be 10 percent. She was quite satisfied: she had enough money for a month's holiday, and she arranged to spend it in Cornwall in lodgings where she would have nothing whatever to do with keeping house or preparing meals.

They lodged with Mrs. Beatrice Carne in Trehemborne, only a few yards away from the converted chapel in which *Pointed Roofs* had been born, and Dorothy was expecting proofs of *Interim* to arrive at any moment. Before the proofs came, she and Alan got in a few happy days of sunshine and adventure. It was a warm September, "a second summer" as she described it in a letter to Owen, almost too hot to bathe. She ventured in, though, unable to resist the "mauve green billows" of the bay, but Alan could not be persuaded to wet more than his knees. He was perfectly willing, however, to walk all day, in and out of the coves and among the dunes. They lost their way again, returning long after dark to a village that had already begun to think about a search party and ropes. They were still foreigners to the Cornish and might easily in ignorance have trapped themselves on the rocks, delayed coming down, and been caught by the swift incoming tide. Such accidents were always happening in Cornwall; and Mrs. Carne, knowing Dorothy and Alan were artists, thought them more helpless than ordinary holiday visitors. In fact, she had been lodging mostly artists for the past few years, especially those with small incomes and some with unstable temperaments. The novelist Gilbert Cannan, who apparently went insane at intervals, had preceded Dorothy and Alan. During his stay he had read the proof sheets of *Time and Eternity,* and had left one set behind in the wastepaper basket. Mrs. Carne had rescued them, and when the Odles came she produced them with pride as reading matter for her new guests.

Dorothy reported all this to Owen Wadsworth, who had decided by then that one of the ways in which he could express his gratitude for her friendship was to supply her with the contemporary literature she had told him she knew so little about. He sent her three novels by Compton Mackenzie, one by George Moore, and a set of the *Little Review* to date, containing the controversial episodes of *Ulysses.* She did not say anything specific to Owen about Joyce but chose instead to comment on the immensely refreshing Mackenzie. She noted that Henry James had singled him out some years before as one of the most promising of the younger novelists, and it seemed to her he was justifying James's praise. She especially liked the evidence in his work that he was "not out to show . . . what he [could] do," enabling him then to feel clever and superior for having done it. One suspects that in this she was contrasting Mackenzie with Joyce.

Not that she objected to cleverness, even when it was directed against her. The sharp-tongued Katherine Mansfield, for example, had reviewed both *The Tunnel* and *Interim* in the *Athenaeum.* In April 1919 she had said that anything going into Dorothy Richardson's mind could be summoned forth again "complete in every detail, with nothing taken away from it—and nothing added." Now, in January 1920, she remarked that since for Dorothy Richardson everything was of "equal importance," it had to be true that everything was also of "equal unimportance." Dorothy said that Katherine Mansfield was "as clever as old Nick," but a woman had a right to be clever, and she liked her.

She was not as good-humored about all the reviews of *Interim,* which was published in December 1919, when she and Alan, after an idyllic month in Trehemborne, had begun to live at Rose Cottage in Trevone. They had arrived in October "bucolic and brainless," she said, and had been forced immediately to husband all their wits for the sole purpose of existing from day to day. In other words, the once desirable Rose Cottage had been unveiled, but only because Dorothy had begun to pay attention to it. There had never been either an inside lavatory or electricity. Like most of the cottages in Cornwall, it was lit by oil and heated by the coal fireplace. To the side of the fireplace in the sitting room was a small oven heated by coal, at which—as in most cottages—the cooking was done. Some cottages had an oil stove in the kitchen as well. Coal was more economical to use than oil though, and Rose Cottage had no other apparatus for cooking than the oven in the fireplace.

It happened that this particular year the Padstow coal was damp, and since it did not burn exceptionally well even when dry (because a good deal of it was stone), cooking with it turned into something of a nightmare. Dorothy claimed she sometimes had to "nurse" the fire for an entire morning, not to speak of "dosing [it] with paraffins, candle-ends, whole candles, sugar, margarine, to achieve anything that [would actually] cook." But the real problem was that she lacked the lifelong experience of the local women with Cornish housekeeping. Neither did she take much pleasure in it. She struggled in her fashion with coal stoves, oil lamps, and flues; and she claimed that Cornwall kept "its spell through thick and thin," even through February, when she saw a copy of the *London Mercury*.

It contained a single review of several novels, *Interim* one of them but with more than a mere notice. The reviewer wrote at length about the indisputably "genuine" quality of all Dorothy Richardson's books. They were written in the way they were, the reviewer claimed, because they had to be—and because, when you came down to it, the mind thus following its natural bent and producing these volumes of *Pilgrimage* was not a normal one. To this reviewer a mind that observed and recorded in such a close, literal fashion could not be normal, so Dorothy Richardson's "impressions of life" could not possibly "correspond to life as normal persons [saw] it."

This review angered and troubled Dorothy enough so that she wrote a letter in her own defense to Edward Garnett. She admitted her own dissatisfaction with all but the first part of *Interim*. It was "thin and badly foreshortened," she said, because it had been written "in a perfect gale of difficulties and disturbances," but she could not understand how anyone could fail to see her books as anything but "quite sane." She thought it damaging, moreover, to be so misrepresented, to have her own view of life described as "fragmentary, abnormal and so on" because she was trying to convey the " 'fragmentary' world of an adolescent." People who

125

had never read *Pilgrimage* would be turned away by such a review, she said, and for reasons without any foundation in fact.

Though she was quite right to object to the confusion of the "point of view" with the author and to admit to the book's thinness, her reaction to this particular review seems excessive, and one surmises that a raw nerve had been touched. She was perhaps more susceptible than most to the suggestion of abnormality or insanity because of her mother's long illness, but this does not account for her response. Her first novel, *Pointed Roofs,* had been described in the *Saturday Review* as the product of a diseased or neurotic mind, and she had not been unduly affected. In the present case, one would guess that her real concern was not so much with the charge of abnormality as with the troubling evidence in this review that the image she was forging of herself was being tampered with.

This was a problem she would face again and again—portraying herself as she wished to be seen and having that portrait viewed and described differently than she intended—but this was inevitable. Miriam Henderson was the girl Dorothy Richardson had been in the past, but she was not the woman who was now recording, shaping, and subtly altering her young self. Autobiography by its very nature is largely history, and when it is transcribed in the form of a fictional narrative told in the third person, it takes on a new and problematic identity. The configuration of Miriam's life remained that of Dorothy Richardson's, but the internal development of her character, when pressed into fiction, took on certain of the qualities of caricature. The lines of Miriam's strong personality followed those of Dorothy Richardson's but had the sharper edges and more heightened coloring of a figure seen through the lens of a camera. Dorothy would not always be happy with the effect, or with some of her readers' interpretations of her. It was a little as if she herself were being taken out of her own hands.

3

Another development that Dorothy was not entirely happy with was the more and more common association of her work with Joyce's, for it must have seemed to her inevitable that she would suffer by it. Yet her two novels of 1919, *The Tunnel* and *Interim,* were very much in the style that would come to be called Joycean. They were concrete, if not naturalistic, and they evoked the city of London, as

Joyce was evoking Dublin, by an accumulation of minute and sensuous detail. London actually comes into one's ears—"in full open midday roar; brilliant and fresh; dim, intimate, vast." But for Dorothy the evocation of London is less an end in itself than a means by which her theme of self-discovery is carried forward.

To this city Dorothy had come in 1896, at the age of twenty-three, and had taken up residence with great excitement and no less great expectations. Now she has her heroine arrive under similar circumstances, at twenty-one, to work as a dental secretary (but in Wimpole Street rather than Harley) for £1 a week and to live on the fringe of Bloomsbury, in an attic room at No. 7, Tansley Street, where Endsleigh Gardens opens out of Gower Place. The house is run by Mrs. Bailey, a widow with four daughters. At first Mrs. Bailey only takes in lodgers (as Mrs. Baker did in Endsleigh Street); then she switches to boarders, as did her counterpart in fact. At the end of *The Tunnel*, Dorothy Richardson has Mrs. Bailey explain that a boardinghouse would give her daughters "a better chance." It wasn't "fair on them, living in the kitchen and seeing nobody," she said, and one of her friends had actually married three of her daughters to boarders.

By the time of *Interim*, then, the companion novel to *The Tunnel*, the house in Tansley Street is full of boarders—Norwegian, Canadian, Irish, Spanish—who give it a cosmopolitan cast and who contribute further, in one way or another, to the education and development of the innocent Miriam Henderson. Having mastered the geography of the city in *The Tunnel*, she herself is taken over in *Interim* by a swaggering, disreputable Spanish Jew whose name is Mendizabal. He tells elaborate and clever stories about himself, his favorite remark is "*Je m'en fiche,*" and Miriam, who has never met anyone like him, is fascinated. She spends most of her free time with him, listening spellbound to his talk on their long evening rambles through London. But as colorful as the story of Mendizabal happens to be, it is more a means than an end in itself, a means by which a pattern of response and involvement is traced and by which two of the major characters in *Pilgrimage* are introduced.

In the first place, as a Jew the Spanish Mendizabal recalls the German Jew of *Backwater*, who had also been attractive and unconventional. He points forward, too, to the most important Jew in Miriam's life, the Russian Michael Shatov with his rich and foreign nature (modeled after Benjamin Grad). In the second place, Men-

127

dizabal's obviously devilish appearance and effect on Miriam (his image obliterates everyone else from her mind) strike a note that serves to link character and theme with structure. And finally, both *The Tunnel* and *Interim* have echoes of a famous classical journey in search of self, Dante's *Divine Comedy*. When Miriam makes friends with Mendizabal against the warning of her friends in Tansley Street, a loose Dantean parallel is suggested as the strange and fiendish, but also comic, Mendizabal guides her on her walks through London.

The Tunnel, the only volume in the entire series with more than fifteen chapters, is divided into thirty-three, the precise number of cantos in Dante's comedy. Moreover, the novel contains repeated phrases that suggest the Italian journey-poem: the "inner circle," the "outer circle," the "rim of the world," the "tiger" of sensuality, the "dense thicket," "selling my soul to the Devil," the sins of pride and sloth. Then at the center of *Interim* is a Dante lecture that Miriam attends. It impresses upon her the absence of love in her nature. It seems to her that she cannot love humanity at large, and neither can she pray—presumably to learn how to love others rather than herself. This is one of Miriam's personal demons, and she feels its close pursuit even as Dorothy had felt it when she was as young as Miriam.

The other major character introduced in these two novels of 1919 is Hypo Wilson, modeled after H. G. Wells, who does not look devilish in the least but whose words and manner would gradually reveal themselves as those of an archseducer—of minds, that is, and unformed feelings. Ironically enough, it would not have occurred to anyone that Miriam needed a warning against him, the clever, rising young writer whose wife liked to quip (with a seriousness lost on Miriam) that the middle initial in her husband's name (he was Hypo G. Wilson) stood for God.

The central encounter in *The Tunnel*—and in the whole of *Pilgrimage*—is that between Miriam and this writer whom surprisingly few people identified as Wells. The point made by W. H. Mallock in his preface to *A Human Document* (though in a purely fictional context) had turned out to be a sound one. Because there was no connection in the public mind between Dorothy Richardson and H. G. Wells, the striking resemblance Wilson bore to his original went virtually unnoticed. Even more to the point than the absence of a clue was the strength of the portrayal as fiction. Hypo

Wilson was so vivid a character in his own right that the readers of *Pilgrimage* were not the least bit tempted to seek an original for him. Though the same holds true for Miriam, the fact remains that Wells was much more famous in 1919 than Dorothy Richardson. His fictional portrait, moreover, continued to be drawn in greater and greater detail through the novels that followed these two, but his identity remained a secret from the general public even after Wells himself had revealed it (in the autobiography he published in 1934). One can only conclude that Wilson was good enough as Wilson and did not need the help of his real-life identity as Wells.

His appearance is the high point of *The Tunnel* and was prepared for as an important stage in Miriam's gradual loss of innocence. London itself had begun the process, which Hypo Wilson will push forward by leaps and bounds. The stage is carefully set by a visit Miriam pays to her friends Jan and Mag (Johnny Schleussner and Mabel Heath) on the eve of her meeting with Wilson. With the note she has just received from her old school friend Alma, who is Wilson's wife, inviting her to their home outside of London, Miriam goes on impulse to the flat of her friends. They live on the top floor of a Bloomsbury building, which they have just learned is a quietly conducted, lucrative house of prostitution. They ask Miriam what she would do in their place, leave or stay. She answers, "I don't believe I should have found out."

In the first three volumes of *Pilgrimage,* the innocence and self-involvement dramatized remained essentially intact. Now in the fourth volume she will find herself challenged to lose those qualities, the nature of the challenge prefigured in an episode that takes place on her way home from Jan and Mag's. She leaves at midnight, humming as she walks across the moonlit square. A man appears in her path. He misinterprets her song and makes an obvious gesture toward her which at first she does not understand, unprepared as she still is for signs of overt sexuality. The scene is meant to linger in the mind during the account which follows of her weekend visit at the Wilson home.

The first meeting with Hypo Wilson is recalled in the one dramatic flashback of the novel; it is introduced as though it had been the most exhausting and threatening experience she ever had, as if in fact "something had brushed across [her face] and swept the life away." In that meeting she had come into touch with a world of writers and ideas so new and foreign to her experience that she felt stunned. At first, however, she had not been the least bit alarmed. Her initial view of Wilson himself had been reassuring. He was a "little fair square man" hardly taller than she, who looked like a "grocer's assistant." But this comforting view faded quickly. Though he remained a little man, he gave her the sense of a "strange direct attack, pushing through and out to some unknown place."

Wilson threatened her, in a "common voice, with a cockney twang," with his absolute certainty about everything. The books of the future, he foretold, would eliminate the relationship between men and women. Science, he asserted, was the most important subject of the present. God, he affirmed, was the creation of cowardly man. He stated facts, not opinions, and Miriam, convinced he was wrong, nevertheless wanted him "only to go on." She barely understood his critical terminology, but she absorbed his meaning through gesture and inflection. As she watched him, she caught him watching her; and she felt, excitedly, that she belonged with him and his world—or wanted to belong. At the same time she sensed, fearfully and oppressively, that "something here"—not yet understood—"was going to tax her more than she had ever been taxed before."

On her way back to London, Miriam told herself alternately that she would not go "down" again to the Wilsons and that she *must* go "down" again. The use of the word "down," perfectly natural to indicate the direction from London, nevertheless connotes a journey to hell. Miriam had already thought it possible that to join the Wilson circle would be to sell her soul to the devil. The farther the train takes her from Wilson, the more certain she is that she will return to him, but once she has reached London, the doubt and fear have crept in again. The thought of Wimpole Street and its respectability assails her. Wilson would never be approved of there: his marriage was irregular (Alma had been his student, and he had left his first wife to go off with her), and his way of seeing things was incomprehensible. Despite the fact that he was a "coming great man" and "a new kind of critic," Wilson and Wimpole Street were like oil and water. It would be impossible, Miriam decided, to convey what she had found in Surrey.

The contrast between the Wilson world and that of Wimpole Street is a fundamental one that operates in one way or another through the whole of *Pilgrimage*. It represents in part the conflict between a young woman's urge to be free and her yearning for the comfort and security of the middle class. Hancock, the dentist, and Wilson, the writer, are one pair of such opposites; Mendizabal and a Canadian doctor in *Interim* are another. And the pairs multiply as Miriam's struggle to choose one or the other continues throughout *Pilgrimage*. It is the same struggle that Dorothy Richardson herself had waged, a struggle she finally concluded by marrying Alan Odle, who happened to be a strange combination of both worlds and both sexes. There is in *Pilgrimage,* as there was in Dorothy Richardson's life, the alternating pull, equally strong, of the male and the female. In *The Tunnel* Miriam said of herself "I am something between a man and a woman, looking both ways," and in *Interim* Dorothy created a character (for whom there is no known model) who seems to have come directly out of this conflict, a young woman named Eleanor Dear. Since the novel was written during the first difficult period of her marriage, it is not surprising that Miss Dear should be a version of Alan Odle.

Eleanor Dear is a nurse who cannot practice her profession because she has turberculosis, which she refuses, however, to acknowledge. As a result she is driven to extreme lengths to support and, in fact, to preserve herself. Without either family or funds, she *wills* her continued existence and holds her life together with gossamer threads, weaving fantasies of betrothal and impending marriage. Miriam, unable to separate Eleanor Dear's delusions from reality without the aid of someone else, watches her manipulations with fascinated interest. Nurse Dear is the feminine artist who produces her own life out of other human material with a mental power which amazes and paralyzes Miriam. In the presence of Miss Dear's strength, Miriam weakens. She allows herself to be preyed upon and maneuvered, going nightly to the ailing girl's room to read to her. So enmeshed does she become that when her own sister Eve comes to London for six months, Miriam can scarcely find time to see her. Even though she learns quickly enough the truth behind Miss Dear's fabrications, she cannot act upon her knowledge to escape from the net in which she is caught. The sheer force of this "helpless" girl's will enslaves her, but so, too, do the shape of her face, the color of her hair, the size of her hands.

So, too, might Dorothy Richardson have felt enslaved by her artist-husband who also refused to admit he was ill. But Alan did not produce art by ensnaring other people or by weaving fantasies of relationship. On the contrary, he produced art by ignoring most people and refusing to enter into relationships with them. Left to his own devices, with neither family nor funds, he would probably have drawn until he died, for it seemed that in him the self-preserving instinct had been channeled into art, which in his vocabulary was another word for life.

In the recesses of her imagination, Dorothy must have been aware of how susceptible she would have been had Alan been more like Nurse Dear than he was; and in fictionalizing what she felt she had narrowly escaped by marrying him, she might also have been trying to reconcile herself to the demands of the life she had *not* escaped by marrying him. At the same time, she often fulfilled those demands as though she were indeed under the spell of a Nurse Dear, as though moreover she wanted to be. It was a way for her to draw back, as long as Alan lived, from the risks she did not want to take, and perhaps was a way even to account for her failure (the difficulties of life, she had already said, were to blame for the thinness of *Interim*). One might describe her marriage in this early period as a combination of self-willed enslavement and release, and in the delicate, doomed girl she had created, with a will as strong as her own, one might see her unconscious projection of both Alan and herself. For in these two novels written after her marriage, it would seem that her current emotional life had begun to infiltrate her fiction and to reshape her past.

CHAPTER NINE

Past and Present

DOROTHY AND ALAN left Rose Cottage early in May 1920, quite according to plan, and moved the short distance up the road to Mrs. Pope's, but without a completed manuscript for volume six of *Pilgrimage*. Dorothy had hoped to finish this volume during the winter in Rose Cottage so their two months with Mrs. Pope might be pure holiday for them both. Now there was no help for it. She would have to go on working; so would Alan, who refused to stop unless she did. She had promised her new book to Duckworth for the summer because she herself wanted volume five followed as quickly as possible. *Interim,* ending more like a chapter and with less finality than any of the other volumes, had made her uneasy, and she hoped the new book would be more solid fare for the reviewers. Thus, with a sense that the winter had foiled her, that it had been too rigorous for words, and that nothing was quite right except Cornwall, Dorothy sat writing *Deadlock* on a "minute rickety table" that needed to be propped to bring it into "some sort of relation to [her] chair." When she or Alan wanted to read the books being used to support the legs of the table, it had to stand "at a drunken tilt."

They had arranged to stay in Trevone Cottage with Mrs. Pope until the end of June, contented simply to be in Cornwall. Mrs. Pope fed them from her own large garden and from the Trenouth farm that was almost at her doorstep; she also allowed them the use of her sitting room—all for £2 a week. Since their winter tenant in Queen's Terrace, who paid them nearly £1, wished to remain through the month of June this year, the Odles felt they could stay in Cornwall longer than usual. But when they left Trevone for London at the end of June, Dorothy still had not finished *Deadlock.* Late in May the entire Pope household had fallen ill, and Dorothy and Alan had once again found themselves in the unexpected position of tending to a cottage—and nursing a family as well.

Then London and the summer greeted them with a rain that fell almost steadily during the next three months. Alan caught cold after cold, gave Dorothy a few of them, and they both began to long for Cornwall under any circumstances. But at the end of November, when the time did come to go back, they could scarcely bring themselves to leave the city, for despite the rain and persistent ills, London by then had reestablished its own strong claim.

One of their favorite pastimes in London (outside of walking) was riding the buses, to make out anew the various shapes the city took from different points of vantage. They had "haunts," as well, that had to be visited each summer: the art galleries, Mudie's, the British Museum, Monizhetti's restaurant (apparently the original of Donizetti's in *Pilgrimage,* whose owner had served the grateful Miriam, on her first timorous entry alone, the mere roll and butter and coffee which was all she could afford), and numerous nooks they had discovered in their wanderings through St. John's Wood. This time, while they made their accustomed rounds, Dorothy was also describing some of them in *Deadlock:* those that were part of her life in the early years of the century. Then she had roamed through London with Benjamin Grad; now it was Miriam's turn with her strange new friend, Michael Shatov; and Dorothy wove into her novel a curious mixture of the past and present.

The Russian Shatov, recently arrived in England, looks one moment like an aged professor; the next like a chubby, determined baby; and, when he walks through the streets eating grapes from a greengrocer's bag, like a "disreputable foreigner." Miriam, shrinking all the while from his "yellow boots" and "voluminously floating overcoat," takes him to the British Museum for a card of admission to the Reading Room. But she will not permit anyone else to patronize him. When the librarian smiles a "self-conscious superior English smile," it soon "sour[s] into embarrassment" under Miriam's hard stare.

The moment Shatov gets his card, he insists upon asking for "Anaka*ray*ninna in English"—shouting his intention to Miriam in an "enthusiastic whisper." He wants to introduce her to the glories of Tolstoy and to Tolstoy's "self-history" embodied in the story of "Layvin." But when he gets the book, he finds the translation "most vile." Sitting at one of the little desks in the Reading Room, he shuffles the pages of the book, muttering, looking for one of his favorite passages as the readers on either side cast angry glances and

Miriam tries to quiet him. But he is irrepressible: his guttural whisper is far more distinct than are his mutterings; and the suffering he causes the fastidious Miriam is drawn by Dorothy Richardson with a mixture of sympathy and scorn. The scene is brilliantly accurate and comic, in the great tradition of realism, and is a synthesis of countless experiences Dorothy had had not only with Benjamin Grad but also with Alan Odle, whose more or less bizarre appearance never went unregarded.

The relationship between Michael Shatov, who is twenty-two, and Miriam Henderson, who is twenty-five, occupies nearly the whole of *Deadlock*. Although it flowers briefly into a romantic engagement, the primary feeling on Miriam's part is protectiveness. Michael may be her equal if not her superior intellectually, but she responds to him emotionally as to a dependent child. The more protective she feels, the greater his claim upon her becomes. The fact that Michael is a Jew even further complicates an already tangled skein of emotions and takes on a prominence it might not have had if the other difficulties did not exist as well. He is, after all, the third Jew in her life, the three of them sharing a distinctly foreign appearance that seems to simultaneously attract and repel Miriam. Her relationship with Michael, however, is more serious than that with the German Jew of *Backwater* or the Spanish Jew of *Interim*. Faced this time with the need to make a decision, she finds her Anglo-Saxon nature unalterably opposed to a Russian Jew who only at odd moments looks tolerably French.

There is more to it, of course, than that. The relationship between them grows and changes in character through the novel. Though Miriam begins by teaching English to Michael Shatov, it is she who learns the most, not only about Russian literature and Eastern philosophy, but also about herself in relation to love and sex. She is drawn at first to his brilliant color and deep voice, as well as to his encyclopedic mind; then in time she comes to see the other side of the coin. A crimson tie and gold watchchain are also vulgar, and a deep voice can bawl at waiters. The knowledge stored in Michael's mind begins to strike her as arid, fastened to dogma, "exclusive." Worse still, though deferential to Miriam, he betrays for women in general a scorn that infuriates her because—so she claims—it signifies his exaltation of race over individual. Nonetheless, when Michael kisses her and declares his love, she feels it is a gift he confers, and she tremulously accepts—becoming again, briefly, the seventeen-year-old girl in *Pointed Roofs* who had dreamed of a home and a husband.

The reversion is brief indeed, for evident at once, after the initial surprising embrace, is Miriam's physical resistance, markedly unlike that of a shy girl. She is more like an unprepared and embarrassed boy, while Michael assumes the attitude of an imploring maiden. Miriam herself senses these reversed roles and her own clumsiness. During the first week of their "strange romance," she tries to justify her refusal to allow his touch: when he becomes less foreign, she will be more able to "suffer his nearness." But when she attempts to right the balance of their relationship by acceding to the feminine role, the result is an uneasy consciousness that her own face has begun to reflect the smug and "irritating smile" of the sort of sexually competitive woman she has always held in contempt. With the desire for the experience of love continually counteracted, she can neither part from him—and leave the "biggest world there is"—nor fully respond.

The "deadlock" is partially resolved (with respect to Michael at least) by his confession of an early encounter with a prostitute. (Dorothy appears to have substituted this kind of lapse for the breakdown suffered by Benjamin Grad, and with it she struck one of the few false notes in the novel.) Miriam feels an immense relief, deciding that her failures of response can now be explained by his past, which must always have stood between them. She is also finally able to react in at least some way—but to Shatov's self-recriminations (he is the image of Russian guilt and self-loathing): " 'Poor boy,' she murmured, gathering him as he sank to his knees, with swift enveloping hands against her breast." She can only feel maternal toward him.

Though it seems forced into play here, the attitude of protectiveness and solicitude has its own lambency. Miriam had been moving in gradual formative stages toward the role she can justify to herself, that of guardian, since the early novel *Honeycomb*. There she had thought of herself as the source of understanding and sympathy denied to her mother, as the "husband" who should have been granted to Mrs. Henderson. In the next two novels, the woman's place in Miriam's consciousness is filled by Nurse Dear, to whom she speaks at the end of *Interim* in a "lover-like undertone." Three years later, however, in *Deadlock,* she has begun to realize her slavish susceptibility to women. Nor does her brief recognition of the man in Michael Shatov produce the equilibrium she hoped to achieve. She is able to come to him as a woman only in the maternal role. Her emotional deadlock remains unresolved: "I'm as much a man as a woman," she says. "That's why I can't help seeing things." The "revolving lights" of the next novel would represent Miriam's intellectual effort to break the deadlock by exploring points of view "the long way round, the masculine way."

Meanwhile, as she worked on *Deadlock* at Queen's Terrace during the summer of 1920, the real London merging with the London of her memory, and her husband physically present in the room, bent over his table, although immersed in the world of *Candide* that he was re-creating, Dorothy carried into her work a blend of the past and present. She had Miriam remember a line from Voltaire and even muse on the subject of an essay she (Dorothy) was preparing to write. The essay about "Women in the Arts" would attempt to answer the question she now had Miriam ask in *Deadlock:* how should one reply to men "who called women inferior because they had not invented or achieved in science or art?" The question, moreover, is made to occur to Miriam when she catches sight of a certain book on a table in the dental surgery at Wimpole Street. Presumably it belongs to one of her dentist employers, a fact (if it is indeed a fact) which fills her with rage. The book is T. W. H. Crosland's *Lovely Woman,* the best-selling attack on her sex by one of Alan Odle's former companions at the Café Royal, to which Dorothy had paid her first visit this very summer. Whether she had known of the book at the time in her life which Miriam has reached in *Deadlock* is another matter. Yet the past and the present manage to blend with perfect ease.

One is led to suspect that more than lines of Voltaire and titles of books have crept out of Dorothy's current life into her past. Her fictional account of the "strange romance" of Miriam and Michael Shatov is modeled unmistakably on her own friendship with Benjamin Grad, but surely there are traces of her marriage to Alan Odle mixed in as well. Miriam's solicitude for Michael was indeed Dorothy's for Benjamin, but it can also be Dorothy's for Alan. There he was all the while, visibly in need of her care but at the same time self-sufficient in a way Benjamin had never been. Yes, Alan needed her, but she could satisfy his needs with no violation of her inmost self. His delicate—and dedicated—mind ensured her of the privacy that had been threatened by the gifted, brooding, unpredictable Benjamin. Her re-creation, in Michael Shatov, of all the color and brilliance she had loved and the melancholy, erratic nature she had feared in Benjamin may have begun to impress upon her how safe she was with Alan, and how wise she had been to marry him.

2

Deadlock was not quite finished when the Odles left London again for Cornwall. They had had a "wild fortnight" of social activity at the end: dinner parties, "crushes," and "innumerable teas"; and the silence of Cornwall during the first week of their arrival was deafening. This winter of 1920 they were renting another bungalow owned by the Ponder sisters of Rose Cottage. Called Cozy Corner, built of corrugated iron and painted red, it lay slightly off the road leading from Harlyn Bay to Trevose Head. Trevone was only a ten-minute walk across the cliffs to the north, but it seemed much farther than that to the Odles. In their Harlyn bungalow, they were surrounded by tall weeds and bare trees through which, from the rear, they looked straight out to sea. Through a glass-paned door at the side they had an unobstructed view of three immense headlands, one behind the other. Across this expanse, in all the varying weathers and skies of Cornwall, one could see the infinite shadings of light. Cattle were sometimes in view, straying about the clifftops and occasionally wandering into Cozy Corner's "paddock." Both Dorothy and Alan were enchanted by their new situation. They discovered unknown lanes to explore and strange wildflowers to gather, and when they did not feel like venturing forth or staring out to sea, they could contemplate the large and mysterious Harlyn House across the road, barely visible through the trees and traditionally said to be haunted.

Cozy Corner was not, of course, without its drawbacks. The well from which the water had to be pumped was a quarter of a mile away, and rain, hail, and sleet fell with a thunderous sound against the corrugated iron of the bungalow. But these flaws were minor. Dorothy finished *Deadlock* at Cozy Corner, and by February 1921 the book was greeted with delight by reviewers eager to report that "something [had] actually happen[ed] to Miriam!" According to the *Times Literary Supplement,* what had happened was that Miriam had fallen in love with Michael Shatov, and the "mere fact" of this constituted "progress." In their hearts, though, many of the reviewers knew that such facts and progress were beside the point, and that a marriage was out of the question.

In more serious moments, several reviewers noted signs in *Deadlock* of what seemed to them a different sort of change. They thought the novel showed "a maturer skill" and contained "episodes and passages of richer beauty than . . . any of the previous books." Though Dorothy had no objection to praise, she felt it was misplaced. When even her fellow novelist E. B. C. Jones, with whom she had recently begun to correspond, said the same thing, Dorothy decided to speak up. She wrote back to "Jones" to say that *Deadlock* seemed more "lucid" because Miriam was now more "articulate." In the earlier volumes she had been "vague," which accounted for the "sacrifices of direct information" that had to be made. But few people ever fully grasped this point: if the books were the expression of a growing, changing consciousness, they could only be what Miriam herself was, stumbling and confused one moment, penetratingly intelligent the next, vague and lucid by turns, with the art of the best volumes lying in the tensions of the consciousness itself.

The point Dorothy was trying to make can be illustrated by means of contrast. Conveniently enough, about this time she had written a short story ("Christmas Eve") concentrating on someone other than herself. The story was published during the winter of 1920, shortly before *Deadlock* appeared. Though it is told in the first person, the narrator exists largely for the sake of the tale, which has to do with the way in which the lifeless spirit of an English Christmas Eve is transformed by a young German woman. The scene of the story is a London residence for young women. The narrator had lived at the residence the previous year and is obviously Dorothy Richardson. Carrying her pilgrim basket, she comes to meet a friend and unexpectedly witnesses the effect of the German woman's determination to reproduce a German Christmas Eve.

Dorothy Richardson considered the story "uncharacteristic" for her, apparently because it dealt only with surface consciousness, the narrator making only the barest observations. Indeed, she would have described the objective, straightforward method of "Christmas Eve" as "indirect." Such was her term for "the method of statement, of giving information." Granting there must be information, she nonetheless felt that the moment it was "given directly as information, the sense of immediate experience [was] gone." It was precisely this sense that above all she wanted to give her readers in *Pilgrimage,* and she knew that "the great and abiding problem of all those who [took] the inward way" was to get things "tremendously there [but] as it were unawares." She did not think she had solved the problem. In her opinion neither had Joyce, whose failure she considered positively "titanic."

Whether she was right or not about Joyce, it was certainly true that her own aim was to implicate the reader in the very process of consciousness. When an editor of the *Pall Mall Gazette* asked her where she thought the "future of the novel" lay, she answered that it lay, in part, in the young current form of fiction as she saw it, which would one day achieve its aim: to weave for the reader "the eternal romance of *his* own existence and demonstrate that aesthetic recreation [was] to be had not only by going far enough out, but also by coming near enough home." She saw this new form as a blend of the realistic and the romantic, finely balanced, as though the novelist were walking a tightrope. But she was aware that while balancing oneself in time and human experience, one might fall into a pit where no one could follow, where human life could not be sustained.

The image of the balancing novelist was an apt one for Dorothy to use. Her remarks on the future of the novel appeared in the *Pall Mall Gazette* shortly after she had finished *Deadlock,* and thus, for the moment, she had performed her own rather special balancing act. Poised from the beginning of *Pilgrimage* between the past and the present, Dorothy had now reached a point in time when the distance between them was growing smaller and smaller. The more mature her heroine became, the closer she would be to Dorothy Richardson at the moment of writing about her. From *Deadlock* on, *Pilgrimage* would begin to reflect a double image; it would offer a contemporary as well as a retrospective portrait of the artist. Corresponding to this added dimension is a change in technique. Beginning with *Deadlock,* one notes an increased use of the direct internal monologue in place of the indirect. Miriam records many of her reflections in the first person, although Dorothy Richardson continues as narrator to lead her heroine to the point at which, in effect, they speak together.

In point of actual time, between *Interim* and *Deadlock* three years have elapsed in the London life of Miriam Henderson. Another three years will pass in the course of *Deadlock, Revolving Lights,* and *The Trap.* Miriam will be twenty-eight in *The Trap,* at a time when Dorothy Richardson was thirty-three. Miriam's experience during six years in London corresponds to ten years of Dorothy Richardson's life in London. In these novels Dorothy condenses and summarizes a segment of her past, as if to distill it, but she introduces as well certain touches of her current life that give the novels the faintly audible undertone of a contemporary voice. The reviewers of *Deadlock* who caught this voice ascribed it to a maturing literary skill, but they did not quite know what it was they heard.

At the heart of *Deadlock* (and this no one missed) is the historical period of the reign of Edward VII. In this novel Dorothy re-creates the world of suffragettes and Fabian socialists, the world of argument and assertion in which she had developed her own mind and personality and had served her apprenticeship as a writer. Her heroine will follow a similar course. She will also be placed at the center of the emotional and intellectual web Dorothy Richardson would spin out of her own existence. But the fictional life would have its own shape and form, with the first line of the novel— "Miriam ran upstairs narrowly ahead of her thoughts"—suggesting the underlying struggle in *Deadlock*: to maintain this slight edge, to prevent thought from interfering with action to the point of total impasse. Each stage or aspect of the struggle is matched by a corresponding prose style: the expository (constricted and heavy) to transmit the process of thought negating thought, the pictorial (flowing and light) to convey moments of freedom and buoyancy. Miriam's alternating moods are also reflected by means of figures out of literary history: Emerson, the philosopher-poet who seems to incorporate all knowledge and to express it in pure English, and Maeterlinck, who creates symbolic atmospheres which suggest a myserious and shadowy essence of life that logic cannot penetrate. In *Deadlock,* structure, style, and meaning each presents the basic problem of irresolution.

Dorothy herself thought there was nothing in *Deadlock* she had to account for or explain away, as there had been in *Interim* and even in *The Tunnel,* the opening of which in her opinion was a total failure. (She had tried "a compressed retrospect and achieved almost nothing at all.") So, although her worldly prospects a month after the appearance of *Deadlock* seemed rather grim, her mood was jaunty. In mock-despairing tones, she claimed the title of this last

141

novel of hers had come home to roost: her English publisher was complaining of the losses incurred by her books. Her American publisher was promising to "hold on" as long as possible. Alan's drawings simply would not sell. The rent of their "crumbling rooms" in Queen's Terrace had been raised. What did all this amount to, she tragically sighed, if not deadlock?

But spring was on its way, and in another month she and Alan had moved from the bungalow in Harlyn to their holiday quarters in Trevone Cottage, where Mrs. Pope took care of them, feeding them the gulls' eggs she claimed were superior to any others because (in her words) they were "lighter than vanity." It was here, moreover, that Dorothy received her first letter from the admiring E. B. C. Jones, which led to a correspondence that surprised Dorothy, for it seemed to her that someone like Miss Jones would soon grow tired of both Miriam and her creator. Jones wrote brisk novels out of what Dorothy saw as a "rich and generous social experience," while Miriam's life (and one presumes she meant her own as well) was by contrast "so threadbare and socially grotesque" that Dorothy wondered how Jones could endure reading about it, remarking that if she were Jones she would want "to shake and smack [Miriam] nearly all the time."

Dorothy's confident and high-spirited mood went on into the summer in London, where she and Alan were rarely unhappy and where, besides, all sorts of new pleasures awaited them. The cinema was one. They went to the "local 'pictures'" once a week, and when the fare was a melodrama, of which Dorothy was inordinately fond, Alan would announce the fact at the start as a signal to them both. By the end, they had usually forgotten it was melodrama anyway, so absorbing to them both was the visual—and dramatic— experience. One particular evening they saw a "submarine melodrama" in which most of the action took place under water and one of the characters was an octopus. When they came home to Queen's Terrace, Dorothy found a copy of E. B. C. Jones's novel *The Singing Captive* waiting for her. She read it late into the night, with the submarine melodrama still moving before her eyes, and somehow began to think of Henry James. It occurred to her that all his books were conceived and written in vast deep waters—indeed, that he himself was a "large pale motionless octopus with huge eyes, suddenly throwing out huge tentacles." But, she thought, he was not actually in the water; he was in a tank "full of holes through which the ocean flows.'' Reporting this sequence of images to Jones, Dorothy hastened to assure her that it was ''no more meant as an insult to the magnificence of H. J. than . . . as a 'compliment' to [E. B. C. J.].'' Nevertheless, her review of *The Singing Captive,* which she entitled ''The Perforated Tank,'' has always been taken for precisely what she said it was not intended to be.

Dorothy's confident spirits extended even to the new novel she had already begun to write. She had high hopes for the sequel to *Deadlock.* The ground for it had been sufficiently laid, and its substance was more dramatic in quality, she thought, than that of any of the novels thus far. This did not prevent her from remarking wryly to Jones that when *Pilgrimage* was finished, she would write ''a novel of incidents by E. B. C. J.'' and Jones could write ''a sceneless book by D. M. R.'' Secretly, however, she hoped the new volume might satisfy at least a few of the readers of fiction who yearned for a modest event or two. Counting on the book coming out reasonably soon, she worked steadily all through the summer of 1921, and her happy mood held up.

This feeling of well-being was bolstered by Alan's contract with Routledge to illustrate *Candide,* which had finally been drawn up and signed, and by several young friends who were coming in for tea and to talk or were meeting her for a simple meal in a restaurant nearby. The newest of these was a sweet-faced girl named Pauline Marrian, who was brought to Dorothy by a journalistic acquaintance of them both. Pauline was not yet twenty, but she had read all the volumes of *Pilgrimage* to date—and a good deal more besides. She was fiercely independent, and she wanted to write fiction herself and to find a way to live at the same time. Pauline bemused and impressed Dorothy by turns, as eventually Dorothy impressed Pauline, and they became lifelong friends.

Then there was Owen Wadsworth, recently returned from India, and feeling at loose ends in England. He had decided to return when the value of the rupee had begun to fall, but he now felt he could not stay in England, where it seemed the only work he could find was a ''clerkship.'' On his visits he sometimes brought a young friend with him; at other times he poured out his heart to Dorothy and Alan, who listened to his chatter and laughed at his tragicomic tones. He would sit at their feet on the floor in Queen's Terrace, looking up at them with his large, expressive, beseeching eyes. Dorothy was growing more fond of him all the time and wanted to give him some

143

help. It occurred to her one day that something she had heard recently from her friend Barbara Low might be of use to Owen. Barbara had alluded in passing to the happy life a literary person might live in Prague. Her own friends, the poet Edwin Muir and his wife, had just gone there with very little beyond themselves. When Dorothy suggested Prague as a place Own might look into, he decided virtually on the spot to go. With an introduction to the Muirs and roughly £10 in his pocket, he left that fall, promising to write and tell the Odles everything.

3

Owen's first letters from Prague went to Cornwall, where Dorothy and Alan were by then installed for another winter in Cozy Corner. They were so much relieved, she said, to hear that at least for the moment he had his own "small nest" and was getting his "daily bread," through a temporary job he had found with the Cunard Line until something better came along. The Muirs, he reported, were most kind to him, inviting him often to stay to tea when he dropped in, and Mrs. Muir thought she might even be able to help him find another job, teaching English in a Czech school. Owen not only got this job but by the time the Muirs left Prague the following year (1922), he had also begun to write for the London *Observer* and for the New York *Dial:* Edwin Muir had steered him into journalism, which would be his lifework.

Meanwhile, Owen was much taken with the soft beauty of Slavic faces, and Dorothy tried to warn him about inferring the inner life of these attractive beings from their outward appearance. She thought "Europeans proper" were often misled in this regard. In any case, she felt in touch with Prague through him, for his letters were filled with details and impressions. She apologized for her own scrappy replies, blaming them in part on the tense lives they were living that winter as Alan worked almost day and night on the drawings for *Candide.* He had grown a beard without knowing it. She thought it suited him but needed as accompaniment (in order to be perfectly pre-Raphaelite) both a negligee and a sage-green tie.

Alan finished the drawings in April, and though he at once dropped a kettle of boiling water on his foot, they both managed to limp into Trevone for three weeks of rest before going to London. Dorothy had in mind a little ambling about the country in a small donkey shay. Alan was dubious but willing, and the temperature

The Illness of Candide in Paris, pencil drawing by Alan Odle to illustrate *Candide or the Optimist* by F. A. M. de Voltaire.

was right. So when they arrived in Queen's Terrace the last week of May 1922, Dorothy felt ready to "pursue"—as she put it—the end of *Revolving Lights*.

Finishing the novel was to be a full summer's work, involving another round of juggling the past and the present that was more elaborate than ever before. The novel's subject was in large measure Miriam's increasingly complicated relationship with Hypo Wilson, and ironically enough, in late summer Dorothy found herself occupied with the real present-day Wells. He was going to stand a second time for Parliament, as a Labour candidate in name but an "independent" in actuality, and Dorothy had decided to endorse him. She waited, however, till almost the last moment before doing anything about it, and when she finally offered her "electioneering stuff" to the *Daily Mail*, they claimed it was too late to be printed. The *Herald* took it instead, identifying her as "a novelist of rare distinction."

Though her article was brief, it is of interest as a public statement made at the same time she was exploring in fiction the private nature of this problematic man with whom over the years she had made a kind of peace. In the *Herald* article she said there were " 'wiser' men than Wells, steadier men," but no one more aware than he of the barriers to a new and better world, and no one more "fertile" in plans for removing them. No other man, she went on, had taught quite as well as he the lesson of thinking of the world as a whole. He stood "for the possibilities of the future more clearly [and] more articulately than any other public man."

Dorothy was also writing about Wells to Owen, who after a year in Prague had worked himself up to a series of lectures on English novelists. She told him of her piece in the *Herald* and remarked that even though Wells shed his opinions every few years (a remark she had Miriam make again and again about Wilson), his "vision" remained. It was that, she thought, which made him "trustworthy." Parliament would not change Wells, she said, but there was a good chance that Wells might change Parliament. As for Wells the novelist, her friend Jack Beresford had written a small book about him in 1915, but as it had been done for a series there was not much in it. Owen, she thought, ought to treat Wells's early work, his "wonderful literary blossoming," the "exuberant fantasy period" that had been "broken into" by his increasing obsession with "life-as-it-is." Though he had produced some fine novels after that, with *Tono-Bungay* the best of them, he had become nonetheless more and more "expository" and less and less an "artist." But to Owen Dorothy said nothing at all of her own fictional portrait of Wells.

As a matter of fact, Wells occupied fully half of *Revolving Lights* in the role of Wilson; and, given the election campaign, it is quite astonishing that not even someone as sharp-witted as J. B. Priestley seems to have caught the resemblance. But he, like most of the reviewers, was interested in other matters: one of them, the great length he thought *Pilgrimage* was reaching, and, another, Dorothy Richardson's own character as novelist. Besides, though *Revolving Lights* was finished by the time of the election (which Wells lost), it did not actually appear until the following spring. One suspects it was deliberately held up.

Revolving Lights contains a good deal more than a portrait of Wells as he was in the early years of the century. Above all, it is the most extended analysis of the character of her heroine that Dorothy Richardson had yet attempted and, as such, offers a fascinating glimpse of her mingling of fact, fiction, and idealization, as well as of past and present. The novel consists of four chapters. The two at the center constitute dramatic scenes in the present. The first anticipates both of these and links them to events in the past. The final chapter completes the third in retrospect and points toward the future. Throughout the novel the movement of Miriam's mind resembles an arc, her thoughts curving backward and forward, but in the unsettled inconclusive present they cannot meet to form a complete circle. In other words, there is no resolution of Miriam's personal dilemma in *Revolving Lights,* though one can see advancement in the course of the book.

Miriam's long, slow, and impeded walk through the whole of the first chapter characterizes the progress in the novel and the form it will essentially take: the lengthiest journey of thought Miriam has so far achieved. Here, at the beginning, in her carefully charted midnight ramble, is the overture to the seventh volume. At the center is a musical analogue: Beethoven's Seventh Symphony, heard in Hypo Wilson's home, where Miriam spends the four weeks of her summer holiday.

Miriam's walk (covering fifty-five pages) begins in the present, to which the London streets keep her bound, curves back into the past under their influence, and ends in the future, with a disquieting confrontation of self. When Miriam reaches her final destination (Tansley Street) after a long inner dialogue and comes upon the figure of an old woman who leers knowingly at her, Miriam sees her own aged face, "set in her path and waiting through all the years." She had been trying in this walk to identify and come to terms with herself after an evening spent among people who seemed so sure of themselves that her own uncertainties crowded even more thickly about her than usual. She had been in a lecture hall, listening enviously to a group of Lycurgan (Fabian) socialists, whom she had met through Hypo Wilson, express their apparently united point of view. Once out in the London night air, she remembers that Michael Shatov was proposing to introduce her the next day to his revolutionary friends just arrived in England. They would represent still another new point of view, and Michael, in his eager way, would present her to them as the embodiment of her country. Wilson also spoke of her as British to the core. Yet here she was, coming into the "narrow winding lane" of Bond Street with but a "hoard of contradictory ideas," a solitary shrouded figure in her cloak, unknown to anyone, even to herself.

So begins the deliberate self-analysis toward which Miriam had been moving since *Pointed Roofs*. The way for it had been cleared in *Deadlock*. There the spell of the street she associated with her mother (the little street through which they had often walked together) had begun to lose its potency: she no longer found herself at periodic intervals suddenly and hauntedly within the same little thoroughfare. One step forward had led to another. She had quite clearly portrayed for the reader from the start the resemblance between her mother and Mrs. Bailey, the frail widow of the Tansley Street house. She was able to acknowledge the resemblance and even to sit with Mrs. Bailey during one of her illnesses. Most significant of all, she could speak aloud of her father, with his "funny old-fashioned English quality from somewhere or other heaven knows," as someone Michael Shatov would like. She got even further than this by actually saying he was "really an intelligent man." Clearly, the stage was being set for the first ray of "revolving lights" to fall upon Miriam's inherited nature as Dorothy Richardson has her see it: "a helpless going to and fro between two temperaments."

Miriam's father was skeptical, dilettante, intuitive; her mother was kindly and irrational. On his side stood an ancestry of Puritanism, which he had renounced along with the family trade but had nevertheless passed on to Miriam. His Puritanism was not narrowly Cromwellian or Roundhead; rather, it was narrowly elegant and fastidious. The tall, gaunt relatives Dorothy gave to Miriam she had already revealed as her own in her first short story, "Sunday," written several years before. In this story she had also revealed the same hate and fear that Miriam remembers she had felt as a child for their consciousness of all-pervading sin. Yet now Dorothy has Miriam remember their distinctive beauty, their "well-shaped hands, alive and speaking amongst their rich silks and fine old laces," and find herself drawn to them, after all the years of escape and denial, much more than to her mother's family.

Mrs. Henderson stemmed from "rounded sturdy West country yeomen." Their features were blunt, their manner jovial, and their voices big. But within Miriam, the third child and longed-for "son," both natures, equally matched, struggle for supremacy. With an eye nurtured by her West country heritage, she would always see the light and the spring. As a Puritan Henderson with an overmastering love for the old "finely-etched" Bond Street through which she is passing, Miriam feels she must look beneath into the dark abyss and fight "the devil every inch of the way." So it was that Dorothy dramatized (and perhaps both idealized and intensified) the primary conflict within herself between the Richardson influence (proud and overbearing as well as elegant) and the more humble Taylor strain.

Dorothy Richardson brings the "heavenly city" of *The Pilgrim's Progress* into Miriam's mind in the surroundings of London, and has her review the sieges of her personal life as though it were Christian's faith being threatened. For Miriam (as it had been for Dorothy), the freedom to determine the shape of her own life is threatened by Hypo Wilson, Michael Shatov, Eleanor Dear. Wilson is the greatest threat of all: his image and the sound of his "interested, mocking, critical voice" are blended in her consciousness of past, present, and future. She can neither wrench herself free of him nor keep pace with his darting mind. She imagines him already making fun of the point of view he had dogmatically aired in her last visit to him. He was forever moving out of her reach, always seeming to void the rare moments of closeness and equality she achieved with him. With a feeling of hopelessness in her revolving mind and in her contradictory desires, and aware that she is entangled by

149

multiforms of love, Miriam turns to something actually within her grasp—the incomparable city, a "mighty lover" embracing her, engulfing her, yet leaving her untouched.

No human being she had ever met is such a lover, certainly not Hypo Wilson. In *Revolving Lights* Wilson is portrayed for the first time in the dramatic present, with the shift in technique signifying that Miriam's relationship with him is changing. Two months after her midnight walk, she goes to spend a four-week holiday at his seaside home and arrives at what is undoubtedly H. G. Wells's Spade House in Kent. Miriam at this point is a strikingly unretouched photograph of Dorothy Richardson. Age is the sole difference between heroine and author in this chapter of *Revolving Lights*. Miriam has reached at twenty-six the stage Dorothy had reached in her thirties, the stage of her early book reviews for *Ye Crank* and *The Open Road*. Miriam has already written the same first review (of a "bad little book on Whitman") and has referred to Wells's *A Modern Utopia,* published in 1905. During her visit with the Wilsons, Miriam writes the very review Dorothy Richardson had written in May 1907. Mary Everest Boole, one of her fellow contributors to *Ye Crank,* is mentioned by name. However, Charles Daniel himself and his wife Florence are transformed into George and Dora Taylor, whose friends are described as "real cranks." The atmosphere of those early years of the century is reproduced with great exactitude, as though Dorothy had turned her camera on the past.

Curiously, Dorothy includes as another visitor present a woman writer who Miriam is told "puts" actual people and events into her books. Miriam is "revolted and fascinated" by such a use of current life. It was a "cheap easy way," she felt, "an impossibly mean advantage," and in her view such a person had no right to be called a "creator." In this Dorothy Richardson was not being coy. On the contrary, she seemed to be saying by implication that the real identity of each of her characters was irrelevant to the roles they played in the novel and the effect they had upon Miriam. As for Wells, the occasional references to him by name added a measure of accuracy to the historical setting of the novel; nearly everyone was talking about Wells in those days. It was also true that Dorothy Richardson's primary concern was with Wells the man rather than with Wells the writer, and by separating the two as she did in the novel, she was able to concentrate on the personal relationship of Hypo and

Miriam. It is the fictional truth of this portrayal that is the remarkable achievement of *Revolving Lights*.

They move warily toward each other in dramatic scenes that form
the artistic core of the novel. When Miriam arrives at the Wilsons'
(with her customary "pilgrim baskets"), she is placed at the center
of the house in a downstairs spare room instead of in her usual
upstairs nook. Within sound of the sea, next to the garden, and
adjoining the rooms of both Hypo and his wife Alma, she rejoices in
her position at the "heart" of Wilson life. The visit would be "a
long unbroken magic," she feels, its spell cast by the "husky
voice" and the "ringed, lightning-quick grey eyes" of the intense
little man.

Her countless changing perceptions of Hypo Wilson become the
substance of the visit. Never before has she had the chance to
observe him steadily from so many different vantage points. Now
she finds that each phase of the day and of her visit reveals him in a
variant state of being: kind and admiring one moment, ironic and
oblivious the next, and never fully attentive to anything except
science. In the mornings, as preparation for work, he listens to the
perfectly appropriate Beethoven Seventh Symphony, yet he prefers
its last movement "because it did so much with a theme that was
almost nothing." She is pleased on the first evening to hear him
express a fondness for Bach, and is appalled to learn that Wilson
finds *women* in Bach's music—where Miriam finds no people
evoked at all. On one occasion he proposed that they spend a night
out of doors and she looked forward to an opportunity for extended
talk, but when the time arrived, Wilson unpredictably wanted to
sleep.

Nevertheless, in spite of the emptiness she senses beneath his
"marvellous phrases and pictures," he continues to fascinate her
more than any other man. He was married to her old school friend,
the dainty and pretty Alma, whom he called Susan (as Wells called
his wife Jane) and who seemed unable to stop behaving "as if she
were still brightly in the midst of people keeping things going."
Miriam endures Alma's social antics but with her eye and mind
follows the "threshing" arms and "destructive conclusions" of the
man who is now always within her consciousness. They were very
different, Wilson liked to tell her. He lived to think, whereas
Miriam thought in order to live. Yet when she hurled a violent and

151

emotional statement at him to gain his attention, he would turn swiftly toward her, understanding and thus "healing her despair." It is clear that above all she wants him to take notice of her.

The visit with the Wilsons is finished in retrospect as Miriam, returned from her holiday, sits at her Wimpole Street desk in the presence of the dentist Hancock. Here, in the setting that has long served as a contrast for the Wilson world, Miriam recalls the final fortnight spent at the home of Hancock's opposite. The dentist is physically present, yet the absent Wilson is dramatically present. In a flashback Miriam describes her retreat from Hypo Wilson after their literal and guarded approach to one another. There had been time during the last two weeks for undisturbed conversation. Wilson had told her he liked having her about, and she had confessed he had a "way" which obliterated other men for her. He had suggested they "explore each other and stop nowhere," and Miriam had felt triumph over other women. She found it immensely gratifying to hear him praise her ability to talk. She had told herself that "if *his* mind could be tackled even though there were no words to answer him with, then anyone's mind could be tackled."

Wilson thought it "easier . . . to talk hand in hand," and Miriam began to draw back from his flourishes of "*deliberate* guilt and *deliberate* daring." Pursued, she turned away. She had responded to the challenge of his "minatory finger" and his devastating wit, but the touch of his hand separated him from her, dispelled his "charm." His attempts at what she considered "coercion" drove her off. "Never since the beginning of the world," she said, "has a woman been mastered." Dorothy Richardson had said much the same thing nearly six years before, at the time of her marriage to Alan Odle. A woman's consciousness was "synthetic," she had written in 1917, and "always made its own world," regardless of circumstances; it could be "neither enslaved nor subjected." She was leading her heroine into the volume called *The Trap*, in which Miriam would narrowly escape enslavement, and at the end of *Revolving Lights* Dorothy seemed to be expressing unconsciously her sense of the freedom she had won from H. G. and had preserved by marrying Alan.

152

CHAPTER TEN

A Borrowed Year

TOWARD the end of 1922, a new name began to sound more and more frequently in the London literary world. It was a name familiar to the French—one that had been among them for more than ten years—but only now did the novels of Marcel Proust begin to make their way in numbers across the Channel. They came, in English translations by Scott-Moncrieff, only shortly before the news that Proust himself was dead. The first to arrive, the two volumes of *Swann's Way,* had been so excitedly discussed that Dorothy told Owen she was prepared to "beg borrow or steal" in order to read them. She had her copies (from Owen) by December, and in the months before her own *Revolving Lights* appeared, Dorothy immersed herself in Proust. He was perfect for the long winter evenings in Cornwall.

While Alan patiently awaited his turn, Dorothy read, reread, and reread again. The design and detail of Proust seemed to her all one, with "the whole of him in every part." He was "a thousand things at once," she said, all of them "overwhelming." But although he outdid everyone in some ways, she thought it inaccurate to say that he was writing "through consciousness." In her opinion he was writing "about consciousness, a vastly different enterprise." It allowed him, as she put it, to "let himself go completely," intimating that this was something she herself could not do because her own novel stemmed from, or came into being through, a young, still developing, and therefore limited consciousness. Just as this distinction may well be, and as different as the minds (and gifts) of these two writers were, they had certain psychological traits in common. They shared an impelling need to re-create if not transform the past. For both of them the past was a world to which they went forward rather than back, thus making of it a future that would one day be the present. Proust hungered more for the past itself than did

153

Dorothy Richardson. She wanted as much to regain the self she had once been as to see that self emerge before her mind's eye as though she were actually her own creator. Egotism cannot go much further than this. Virginia Woolf had already noted in her diary the "danger [of] the damned egotistical self" which to her mind was ruining both Joyce and Richardson. In a few months D. H. Lawrence would claim it was killing the novel. He could hear the "death-rattle," he said, in the throats of Richardson, Proust, and Joyce. Dorothy, unmoved by Lawrence's diagnosis, felt that someone was always announcing the decay of the novel; it was another "sublime shibboleth," she said, like egotism.

1

Lawrence's piece appeared in April 1923, along with a variety of reviews of *Revolving Lights* that were, in Dorothy's words, a mixture of "guarded appreciation and unguarded scorn." She herself was just as scornful, referring with utter contempt, for instance, to someone like Middleton Murry, who had finally realized that the modern novel was "ceasing to be primarily a story." But remarks such as Priestley's, that half the time she was not even a novelist and that her books lacked any kind of construction at all, made her angry. Moreover, she resented the complaint that kept recurring— that each new volume placed an unconscionable burden on the reader, since he had to remember the volumes that came before. Under the circumstances fan letters were more welcome to her than ever, and she proceeded to translate the decent number she actually got into a "huge mass" when H. G. Wells irresponsibly remarked that the sales of her books in America *had* to be greater than the small figures reported by Knopf. Dorothy, who wanted to believe he was right, wrote to Knopf and told him what Wells had said. Knopf replied that he was too proud to prosecute Wells and he had already lost so much money publishing her books that he could no longer set them up himself. From then on, he said, he would buy sheets from Duckworth.

The entire business mystified her. Wells had been so persuasive, and Knopf was so new a name in the publishing world. She clung to her suspicions a bit longer and asked Owen, who that summer was on his way from Prague to the States, to keep his eyes open. It does not seem to have occurred to Dorothy (who always imagined herself more businesslike than she actually was), or to Wells either, that when admiring readers reported how popular *Pilgrimage* was in America and how difficult it was becoming to get her books, the reason might very well be the truly small printings rather than supposedly hidden large sales.

The row with Knopf, fresh in her mind when she and Alan came to London in June 1923, faded as the summer and a new idea—the possibility of a trip to Switzerland—took hold. Once planted in Dorothy's mind, the idea was lodged there permanently, since she had not been out of England for fifteen years and Alan had never had the experience of a country other than his own. It seemed to Dorothy that Alan's first view of the Swiss mountains would knock him sideways; and the more she thought about it, the more determined she was to go. She thought about it virtually all the time.

It all began early in the summer with a letter from Paris, from Sylvia Beach, owner of the famous bookshop Shakespeare and Company, and publisher of the first edition of *Ulysses* the year before. She had written Dorothy to introduce a young woman named Bryher who wished to meet the author of *Pilgrimage*. With the letter came a note from Bryher herself, composed—she would later say—"as if it were the first chapter of a novel." The answer to this, the "reward" in Bryher's word, was an invitation to tea at Queen's Terrace.

There, in a room crowded with books and drawings, with faded postcards of the gargoyles of Notre Dame ranged on the fireplace mantel, the expectant Bryher found the woman she took to be Miriam wearing a "stiff" blouse, "a mass of gold hair piled on the top of her head." Alan sat smoking and smiling, watching with "brown, draftsman's eyes" either the visitor or the way the light fell on the door. He took little part in the conversation, which concerned mostly books and travel. Bryher herself had written a book entitled *Development*, which recorded with great fastidiousness the efforts of a young mind to gain both control over itself and freedom to grow without hindrance, a book that Dorothy thought "strange and somehow tremendous." She understood why Bryher felt such kinship with the heroine of *Pilgrimage*, for she had read the early volumes while waging her own similar struggle for independence, although the economic circumstances of that struggle, as well as the life which Bryher now led, were vastly different.

The daughter of a millionaire industrialist, Sir John Ellerman, Bryher had taken up residence in Switzerland the year before, traveling frequently—to the Scilly Isles (from one of which she had taken and eventually legalized the pen name of Bryher), to Egypt, Greece, Italy, France, and America. She was married to an American, Robert McAlmon, the owner of the Contact Press, but it had been a marriage of convenience which had allowed Bryher to separate from her family. Her closest relationship was with the American poet H. D., whose own marriage to Richard Aldington had broken down. Bryher had come into H. D.'s life by writing to her about her poetry; now she stepped into Dorothy's lightly but resolutely, almost at once feeling in that tight and crowded room a need for enlargement. They ought to go abroad, she said.

Dorothy did not need much urging, and she had been quick to note Alan's interest in the idea when Bryher brought it up. The chief problem, of course, was money, though Dorothy also felt uncertain about Alan's health. He had been doing well on the Cornish coast. Would the excitement of travel, perhaps even the Swiss air, do him harm? She wished to spend six months abroad, from the end of October until the end of April, so she was not planning a brief stay. She felt an undertaking such as this would require all her organizing powers, not to mention courage, for as much as she would have liked to travel with ease and style, the whole affair made her very nervous. She set her heart on it nonetheless, for somehow Bryher's words—this was the year to go—had struck exactly the right note.

2

Dorothy's final decision to go was made in September, leaving two months to make all arrangements. First she proposed to Clement Shorter of the *Sphere* (who had helped Bryher publish *Development* in 1920) a series of articles about Switzerland. When he agreed, she took his commissions to the publicity department of the Swiss Federal Railways and suggested they underwrite her travel expenses. After endless interviews in Piccadilly, Dorothy actually got first-class traveling facilities for herself and Alan, a fact she announced jubilantly. They would leave from Victoria at 11:00 A.M. on the first of November and would arrive in Montreux (via Calais, Paris, and Lausanne) at 9:00 the following morning. Alan was going to see his first mountains in the early morning light.

Once Dorothy had the tickets, a hundred other things had to be done. She intended not to remain in Montreux but to move on after a few days to Château d'Oex, where she had stayed nearly twenty years before. It was windless, sufficiently exposed to sunlight, and dry, so it seemed to her a reasonably safe place for Alan. She thought at first that from Montreux they could explore Château d'Oex for quiet quarters, but instead she decided to write to a small pension called Les Hirondelles. She learned that, in the interim since her last stay in Switzerland, a second chalet accommodating about sixteen people and providing separate tables had been added. What ideal conditions!

The proprietress offered her the "best, balconied, south room at 7 fr. each. *tout compris,*" but she confessed at the same time that next door to the room was an "auxiliary salon," which she did not think would be used much. Dorothy considered the possibilities inherent in such an arrangement. Would the little salon emit distracting sounds? Moreover, what might be heard from the big salon? She feared distant noises most of all—for instance, the sound of jazz she had only "smelled" until now, but "hints and suggestions" had made her "dead drunk on the instant." She could work, she thought, in the middle of an orchestra but not within hearing distance of it. Despite all this, the rates were too attractive to resist, so she wrote back and reserved the room for a month's trial.

Money, of course, was their chief problem. Though Bryher had helped with a "beneficent loan" and had invited them to stay with her when they got to Montreux, there were clothes to buy that a winter in Cornwall did not require. Dorothy raced about thundery, wet London bargain-hunting for Swiss outfits. She tried, also, to draft the Swiss articles before they left, so she would have time to work on the next volume of *Pilgrimage* while they were away. She had done very little work on it since the winter in Cornwall. Instead, she found herself writing poetry.

When Bryher asked to see the poems she had written, Dorothy demurred, saying: "I think you would call them herd poems." But Bryher persisted, and Dorothy confessed it was her "vanity fearing exposure." She knew she was untrained, indeed altogether ignorant of the technique of poetry, and her efforts were invariably couched in "sober blank verse." Bryher, moreover, delighted in the poems of Marianne Moore and H. D.; alongside theirs Dorothy felt hers were ponderous. But, she said, if the "little editors of bourgeois magazines [were to] print them and they presently made a volume," then Bryher could read her poems. It was not long before Dorothy relaxed her conditions and was defending her poems against the criticism she had asked Bryher to make without regard to her feelings. She agreed with Bryher's comments—"but only in the abstract."

Dorothy could find no "diffuseness" in her first poem. "Whatever it isn't," she argued, "it's as tight as anything ever written." However, Bryher had seen that the seven-line poem spread outward, even though rhetorically it moved to a pointed close. Their dispute continued in bantering tones. When Dorothy sent two poems to *The Smart Set,* Bryher could not suppress a smile. She wrote a letter—which Dorothy signed—to Harriet Monroe of *Poetry* to accompany another pair of poems. Two months later, from Switzerland, Dorothy reported triumphantly that *The Smart Set* had offered her $25. She suggested that Bryher "eat [her] sniggerings." But the poems did not appear. At the same time, Miss Monroe accepted the poems submitted to her, actually paid $25, and published them in June 1924. Dorothy announced with glee, "I shall have my heels made higher and wear a sombrero."

In an equally joyful state, Dorothy and Alan left London—on the second instead of the first of November—after weeks of last-minute excitement. Life had been a "storm," Dorothy said, "people coming all day and staying all night." There were parties as well, at the Café Royal and the Brasserie Imperial. Only two days before their departure, the portly, thick-lensed Edward Garnett called and found them, as Dorothy had warned him, "girt for departure, seated on [their] packing cases." Through it all Dorothy felt young and full of vitality. Bryher could not help seeing her as the seventeen-year-old Miriam, an image that never seemed to fade from Bryher's view.

Dorothy and Alan were Bryher's guests in her chateau at Territet for a "long dizzy month." Territet, to which the general name of Montreux was often applied, was one of the villages along the east shore of the Lake of Geneva. From Territet itself a mountain railway ran past Glion and Caux nearly to the top of the Rochers-de-Naye, more than 6,000 feet high. Also accessible, by means of the Montreux-Bernese-Oberland railway from Versoix, was the Gruyère portion of the upper Sarine valley. Dorothy and Alan could thus make full use of the free transport within Switzerland she had secured for both of them. Alan was eager to look at everything. Here in Territet, in the autumn splendor between the snow peaks and the blue lake, he prowled about, absorbed and delighted, showing not a sign of even the slightest warning symptom.

Neither Dorothy nor Alan did any work during the entire month of their arrival. H. D. was there, as was Robert McAlmon. Dorothy and Alan had already met both of them in London. McAlmon had called at Queen's Terrace and had talked with them for hours—in the spirit of "young America," Dorothy thought. He spent most of his time in Paris, where the young literary world consorted in 1923. There Sylvia Beach's bookshop in the rue de l'Odéon, which also served as a General Post Office, was the most popular meeting place. There Joyce might be seen at a late hour of an afternoon, and there McAlmon (who Bryher said had a gift for meeting people) collected his stories about Paris and its "Franco-Anglo-American" communities of writers. Their appetites whetted by McAlmon's tales, Dorothy and Alan sat with him, Bryher, and H. D. in the Montreux café called "Sports," savoring the Swiss-French accents around them. The question of the moment, however, concerned not Paris but Florence, where by the third week of November Bryher was urging that they all go. Dorothy had virtually agreed to a brief spell in Florence before "settling down in the snow," but Bryher and H. D. ultimately left without the Odles. Alan suddenly began to cough, and Dorothy hurried him to the higher altitude of Château d'Oex.

They did not go at once to Les Hirondelles but instead to another pension Dorothy had learned of while in Montreux, a small chalet recently built by the local woodsman, where they stayed for a month and a half. They were the first *pensionnaires* at the Châlet Marie, at "frightfully reasonable" rates, Dorothy claimed; but they found the accommodations cramped. They had a sitting room, a bedroom, even a balcony and a winter garden—all of minute proportions. The heating was by stove, so—Dorothy told Bryher—the temperature alternated "up and down the scale between zero and asphyxiation." Out of doors, though, they could discard their coats and bask in a brilliant sun. Within a few days they both were sunburned and Alan's cough had vanished.

Alan was even more enchanted with Château d'Oex than Dorothy had hoped he would be. At first they did little more than "commissions": they went to the post office, had their boots clumped and sprigged, chose post cards for Christmas, found the cigarette and match shops. They also stared into innumerable shop windows. But Château d'Oex was so scattered and winding that to do all these things meant long walks, and Alan loved marching along the roads and pathways without a flapping coat. Snow was everywhere, "white peaks cutting violent blue skies," and a "pure hard light" made everything so beautiful that the village looked like a "shallow sun-filled cup."

A regular daily regimen was established. They rose at 7:30 A.M., separated after breakfast to work until lunch at 12:15. After lunch they went out to climb or toboggan, mainly for the sun, until tea at 4:30. They spent the interval after tea reading and talking until supper at 6:45 and then worked after supper until retiring at 9:00.

Alan seemed to thrive with this kind of organization. He settled down to work almost immediately ("Absence of Mind," he explained). He worked mainly on pen drawings and lithographs for *The Golden Hind*, an elaborate folio-sized quarterly devoted to art and literature, published by Chapman and Hall. It first appeared in October 1922, as clearly committed to draftsmanship and calligraphy as to prose and poetry. Alan was attracted to it at once for the rare opportunity it offered an artist to have his drawings reproduced close to their original size. For sheer movement and power, the work he contributed to the quarterly during its two-year existence was extraordinary. Dorothy often said she could "hear" his drawings as he worked on them.

Dorothy, however, had trouble settling into her work. Perhaps to avoid the sound of Alan's drawings as he worked on them at the sitting-room table downstairs, she sought the aid of her young hostess, the woodsman's wife, to establish herself upstairs at a "nachttische," with heat and a light "just above [her] nose." She later claimed that the upstairs room did not really warm up until the sun came in at eleven and that once her "brain and hands [were] serviceable" it was time for lunch. Too, she found that the few days the room was warm between five and the supper hour were not enough. "Not one fresh word" was added to *The Trap* in Châlet Marie. Instead she worked over the chapters already written and jotted down a few short pieces she hoped would be "pot-boilers."

Ten days before Christmas 1923, the snow began to fall and the mountains disappeared. The village and valley grew "whiter and still more thickly white," and the record snow went on. It stopped briefly on Christmas Day "to let the sun through," then began again harder than ever. The misty impressionistic scene was astonishingly beautiful. So was the burst of clarity that came with Christmas.

The Odles spent the moonlit evening seated within a small group around a tall, brilliantly colored tree, listening to the Swiss natives among them sing hymns and ballads with yodeling refrains. The singers were their host and hostess—the woodsman and his wife— two *pensionnaires,* and the chalet's small servant and large washer-woman. Afterward, when all rose to sing the Russian, Swiss, and English national anthems, the Odles joined in. The festivities struck Dorothy as being at one and the same time incongruous and "very grave and moving." Both she and Alan were won over by the sim-plicity, spontaneity, and strength of the rich, uncultivated voices.

The next day they began to see and hear another phenomenon of Switzerland: avalanches of snow. Their landlord, who sang so blithely at the holiday festivities, was cut off with all his men for four days. They had gone high up into the mountains to get wood, and it took twenty men with the aid of horses—men and horses roped together in a long line—to cut their way through a hundred yards of snow "house-high on a path overlooking a precipice" to rescue them. They had been caught unawares, for these avalanches were but a sliding about of premature snow, unbound by cold, anywhere and everywhere, and not the expected avalanches of spring with their "known haunts." The snowfall during the next ten days was followed by more avalanches and magnificent sky sce-nery: "Cloud masses. Sun and stars in the gaps." Underfoot, though, slush prevailed. They wallowed in it.

The temperature began to drop slightly just before they left Châlet Marie in mid-January 1924, but after a few days in the new pension, spring once again seemed to be in the air. Within doors, nonethe-less, Dorothy was grateful for the central heating of Les Hirondel-les, where they had a large room with three windows and a balcony, a radiator, a stove, an electric range for cooking, and cupboards. When they saw their room and the crowd of guests at the new pension, they rushed out to buy all the implements for tea. Les Hirondelles was completely full, and meals—in the company of Anglo-Indians, Scotch, Irish, Hampsteadians—were "a sin of top-ics," which ranged from politics and the Roman Church to psycho-analysis, Mr. Wells, and imminent disaster in England. Dorothy commented dryly that she had "taken up" *The Trap;* and Alan must have woven these mealtime scenes into his lithographs.

The other guests at Les Hirondelles appear to have been almost exclusively women, whom Dorothy took to describing as "The Fifteen Virgins." They were scandalized, she said, by the arrival of a package addressed to "Dorothy Richardson c/o A. Odle." Both she and Alan were a bit unkind to them. Some of the women gathered in the small salon or smoking room adjoining their own room that Dorothy had speculated about. From behind walls "perfectly porous to sound" she now heard them, having French lessons in the morning, tea parties in the afternoon, and "indignation meetings" in between. But after a while she learned how to work in a "beehive," and during February she felt closer to *The Trap* than she had been since she had begun it. As a result, she decided not to stir from Château d'Oex (unless she had to) until the end of April. Alan was putting on weight and was producing "mighty work." They went tobogganing together every afternoon, and Dorothy remarked that they would toil up the mountainside for two hours and then slide down in five minutes.

The only thing that might force them to leave Château d'Oex earlier than they wished was their financial situation. Here they found themselves spending more for charges they had not anticipated: an additional charge for heat, a *Kur-taxe* on visitors, and a variety of odds and ends that left them at one point with "exactly three weeks living in hand." Yet Dorothy did not seem seriously concerned. She described their precarious financial state in detail to Owen, who wanted to visit them briefly on his way from America to Vienna; but she urged him to come nonetheless, even insisting that he be their guest for three days if an expected sum of money reached them before his arrival. As it happened, aside from this sum, Dorothy persuaded Duckworth to advance £25, and Bryher sent a check.

But by that time there was another matter of real concern. At the end of February, after a short visit from his painter-friend Adrian Allinson, Alan once more began to cough—indeed, to reproduce his most frightening symptoms. Dorothy thought they might have to leave after all, because two children had come to stay in the house. Yet the pension had two chalets, and the children could be kept away from Alan. The *hausfrau* agreed to this, and they decided to remain until the end of April as they intended. Then they would go by the easiest possible stages to Cornwall.

During the next few weeks, especially when Owen was there, Dorothy feared Alan might collapse at any moment. The least excitement brought on a paroxysm of coughing. She attributed the recurrence in part to the spring. His health during the cold weather had seemed the best she had ever seen it. It gave an "illusion of inexhaustible strength," which she thought had tempted him to do too much. But she felt the visit of Adrian Allinson was largely responsible. She was convinced that the talk, laughter, and late hours had exhausted him. Now, although they did not talk about it, she felt the need to prepare for a crisis.

Dorothy never really knew whether Alan was aware of his illness or that she knew that he was ill. She believed he would continue to behave as though nothing were wrong until the last possible moment. Accordingly, they began to enact a drama without knowing whether the script each of them followed was the same. Alan went about his routine seemingly without the slightest intention of altering it, and Dorothy devised reasons for various small changes that would curtail his activity and avoid contact with the children.

Owen arrived at the very beginning of this without the slightest idea that anything was amiss. Dorothy was determined to avoid a repetition of Allinson's visit. She knew Owen would want to talk endlessly about New York and Boston, and he was only staying overnight. She made the most of a request made by people in the room upstairs for quiet after 9:00 P.M. and managed to keep the atmosphere subdued by carrying on the conversation with Owen herself as much as possible. As she explained to him later (assuming he had noticed nothing), Alan ought to have been in bed all the time, and if a doctor had seen him then, he would have put him there. But she was convinced that a doctor would *finish* him.

Whether she was right or not, Dorothy watched and waited. Understandably, she had little heart for *The Trap*. Moreover, in the midst of the most alarming period of Alan's illness, she learned that an American writer also named Dorothy Richardson had published a novel that had been reviewed mistakenly not only as hers but as her best book thus far. "So that I think about finishes me," she remarked to Bryher. "I shall try advertisement writing."

But Alan rallied. By the end of March he was better, and Dorothy's spirits rose. Now that they might not have to crawl back to England wounded and spent, she was full of plans again. When she discovered that the chalets were to close on April 15, she decided to leave on that day, provided of course that Alan continued to improve. They would descend to Montreux, rest there for a fortnight, then begin the journey home. Meanwhile they reveled in the sound of the genuine spring thaw up above—"a thousand sunlit torrents''—the smell of which she admitted was "a little rank for fastidious snouts.'' Pigsties and cattle sheds were being opened. But the scent of pine woods also hung in the air, coming in at the windows to mingle with the "radiant'' perfume of the indoor hyacinths.

For the moment, virtually everything began to improve. Dorothy's essay "About Punctuation'' appeared in the April issue of *Adelphi*. Its editor was Middleton Murry, at whom she had poked fun the year before; but he paid her £6 for the essay and asked her to contribute regularly. One of her Swiss articles had been printed in March, and a second appeared in April. And the current issue of New York's *Vanity Fair* ran her short essay, "Women and the Future.'' She planned several more articles for both *Vanity Fair* and *Adelphi*, especially for the Contributor's Club feature of the *Adelphi*, for which Murry paid about 15s. to £1 per page. If she could learn to produce these things quickly, the small sums would be very useful. Yet no matter how many pieces she wrote, she never became a practiced journalist.

Meanwhile, in 1924, as she approached her fifty-first birthday, she described herself to Bryher as "burly'' (she had put on fourteen pounds in Switzerland). Bryher was suggesting that Alan might profit from a summer in Châteaux d'Oex. Dorothy said the only way she could manage that would be to feign illness herself, but being as strong as she was, she could accomplish this only by breaking a leg. Alan already had his eye on London, though Dorothy, knowing he could not be exposed this year to its damp spring air, was counting on going straight to Cornwall for a month or so.

They began the homeward journey on April 15 as planned and spent two weeks in Montreux's Hotel Richemont. There they got more rest than they had bargained for. It was sweltering in Montreux, and most of the time they sat inert in the Sports café, barely able to watch the chestnuts bloom. Bryher was away, but occasionally H. D. happened in. One afternoon they wandered off alone to Clarens and found themselves in a suburban world, "the statelier, deader part of Hampstead.'' They turned and fled. In spite of the heat and thunderstorms, they were charmed again by the "lace-trimmed'' Lake of Geneva and the sophisticated look of Montreux, "all airs and graces,'' Dorothy said, though in her mind's eye it was really Paris she had begun to see. They were to have—through Bryher's generosity—ten days in that glorious city.

3

A quarter of a century later Dorothy would recall landing "bliss-fully" at the Dôme at one in the morning on April 30, 1924. They sat in the famous Quarter café, alone and quite content, until the small hours. The Hotel de la Haute Loire in the Boulevard Raspail, in which Bryher had booked a room for them, was nearby. And, just as Dorothy had warned Bryher they would do, they had breakfast and lunch served in bed and did not appear in daytime Paris until the tea hour. By evening they were "ready to face the world."

The world they faced that evening was a small, young, vibrant group gathered at the Dingo by Bryher and Bob McAlmon. Seated at a long trestle table were Ernest and Hadley Hemingway, Mary Butts and Cecil Maitland, Mina Loy, and others of the Montpar-nasse group.

Alan, seated at the end of a row, found himself beside a woman with lively blue eyes, red-gold hair, and ivory skin, who kept up a stream of chatter. He took her for a lady of the town, not recogniz-ing her to be Mary Butts, who was then one of the most gifted young women in Paris. Her collection of stories, *Speed the Plough,* had appeared in 1923, and her novel, *Asshe of Rings,* would be pub-lished by McAlmon's Contact Press in 1925. Ford Madox Ford thought she had a streak of genius, and Douglas Goldring called her a "living embodiment of surrealism." Yet Alan Odle, former habitué of the Café Royal, failed to recognize her as a current bohemian. She was then thirty-two years old, had separated from her husband, John Rodker, and was living with the brilliant but eccentric Scotsman, Cecil Maitland, with whom she dabbled in the occult among other things.

Dorothy was seated opposite Maitland, but she had no idea who he was. At a quiet moment, he leaned across the table and asked her, "What is your favorite book?" She admitted afterward that she had "suspected an intellectual," so she had said, *"The Three Mus-keteers."* "God be thanked, it's mine, too," Maitland had re-plied. "I always wanted to meet you and now I know why."

It did not take long for Dorothy and Alan to slip into the spirit of Montparnasse, which, according to Bryher, "adopted" them at once. They went to a midnight party at the Boeuf sur le Tôit. They watched a classic Quarter fight from behind their café table. They had coffee with the Hemingways in their little flat and, when Bryher and Bob McAlmon left for London after a few days, spent several evenings with the engaging young writer. Hemingway had already written most of the stories soon to be collected as *In Our Time*. Dorothy liked them very much and encouraged him to send some of them to English magazines. They also met Nina Hamnett, whose drawing of Alan's back had appeared in the first issue of *The Gypsy* years earlier. She was known as the unofficial hostess of the Quarter, having supposedly introduced Rudolph Valentino to James Joyce one day, only to find that neither had ever heard of the other.

To Dorothy's disappointment, she did not meet Joyce. Since the previous August, he had been living at the Victoria Palace Hotel in the sixth arrondissement, and could often be seen at dinner with his family in Michaud's. During the Odles' stay, however, he was suffering from recurrent eye trouble and would undergo another in a series of operations in June. (But Dorothy bought a copy of *Ulysses* for a friend of Owen and smuggled it into England packed among her lingerie, a hiding place both Leopold Bloom and Joyce himself would have relished.) She missed Ford Madox Ford as well, who was then editing the new magazine *transatlantic review*, in which the first fragment of *Finnegans Wake* had recently appeared. Ford had gone to America, and only a month later would ask Hemingway to put out an issue of the *transatlantic*. In answer to a charming appeal from Hemingway to Dorothy for a contribution ("Please don't get English and say that you haven't anything that would be of use to us, because I would be very happy to have any story of yours"), she sent a sketch entitled "In the Garden."

Paris itself was as magical as they had expected. They wandered about during their ten days, "*smelled*" their way to the Louvre, browsed among the bookstalls, gazed at Notre Dame and its familiar gargoyles, ambled through the Bois de Boulogne and Montmartre. They saw at least five Parises, Dorothy counted, and loved them all, including the Paris of the tourist. For them it was the high point of the year; for Dorothy it was the high point of the decade. She was never again to feel quite as celebrated as this. She would talk for years about returning to Paris, though the particular time was always wrong. The truth was that nothing would ever be as right as this again, and when they crossed the Channel in May, Dorothy must have known she would not return. The psychological odds were against it.

CHAPTER ELEVEN

Ironies and Ambiguities

ON THEIR RETURN from Paris in May 1924, Dorothy and Alan remained in London only long enough to store most of their things at Waterloo Station. Their Queen's Terrace rooms were still occupied, and to go to Cornwall encumbered with all their baggage for but a short stay seemed senseless. They spent one night in a hotel near Waterloo, and the following morning, with only two small bags, they took the "sweet shabby open-windowed south-western train down to hawthorn, gulls and gorse."

Cornwall greeted them equivocally. Dorothy felt sure it "*resented* [their] winter's absence" and was taking revenge with a gray misty rain that kept falling, a low gray sky, and a steady driving wind: "wintry effects" to remind them that Cornwall expected loyalty.

Dorothy and Alan had come back to Trevone Cottage and Mrs. Pope, planning to stay for three weeks, until June, when Dorothy thought it would be safe for Alan to be in London. He was holding his own, showing no sign of the symptoms that had been so marked in Château d'Oex; but Dorothy, while hoping he would go on in Trevone as he had begun—lounging by an open window and reading contentedly instead of working—feared that if he caught *her* at work (which was what she wanted to do), he would follow suit, which meant she had to "scribble surreptitiously." Upstairs, in the little rear bedroom looking out on Mrs. Pope's quarter of an acre of garden, she pretended to be writing letters only. She actually did write a few, and she sent Alan to post them one by one, "profiting by his pristine innocence as to the hours of collection" and counting on exchanges with friends met in the lane to occupy him further. All this meant that she had been frightened more than she had thought possible by the episode in Château d'Oex. It had begun to dawn upon her, somewhat hazily at first, how necessary Alan was to her

167

life, and that she had to take care of him as much for her own sake as for his.

Meanwhile, the work she had in mind was the last chapter of *The Trap*, in addition to roughing out the articles she would write when they moved to London. Except for a piece about Paris that she said she wanted to do but never did, three others she planned to write occupied her during the summer. "A Note on George Fox" appeared in the *Adelphi* of July 1924; the two others, "Women in the Arts" and "Antheil of New Jersey," were published by *Vanity Fair* the following year, in May and November.

Her essay on George Antheil, a twenty-three-year-old jazz musician, was only indirectly a product of her visit to Paris. He had given a concert there in 1923, and when Dorothy and Alan had arrived there in 1924, Paris was still talking about the new rhythms of the young man who looked like a child and lived like an anchorite. But Dorothy had already heard him performing three of his sonatas in London and had spoken to him afterward. Now she described him as "an innocent and helpless innovator. In other words a very disturbing person." Her interest in Antheil was only mild. He was a phenomenon, the so-called "bad boy of music" who seemed to have been a less gifted and less demoniac musical counterpart of James Joyce. (Indeed, Antheil had promised Joyce, but never actually composed, "an electric opera" with the Cyclops episode of *Ulysses* as libretto.)

The subject of her other essay for *Vanity Fair* was more important to her. On the surface, "Women in the Arts" was an attempt to explain the absence of "first-class feminine art." To Dorothy Richardson it seemed that artistic achievement required certain "absolute conditions." One of them was quiet, and the other was solitude "in the sense of freedom from preoccupations." But even if a woman paid any price for these, she would not get them in the way a man would, for a woman could never find the equivalent of the devoted wife or mistress, nor could she employ "the most neglectful char known to man." When women served women, Dorothy was convinced, the service was as different from that given by women to men as chalk was from cheese. If it were hostile, it would manufacture difficulties; if friendly, it would demand an "unfaltering response." Here was Dorothy's central point: a woman could not help but respond to "the human demand," which would besiege her wherever she was, clamoring for what Dorothy called "an inclusive awareness." Men, she insisted, were "exempt" from it, "for good or ill."

On a deeper level, the essay was in the nature of an apologia. A novel such as *Pilgrimage* could only be written by a woman; and because she was a woman, she could not produce *Pilgrimage* at the rate a man might be able to and under conditions he could achieve. Furthermore, if her novel was not absolutely first-rate, it was because she could not ignore "the human demand" that life—in the form of Alan—made upon her.

On the deepest level of all, Dorothy Richardson seemed to be expressing a veiled fear of achievement. In trying to account for the "overwhelming superiority" of the male artist, she brought up the matter of ambition, that "elusive and enormously potent factor," which she defined in terms she had used before. In her essay "Women and the Future," published in *Vanity Fair* in April 1924, she had described ambition as a "subtle form of despair," but without further elaboration, because the burden of her theme lay elsewhere.

Now, however, she developed the point. "In a lifetime," she wrote, a man might move "from the desire for personal excellence, the longing to be sure that either now or in the future he shall be recognized as excellent, to the reckless love of excellence for its own sake, leaving the credit to the devil," and he would go on to become—behind his own back as it were—"one with his desire." In the case of the artist, she went on, though his ambition was not necessarily personal, he was most apt to suffer in the absence of recognition. Agreeing that the "quality of a man's ambition" need not lessen the "intrinsic value" of his work, she maintained that ambition, to the extent that it remained "a thirst to be recognized as personally great," seemed to her "a form of despair." It was a form of despair to which men were "notoriously more liable" than women. She seemed to be saying, in other words, that in the face of the natural creativity of women (their childbearing and homemaking), men could indeed feel hopeless and try to perpetuate themselves by the means available to them: achievement and recognition.

In suggesting such a cause-and-effect relationship between personal ambition and despair, Dorothy Richardson revealed what appeared to have been a conflict within herself. On one hand, she wanted to be known and admired. On the other, she seemed afraid of the consequent demands that might be made upon her, demands that she could not fulfill. She maintained, more emphatically than seemed warranted, that despair went hand in hand with ambition. To avoid despair, which she thought men could not help but feel because they had *to do* rather than *to be,* she herself would try to suppress ambition, since it might take the form of a desire for personal recognition and thereby become despair. What she perhaps concealed from herself in this way was a deep fear that the achievement of fame would bring with it personal failure. On the other hand, to be Alan Odle's wife par excellence—to give priority to *being* over *doing,* i.e., over producing *Pilgrimage*—was to ensure a personal triumph. At the same time, one must add, it was her very being that she was engaged in producing in *Pilgrimage.*

2

During these three weeks of Cornwall in May and early June while she tried to finish *The Trap,* the title of the new volume took on a significance that spilled over from the life of her heroine into her own life. There had been signs even in Switzerland that the book was becoming something of a problem. "The Trap is closed against me," she had written to Bryher from Les Hirondelles. "I can't get inside." But once she did get inside, she could not get out again. In the novel, Miriam was being held captive by a relationship she had hoped would be a "marriage of convenience" but which had turned into an "active involvement." So, too, Dorothy seemed to be approaching—slowly and inwardly—the awareness of a tie to Alan that might involve not only the sacrifice of herself but also some of her deepest feelings. Yet the nature of the feelings involved was far from clear to her; she had not perceived the psychological fact that, like her heroine, she found herself in a trap that she had chosen as a refuge.

In spite of her incomplete awareness of this, Dorothy showed her sense of confinement in ways that were safely neutral. For example, shortly after arriving in Cornwall, when the precariousness of Alan's health was still uppermost in her mind, she received a letter from Jane Wells telling her of a reunion of their classmates at Southwest London College. It was to be held at the British Museum, where the husband of one of them was in charge of the Greek and Roman antiquities. Dorothy wrote to Jane that she longed to go but could content herself only with a "prance" to Padstow and a ferry

The graduating class of 1890 at Miss Sandell's "ladies' school" in Putney. Dorothy Richardson is standing in the back row at the far right; next to her is Amy Catherine Robbins, the future wife of H. G. Wells.

ride across the estuary. A few days later, Jane wrote again to describe the reunion. The head of the college, Miss Sandell, had been there and, to Dorothy's regret, her old music master, Herr Froude, as well. Dorothy would have liked to hold his hand, she said, and "confess the love that filled to bursting [her] little eight year old heart." Though it was a somewhat older heart than that (she forgot for the moment a few rather unpleasant years in Worthing), the displacement of her emotion from dangerous objects to safer ones is evident. She was bound to Alan, whether in Cornwall or not, and whether the distance between what she had and what she wanted was 250 miles or the extent of her doubts about herself.

A gap she *was* able to close was the one created by time, separating her from the girl who had been happy at Southwest London College on Putney Hill. She could feel her way back, not only to Putney and the eager piano student of Herr Froude, but also to Abingdon and the much smaller child who had loved her garden in Albert Park and had lost it. In a sketch Dorothy wrote in June, when her classmates were meeting without her at the British Museum, she retrieved the Abingdon garden and the sense of freedom, of solitude, of safety it had briefly given her. She projected herself into the infant consciousness of her earliest years, writing the sketch as the sensuous little being she had been and ending it with the child's fall—with a "Bang. The hard gravel holding a pain against her nose"—when she ventures beyond the permitted boundaries. Such was the punishment waiting for one who leaves a garden even temporarily.

The Abingdon garden had disappeared permanently from her childhood life when the family moved to Worthing for two years. Now, as if with the need to relive that loss and the intolerable change which succeeded it, Dorothy went on to write about her feelings in the Richardsons' "hired house" on the Channel coast. Although "What's in a Name?" was not published in *The Adelphi* until December, whereas her Abingdon sketch appeared in Hemingway's issue of *transatlantic review* in August, both resulted from a similar impulse: to bridge the "gulf" between desire and actuality, which she was also writing about in *The Trap*. Indeed, these pieces served as antidotes to the restricted life she was leading in fact as well as in fiction. To write of her early childhood at this particular time was not so much to escape into the past as to assert the freedom and power of her mind. It is not by chance that in "What's in a Name?" she chose to illustrate the "first assertion" of her eight-year-old mind: having balked at the sound of the name of the church to which her parents took her, she refused to walk down the path leading to the hated St. Botolph's, because it was "treeless" and lined by houses with "high walls that allowed no glimpse of gardens."

Nor was it by chance that during this same summer of 1924 Dorothy undertook to review a book about dreams: Mrs. H. A. Foster's *Studies in Dreams,* published in 1921. Dorothy's reaction to the book was politely negative. She did not like its position that "effective dreaming" could be attained, under certain conditions, by following Mrs. Foster's outline to enable a person to bring dreams about. Dorothy said wryly that Mrs. Foster had "achieved nothing less than the destruction of the dream as a freebooter and its reconstruction as a controllable human faculty," neither of which achievement made her happy. She confessed that, given the choice, she for one would choose not to dream. Not only was there no attraction for her in "the art of dreaming," but she had an "aversion so strong that [she was] aware, while a dream [was] in progress, of an annoyed sense of being derailed, of wasting time." Most emphatically, she did not wish to learn to dream.

And why not? Her answer was that she preferred "the chance of profound unconsciousness" to a "dreamland," however "magically real." She then proceeded to try to convey what she meant by "profound unconsciousness." Her own experience of it had "prevailed in perfection" on only one occasion, when she awoke undisturbed from a deep sleep to find herself (she could put it in no other way) "busily alive in the past, and at the same moment onlooker at [her]self living." It was a moment, she felt, of the most intensive living, during which "as onlooker" she had "an inquisitorial view both backwards and ahead." Her "known self" was the "actor," living through whole strands of life, not in succession, but . . . all in one piece." At the same time, this known self was aware of an inquisitor presenting the strands of life, sharing them, and making judgments "with a gaiety bordering on amusement and enchanting altogether." It would seem, however, that what Dorothy was describing was an experience of profound *consciousness*—such as might come to a psychoanalyst turned upon himself and purified of all resistance—a sense of staggering self-sufficiency.

She wanted even more than this. Her ultimate aim, as revealed in the review, was to be in "current possession, from a single point of consciousness, of [her] whole experience intact," and consequently—from the vast synthesis in her mind—to be able to arrange "the immediate future." Not the long-range future, only the immediate future. There are echoes in all of this of both Freud and Wordsworth. Only a few months before, she had written a brief essay on Wordsworth and Coleridge, and she would one day review a pair of biographies of Wordsworth. But the Freudian echo dominates and is ultimately more pervasive. In 1920 she had reviewed Barbara Low's *Psycho-Analysis: A Brief Account of the Freudian Theory* positively enough at so early a time as to prompt the editors of the magazine carrying the review to append a note detaching themselves from her views and expressing their own opinion that "the followers of Freud [were] pushing things too far."

Yet Dorothy felt ambiguous about psychoanalysis. In the corpus of her letters (especially those written to Bryher, who was analyzed by Hanns Sachs from 1928 to 1932), she criticized Freud and the movement, declined to be analyzed herself, and at one point declared that she knew what an analyst would find out about her. Perhaps just as she had chosen in 1912 to write a novel about her own life because it was all she could claim to know, so, too, she was convinced that only she could claim to know herself and her life. Moreover, in the very last pages of *The Trap*, she has her heroine declare that she must create her life, using "self and circumstances" as the "raw material." If Dorothy herself had really succeeded in carrying this out, then during the months in which she was bringing Miriam to the point of making the same declaration and setting herself the same task, she might also have been saying in various ways that only the artist can claim to know his own creation. But the evidence seems to point to her growing less and less sure who was really in control of what.

3

Early in June 1924, Dorothy Richardson returned to London with Alan and the completed but unrevised manuscript of her eighth volume. It was "congealing" in her hands, she complained, even though she tried to work at it every possible moment. But there were not enough possible moments, and she had the distinct sense that life in the world was obstructing the life and identity within *The Trap*. Waiting for her at Queen's Terrace, she found a flattering letter from the editor of the *Sphere* and also a note from Wells to tell her that the American Dorothy Richardson was still being confused with the English, for in a recent issue of the *Observer,* her namesake's *Book of Blanche* had been cited as "an early essay" of her own.

Dorothy took the opportunity to write a disclaimer expressing her regret that since there was no copyright for authors' names she could not protect those who preferred her namesake's work to her own from mistakenly buying or borrowing her own books. She said that this was her "first and last contribution to the enlightenment of [her] friends the reviewers." She was canceling her press-cutting subscription, since the income she derived from her books was not enough to pay for the "entertainment" of reading her namesake's reviews, which were being sent to her along with her own. The deepest irony in all of this was that in the very act of struggling to reproduce in *The Trap* the arduous process by which she became the author of *Pilgrimage,* Dorothy Richardson had to fight to preserve an identity that had been, as it were, doubly carved—in life as well as in art. It was a bitter pill to swallow.

It seemed the season of ironies. One reason her revision of *The Trap* went so slowly was that she spent so much time writing essays and reviews. Eleven of them appeared in 1924 alone, of which six were published by Middleton Murry in the *Adelphi,* leading Dorothy to fear she might glut her *Adelphi* market. To prevent this from happening, she adopted a pseudonym, R. Theobald, which she took from the name of the London road that led out from Southampton Row and Upper Woburn Place, where Miriam was living in the course of *The Trap* and where she herself had lived when she was young and unknown. In choosing a name linked with her London life, was Dorothy declaring that if she *were* to become someone else, she alone had the right to determine *who* she would be?

Involved as she was, then, in the increasingly more complicated matter of private and public identity, how ironic again that another reason for the delay of *The Trap* had to do with Wells. While in Switzerland, she had agreed to read some of the proofs of an edition of his collected works. There would be more than twenty volumes in all, and Wells had offered her £20 to read the first two, which were ready in the spring when she and Alan came down to Montreux from Château d'Oex. Now, in the summer, she was reading two more volumes, calling out the best passages to Alan, while her own novel languished.

Alan, too, was playing a part in the curious affair of the stymied *Trap.* He and Dorothy had come up from Cornwall to find the early

June weather in London disabling. A cold wind blew perpetually, a cold rain fell, and thunderstorms struck regularly. Dorothy, who feared the effects the dank air would have on Alan after his spring attack, took advantage of every moment the sun shone to go out with him. She felt both anxious and burdened. Then by July, London was serving up entirely different fare—"roasting weather," which Alan did not take any better. They went out as often as possible for bus rides in the evening, but during the day even Dorothy was almost too limp to do anything. Yet on the afternoon of what turned out to be—as the West End sandwich men helpfully informed them—the hottest day to date, Dorothy and Alan took themselves down to the Leicester Galleries to see an exhibition of Gauguin's Tahiti work.

"Sickness," Dorothy described it to Bryher, "but a magnificent sickness." It seemed to her that Gauguin had suffered everything an artist could suffer, and she was filled with wonder and pity. At the same time, a painting such as "The Agony in the Garden" stirred her to revulsion. Gauguin had put himself in a Tahitian garden and sketched in around the corner both the spires of Paris and the European disciples hiding from him. "A man may give his life for his truth," Dorothy conceded, "but a picture of himself doing it" struck her as going too far. Whether Alan shared her opinion she did not say, for his response to Gauguin is conspicuously absent from her account of a tropical afternoon devoted to tropical pictures and spent largely on his behalf, as if he were a silent and passive charge who had to be periodically "trotted" out. The verb is Dorothy's.

4

London in August began as its customarily gray, cool self, and the mass weekend departures for the sea lost some of their earlier frenzy. But before the month was three days old, Dorothy had found another outlet for the feelings of constriction and despair which pervade *The Trap*. On August 3, the novelist Joseph Conrad suddenly died. Although she had never met him, once at a large party his back had been pointed out to her and she had decided on the instant that it belonged to an interesting person. For some reason his death cut into her as an enormous fact that was "not possible," she said, but "merely true."

Years afterward, during Wells's last lingering illness, when it seemed to her everyone was waiting impatiently to publish the obituaries, Dorothy would remark with some rancor that Conrad's death had gone almost unnoticed, remembering the reaction, by contrast, as offensively small. She had been deeply affected by his death, and for reasons it is difficult to fathom, even though Conrad does seem to have been associated in her mind with her own beginnings as a novelist (she liked to think that Edward Garnett had "discovered" her as well as Conrad). Shortly after hearing the news, she wrote a poem that offers a small clue to her state of mind. The poem, entitled "Disaster," describes the sudden sinking of a ship that only in the moment before it sank was perceived in all its majesty. A mixture of feelings seems apparent in the poem. A wish to pay homage to the dead novelist is its primary impulse, but another wish is expressed obliquely: a desire to be seen someday as she was seeing Conrad then, not on the small, equivocal scale she had thus far experienced, but in the regal manner she envisioned as Conrad's final due. Might this be the dangerous ambition slipping through that Dorothy seemed to think she had to guard against—for at least one good reason, that it was unlikely ever to be satisfied?

Dorothy herself revealed some of these hidden and mixed feelings in another connection. The day before Conrad's funeral, she and Alan paid a visit to their old friend Crosland, who was very ill. The old "jobbing poet" clung to his slum off the Edgeware Road, refusing to "make for the sea" as Dorothy claimed the doctor had ordered, and he sat up in bed "cadaverous but mighty still," entertaining his guests with unfaded wit until they simply had to leave to quiet him down. At one point Alan told Crosland of the other Dorothy Richardson, and to the immense gratification of the one present, Crosland exploded with rage. He swore to recover if only to "blow her and her publisher to smithereens." Dorothy had no idea Crosland read any novels at all, much less hers, yet beside his bed was the copy of *Deadlock* she had sent him at Christmas, and it looked to her as though it had been read more than once. She was touched that Crosland, who had spent his life cursing everyone and everything, now solemnly gave her his blessing. At this point, Crosland merged with Joseph Conrad in Dorothy's mind. Breaking off her account of Crosland's unsuspected devotion, she took up the lament with which she had begun this letter to Bryher: "But— Conrad is dead," she exclaimed. "Joseph Conrad, is *dead.*"

177

CHAPTER TWELVE

The Trap

CROSLAND'S miserable circumstances moved Dorothy to write Wells, who had known him for years, for help. She told Wells that Crosland was dying and that it would be pure charity to send him a few hundred pounds that would enable him to spend his last months in comfort outside of London. Wells responded with a tirade. He did not believe Crosland was dying, and in a vilifying letter he took Dorothy to task for her sentimentality and simplemindedness. The letter reached her shortly after the news of Crosland's death; it had been written while the old man lay dead in his slum. Dorothy shot back to Wells her bald opinion of him. When she received no answer, she wondered if her proofreading would now cease.

Though Wells continued to remain silent, the proofreading went on. Dorothy sent him a peace offering in the form of a book she thought he would like, and they were soon on the old familiar terms again. But whether she knew it or not, her own position had been shaky. By the time she had written to Wells about Crosland, a few months had passed and she was already in Cornwall. Her appeal might have had more effect on Wells—besieged as he constantly was by letters and requests of all kinds—if she had been able to say she had just that moment seen Crosland. However, by the time she wrote in December, Crosland had managed to remain alive for more than four months, and Wells was understandably skeptical. His abusiveness followed as a matter of course.

Dorothy had not been able to focus on Crosland's condition until December because of other concerns. *The Trap* had finally reached completion by October 1924, when she and Alan left for Cornwall, but nothing else seemed to go right. London had been dark and dreary throughout September. Dorothy could not find a winter tenant for their Queen's Terrace rooms. And Alan's elder brother Sidney was in the last stages of tuberculosis. Alan had gone to Hastings to see him, and while he was away, Dorothy had begun to pack for Cornwall.

London was in a thick fog when they left Waterloo Station for Cornwall. As their train moved west, Dorothy might well have conjured up a recent dinner party at May Sinclair's that had been one of the few bright spots in the past two months. Sinclair Lewis, who had been the principal guest, had made a shambles of the formality cherished by his hostess. Dorothy was sure that until then no guest at a May Sinclair dinner had ever placed his cigarette case and matches among the almond and olive dishes in front of his plate or rested his elbows comfortably on the table after the soup or lit a cigarette the moment he had swallowed his pineapple. In spite of all hints dropped—less and less gently—Lewis could not be moved from the dining room to the drawing room for coffee. Dorothy would never forget the "horrified" maid trying to clear the table under the noses of the guests and virtually screaming ("such was the din") into May Sinclair's ear a query whether she should serve the coffee "in HERE." The Odles would laugh at this again and again.

Meanwhile, the train moved out of the murky fog into a brilliant sun that shone over five counties and went down at last behind Dartmoor. A few hours later they arrived in Padstow in a dark-green Cornish night outlined by the moon. The estuary shimmered in pure light, and palmlike trees on the station hill were etched against the sky. Then, in a black-and-white setting such as Alan himself might have created, they set out, with all their baggage, across fields of tall spire-grass to Harlyn four miles away.

The moment they reached Cozy Corner, the soundless night erupted, as two sheepdogs from a nearby farm "made a frantic scene." Dorothy interpreted this to mean they had not liked the tenant the previous winter. Once the dogs were quiet, the Cornwall Dorothy and Alan had missed the year before asserted itself: the sea swished behind them just across the dunes, and they could see the ring of trees, slightly elevated, just visible from their door. Tired as they were, instead of retiring at once, they stood there watching the moonlight on the bare branches that patterned the sky and listening to the sound of the bells in the tide.

The morning scenery was all they could wish for: the coast and sea were radiant in flawless sunlight. Harlyn itself was green and gold and scarlet. The bungalow, with windows everywhere, from a distance appeared to be nothing more than a large, colored looking glass. Ambition, fame, and failure all were negligible in the midst of brilliant sky and seemingly eternal gulls. They stared at Cornwall for days, while everything else waited. At times like this, it seemed the loveliest—and safest—place of all.

2

In due time Dorothy picked up the eighth volume of Wells's collected edition, which had arrived in Harlyn before she did. She had not yet had her confrontation with Wells over Crosland. She was also bent on beginning work on *Oberland,* the next volume of *Pilgrimage,* which would record Miriam's first trip to Switzerland. Although she anticipated none of the difficulties she had encountered with *The Trap,* she was having trouble with her publisher. On the one hand, he wanted the volume within the year; on the other, he refused to advance the money that would free her to produce it.

The Christmas season crept near, as Dorothy fumed at autocratic publishers and Alan worked quietly day after day on drawings he hoped to show at a group exhibition in the spring. The exhibition, at this point still largely an idea in the minds of four *Golden Hind* artist contributors, was taken as fact by Alan, who worked accordingly. Whereas Dorothy found herself constantly tempted to slack off, she had to coax him into taking holidays. Bryher had sent her several more volumes of Proust, and she could not resist reading them, even in French. Every day after breakfast she translated a few pages for Alan into what she called her "best Moncrieff." Along with the Proust, Bryher had sent a promise that a hamper would arrive for Christmas. Dorothy, writing to thank her in advance, said she had not told Alan about it, because she wanted him to be surprised. She thought its arrival would help to distract him from the memory of the hampers his father had sent every year until his death. Having been abroad last year, he had not missed the ritualistic package, but this year Dorothy was sure he would have felt it.

The plan to surprise Alan nearly backfired, though, for by the morning of Christmas Eve nothing had arrived except bad news. Crosland, who had suffered "horribly" at the end, was dead. Sidney Odle, whose condition had worsened by autumn, seemed to have rallied for the moment, but it was clear that he could not recover. Dorothy found it hard to feel festive, but as the day—soggy and warm for December—wore on, she cleared away all signs of work and began to prepare tea. The afternoon post brought two circulars forwarded from Queen's Terrace. When Alan came in from his walk, they sat down to tea and were immediately interrupted by a furious banging on the back door, which Alan went to answer. In a few moments, Dorothy heard him making the "polite social noises" he resorted to when he could not understand a word being said and did not wish to be so rude as to admit it. She rushed out and found Alan exercising his urbanity on a village lad who was emitting "floods of pure Cornish." Beside him, in the mud, stood a huge packing case. Alan, who expected nothing, had decided it could not possibly belong to them. Dorothy, after listening to a long Cornish story about a "carrier," in response to the lad's final singing words, "Hoggle, she'm f'you, eenut, areckon?" said quite firmly, "She'm fer we." The packing case was soon moved to the sitting-room floor, and in it, Dorothy reported to Bryher, was "a feast for a king"—as well as, undoubtedly, for a queen.

Harlyn was a wild place for several days after Christmas. All the elements raged together night and day. The tide, waves, and wind roared, and rain drove in through the casements. Dorothy and Alan tried one afternoon to go down to the sea at low tide, but when they felt themselves plummeting down the lane, they turned around ("to escape being blown into the sea") and fought their way back inch by inch to the safety of the bungalow. On their return trip, the wind was like an impenetrable wall. A milder storm began to brew when the elements ceased to rage.

The correspondence between Alan and his fellow artists increased, and by the second week of January 1925 it was decided that the show would go on. A mass of details had to be sorted out. This was no simple task with Alan in Cornwall, John Austen in Kent, Harry Clarke and Austin Spare in London and Dublin. Dorothy plunged into the discussions, helping Alan weigh the various possibilities and writing his letters, but she felt dubiously rewarded when they all asked her to write a preface for the catalog. In spite of protests that she knew nothing about art, they insisted, and she began to make a few notes. Ultimately the gallery hired an art critic to help prepare the catalog, and Dorothy put her notes aside, thinking they could someday be turned into an article.

The biggest problem of the moment, as usual, was money. Somehow Alan would have to bear his share of the show expenses. Then, with what Dorothy repeatedly (and sometimes resentfully) called his "pristine innocence," he proceeded to add to his contribution to the show a few lithographic drawings which, for preservation, required reproduction by an expensive process as soon as possible. If he had worked unstintingly before knowing the show would actually take place, he now worked frantically. The sale of just a few drawings would provide enough money for him to share respectably in the expenses of living, and the sale of one or two would at least pay the costs of exhibiting. But if he could sell a "heap of drawings," he kept saying, they might be able to go again to Paris.

His hopes were high, but Dorothy began to feel "rather white-haired" under the strain of witnessing both his hopes and the furious pace at which he worked. One of Knopf's periodic reports arrived amid these preparations. When it indicated only "two whole dollars" due her in the spring and "calmly" stated that the first five volumes of *Pilgrimage* were out of print, she was not really surprised. Soon after this Alan's cough reappeared, and the symptoms of the previous year in Switzerland began reproducing themselves. Dorothy immediately asked one of the other artists to undertake hanging Alan's drawings so he could remain in Cornwall until the last possible moment, and she accepted an offer of help from Bryher to tide them through the show, if not perhaps the year.

The opening date of the exhibition was set for May 21, later than originally planned. Before this, Dorothy had been thankful that all Alan's drawings would have to be sent to town by the beginning of April. Now she felt that, with an extra three weeks, he might be persuaded to slow down. They could remain in Harlyn until the end of April, working under reduced pressure. Then they could take a fortnight's holiday at Trevone Cottage before appearing in London on May 14. Meanwhile, she plied Alan with eggs and Cornish cream and, in spite of everything, looked forward to the show. She pictured herself and the four artists gathered every day in "low haunts" where, with beer in hand, they would speculate, forecast, analyze, and "shiver over the fate of their works." She wanted Bryher to join them, especially to meet Austen and Clarke. "You shall come around with a large cigar," she instructed, "and drink a tiny little stoup of ale." It would all be an immense "lark."

As a result of Bryher's help, no doubt, Dorothy and Alan moved to Trevone Cottage in the early part of April for six weeks instead of two. Although they would still work until the final fortnight,

Dorothy was relieved of household chores and of the responsibility of feeding Alan. Now she turned to her Swiss novel. If she finished it by autumn, Duckworth could publish it during the winter, which she thought might help its sales. She had stopped fretting about the unreasonable demands made by publishers.

Trevone seemed as efficacious as Dorothy had willed it to be. As May approached, bringing with it a gorse spring that flamed everywhere, Alan was coughing less and looking not quite so pale. Dorothy packed and sent off all his exhibits, plus all of the material required for the catalog—the price list and the personal information. There remained a poster to be designed and sent out for reproduction, which would take Alan only a few days. Moreover, *Oberland* was one-third complete. It might actually be finished, revised, and typed within the year, even allowing for "exhibition dementia." And a telegram from Bryher informed Dorothy that *The Trap* had finally been published.

In quiet Trevone, Dorothy also hatched a plan to translate the journal of the Goncourt brothers, which she had heard would be published in September and which she was sure would be a classic. Work such as this would have none of the uncertainty of writing articles that, when completed, had then to be placed. All that was needed to secure translation rights was a London publisher, so Dorothy wrote to a literary agent, outlining the venture in all its native appeal. The answer she received, she thought, was devastatingly stupid. The agent had said he could not approach publishers, but he would gladly handle the book for her if she could secure the rights. "Fool," she exploded. How could she, from Cornwall, telephone all the publishers? There was not enough time to *write*.

The naive agent had touched off a small outburst, for by this time Dorothy was not feeling well. She had been bothered with an aching tooth since the beginning of the year—"payment," she admitted, for "neglecting the dentist since Tunnel days." The ache became worse and worse during the final fortnight in Trevone Cottage, and both sides of her mouth were affected. She was sure there were exposed nerves that, by the time she and Alan arrived in London, had caused her face to swell painfully. Before anything could be done about her teeth, she came down with influenza, and since Alan was not only an inept nurse but also frightened by the illness of anyone—but especially of Dorothy—she went into a nursing home. She emerged after ten days more or less recovered from the flu, but she was still reverberating from the small operation that had been performed on her teeth.

The show opened at the St. George Gallery two days before Dorothy returned to Queen's Terrace. She arrived at the gallery to find Alan's drawings badly hung, the best of them crowded out. Her *Trap* press was "mostly brickbats and vitriol." Duckworth plaintively asked how many more "Miriams" there would be. He offered her £25 for *Oberland*, and Knopf decided to purchase sheets for an American edition of *The Trap* as small as the one of *Deadlock*: 500 copies. "So that's that," Dorothy remarked—but it was not.

Within a few days Alan's work began to draw crowds and to create a stir. When his brilliant nose-thumbing and breathless satire attracted a great deal of attention, he dared to hope some of the drawings would sell, even though the critics ventured only to predict that someday there would be a "rush . . . to secure Odles." Unfortunately, no one seemed ready "to secure Odles" now. When the exhibition closed in the middle of June, not a single Odle had been sold.

Nor had Dorothy fared better. Much of *The Trap* criticism was vehement, perhaps best summed up by the title of the *New York Times* review in August 1925, "Much Ado about Little." Dorothy said she understood the "bewilderment" (resulting from lack of imagination) and the "boredom of most men in a world of which they know nothing." But what puzzled her was their "Fury," which certainly had an effect on Duckworth. He listed the volume only once, with no comment at all.

Throughout the summer, Dorothy tried to work on *Oberland*, and Alan turned to illustrating Rabelais. "Strange young people" sent their manuscripts to Dorothy and came to call on her. "Thus," she noted, "one has all the taxes of a certain measure of notoriety" and none of its "rewards." Both she and Alan, by totally different means, had arrived at the same impasse.

3

Dorothy was mindful of the strange fate that had befallen her past self. In *The Trap*, as Miriam, she had relived the year spent in Woburn Buildings with the proper, spinsterish Miss Moffat, who had disapproved of Dorothy's affair with Wells. Miss Moffat, translated to Miss Holland (Miriam can never address her as Selina, just at Miss Moffat's Christian name seems lost forever), becomes in *The Trap* a kind of social worker, giving moral lectures in the evening to the East End poor and gradually discovering that Miriam, despite her elegant bearing, is an unreclaimable lover of life and of men. The awful truth breaks in upon Miss Holland when Miriam forgets to keep a promise to her. With outrage and spite in her "most fastidious voice," Miss Holland draws the inescapable and damning conclusion, "Had it been made to a *man,* your promise would at once have been carried out." But this is as far as Dorothy allows Miss Holland to go in expressing her disapproval of Miriam; and only in Miriam's thoughts does Hypo Wilson appear, playing by implication the part Wells had played in Dorothy's life at an earlier rather than corresponding time. They are not yet lovers in *The Trap*.

At this stage, absent though he may be as a lover, Wells is unavoidably present as both himself and Hypo Wilson. Miriam's relationship with Wilson occupies a prominent place in her thoughts, with the chance at any moment that a scrap of his conversation or a note he had written might float into her mind, a remark he had made might be echoed in one of her own. But Miriam does not identify Wilson by name, since *she* knows who she is thinking about. So would a reader of *Deadlock* know, for in that volume Hypo Wilson had begun his "systematic pursuit" of his wife's young friend. But a reader of *The Trap* alone would not be prepared for such an unidentified message from Hypo as this: "You were a lovely person in your blue gown. . . . I've seen you look charming, in Miriam's quiet way. Didn't know you could be splendid. Don't fly out. It's all right. I'm staying friends. Honour bright. For the present." No wonder the *New York Times* reviewer complained that Dorothy Richardson expected her readers to "remember perfectly and in detail" the earlier volumes of *Pilgrimage*. Yet if the novel had made him aware of the requirement, then it was not entirely obscure.

What no reviewer unacquainted with Dorothy Richardson herself could possibly perceive was the subtle blend of fact and fiction in *The Trap*. The historical world of 1905 in which Dorothy Richardson lived has become for the most part the imaginary world of Miriam Henderson, who goes to lectures sponsored by the Lycurgan Society and overhears at one of them a remark she will pass on to Hypo for his amusement: "Now Mrs. Wilson *is* charming. . . . A far more charming personality than he." Dorothy Richardson must have heard similar remarks about the Wellses and passed them on to H. G., but the flavor of *this* reality cannot be tasted without knowing that Wilson is Wells. Although Dorothy Richardson did not want this to be known, she *did* want the historical basis of her novel to be recognized. What better way to achieve such recognition than to have her heroine read *The Ambassadors,* live opposite Yeats, and also think about and mentally argue with H. G. Wells as so many people were doing in 1905?

Was she, in being a woman, "one of Wells's crawling cabs waiting to be hailed?" Nonsense, Miriam answers in her mind, but with a touch of defensiveness and uncertainty. Why, in spite of her "new life" in an unconventional world, with her strange friend Michael, who sat in lecture halls "crackling" his bag of hardbake, and her curious vegetarian friends the Taylors, did she find herself drawn, as she always had been in her youth, to Philistines? She knew their "mental immobility" was deplorable. Yet within their own world, she saw them as somehow "rich and racy": their life had an "essence" to be savoured, and did not their critics, missing this, miss as well "the essence of all life whatsoever?" It seemed to her that their critics were afraid of the *"power* of the Philistines." And what was this power they and Miss Holland had in common with Hancock's relatives and the girls at school with her long ago in Barnes? It was the power to stifle freedom.

But had she not come to London precisely for the sake of freedom? Yet what had Wells just shown in *A Modern Utopia?* That "freedom, unless people become samurai, slid down into a pit. Perhaps these clever, scornful ones, the moderns and the Lycurgans, were all escaped Philistines?" She herself was one, and perhaps they were as dissatisfied as she was. Thus, into the fabric of Miriam's mind Dorothy Richardson wove the struggle of an uncertain, tentative, modern consciousness to escape from the sure, solid, formidable nineteenth century; and she knew this could not be done realistically without Wells as Wells—the arch-iconoclast—rather than the fictional Hypo Wilson.

Nor could the Lycurgans be fully realized as the Fabians without bringing into view two of the most prominent men among them: Wells and Shaw. So Dorothy Richardson has Miriam attend a Lycurgan Christmas dance at which she sees Shaw present and "religiously enduring. Coming to Lycurgan gatherings as others go to church." Also distinguished from the crowd is a worshipper of Wells named Arnold Englehart, whom Miriam describes as sharing Wells's militant, controversial, and un-Fabian view that socialism can be brought about "in a fortnight." But Dorothy Richardson does not bring Englehart and Wells together at the dance. As a matter of fact, Wells is not actually there; he is present in name (someone is always referring to him) and in the person of one of his own fictional characters. Thus "Wilkins the author, gesticulating greetings, came up and hooked Englehart away by the arm." Wilkins, an alter ego of Wells who appears in several of his novels, would have been recognized, but only by those who were familiar with the Wells novels; and it is difficult to believe that Dorothy Richardson felt she could count on such knowledge.

Oddly enough, in the time scheme of *The Trap,* the appearance of Wilkins is anachronistic: Wells had not created him until 1909, in his notorious novel *Ann Veronica.* But it seems unlikely that Dorothy Richardson erred, engaged as she was in proofreading Wells while writing her own novel. It is much more probable that she could not resist summoning up Wells in such a cagey way, and that she was aware, too, that at least readers familiar with Wells's work would recognize Wilkins the author and relish her little joke. In effect, she created a curious atmosphere for *The Trap,* a blend of historical and fictional reality derived from equally mixed sources, somewhat like an actual photograph of long ago which nonetheless seems unreal.

In such an atmosphere, Miriam Henderson takes on some of the qualities of a touched-up figure in an old photograph, her reality striking one as questionable. On the surface she might almost seem a parody of the "new woman" who in 1905 had achieved a measure of independence from the Victorian family and had begun to discover that freedom did not go hand in hand with independence. But to look at Miriam Henderson closely is to see the kind of authenticity that in its own time breeds dislike—as Miriam's did—and in later years breeds something like suspicion of, if not contempt for, such a seemingly outmoded struggle.

There is no doubt that Miriam is preoccupied with herself, and Dorothy Richardson makes no effort to mitigate her egoism, which in fact, as the underside of the need to honor oneself, is one of the constant themes of both her life and her book. Miriam has moved into Flaxman's Court with Miss Holland (as Dorothy had moved into Woburn Buildings with Miss Moffat) to escape the boarding-house at Tansley Street and its threat of personal relationships, with all their demands of feeling and responsibility. She had met Miss Holland only twice before they agreed to live together, but Miriam felt sure the arrangement would be businesslike and comfortably outside the range of feeling. At the same time, though Miriam does not mention this until much later, when she is ready to leave Flaxman's, she thought that a "marriage of convenience" with Selina Holland would permit her to economize. By living more cheaply, she could help her family. Dorothy Richardson does not allow Miriam to specify, but there is only one person she could possibly mean—her father, who, like Charles Richardson in his difficult old age, was being cared for by her eldest sister. Yet when it becomes apparent to Miriam that neither Miss Holland nor Flaxman's Court will do, she also realizes the impossibility of remaining there simply to be helpful. Instead she faces her "deeper self" and takes "responsibility" for it. Her own needs come first. As she herself puts it, "There is not a soul I would sacrifice myself for."

A "disagreeable" girl most reviewers of *The Trap* called her, and from a certain point of view they were right. It is hard to be agreeable when one finds one has made a series of errors in judgment. First of all, Miriam discovers that Flaxman's Court, which had always "drawn her eyes" as a "scrap of old London standing apart," is not a pleasant place to live. Her new rooms are damp and insect-ridden. From the ground floor, periodically, come the sounds of the occupant beating his wife. The "dismal court" resounds with "curses and blows," which reach their peak during the summer months when all the windows are open. Though Miriam's room-mate seems not to notice any of this, she does manage to learn that the young couple living immediately below them are not yet married and are expecting a baby. Their presence leads Miss Holland to conclude that she and Miriam are in "*strange* surroundings." She also assumes without question that Miriam agrees completely with her, not only about the young couple who, she complains, are "*quite* without circumspection," but about everything. Nothing could be farther from the truth, yet it takes Miss Holland a good while to note the gap between them.

At first Miriam says nothing to enlighten her. Unhappy as it makes her to hear Miss Holland gush with delight at the news that W. B. Yeats lives directly across the court and would therefore be writing poetry "so near at hand," so close indeed that if one looked hard enough one could see "verses on the air between the opposing windows," Miriam does not try to explain her own sense of responsibility for preserving Yeats's privacy. Instead she diverts Miss Holland's attention by telling her the story of her moonlight meeting with Yeats in Bloomsbury Square, the same story Dorothy Richardson would tell about herself years later when Yeats was dead. But Miriam's patience gradually gives way in the face of Miss Holland's standardized Philistinish self-assurance.

Besides, Miriam is unwillingly and uneasily attracted to Miss Holland. She finds herself drawn to the large, imposing figure she makes indoors, with eyes that were really quite beautiful when the light did not show the "tired muscles" around them. Outside or among other people, Selina Holland looked "thoroughly dowdy" and "flat-haired," with "no style but [her] set of beliefs"—but strangely enough she only appealed to Miriam the more.

There was something in the dowdiness of women like Miss Holland which drew Miriam to them; "her heart went forth with mysterious desire" to all the comfortable, secure, "upright and insulated" Selina Hollands. Even their voices, constricted and contemptuous as they usually were, attracted her subtly, even aroused her envy of the "mode of being" that produced their distinctive way of speaking. It was a mode that involved a "disdain of life's external processes, of everything but high ends, any kind of high end, from the honour of England to the dignity of the speaker and of the person spoken to, that everything in life must be moulded to serve." By contrast, Miriam lived for nothing but low ends, if not the lowest end of all—her self—which she vaguely felt Miss Holland threatened by her very attractiveness. Miriam was aware that she craved the single-mindedness and certainty of this woman, who, she knew quite well, was also devastatingly dull.

The turning point in Miriam's ambivalent feelings comes when Miss Holland loses her composure, reveals "a volcanic temper and a spiteful tongue," and bursts into tears—all because of a forgotten promise. The fit of weeping is more than Miriam can bear, involving her as it does in the "meanest of all abandonments," the "soft feebleness" of femininity, which she loathes. But it also frees her from the trap of her own susceptibility.

This, however, is not the only trap in which Miriam is caught. She struggles also with her equally mixed feelings for the young society doctor who wishes to marry her. The prospect of becoming his wife both attracts and repels her. On the one hand, life with him would be "gay and easy," full of solace and protection. On the other, it would be full of "unconsciousness" and a "loneliness beside which the loneliness of the single life was nothing." She would want companionship, and he could not provide it. Yet all he does offer tempts her, for it seems to her that marriage with him would mean "launching into life as [her] people have lived it." Here, in the pull toward precisely what she is trying to escape from the most—her family—lies the most insidious trap represented in the novel.

Ultimately Miriam rejects Dr. Densley, throws off Miss Holland, and decides to leave Flaxman's Court, the "corner" that seems filled with "the sense of death." She realizes that life, like art, cannot be left to chance. With her own self and her own circumstances as the "raw material," she will have to create her life—but only her own life. She can do nothing for other people. If their lives remain uncreated, it must be so. She can take responsibility for no one except herself. But while she hammers out these conclusions during the last scene of *The Trap,* as the stonemason on the ground floor curses womanhood and "its physical manifestations," she comes to a realization of several flaws in her reasoning. Michael Shatov, with his imperious claims upon her, is one; Hypo Wilson, with his equally imperious demands, is another; and she herself, with her inability thus far to be "actively involved" with anyone, is a third. *The Trap* ends on this note of precarious if not deceptive freedom so thoroughly familiar to Dorothy Richardson. Dorothy would play the same note again and again, until her heroine knew it as well as she.

CHAPTER THIRTEEN

"A Life in Duplicate"

THE SUMMER of 1925 took on for Dorothy and Alan a much more colorful hue in July than would have seemed possible when it began. In June, the show had practically failed, and *The Trap* had seemed destined for the same fate. But the months that followed were a distracting "whirl of social life" that reached a high point during August, when Dorothy and Alan were visiting at Wells's home in north Essex.

For fifteen years Wells had been living with Jane and their two boys at Easton Glebe in the village of Little Easton near Great Dunmow. Their house, originally the Little Easton rectory, stood at the edge of the vast park belonging to Lady Warwick of Easton Lodge. Wells had not only renamed the rectory but also greatly refurbished it. He had turned the ancient barn, for example, into a ballroom with parquet floors and a pianola; and to fully satisfy his taste for the incongruous, he had added a ping-pong table as well. He used Easton Glebe, moreover, in his novel *Mr. Britling Sees It Through* (1917) as the model for his patriotic hero's Dower House; and he put into the mouth of an American visitor sharp criticism of renovations similar to his own:

> "There's one thing I would like to remark about your barn, Mr. Britling, and I might, while I am at it, say the same thing about your farmyard. . . . the point that strikes me most about all this is that that barn isn't a barn any longer, and that farmyard isn't a farmyard. There isn't any wheat or chaff or anything of that sort in the barn, and there never will be again: there's just a pianola and a dancing floor, and if a cow came into this farmyard everybody in the place would be shooing it out again. They'd regard it as a most unnatural object. . . ."

Despite the touch of self-ridicule, Wells took immense personal delight (as Britling did in his Dower House) in the sweeping grounds of Easton Glebe, in the various walks and spacious gardens, in the tall blue cedars overhanging the great lawn, and in the square red-brick Georgian house itself. He liked Essex, too. In no time at all, his rather rotund figure had become familiar in the villages surrounding Little Easton. Nearly fifty years later, a resident of Saffron Waldon would remember Wells "struggling and sweating for twenty minutes to make his old car work when it broke down in the main street at Thaxted, and when a country boy stepped forward and got it going in a few seconds, H. G. W. tipped him and roared with laughter."

By 1924, Wells found himself experiencing one of his all too familiar "fugitive impulses," the urge to "get clear," to "get away . . . and think and then begin again." He had tried to satisfy his desire for renewal with the creation of Easton Glebe, but it was only a partial success from the start. In 1911, the year after he moved in, Wells had published *The New Macchiavelli,* the story of Richard Remington, who leaves his wife and goes off to Italy with the other woman he loves, to "write in lofty tranquility of politics in the abstract" as he himself wanted to do. By this means, in the person of Remington, Wells had "relieved [his] tension vicariously." But in 1924 another Remington would not do, and Wells began to lead—as he later put it—"a life in duplicate." At Easton Glebe he conducted his correspondence and dealt with his business. At a *mas* or farmhouse called Lou Bastidon, situated near Grasse in the Maritime Alps, Wells cut himself off in fact (as Remington had in fiction) from the "daily urgencies of England" and began to "sift [his] thoughts and purposes in peace." He was not alone. The journalist Odette Keun, who had sought him out just when he needed the excitement she was ready to provide, was living in the farmhouse with him. Here he began to write another novel in the autobiographical form of *The New Macchiavelli,* but instead of wishing himself into the new character as he had into Remington, Wells "dramatized" himself as William Clissold, who is also "in retreat," surveying the world from his farmhouse near Grasse. Such was the general state of his life when Dorothy and Alan Odle went to Easton Glebe to spend the month of August in 1925.

2

During their stay Wells shuttled back and forth between Essex and Grasse. Whether he was there or not, Jane filled the house with weekend guests who often stayed until Tuesday morning. During the week people from "round about" came in for tennis and tea. "Its all revue," Dorothy wrote to Bryher, "continuous performance, in an ideal setting; all doors & windows opening on to sudden drama; several James novels at once, musical comedy thrown in, & for everything a . . . beautifully inclusive cast." There was "the County," she went on to describe, "the lesser gentry (still Whig though moribund Whig), Industry, wearing the scars of battle, rampant communism posed for the final barricade, the stage (Basil Dean & Coward who looks much more like Beresford than like himself), the film (hopefully experimenting in a studio hidden in Buckinghamshire), the law (a barrister who caricatures himself & has a sound theory of aesthetics & plays Bach like an angel) & washing all round & in & out the amazing New Independent Labour Party staying at Lady Warwick's & apparently consisting of seceded aristocrats."

"You think we missed Bank Holiday?" Dorothy continued with glee. "It began here on Saturday." All that day they had watched caravans and traction engines wind by, and the results on Monday had been a flower show and an amusement park with shooting galleries, roundabouts, sports, scarecrows, and all kinds of sideshows, including "Terrors of the Jungle," such as limp snakes in a pit, charmed by a spangled lady who talked broken English to them with a strong cockney accent. They all got drunk on ginger beer, Dorothy said, and had a thoroughly good time.

In spite of the hectic atmosphere, which Dorothy obviously relished, she managed to mix some hard work with the profuse play that went on at Easton Glebe. Jane provided her with "an indoor and outdoor study locked & inviolable & solitary"; it was "like working in heaven," she said. What Alan, in turn, was doing, one can only guess. There must have been a table somewhere in Easton Glebe at which he could draw if he wished. It is more likely that he spent his time gathering the material for drawings, storing up satiric scenes as he sat on the lawn in his stout, laced boots, his long legs floppily crossed in their wide, loose trousers. With the invariable cigarette between his long, darkened fingers and the brim of his battered trilby hat pulled down to shade his eyes, he would have looked inscrutable.

What the Wellses made of Alan, they never said. (Alan himself was greatly impressed by the whiskey and soda always at the bedside of their guests.) H. G. seemed interested in Alan's work and even began to speak of himself as a kind of "patron." He bought another of Alan's drawings and maintained that beside it everything else he owned looked feeble. The wild hope entered Dorothy's mind that H. G. would take care of Alan. He was being so kind and encouraging that all her fondness for him, and her belief in his great powers, returned. When she and Alan spoke of going back to London, "H. G.'s persuasive voice" bid them stay, and they stayed. It was like the visits of old, when she had gone to Surrey and then to Kent on a Saturday afternoon, and on Sunday evenings had found herself giving in to Wells's voice urging her to spend another night, to miss the morning's work at Harley Street. Here again was H. G. talking about her situation, her writing, her prospects. Duckworth, he said, was not enterprising enough as a publisher. Of late he had advertised *Pilgrimage* less than ever. Her books would fare much better, he felt sure, if they were handled by someone else. He would look into the matter and let her know.

These were soothing words to Dorothy's ear, and she took them seriously. When the Odles did at last return to London, Dorothy felt buoyant and almost carefree. This buoyancy, which remained through September and even into October, helped to make her first meeting with D. H. Lawrence and his wife a joy. She and Alan spent an evening and a long afternoon with them in Hampstead, which Dorothy duly described to Owen Wadsworth, who revered Lawrence as a god. A few months later, however, when the glow of a good summer had faded, Dorothy commented, again to Owen, that she was glad Lawrence thought of *The Rainbow* as his best book, because "There's an insolence in all the later ones that gets wearisome."

3

Back in Harlyn when she wrote this about Lawrence, Dorothy claimed she was "ostriching, ignoring rocks ahead & concentrating . . . on *Oberland*." It was clear that several kinds of trouble loomed. One was the problem of publishing the finished book. Out of Wells's immediate range, she doubted that anything would come of his plan to find her a new publisher. Yet she agreed with him about Duckworth, who wrote her "affectionate" letters, she said, but offered no money worth speaking of—or even the prospect of any. Another grim certainty was the impending death of Sidney

Odle, who she thought could not last the winter (though he did). Finally, trouble was brewing at the London home of Veronica and Benjamin Grad, and Dorothy knew it would involve her deeply.

By January 1926 she had come close to finishing *Oberland*. Part of it still had to be written and a good deal of typing remained to be done, but she felt confident that the book could be published in time for the 1926–27 winter season—that is, if it had a publisher. Wells had come up with nothing. She began to think the sensible course was to reason with Duckworth, but she seemed unable to act, perhaps immobilized by the suspense of waiting for the Grad household to erupt.

Early in April a frantic Veronica reported that Benjamin had disappeared and that she did not know how to reach their seventeen-year-old son David, who was not at home. Apparently she wanted Dorothy to broadcast for David, but this course of action was permitted only in a case of mortal illness. Dorothy tried to calm Veronica from Cornwall, but she had little success. She herself felt "tied up in knots." She felt liable for the Grad family as something she had created, and both Veronica and Benjamin (whom she persisted in calling Michael) seem to have felt the same way. Veronica always turned to Dorothy when she was in trouble, and though Benjamin did not communicate with Dorothy before he left home, he would write to her first (two years hence) when he was ready to return. But now Dorothy had Veronica to cope with. It was one thing to exchange letters with her and quite another to confront her in person. Dorothy tried to postpone this meeting with the distraught Veronica for as long as possible, by insisting on her need for two months of quiet—and safety—in her spring refuge at Trevone Cottage.

Dorothy and Alan moved from Harlyn at the end of April, carrying with them their winter's work: the nearly completed *Oberland* manuscript and a fat pile of Rabelaisian drawings. For several weeks, despite the ominous general strike in May and the threat of a coal shortage in Cornwall, things went reasonably well. Dorothy finished the novel, "wedged in," she said, "between the hyacinths and the fireplace." Then, without fully understanding why, she felt a sense of utter despair. The only explanation she could offer had to do with *Oberland*. She knew the novel was "alive," but she feared it wanted a few more "coats" of color—for which she used the French word *couches*, a word whose primary meanings and associations suggest a very different world: the world of marriage, of child-bed, of swaddling clothes. Indeed, it suggested a world in which she had long been closely related to the Grads. It would seem that the refuge in Trevone was not impermeable and that, despite her wish to maintain her distance from Veronica, their ties were too deep and too complicated to be set aside even temporarily.

Nevertheless, she set to work revising the novel, and when her typescript became unreadable in the process, she decided to wait until they got back to London, where she could have a new typescript made. She felt there was no hurry now. She had no publisher except Duckworth, and he seemed in no mood to stir himself for another Miriam novel. Dorothy herself was curiously languid about publication. She seemed glad that *Oberland* was not to be flung to the reviewers at once. More than likely, though, she was anticipating with alarm the prospect of at last confronting Veronica face to face.

As Dorothy and Alan prepared to return, even London itself assumed a fearful shape. They did not know what the city would be like after its nine-day siege; and to add to their concern, they learned that the tenant of their rooms in Queen's Terrace had decamped, leaving the rent unpaid, and had taken with him the house linen at the least. What else he might have taken, they had no idea. As a matter of fact, they had given him money for materials to decorate the rooms, a project he himself had put forward as mutually beneficial, and they did not know at what stage of the work he had gone off.

They made the annual trip to London, then, with good cause for trepidation. Upon their arrival, the city looked roughly the same to them, and at Queen's Terrace they found their belongings safe. No books or drawings had been taken, and the rooms had actually been redecorated. To their great surprise, the landlords (the Eyre Estate) agreed to reimburse them for nearly the entire redecoration cost.

The rooms themselves, as well as the landlords, now became a subject of endless discussion with Veronica. With her husband gone, she wanted to give up her home and store some of her furniture, for the time being, in Dorothy's rooms. Dorothy weighed the idea carefully, as though it had a metaphysical significance, but really as a way of calming Veronica. She went through the various possibilities of Veronica's plan meticulously. Their furnished studio-bedroom in Queen's Terrace contained—among other things—"chairs no one [could] sit on and live," yet they paid a higher rent for furnishings such as these. What a boon it would be to pay rent instead for bare rooms, and then be able to ask a higher price of the winter tenant for the use of Veronica's better furnishings. The important question was whether the landlords would agree to a lower rent. Nearly anyone but Dorothy would have known the answer, and at another time and in less trying circumstances, she too might have known it.

Although nothing came of the idea, Veronica was occupying a prominent place in Dorothy's current life just when she had reached, with the novel that would follow *Oberland,* the time of their first meeting in the past. In her fictional form, Veronica's name would be Amabel, she would be given French nationality, but her personal importance would be unchanged. Her place in the novel can be gauged by the title Dorothy first gave it—"Amabel"—a title she kept for some time. The book would finally appear as *Dawn's Left Hand,* however, and would contain the equally prominent figure of Hypo Wilson. Strangely enough, after her unexpectedly dramatic involvement with Amabel's original, Dorothy and Alan received another invitation to visit Easton Glebe, as if for a last-minute review of Wilson's original.

4

When the Odles went again to Essex, exactly a year had passed since their last visit. This time Wells was at home during most of their fortnight's stay, entertaining his guests lavishly. The weekends were crowded, as they had been the year before, with all manner of people and events. One Sunday even brought a preview performance of *The Constant Nymph,* with Edna Best in the role she would play on both the London and the New York stage. Basil Dean, who had coauthored the dramatization of Margaret Kennedy's novel, was among Wells's guests at the performance. Dorothy had met him there the year before, and this time she picked up with great delight a number of theatrical tidbits in conversation with him.

But the day after the performance was even more fun. After everyone else departed at dawn, Dorothy, Alan, and the Wellses settled down, each to his own work, with "nothing in sight" except a visit from some local people for dinner at eight. By lunchtime Wells was restless, and since an empty afternoon bothered him, he proposed a visit after lunch to a few of the old churches in the neighborhood. Just as they were starting out, someone came in with an invitation to tea. They would return then at tea time.

Thunderous and gloomy weather marred the church-seeing, and when the sun broke through, Wells was determined to take advantage of it. They would keep on going, all the way to Bury St. Edmunds in Suffolk. They "did" Bury thoroughly, shopped, had "an excited trippers' tea," and raced home to find "starving and puzzled guests" waiting for them when they arrived back at 8:30. The servants, who had been left no message, were as mystified as the guests. *That,* Dorothy said, was H. G.; "but he more than made up" for the tardiness and unexplained absence during the rest of the evening. In fact, Dorothy had not a single critical word for H. G. during the whole visit.

Wells had not found her a publisher for *Oberland,* though he did make suggestions, the latest of which was Hodder and Stoughton. At the time of their visit, he was trying to get Dorothy a Civil List Pension. (It turned eventually into a Treasury Grant of £250, which, for some reason she never understood, she was not supposed to divulge to anyone.) So Dorothy praised Wells to Bryher as someone who was constantly besieged but was kind and charming in spite of his eminence. She was eager to have Bryher meet him. Though he would not have time for the evening party she had hoped to arrange in London, he promised to reserve the one free afternoon he would have when he returned from France in September. In reporting this to Bryher, Dorothy added cautiously that she hoped Wells would keep his promise, and she took care to imply that if he did not, it would only be because so many demands were made on his time. The meeting does not seem to have taken place.

Dorothy knew that Wells was planning to build himself a house in France, near the rather primitive one in which he had been living; but how much more than this she knew, she did not reveal. The novel Wells had written at Lou Bastidon, *The World of William Clissold,* had recently appeared, containing a fictional account of his relationship with Odette Keun. It was she, of course, with whom he would live in the new, more modern house—Lou Pidou—but Dorothy did not speak of this at all. She did not even record the offer of Lou Bastidon that Wells was supposed, according to one of his biographers, to have made to her, an offer "gratefully declined."

Wells's novel happens to be more interesting than anything else going on at the time. It is a curious fact that while Dorothy was engaged in drawing portraits of both herself and Wells that no one seemed to recognize, everyone assumed that Wells's heroes were all thinly veiled projections of himself. This proved to be more and more of an annoyance to Wells, who gave querulous warning in "a note before the title-page" of his new novel that Clissold was not to be confused with his author. "Naturally his point of view is like Mr. Wells'," he said. "That was to be expected. How can one imagine and invent the whole interior world of an uncongenial type?" Wells was tired, on the one hand, of the accusation that his novels were photographic reproductions of himself, and, on the other, of the charge that he was inconsistent because the opinions of his heroes varied "scandalously" from book to book. Would his readers do him the courtesy of accepting Clissold as "nothing but a novel," and if they found it impossible to do so, would they "please leave it alone"?

Wells's eight-page note was a mixture of bad temper, special pleading, and reasoned argument that touched on matters close to Dorothy Richardson's heart. Harassed by what he felt to be the voyeuristic way in which his novels were being read, Wells denied that Clissold was either an autobiography or a *roman à clef*. He took care to point out, for the benefit of those who would try to find it, that the *mas* in his novel was similar to one within a few miles of Grasse, but no one would ever find "the actual mas," "the precise rooms," or "the exact view." Wells claimed that they did not exist, just as Mr. Britling's Dower House did not exist, and that precisely the people who knew his home least were most certain that Dower House was an exact replica of Easton Glebe. In the same way, the less people knew him, the more sure they were that Britling was Wells. He heaped scorn on the "enthusiastic strangers" who wanted to see "the place where he [had] wept when he heard that his eldest son was killed."

But not all of his readers were so unsophisticated as that. They did not all believe that the lives of his heroes corresponded exactly, in every physical detail, to the life of Wells. Some of them might well have perceived—though perhaps not fully—the importance of Wells's own qualification in his mandate that Clissold was not to be confused with himself: "He is (to the best of his author's ability) his own self and not his author's. . . ." Truly, in this respect, Wells's ability was not great. He could not help projecting his fictional characters as variations of himself, and the variations are autobiographical. They fulfilled his wishes, expressed his anxieties, or—as Dorothy Richardson realized—satisfied his "impulse to confess." But Wells insisted that, because he did not consciously intend to write autobiography or novels with keys, he was not doing so, and no one had the right to find in his books what he himself did not know was there. At the same time, he argued incontrovertibly that "all novelists use actual experience in their work," and he then went on to speak as if no such experience could be used if it was not part of the writer's conscious awareness. Yes, he said, the novelist would "rearrange, sublimate, intensify"—but almost knowingly, as if the pages of his memory sketchbook could be turned at will and the material there recorded could be lifted out to serve his current need. Though he did not deny the role of the imagination, it seemed to exist for Wells as merely an adjunct of his all-controlling, never-sleeping mind.

Dorothy Richardson did not argue about autobiographical fiction. She wrote it with a fuller consciousness of what she was doing than Wells ever achieved, because she knew and accepted herself in a way he could not: as her own creation. Wells, unable to decide who he wanted to be, repudiating identity after identity, suffered from his "fugitive impulses." He built selves as well as houses and cast them (in his own words) "as a snake casts its skin." In sharp contrast to this prodigality, Dorothy Richardson prudently refined her image, creating a character who could stand on her fictional feet unsupported by the fact of her identity as Dorothy Richardson. Miriam's independence, in turn, allowed Hypo Wilson's, Michael Shatov's, and—in *Dawn's Left Hand,* which Dorothy worked on at Easton Glebe—Amabel's. Her readers did not engage in a search for originals, the kind of search that maddened Wells. Instead, the reviewers of *Pilgrimage* were preoccupied with the character of Miriam, and at least some of them recognized that a host of vivid portraits were being drawn for their own fictional sake. Granted, Wells was a world figure, and Dorothy Richardson was not. Yet he seemed to invite precisely the kind of attention he claimed to despise. How else did the fictional portrait of so world-famous a figure as the original of Hypo Wilson escape recognition?

As a matter of fact, the portrait in *Dawn's Left Hand* would not be flattering, even though in Essex Dorothy found herself again under the spell of his charm. She no longer felt dependent on him as she had in her youth; with her status now defined by Alan and by *Pilgrimage,* she could simply enjoy the richness of Wells's personality. But she had not for a moment lost the sense of the past or of her emotional entanglement with him. She was ready to plunge into a full-scale analysis of his limitations as a human being and to present, rather than "a life in duplicate," a man who lived outside himself.

CHAPTER FOURTEEN

A Matter of Identity

THE VISIT with the Wellses came to an abrupt end on a Saturday morning late in August. Dorothy awoke to find Alan in the midst of an attack of asthma, and she rushed him back to London. "Too much society, wrong food & the heavy Essex air," were to blame, she decided. The following morning he suffered another attack, but after a few days of quiet at Queen's Terrace he recovered his equilibrium.

Alan's alternations between apparent health and sudden breakdown were puzzling. Whatever their cause—whether the interruption of his accustomed routine or his fear that Dorothy's attention was being withdrawn—his illnesses usually disappeared once he was reestablished in a familiar setting under her watchful—and frightened—eye. During the rest of the summer of 1926, he seemed perfectly capable of social activity. They dined out, went to parties, and even entertained on a small scale in Queen's Terrace. But he was securely based at home, and Dorothy was always there.

They planned to leave London in October as usual. Until then, she tried to find a publisher for *Oberland,* her apathy toward it gone. Hodder and Stoughton had backed down after a show of interest. Then Wells had suggested Ernest Benn, whose firm had published *Clissold* and was bringing out the Essex edition of his works. Benn was thinking about *Oberland,* and Dorothy could not expect a decision for at least two months, so unless he took *Oberland,* it did not seem likely that the book would appear in time for the winter season. Under the circumstances Dorothy decided to publish a selection from *Oberland,* if she could. She thought she knew of a way to bring it about. In July she and Alan had accepted an invitation to meet and dine with Louise Morgan Theis, the journalist-wife of Otto Theis, who was the literary editor of *Outlook.* Now, early in September, Dorothy invited Mrs. Theis to tea at Queen's Terrace. Not

Dorothy Richardson and Alan Odle in the 1920s.

long afterward she sent two small excerpts from her novel to *Outlook* and wrote a letter to Mrs. Theis—whose admiration of her she had already confirmed—"just to say with all the emphasis of which words are incapable that I am Quite prepared to find both the scraps I have sent with due formality to the Outlook's Lit. Ed. considered by him as Quite unsuited to that paper, & will undertake not to feel crushed & spurned if they come back accompanied by the usual printed slip." As she had probably gauged, there was to be no rejection. Theis agreed to print one of the selections, but he said he would "cut it down a bit." The December issue of *Outlook* would carry a few pages from *Oberland*—a description of Miriam's arrival at her mountain hotel—to which Dorothy had given the title "Sleigh Ride."

Getting "Sleigh Ride" into *Outlook* was only a small success, yet it made Dorothy feel a little less at the mercy of the publishing world. But when they arrived in Cornwall, all the frustrations of life seemed to have come with them and to have settled in for the winter. First of all, they traveled down with the news that Sidney Odle had died on October 5. Second, they came to a new cottage, which struck Dorothy at once as an unmitigated disaster. It was only a short distance from the old one on the winding Harlyn road that led to the lighthouse at Trevose Head. In Cozy Corner they had been nearly on the road itself. The new cottage, Meadowcot, stood at the end of a lane leading down from the road, with a splendid view of both Harlyn and Trevone Bays as well as of the wide sea beyond them. Dorothy had thought it would be more "convenient & commodious" than the smaller Cozy Corner and, because of its wooden frame, more peaceful than the corrugated iron bungalow. She was quite right about that; she had not misjudged the advantages of Meadowcot. But when they moved in, she found it icy cold. There seemed no spot in the house where she could feel warm and dry. The place "*leaks* air all over," she complained; it was "all draught, like sitting in water up to your knees."

She did not know what to do. If she moved about all day, wearing two pairs of stockings, boots, and knickers, it might be bearable. But to sit, even wrapped up, and try to concentrate was to feel "the stealing airs from below." Alan seemed not to mind, although he did admit that Meadowcot was "less warm" than Cozy Corner. Dorothy, who set down his indifference to his "first-class circulation," feared she herself would not be able to write a line in such a place. But to look for another house and make yet another move would be to waste precious time. She would try to endure it—that is, if Alan remained well. After a few weeks, with Alan still all right, Dorothy decided that the kitchen was the most tolerable room in Meadowcot. She established herself there, and she put Alan in the least drafty part of the sitting room, where he worked contentedly; but she "pine[d] for [the] weather-beaten rain dripping shanty with its noisy *warm* iron jacket." As far as she was concerned, they could never stay in Meadowcot again. Neither its size nor its view could compensate for the dampness that almost visibly seeped into both the house and her.

The rooms in Meadowcot were too large for Dorothy to clean without help. Fortunately, a woman who lived nearby, Mrs. Stanley Bennett, agreed to come in once a week. The arrangement turned out to be such a satisfactory one that Mrs. Bennett continued to work for Dorothy until 1939. In her thirteen years of service, Mrs. Bennett gathered a good deal of food for thought about the "lady and gentleman" who came down to Cornwall every winter and roamed about together, always in the direction other people did not take and often looking for wild parsley and sea spinach. She thought at first that they were both writers, surrounded as they seemed to be by books and papers, pencils and pens. Then one day Mr. Odle showed her some drawings he had done. They were filled with "horrible faces," and she tried not to show her distaste. "I wonder where you got them from," she murmured. He gazed down at her from his great height and said in his kind, cultivated voice, "Mrs. Bennett, I look in the glass every morning, and there they are." What could she say to that? With a quick nod of her head, she went on cleaning—and wondering. He was such a nice gentleman. And the "missus" never forgot her or her three children at Christmas. But she would have liked to know why they spent their winters in Cornwall when everybody else who did not belong to the West country came down for summer holidays. Mrs. Bennett might have wondered aloud (she would never have asked), for one afternoon Mrs. Odle explained to her that the reason they came to Cornwall was that a relative from America rented their London house every winter.

2

The matter of identity had become a pressing one indeed. The fantastic explanation she gave to Mrs. Bennett may have had its immediate source in one of the articles, "The Passing of England's Stately Homes," she was then trying to write for *Vanity Fair*. The titles of the others testify, as well, to similar and related currents in her mind at a time when she felt more and more thwarted by the world. "The Siege of Society" was one, "Egoism in Men and Women" was another. She planned also to write an essay "On Putting Woman in Her Place," and still another entitled "Are Women Running the Novel?" None of these ever appeared.

What did appear was an essay, written by someone else, which briefly raised Dorothy's hopes that life would take a turn for the better. From Owen Wadsworth, who had gone to America again, she learned that a substantial article about women writers—Virginia Woolf, Katherine Mansfield, and Dorothy Richardson—had appeared in the *Atlantic Monthly* of September 1926. The article had praised *Pilgrimage* highly, and Dorothy thought she could somehow use the essay to find a publisher for *Oberland*. It even occurred to her that Knopf might be roused by it to "fresh efforts," to advertising *Pilgrimage* and reissuing the volumes out of print in America. She admitted, of course, that it was unlikely Knopf would see the article, and apparently she did not have the courage to send it to him herself. Yet she seemed to believe that if he were somehow to see it, he would certainly be moved to act. Here was willful if not desperate naïveté.

In no time at all, anger was expressed as well, both directly and obliquely. As Dorothy saw it, her negotiations with a publisher had become a "circular wrangle," with nothing but "impasses" created by "despotic efficiency." Ernest Benn had decided against publishing *Oberland*. Hutchinson, in turn, spent two months thinking about it, and only then asked to look at *Oberland*. "Meanwhile," Dorothy snapped, her novel was "eating its head off." Other writers had their own problems, she knew, and she felt sorry for them. Joyce, for example, seemed helpless in the face of a blatant act of piracy. *Ulysses,* unprotected by copyright in the United States, was being published in Samuel Roth's magazine *Two Worlds Monthly* without payment to the author. Dorothy learned of this from Bryher, who also informed her that even though legal action had been started against Roth, an international protest had been drawn up as well. Copies of it were being sent all over the world for signatures. One copy reached Dorothy late in December. She reported its safe arrival to Bryher and expressed her rage at the unscrupulous Roth. Joyce's situation struck her as being indeed pitiable, but though she did not say so, she thought her own deserved quite as much pity as his.

In the same letter to Bryher, as if a further connection might have formed in the recesses of her mind, she proceeded to describe in detail how everyone in the parish was killing pigs just then. Two of the "executions" had taken place only a few yards from the windows of Meadowcot. One of them had gone on while the Odles were eating their breakfast with their curtains closely drawn. The other Dorothy seems to have witnessed, even though she had been duly warned. The family involved had risen at five to try to get the worst over before the Odles were up, but the crackling of the huge bonfire had wakened them. Through their open casements they could see the debristling, still done in 1926 by a man with a small knife who was helped by another who went to and fro with red-hot twigs. The operation took hours. Finally the carcass, drawn up on pulleys, hung from a kind of gibbet. Next the woman of the family set to work, slowly and carefully removing the "choice internal bits." Not until the end of the day could the "sawing up & carving" be done, and the wife spent the next two days indoors, preparing a winter's food for her family. Dorothy was invited into the kitchen to see the great barrel of salted pork. Her neighbor, who had warned her of the slaughter beforehand with tears in her eyes, now patted the top layer of the barrel affectionately: " 'There's my piggie' she chirped." The whole affair fascinated Dorothy. It was "horrible piteous au*gust*," she wrote, and she thought the men and women who engaged in it both hated and loved it. Apparently the slaughter had taken on some obscure significance that she could not express except in its own graphic terms.

3

The new year brought with it a "north-east wind, bitter bleak & black, & a thick gray snow-filled sky." Nevertheless, Dorothy's fluctuating spirits began to lift. Hutchinson was talking about making Duckworth an offer, presumably for all of *Pilgrimage*. Bryher was planning to publish—with Kenneth Macpherson, the man who would be her second husband—a monthly film magazine to which she hoped Dorothy would contribute regularly. And, *mirabile dictu,* Alan had been informed that once his brother Sidney's affairs were settled and duties paid, each of his surviving relatives could expect to receive about £100. Dorothy estimated that the sum would be enough to "boil his side of the pot for eighteen months." When the legacy came, Alan was jubilant. He wanted to post it immediately to the bank, but he would not trust the local substation or even the ordinary post. He insisted on having the envelope registered and took it himself to the post office at St. Merryn. Dorothy calculated that, if *Vanity Fair* took all the articles she planned and if European credit did not collapse, she and Alan would have not only enough to live on through this year, but a little left over for 1928 as well. That would mean "serenity," she said, which, according to Rebecca West, was "part of a writer's stock-in-trade."

Nothing seemed to have disturbed the prospect of serenity by the time they left Meadowcot for their annual spring stay in Trevone Cottage. They felt they could afford to romp, to spend entire days in all their "old excursions." They would leave immediately after breakfast, taking with them a packed lunch, and would not return until the sun was dipping into Trevone Bay. Yet as beautiful as the sea and coast of Cornwall were, Dorothy could not help yearning sometimes for the Weymouth she had known as a child on visits to her Taylor grandmother. She would have liked to be there again, on the Dorset coast, "with lodgings on the *Front*, a deck chair not too near the bandstand, waltzes sounding out across the sparkling sea ... [and] English people all about, of the kind with one type of consciousness." During the last few years the summer visitors to Padstow and the bays had become more and more "sophisticated" and "literate"—what Dorothy described as the "Golder's Green variety." This spring, moreover, "the whole neighbourhood [had] its nose in the air." The Prince of Wales was coming for a brief stay at the Metropole in Padstow.

In the same vein, harping on her dislike for certain kinds of sophistication and society, Dorothy began to demur about writing for Bryher's film magazine. She could not see herself contributing, she said, with her penchant for Wild West drama and simple senti- ment. "Now Alan," she went on, had "*Ideas*." Nonetheless she would look up some notes she had "somewhere" or other. By the beginning of June, with Bryher's encouragement, she had come around fully, but she claimed not even the "smallest thing" could be ready in time for the first issue. There would be no chance at all to prepare it, with the pending trip to London on the eighth and "getting straight" at Queen's Terrace. When *Close Up* appeared in July, however, published in Switzerland at Bryher's Riant Château in Territet, it did contain a contribution from Dorothy.

The title of her piece, "Continuous Performance," was to become the covering title for a series of twenty-one essays, published between 1927 and 1933, as long as *Close Up* lasted. The essays ranged in subject matter from the civilizing value of the new medium to the architecture of movie houses and the demerits of "talkies." In them Dorothy sometimes took issue with Robert Herring, the periodical's London correspondent, about voices in films, or with Wells, who predicted that the "art form of the future" would excel the written word if not doom it. Most of the time she argued for the cinema as an unlimited means of enlarging the personal, social, and aesthetic consciousness of those who attended—from the tired housewives and middle-aged men to the children sitting in the front rows shrieking at the sight of danger on the screen. This was the kind of response, she said, spontaneous and genuine, that Chaplin listened for when he was testing a film. She watched her fellow moviegoers carefully, and she reported that over a period of time one could see them grow "in critical grace." They no longer became "dizzy and breathless" at dramas whose stock characters had become familiar to them, and they could "predict developments." Not even a new situation disturbed them very much: they paid careful attention, refused to be puzzled, and watched for the working out. Nor did she see them bored by good films above their heads; it was the bad films that made them fidget, giggle, yawn, wail, and gnash their teeth. Dorothy believed quite firmly in the capacity of the ordinary filmgoer to distinguish between the spurious and the genuine.

She also felt that the cinema made for social growth, by admitting the people of towns to "a generalized social life, a thing unknown in slum and tenement, in lodging-house and the smaller and poorer villadom." It extended their "cramped consciousness," led them to live "new lives" and to grow—but from illustrations rather than sermons, illustrations "encountered innocently, unguardedly, in silence and alone." As for rural areas such as Padstow, Dorothy said that a year of the "pictures" had wrought observable changes, especially among the younger generation. They were "in communication with the unknown"; they were becoming "world-citizens"; and she felt that in time they would be able to participate in "the world-wide conversations now increasingly upon us."

209

It is not surprising that the author of *Pointed Roofs* and *Oberland* should have taken to the film medium so enthusiastically and with such high hopes for it. The final scene of her very first novel, in which Miriam stands at the window of her departing train and watches the platform of the Hanover station go by, anticipated the "camera-eye." In 1924, when Dorothy had been attending the local picture shows near Queen's Terrace for at least three years, she gave Hemingway a sketch for the *transatlantic review* which showed how sensitive she was to the new art form. The photographic effect of "The Garden," the moving picture of consciousness, and the use of synesthesia to convey the child's relationship with things about her all suggest that for Dorothy Richardson the cinema was not merely a means of entertainment. In *Oberland,* the novel written after the small sketch, Dorothy revealed how well by then she understood the techniques of the cinema. *Oberland,* her most pictorial fiction, was almost pure illustration of the theoretical text she would publish later in *Close Up.*

In the essays devoted to the film, she was once more concerned with the achievement of a state of relation (as she had been twenty years before, in her early reviews and sketches). It seemed to her that in the cinema an onlooker could become an artist by collaborating with what he saw and discovering his own "creative consciousness." When an audience forgot itself as audience and fully participated in the film, a living and real work of art came into being. In her opinion, such a result could best be obtained with but a single accompaniment to soundless film and audience: music. She preferred a piano played by someone capable of improvising "connective tissue" for "varying themes." Music of any kind, however, was essential to her, for without it she felt there was neither light nor color. Indeed, she claimed to remember an accompanied film as in color (even though films at that time were only in black and white) and one lacking in music as without color. The piano, she maintained, would not be an "alien element of sound," as some people seemed to feel, if it were blended with the performance and just as continuous.

In many ways she had made of *Oberland* a moving picture in words, with the harmony, color, and continuity she wanted in a film. Miriam's fortnight among the "fresh vistas" of the Alps is the material of the novel. But its technique is cinematic. The mountains are approached in the first chapter and they recede in the last, as if a camera had been brought into focus and then withdrawn, always in a flowing and even movement. The ideal of "continuous performance" is achieved. So closely do the chapters follow one another in mood and time that the words beginning the third link with those ending the second. Miriam falls into "the uttermost depths of sleep" at the close of chapter two, which is the end of her first evening in *Oberland*, "From which she awoke in light" to open chapter three, beginning her first full day in the land of the Alps.

The illusion created is of an uninterrupted state of consciousness, set into motion when she comes within sight of the mountains. Her first view of them is of "a picture sliding away, soundlessly, hopelessly demanding its perfect word." She finds that perfect word, after a half-day climb to the Alpenstock Hotel, in the language of music. To her rooms comes the voice of a piano from somewhere unknown. It speaks the Chopin Ballade that Miriam had not heard since the time of Hanover and "pointed roofs," and it plays again in just the same way, "slipping it into the stillness." The effect of the music is to carry Miriam smoothly back in her mind through merging scene after scene until she feels herself to be everywhere in Hanover at once—in the *saal,* the garden, the summerhouse, and beyond the walls in the light along the wide streets. But she never loses the sense of being in Switzerland at the same time. The night and the snow around her blend with the image of a dark *saal* and the gleaming white dress of one of the girls. The pictures, suggesting to Miriam that some part of her had lived "continuously" there in Germany all these years, have been set into motion and fused into a whole by the musical accompaniment.

Oberland is linked to the film essays in still another way. Dorothy said in *Close Up* that "actual drama moves silently, speech noting its movement." She thought pantomime was the primary character of a film, and in her film-novel she made the dramatic moments speechless. Her heroine must speak in order to note movement, but the drama that Miriam watches—involving a precocious child named Daphne and a rather stolid man named Eaden—is essentially a pantomime, a dumb show from which she tries to remain aloof, wanting to keep her vision of Switzerland clear of human feeling. But Dorothy does not allow Miriam to succeed at this, and her decision serves to link the novel with the time of its composition.

She had been writing the end of *Oberland* in Cornwall when word of the crisis in the Grad household reached her. Veronica had immediately wanted all of Dorothy's attention, whereas Dorothy wanted to finish her book. This would not have been the first time Dorothy was accused of caring for no one, of putting her books before everything and everyone, and of treating people as though they were nothing but material for fiction. Indeed, Dorothy wove both Veronica and her accusations into the story of the precocious, tyrannic little girl of *Oberland* who makes Miriam feel small and selfish. The child loves, as Veronica does, in a single-minded and appropriative way. The object of her love is not Miriam, however, but a prosperous and overworking landowner on a brief and reluctant holiday, who comes to realize his moral responsibility to the child for her love. He realizes it most fully when Daphne, to prevent his scheduled departure, cuts her finger with a razor. Miriam herself becomes involved by failing to help the child reach him to say goodbye when he finally does leave. Daphne had been detained by a broken toboggan cord, and Miriam unthinkingly had come down the run without her. Even the landowner reproaches her for this. The child, who arrives just a few moments too late, turns her "wrath-blazing eyes" on Miriam and sees that she knows the "simple selfish truth" about herself.

The story of Daphne is emotionally autobiographical. At a time when Dorothy felt both pressed by and responsible for Veronica, she sought relief in working out this drama of a strange and unequal love. It was a triumph of art over life. Veronica's disguise in *Oberland* is virtually complete, and Dorothy could give herself up freely to her characterization as Daphne. But in the novel she would write next, the one originally entitled "Amabel" and finally turned into *Dawn's Left Hand*, Veronica's identity as Amabel would be all too clear. Worthy of note (perhaps in part because of this), Dorothy would have great difficulty: she was to spend more than five years writing *Dawn's Left Hand*.

4

During the summer of 1927, Dorothy could not focus on the new novel. She thought about it, spoke of it, and worked at it sporadically; but she seemed at heart unwilling to write it. She occupied herself with *Oberland* instead, the still unpublished book that no one seemed to want. Dorothy had decided, even before arriving in London again, that Duckworth would have to bring it out after all; she could wait no longer. After an entire year, only three other publishers had been approached, and all of them had refused to take the risk. She began to wonder whether Duckworth would now close *his* door. With trepidation she went to his office to meet with him in person for the first time in all the years he had been her publisher, and to her great relief she found him willing to take her back and to publish *Oberland* in October. In addition, he promised to "release" her if an enterprising firm should wish to tackle *Pilgrimage*. For all of this she was grateful. But Duckworth would offer no more than £10 for *Oberland,* and Dorothy said she had to agree, for the book had to come out.

At the last minute, Duckworth had a change of heart and offered her half-royalties (71/2 percent) instead of the flat sum. He also did his best to advertise the novel, and Dorothy tried to play her own small part. Convinced that the book would sell if it were displayed at the winter sports centers, she mailed copies to the pension in Château d'Oex where they had stayed, for its circulating library, and to the Swiss literary papers. To the English Library at Montreux she sent a marked Duckworth catalog, and Bryher agreed to ask the Montreux bookseller if he would display the book during the season. Alan's painter-friend Adrian Allinson took a copy of the book with him on a holiday to Mürren with instructions to "dangle it about." Then Dorothy waited for results.

The first reports of the sales were not encouraging. By late December there had also been very few reviews, which Dorothy described as mostly "vitriol" anyway. Then Duckworth told her that Knopf was taking 500 sewn sheets for an American edition and was paying her a royalty of 10 percent. This was the first bit of heartening news she had had. The American *Oberland* came out in March, and the American reviews followed. On December 11, both the *Herald Tribune* and the *Times* paid considerable attention to the book. On the basis of the *Tribune* review, written by G. B. Stern, Dorothy concluded that "you can't beat feminine cruelty to women." Miss Stern, who clearly preferred Katherine Mansfield and Proust to Dorothy Richardson, argued that psychology—or "descriptions of a state of mind"—do not belong in a "saga," which was what she labeled *Pilgrimage*. Proust's novel was an exception, she claimed; one did not "tire" of it. But Dorothy

213

Richardson, she wrote, "solemnly and reverently peeled [an incident] to its coreless conclusion, like a psychological onion." This, Dorothy felt bound to admit, was "brilliant vitriol."

In contrast, the *New York Times* was "ecstatic" about *Oberland,* in one of the most admiring reviews she had ever received. It was gratifying indeed to read that *Oberland* was "like a Whistler drawing" and that for anyone with an experience of Switzerland, or for that matter any of the northern mountains in winter, the book would be "a perpetual joy." This was just what she had hoped would be said. But her gratification was mixed. Though the *Times* reviewer felt that readers who discovered Dorothy Richardson with *Oberland* were very fortunate, his newspaper printed a photograph not of Dorothy but of the American writer with the same name.

It was not easy to dismiss such an error with a philosophical shrug of the shoulder, and Dorothy scarcely tried. "I admit that it hurts me," she wrote to a surprised and puzzled Owen Wadsworth, who wanted to know how someone he had never seen before had become Dorothy Richardson. "I don't mind being represented elderly," she went on, having reached, after all, the age of fifty-five, "but I do very much mind being woe-begone & thin-lipped & 'brainless' & '*refeened.*'" Moreover, whether to be fifty-five was to be elderly or not, her own hair had no grey in it, she carefully pointed out. What bothered her most was not so much the nature of the identity foisted upon her as the negative climax to all the years she had vested in the creation of a fictional self who now seemed to possess a greater reality than her own—and who called down upon her a patchwork variety of abuse.

Part Three
1928-38

.

CHAPTER FIFTEEN

"The Shock of July"

THE winter that was just ending when Dorothy saw the American reviews of *Oberland* had begun with news of the death of Jane Wells. Her "disappearance," Dorothy said, mattered greatly, and would always matter, even though they had shared almost nothing. Yet, as Amy Robbins, Jane had belonged to Dorothy's idyllic Putney girlhood, and her death in middle age brought home sharply to her school friend an awareness of her own time of life. Thus the photographic error in the *Times* a few months later would serve to irritate an already existent wound.

Jane's death made it even more difficult for Dorothy to work at her novel that winter. She was one of the characters in it, and Dorothy could not bring herself to re-create the Jane of twenty years before when no Jane at all existed. In time she would succeed in regaining her image of that earlier Jane and in projecting it as the fictional Alma, the bright yet always shadowy figure of Wells's wife. For the moment, however, the new novel seemed an enormous problem that it was best not to touch.

The Odles spent that winter in a new, *dry* Cornish bungalow in Constantine Bay, not very far from Harlyn, but quite different nevertheless. The bungalow (named Lynx) had been built recently by Mrs. Dawson-Scott, the novelist, whom Dorothy had known for some years (and who had founded the P.E.N. Club in 1921). Lynx too stood in the midst of tall spire-grass and hummocky dunes, but it was "in the sun's eye," and its dryness alone compensated for the loss of Harlyn's open sea and headlands.

One can follow the turns of Dorothy's mind during that winter by noting what she said she wanted to do and what she actually did. At Lynx she thought of writing a series of twelve articles about the six winter months she had spent alone, as the guest of Jack and Beatrice Beresford, in the "haunted" cottage they had rented in

Cornwall, where she had written *Pointed Roofs*. There is no sign that she even began to work on this, but the idea suggests the direction her mind was taking, a direction borne out by the piece she did write, "Journey to Paradise," which was published in the *Fortnightly Review* of March 1928. The unwritten articles reflect a wish to go back in time to a period filled with promise, to the period of the launching of *Pilgrimage*. In a rather trying present, she wanted to fix a happy moment of a hopeful past. In the essay for the *Fortnightly Review* she went even further back—to the journeys she had made as a child to Dawlish, where no other father but hers took his fortunate family. Her thoughts had turned, then, from her novelistic pilgrimage, whose originality had seemed to pall of late, to the trips to Devon, a still earlier example of uniqueness. *There* was a paradise that had not been tarnished. And *there* was a child with an unlimited future before her, rather than a middle-aged novelist who felt abused by life and tapped on the shoulder by time.

1

Two months after the reviews of *Oberland* had appeared in the *Tribune* and the *Times,* the *New York Post* carried a review that was also an estimate of *Pilgrimage*. It was written by the young American poet Conrad Aiken, who suggested that *Pilgrimage* would earn for Dorothy Richardson "as precise and permanent a place in the history of literature as it is ever possible to predict for a living author." Yet, he went on to say, she was "curiously little known," and he offered as the most likely reason he could think of the exclusive presence in her novels of the mind of a woman.

Aiken had no objection to a feminine point of view per se, but he did have reservations about Miriam—and by induction about Dorothy Richardson, too. It seemed to him that "one of the curious features of her portrait of Miriam Henderson [was] her insistence on the superiority of her heroine's mind—on its . . . richness and power and depth, as compared (frequently) with the minds of the men whom she meets." Aiken thought there was "something a little pinched and sour and old-maidish in this" and that, moreoever, Miriam's attitude might be Dorothy Richardson's as well. He felt sure that it was "a feminist attitude," but one which, "rightly or wrongly, the mere male feels to be the natural withering of the spinster." Indeed, he thought "the air of challenge" marking the

The converted chapel in Trehemborne, St. Merryn, Cornwall, where *Pointed Roofs* was written. Dorothy Richardson is standing just outside the gate; inside the courtyard are a maid and Mr. and Mrs. J. D. Beresford.

behavior of such a woman was "dictated by a sense of inferiority," and that it produced "a kind of dry intellectual hypertrophy, an intellectualism which is curiously thin and bloodless." Aiken found this quality "annoyingly" present in Miriam Henderson.

If Dorothy Richardson had "detachedly projected" this quality, then her "skill in creation" deserved high praise. But Aiken felt a "sneaking suspicion" that Miriam's character lay "pretty close to home"; and he resented all the more the "provincialism and small-ness" that she betrayed. Most distressing of all was Dorothy Richardson's unawareness, "at times, of her complete failure to sound the real note of the masculine." Yet, as if he were uncertain whether she deserved all the blame, Aiken let his sharpest criticism fall upon "poor Miriam," who "thinks she knows so very much and, alas, . . . knows so extraordinarily little." Indeed, it appeared to him that "the whole dark, strange, horrible, fascinating, mas-culine mind remains an absolutely closed book to her."

As quaint as some of this may sound half a century later, Aiken's dilemma was very real. (It resembles the problem of separating James Joyce from Stephen Dedalus.) Aiken did not want to deny the possibility that Dorothy Richardson knew how little (in his opinion) her heroine knew about men. But how could he distinguish between author and character in a book whose method uncompromisingly presented only Miriam? Yet he felt he should try to make such a distinction or at least to suggest that there might—and might not—be a difference. This was only fair, and he could hardly do more with no knowledge of Dorothy Richardson except through *Pilgrimage*.

Not even Conrad Aiken, as scrupulous and sensitive as he was, seemed to bear in mind that the action of *Oberland* had taken place more than twenty years before the time of his reading of it, and that, following from this, Miriam was a projection of a Dorothy Richardson nearly thirty years younger than Dorothy Richardson the author of *Oberland*. At twenty-eight she *had* thought she knew a great deal about life and men. Indeed, with the burden of her knowl-edge, she had lectured to an amused H. G. Wells and had felt herself climbing to the heights of the wisdom of middle age. But at fifty-five, Dorothy Richardson was aware of some of the depths of mid-dle age. In the midst of dramatizing her young and irritating self in all its unawareness, she felt the need to come to terms with her time of life and with the person Miriam had grown to be.

In May, the month in which Aiken's review had appeared, Dorothy began to contribute to a magazine published by her old friend Charles Daniel. Since 1926 he had been bringing out another of his curious monthlies, this one entitled *Focus: A Periodical to the Point in Matters of Health, Wealth & Life.* It would cease publication in December, but from May until then, it regularly carried an essay by Dorothy that was tied, sometimes rather lamely, to the month in which it appeared. All her pieces, however, show a concern with the natural processes of life in an individual and with the adjustments of consciousness to physical change. The voice heard in the pages of *Focus* is sometimes Miriam's and sometimes Dorothy Richardson's—as though she were at two stages of her life almost simultaneously: in the past, approaching the middle years; and in the present, nearing the age of sixty. As Miriam, she anticipates an experience that Dorothy Richardson has already had and now describes. Ultimately, though, it is the voice of experience that prevails, that rings with conviction and authority.

"The shock of July, of middle age," Dorothy wrote, "is a threshold shock. A door is closing behind us and we turn sorrowfully to watch it close and do not discover, until we are wrenched away, the one opening ahead." Waiting there for us, she went on, is the realization that "a moment in the consciousness of middle-age is wider and fuller than a moment in the consciousness of youth." Contrasting with these words are those remembered by Miriam in the opening chapter of *Dawn's Left Hand,* which had already been written when the *Focus* essay appeared. Miriam recalls having once said to Michael Shatov (about the dentist Orly at Wimpole Street): "One *moment* of my consciousness is wider and deeper than his has been in the whole of his life." But now, at the time of *Dawn's Left Hand,* the statement seems not only "meaningless" but also "monstrous" to an older Miriam. The truth about Orly, she has come to realize, is rather that "he was unconscious of his consciousness," that he had been "trained away" from it.

In the pages of *Focus,* the still mellower voice of Dorothy Richardson speaks of life, of consciousness, of experience from a vantage point Miriam had not yet attained. But she sometimes illustrates her ideas with material already filtered through her heroine in one of the novels, as, for example, in the scene of the Fest in *Oberland.* She had had Miriam "film" her picture of the champion skier Zerbuchen, "poised against the sky," in terms of his color, his movement, and his dreamlike attitude. In her *Focus* essay "Decadence," she described the same event in order to make the point that reflection is impossible at the moment of experience, that it can only follow as a "harvest" reaped by the "thinker." When the actor becomes the thinker, he enters also into what she calls his "decadence." Thus experience—acting—is the spring of life; reflection—thinking—is the autumn or decadence. Zerbuchen, during his run, had not been aware of himself; hence Miriam's feeling of his dreamlike state. Afterward he was self-conscious once more, and a "separated entity" rather than one that was "caught up into an eternal way of being." He was then, according to Dorothy Richardson, "in a state of decadence and of the enlightenment that accompanies it." Decadence and enlightenment are the key companion words. They correspond to the dissolution and opening with which she characterized middle age and to her own middle-aged role as the author of *Pilgrimage,* which was (ideally) the "harvest."

Pilgrimage, then, was meant to be not only a re-experiencing of her life but the chance to be her younger self once more and to stem the tide of age and decay. It allowed her also to reflect upon her life and to reap the reward of enlightenment. But whether such a reward was truly reaped, only the rest of her life would show.

At the moment, on a spring day in 1928, Dorothy sat in Mrs. Pope's garden in Trevone, in the large, one-window shed that the old lady had built, and thought about the essays she had already begun to write for *Focus,* the American reviews of *Oberland,* and the next volume of *Pilgrimage.* As if it followed naturally, Dorothy found herself picking up *Oberland,* to *read* it for the first time. It was, she decided, "a delightful thing!" And the crisis had passed.

2

One of the first things Dorothy did when she and Alan arrived in London in early June was to send to Middleton Murry, for *Adelphi,* a sharp-tongued review entitled "Das Ewig-Weibliche." The review considered two books, one by a Danish professor of jurisprudence, the other by Viscountess Rhondda, both of them on the subject of women. Their authors, however, had little more than this in common. The thesis of the professor was that women were indeed inferior to men and had become, in his time, a literal menace to society because of their attempts to deny it. Lady Rhondda concurred that in their present condition, without the full citizenship symbolized by the franchise, women *were* a menace. As mothers and as teachers, they could not bring up their girls to be responsible citizens until the world signified that it wanted and expected them to be such citizens. Dorothy had no quarrel with Lady Rhondda; nor would she stoop to wrangle with the Dane. She merely pointed out that the professor lacked "judicial impartiality" and that if one approached data—as he did—with "uncontrollable fury," one was certain to "cut" rather strange "capers" among them.

By this time she had quite recovered her sense of self. The review for the *Adelphi* launched an unusually busy summer. Early in July, after a series of telegrams announcing his arrival, the editor of *Vanity Fair,* Frank Crowninshield, came to tea at Queen's Terrace. Dorothy seemed proud of that fact and said he even looked happy to be there. He liked their rooms, which rather puzzled her, since they had the look of old desperation that the entire house shared. But this might well have been what appealed to Crowninshield—the flavor of the declining house, its eighteenth-century origins struggling against an inevitable and total eclipse. Dorothy apparently thought of Crowninshield as completely American, as one who would find Queen's Terrace nothing less than a blight after the Savoy Hotel where he was staying. She did not seem to know his background, that he was the son of a painter living abroad and that he had been born in France and educated in European schools. The chances were that he felt quite at home in Alan's studio bedroom. But if he had not, he would not have shown it, since he was also—in the words of Dorothy Parker—"the last of the species known as gentlemen." At any rate, Dorothy Richardson was dazzled by his flying visit to her. "He is off to Paris & Berlin," she reported—almost as if to suggest that he was embarking from Queen's Terrace.

Soon after this Dorothy had another caller who was to occupy a permanent place in her life. A young woman named Peggy Kirkaldy had written several admiring letters to her and had then finally asked to meet her. Dorothy invited her to tea on one of the Thursdays when Miss Kirkaldy said she came up to London from her cottage in Essex. As customary, she warned Miss Kirkaldy that she might be disappointed, and that she herself was taking the "risk [of] losing a reader." "Writers," she went on, "are boring people, banal beyond belief." But young Peggy Kirkaldy, filled with trepidation and

223

bearing a bouquet of flowers from her Essex garden, found Dorothy Richardson all she had expected her to be. She sat at the colorful tea table, listening to the talk that flowed between Alan and Dorothy and feeling that it was—as it ought to be—"far above [her] head." She watched their "pallid and unusual" faces, intent on a conversation she heard as "strophe and antistrophe." Alan rolled his perpetual cigarette and lit Dorothy's when it went out, all without the slightest disturbance of the talk. In due time, Peggy mustered the courage to speak—about herself and about Tollesbury, the little fishing village where she lived, on an estuary of the North Sea. Her cottage there, with its sizeable garden, was her refuge from the London that Dorothy agreed had become "one eternal scram." Peggy dared to invite Alan and Dorothy to come to Tollesbury, and to her great surprise they accepted at once.

Although Peggy Kirkaldy was not a writer, their friendship flourished. She had no literary—or even intellectual—aspirations. She merely had read *Pilgrimage* and had felt—as had Bryher and Pauline Marrian and a young girl from Michigan named Bernice Elliott—that the books had spoken to her in a voice she understood. Dorothy responded with gratitude and affection. Letters to Peggy, which almost at once reflected a warm and easy relationship, became part of her life. And for the next ten years she and Alan paid an annual summer visit to the cottage in Essex, first at Tollesbury, then at Colchester, where Peggy moved. Often Dorothy came with work to do, with something in progress stuffed into the big bast fish-bag that Peggy had made for her. But she came to play as well. Peggy never forgot the way in which Dorothy would rise from her deck chair in the garden to twirl about in a dance she had invented herself. Alan would watch her, grinning inscrutably, his hat tilted to shade his eyes. When Dorothy sat down again, they simply resumed their talk. Peggy felt herself a privileged being.

She introduced them to the fishing village, took them for a stroll along the weaving old railway line, which was no longer in use and was overgrown with grass, to the old, disused pier. She also introduced them to Walton-on-the-Naze, a small, recondite Victorian seaside place less than twenty miles from Tollesbury. It was just what Dorothy had been looking for to replace her childish memories of Weymouth. She and Alan began to stay there for a few days before or after their visits to Peggy, who often drove to Walton to meet them. Peggy would find them sitting at a café on the sea front, under a red-and-white striped awning, having their breakfast of rolls and weak coffee. Dorothy would be watching the glittering sea out of shaded eyes narrowed to a slit, and Alan would be smoking complacently.

As much as she liked Walton, though, Dorothy said she would go to one of the marshes in Kent if she ever had to give up Cornwall. Alan's fellow *Golden Hind* illustrator, John Austen, had built what Dorothy called "a houselet with studiolet" in Kent, on Romney Marsh. They visited the Austens in August, with a friend who drove them down through Wrotham and the Weald, and Dorothy found their situation enviable: "endless distance, with endless far-off things taking the light." Furthermore, John Austen had a "carlet," in which he took them for a "purring leisurely tour . . . through Conrad's country," and they stopped for beer at the Walnut Tree, a "perfect old brown Tudor inn." The drive back to London was spent—or so it seemed—passing hop lorries on the road.

After these short stays on the East coast, Dorothy and Alan remained in London until the first week of October. Dorothy finished her articles for *Focus,* read Clive Bell's *Proust,* which Murry had asked her to review for the *Adelphi,* and went to the cinema and to the theater. In September the *Evening News* asked if she would care to respond to an article by her fellow novelist Storm Jameson that they were about to print. The piece was an attack on suburban wives. Dorothy was amused by the whole affair, but although she was hampered in her communications with the newspaper because she had no telephone, she finally agreed to tackle Miss Jameson. The two were well matched. Storm Jameson, who was rather pugnacious and persistent, was then only thirty-one and had already published eight books. She had begun a trilogy of novels about a Yorkshire shipbuilding family similar to her own, and she would carry on the story of the descendants of this family in later novels. Moreover, she was often accused, as Dorothy was, of "skipping her big scenes," of having them take place off-stage. In retaliation, she suggested that "reviewers as a class be abolished" because they discouraged authors. Her interests—and her talents as well, she herself said—were more than literary. She enjoyed physical activity, loved ships, and in later years insisted that she would have been much happier as an engineer. All her life, apparently, she had nothing but contempt for idle, passive women, and she lashed out against them in her article for the *Evening News* entitled "Bored Wives."

Dorothy agreed almost at once that Jameson's sketch of a bored suburban wife had some truth in it. She said it had an "air of verisimilitude" that could be tested by "anyone rushing about in the world of to-day," as she was sure Miss Jameson had rushed about, collecting her material. The material was to be found in any shopping center. There, indeed, the women Storm Jameson described were "moving sluggishly along the pavement, not buying but just staring, a glutinous mass of femininity." Most of us, Dorothy freely admitted, have roundly "cursed these crowds" when we were in a hurry and were trying to get through them. Still, were there not other women in the crowd as well, "wandering at leisure," true, and staring, but with various purposes in mind, ranging, Dorothy thought, from ideas for home dressmaking to ways in which to keep themselves beautiful? It seemed to her that only a small proportion of the crowd represented "the vacuous automatism credited by Miss Jameson to the whole."

Dorothy was being tolerant, and she was enjoying the role, having not too long before, in *Oberland,* shown scant mercy to the girls from suburban Croydon, not one of whom could offer Miriam a single personal impression of Switzerland. In the *Evening News* Dorothy took issue with Storm Jameson's presentation of a little drama of home life in which a married couple sit together in silence after dinner, having already exchanged the "news items" of their separate days. According to Miss Jameson, the husband "pines" for his club or the next chapter of his Edgar Wallace novel, while the wife alternates between "resentment and self-pity" at having married such a dull man. The feelings of both merge as she offers "her equally wretched and equally unheroic mate a penny for his thoughts" and he "snaps" at her, and then "the evening is in ruins." Here, wrote Miss Jameson, was an unfortunately universal scene: modern woman suffering from the "boredom of the brainless unemployed," and modern man "from the demand for entertainment to be supplied at the cost of his personal relaxations."

Dorothy challenged this indictment of the woman. "Even in Suburbia," she said, "there are entertaining wives, witty wives with plenty of ideas, and wives not over-burdened with ideas but . . . with an ample store of wisdom" nonetheless. There were also plenty of working wives who at the end of the day were "only too glad to take refuge in whatever form of private recreation they prefer." Dorothy did not deny that empty-headed and demanding women existed; she stated that they were in far smaller number than Miss Jameson allowed. Her picture struck Dorothy furthermore as a period picture, of "pre-war, pre-wireless, pre-gramophone, pre-cinema, pre-dance hall Suburbia." Yet even if one supposed, for the sake of argument, that the married couple in "Bored Wives" had numerous counterparts and that there were indeed childless homes and people who were miserable and isolated, Dorothy insisted that the party to be arraigned was not the wife but society and the education it provided for girls. Finally, Dorothy retorted that Miss Jameson, in maintaining that when both husband and wife were equally stupid and bored the wife was "to be blamed for not rising superior to the occasion," was "all unawares" paying the lady "a very large compliment."

Among her friends Dorothy alerted only Owen and Peggy to the appearance of her defense of wives in the *News*. She said she thought Peggy would find it amusing, and she told her also that she had consented to the paper's request for a photograph of herself and had, in fact, sent one that Peggy had taken recently. The photograph was not used after all; but she had actually supplied one, after years of refusing to do so. To be sure, this was one way to avoid an error such as the *Times* had made. On the other hand, she now realized the importance of a candid photograph in reproducing reality—in this case, the reality of her age. She was apparently absorbing "the shock of July," and was even beginning to dispense the "wisdom" of it. She had challenged youthful vitality in the person of Storm Jameson with a newly found weapon—her somewhat pointed tolerance—and she was very pleased with herself. Moreover, the *Evening News* had paid her £12 for doing so.

3

This mood lasted well into winter. She and Alan were once again in Mrs. Dawson-Scott's bungalow at Constantine Bay when they learned that *Oberland* had been nominated for the French Femina-Vie-Heureuse prize. One of its two competitors was H. M. Tomlinson's novel *Gallions Reach,* which Dorothy felt sure would win. The reading public for Tomlinson's novels and essays, she knew, had recently been growing; and with *Gallions Reach*—the tale of a young man who finds maturity on the sea and in the Malayan jungles—Tomlinson won a measure of fame that allowed him to devote all his time to writing books. Before this he had been a shipping clerk, a seaman, a war correspondent, and literary editor of *The Nation and Athenaeum*. It was evident enough that he had achieved success neither easily nor early, for he was Dorothy Richardson's exact contemporary. Dorothy was right about the French prize: it went to *Gallions Reach*.

By the time Dorothy learned of the award in the spring of 1929, Alan's fortunes seemed to be taking a turn for the better. His friend John Austen, convinced of Alan's need for someone to handle his work, had put him in touch with an agent, a man named Sharmin. In no time at all Sharmin had opened negotiations with a firm called the Fan Frolico Press, which was headed by Jack Lindsay, who was then planning an illustrated edition of the mimes of Herondas. Sharmin saw that such a work—filled with scenes depicting the seamy side of city life—was eminently suited to Alan's pen. Lindsay saw this too, and asked Alan to begin work on the project as soon as he could, the financial terms to be worked out in due time. The first contract he drew up, however, was not very good. Sharmin argued for a better one. The second was equally inadequate. Lindsay promised a very, very good third one and begged Alan to devote himself to Fan Frolico Press "exclusively." Alan was so delighted with the mimes and so touched by Lindsay's appreciation of his work that he cleared his drawing table of Rabelais and set to work illustrating Herondas.

With this going on, Dorothy was full of hope that the mere fact of *Oberland*'s nomination for a prize would help its sales. But the news of the award to Tomlinson was followed hard by Duckworth's quarterly sales report. It showed an all too familiar state of affairs. *Oberland* had not even sold enough copies to cover the advance Duckworth had finally been persuaded to give her, and part of it would thus be added to her mounting debt to him. From this only one conclusion was to be drawn, she said, namely that her books could not be counted as "any sort of asset." She felt that even their originality had lost its force: "there were so many young people on the same tack" that it no longer mattered.

Obviously, it mattered a great deal. While possibly she had reached a hard-won accord with her middle-aged self, as a writer she had yet to gain more than the dubious satisfaction of being known by name, of being sought after, of being intensely admired and intensely disliked—though in solid truth she was a publisher's liability. Describing her novel as "superfluous," she did not touch the current volume at all during their spring stay in Trevone Cottage. Instead, while Alan drew for Fan Frolico, she worked at an odd assortment of pieces: a review of a book on handwriting; an essay on marriage, which she saw not as a "processional" with one member or the other leading, but as a "triangle" with the man and woman "side by side, forming the base"; an article in her *Close Up* series; an essay for *Vanity Fair* that was printed alongside a satirical drawing by Alan. They both were also reading Aldous Huxley's new novel, *Point Counterpoint,* and were finding themselves disappointed. Dorothy felt it was "grossly intellectual, a monument to top-heaviness." She objected in particular to the fictional treatment of Middleton Murry, claiming that Huxley's information had been acquired "second-hand & inaccurately" (that is to say, from D. H. Lawrence). As a result, the portrait struck her as "disgraceful without even being funny."

Whether she was right or not, she now took a kind of pleasure in severity, especially when it was directed at someone else. She and Alan spent several evenings hunched over in laughter at four numbers of a magazine called *The London Aphrodite,* which had been sent to them by the Fan Frolico Press, its publisher. The issues contained what Dorothy thought were "screamingly funny" attacks on Wyndham Lewis, Wells, and the whole group associated with the *London Mercury,* a magazine that had carried consistently harsh reviews of *Pilgrimage.*

With these few outlets for aggression, by the second week of June Dorothy felt ready for London and society. When they got back to Queen's Terrace they found their rooms a shambles, with half the belongings of the winter tenant strewn about. From the start Dorothy had thought of him as neurotic, but she was unprepared for this. She was also unprepared for the letter she found waiting for them, a letter she had been warned by a friend to expect from John Cowper Powys. She was familiar with his brother's book, the already beloved *Mr. Weston's Good Wine,* published in 1927, but she knew nothing about this Powys except that he lectured on literature. He described himself as an Englishman who lived in America and was on a short visit to Europe. He said he had hoped, while in England, to meet a writer whose work he admired very much. To

Dorothy's great relief, she and Alan were committed to leave London almost at once for family visits, so there would be no time for Powys to call. Within a week of their arrival they left Buckinghamshire, to stay with Alan's brother Vincent at Iver; afterward they went to Surrey, to visit Dorothy's sister Kate at Long Ditton. Back again at Queen's Terrace on June 24, she wrote to Powys in her customary fashion. "I think on the whole I agree with those who feel it is a mistake to meet writers whose work one likes. There is so rarely any apparent correspondence. The enquirer risks losing 'illusions'—the writer a reader. Truth is served however and that, no doubt, if one can face it, is great compensation." She added that she was at home on Sundays after five o'clock.

The letter unnerved Powys. He could not bring himself to act upon the ambivalent—and lugubrious—invitation. When he finally did, it was to ask for a meeting on the day of his scheduled sailing to New York. As it happened, Dorothy had planned a luncheon engagement with Peggy Kirkaldy, so she exchanged the proper regrets with Powys and considered the matter closed, feeling obscurely that she had escaped a trying experience.

The month of July passed quietly enough. She restored their rooms to a semblance of order, wrote her essay for the September issue of *Close Up,* spent some time in the British Museum, and kept an eye on Alan, who had suddenly begun to cough again. Then, in early August, Powys announced that he had not sailed after all. He would come, if she was still so kind as to permit him, on the following Sunday.

At the appointed time the tall, thin, slightly stooped Powys climbed the short flight of stairs to the front door of 32 Queen's Terrace—"a dingy old house," he thought. He pulled at the large, ugly knocker. In a few moments the door was opened by a man even taller and thinner than he, who, moreover, looked fragile and delicate, as he did not. Powys followed Alan up the inner stairway, around a corner, and, with another step or two, into the flat. There Dorothy, dressed in black velvet, was waiting for them. At her side stood a young man, a "lovely youth," Powys thought, whom she introduced as David, "Michael's" son (i.e., David Grad).

When they were all seated, Powys fixed his attention on the woman behind the letter that had put him off. She was not handsome, he decided, but her eyes were humorous and kind through the pince-nez, and her figure was sturdy rather than plump. He noticed that she had a thick white neck and a rather snub nose, to which she pressed a finger as if that helped her to think. Her hands, he saw, were firm and large, with fingers widely spaced. He could feel the resoluteness in her hands, for she placed one of them on his shoulder several times. In the midst of preparing tea, she would come back into the sitting room to stand beside him, holding her teapot, while he talked with Alan. Powys was surprised to find that the tea, when she served it at last, was good.

He found Alan Odle "enchanting," a "charming wraith—hardly a human being" at all. Otherworldliness had a strong appeal for the author of the romantic novel *Wolf Solent,* which neither Dorothy nor Alan knew anything about. Indeed, if Powys had been less modest than he was, he would have recognized in Alan Odle not only a kindred spirit but also potentially one of his most fervid readers. As soon as Alan discovered the novels, he devoured them, but Dorothy was never able to finish one. As this Sunday afternoon lengthened into an evening at a café, Powys did not breathe a word about his novels or, for that matter, about any of his books: on *English Novelists, Shakespeare's History Plays, Psycho-Analysis and Morality,* and *The Meaning of Culture.* He preferred to talk about Dorothy's books and Dorothy's life and, of course, about literature and life in general. This preference alone might have won for him Dorothy's good will, but his extravagantly humble heart won her affection as well. She had placed her hand on his shoulder out of an immediate fondness that lasted the rest of her life, a fondness that would have sprung up just as quickly had she known that after a few moments in Queen's Terrace he had guessed her age. That he never revealed this to her suggests that she had come upon a man who was akin to Alan, another man with as delicate a sensibility as he had.

4

In different ways, John Cowper Powys's appearance was as striking as Alan's. His tightly curled hair, which had turned gray (he was nearly fifty-seven), still dominated his face, coming down his forehead in a peak and spreading outward in a mass from his temples. His black eyes were deep-set and fiery; and his sharp features gave to his profile a hawkish look. He communicated intensity, which both Dorothy and Alan felt at once.

He wanted to know as much about them as they would tell him and he could observe. It interested him that Dorothy ate meat only "because Alan must have it"; that she thought women "plunge[d] into life at first hand," whereas men "dealt with things"; that she had "a terror of explosive noises"; that she agreed with him about the existence of "a worse evil than Sadism—a brutality of an unconscious kind"; that she liked to know the names of waiters serving her; and that she believed there was in all of us an "immortal part [which] never changes and cannot die." He noticed that she wore green earrings, that she did not wear a hat when they went out to the café, and that she guided him very carefully across the roads while keeping watch over Alan and David at the same time. He had already divined her protective instinct as part of her motive in coming back, while making the tea, to hear what he was saying to Alan, so it did not surprise him that, when she described her first meeting with Alan in this very house, Alan remarked, in a tone of voice suggesting the unassailable truth of the fact of the color of Dorothy's dress, that he would have been "dead long ago but for [her]."

Powys questioned her about books, and though she claimed to have been "ignorant of literature" before marrying Alan, she delivered her judgments firmly. She praised Proust and Mann, defended both Maeterlinck and Wells, laughed at Ford Madox Hueffer, and labeled Lawrence "a surly artisan scowling" (who was responsible, she said, for Aldous Huxley's attack on Middleton Murray in *Point Counterpoint*). But when Powys challenged her assertion that Joyce was trying to express feelings in sounds as Montaigne did, she could not explain the analogy. She said it had not been made by her conscious mind.

She told him also that the writing of *Pilgrimage* had not been premeditated. A sudden urgency had driven her to write, but she had had no idea how she would do it until she began, and then the writing had possessed her. *Pointed Roofs* had been the result, after five months of solitude and near-starvation in the "haunted" house at Cornwall provided by the Beresfords. But Edward Garnett, she said, had discovered *Pointed Roofs*, as he had discovered Conrad's *Almayer's Folly*; he had, she thought, an extraordinary power of insight. Forgetting for the moment that Garnett had described her book as "feminine impressionism," she complained to Powys of her annoyance at being labeled an "impressionist" or a "futurist" or, for that matter, anything at all. And she positively loathed the phrase "stream of consciousness," which May Sinclair had attached to her.

Dorothy warmed to the subject of her books and what had been said about them, which in her opinion included very little of value. G. B. Stern's attack, for example, had been "malicious and unkind," she thought. And a French, rather than an English, critic—Abel Chevalley—had made the most intelligent remarks about her thus far, in his book on the English novel published in 1925. Dorothy said that he had rightly emphasized the close relationship she considered so important to establish between the writer and the reader of a novel, and he had seen that, although as writer she asked a great deal of the reader, she also gave a proportionate return. As Chevalley put it, in the way that one finds only what one brings to love and marriage, so a reader brought to her books and found in them certain "treasures that one had thought lost since infancy." Elsewhere, she said, Chevalley maintained that she was more Proustian than Proust himself.

Powys would have understood her to mean that both she and Proust were engaged in the similar enterprise of recovering not only the past but also their sense of self in that far-off time now buried beneath the weight of the present. Powys's own fictional heroes, whom he did not disclose to Dorothy, were often engaged in an elaborate quest for their mythic, historic, and personal identities. Wolf Solent, for example, whom he had just created, returns to his Dorset birthplace to find out whether he is the spiritual son of his wild and lusty father, who is buried there in a pauper's grave, or of his powerful, beautiful, wronged mother. Dorothy would have been disconcerted, if not repelled, by the way in which Powys translated his understanding of such quests into extravagantly unrealistic tales, if she had not seen that he grasped what she meant by art as a collaboration between the conscious and unconscious.

She could not have divined, though, the mode he would ultimately choose for interpreting *her*. As she sat smoking constantly, first in the sitting room at Queen's Terrace and later in the small café to which they had adjourned, she was not fully aware of his recording mind. She did not know that he was registering *everything*, whether it was flattering or not: her age, her "rather malicious" mimicry of people, her evident fondness for gossip. At the same time, his imagination was beginning to play on the author of *Pilgrimage*, whose figure was "square and solid," who knew the graves in St. John's Wood churchyard as well as he, and who guessed without hesitation exactly where his ideal America was (the "southwestern portion of the Middle-West," as Powys later divulged). He had begun to make of her a "modern priestess," a "Pythian soothsayer," and when he wrote the essay about Dorothy Richardson that no one could have foreseen, it would leave her not quite sure whether to be jubilant or horrified.

CHAPTER SIXTEEN

Openings and Closings

THE September 1929 issue of the *London Mercury,* which Dorothy happened to see, contained a long, flattering article about John Cowper Powys. She was abashed to learn of *Wolf Solent* and of his other books as well. "Dark horse," she said, "he never mentioned them." She would have to acknowledge her abysmal ignorance. Meanwhile, looking through *Wolf Solent* and reading some of it, she wondered what to say to John, whose letters from America she had promised to answer.

The first letter arrived quite soon, in late September, and Dorothy chose to say that it was a good thing she had not known of the existence of *Wolf Solent.* "I am an extension of him, he is an extension of me, as you will. Both. When I have fully read I may have more to say." What she added three months later was largely extravagant praise from Alan, who was perfectly sincere.

John asked her to "pour out" her thoughts and feelings to him. He wanted to know everything, including what went on in her mind at night as she lay next to Alan. This was not her customary mode of communication, but she understood that Powys wanted to establish a "connection" with her, and though she steered clear of intimate personal matters, she made an effort to talk about things that would link them. If Powys felt frustrated, he never mentioned it.

That fall, Dorothy met still another member of the Powys family. During an evening at H. D.'s flat in Sloane Street, Dorothy noticed someone across the room who was unmistakably a Powys. She knew it could not be Theodore, the creator of Mr. Weston, because he never went out. Indeed, she had heard that a bus ride made him ill for a week. So this Powys had to be the youngest brother, Llewelyn, and it was. He leaped from his chair to tell her how "good" she had been to John and how amazing it was that he had visited her, since he, too, "*never went anywhere.*" They chatted as though they were old friends, Llewelyn confiding to her that he was thinking of making a trip to New Mexico to improve the health of his lungs. Since Dorothy had heard of the effect New Mexico's air had had on D. H. Lawrence, she wrote to John at once to say that he must not permit Llewelyn to go. She did not tell John that Alan's condition had been precarious all summer.

Instead, she confided this to Peggy, along with the feeling that she really ought to protect Alan from London social life. But she herself enjoyed it so much that she could not give it up. Moreover, there were ways in which Alan was as fond of it as she was, so one could argue that it was good for him. In any case, their calendar was full until they left for Cornwall in October. They spent evenings in London with Peggy and had a visit with her at Mell, her cottage in Tollesbury. They dined with May Sinclair (whom Dorothy continued to mimic and pity) and with the aging Violet Hunt (whom they had met at May's) in South Lodge. They had an outing with Adrian Allinson (which Dorothy claimed she endured entirely for Alan's sake) and a week's stay in Romney Marsh with the Austens. It was the kind of summer Dorothy especially liked: it made her feel almost celebrated, as she had felt in Paris.

1

The move to Cornwall this year was slightly more complicated than usual. They could not take possession of the bungalow at Constantine until the end of October. Mrs. Dawson-Scott had let it for the entire month to a member of the P.E.N. Club. But rather than prolong their stay in London, Dorothy arranged to board for three weeks with a Cornish family named Tippett. She hoped to spend this time working on her novel, but it was not as easy as that to find her way back into it. Besides, the Tippett house, standing as it did in the middle of a field on the "crest of a rise," seemed to Dorothy to "howl at every pore." She complained that everything waved and flapped, and although she found it good to be "tended," she felt cramped and inhibited. The real trouble with starting again, however, was that Miriam was "slow in coming to the surface."

The Odles did not actually get into Lynx until November 5, and once there Dorothy occupied herself with the cause of film censorship. She had been involved with it for months, ever since the staff of *Close Up* had raised the issue at the beginning of the year. They had drawn up a petition in the hope of presenting it to the House, asking that a special category be created for films of "artistic, scientific and educative value." Dorothy had worked assiduously from the start, circulating the petition for signatures. Her one large failure was Shaw. He had refused to sign on the ground that what was being sought was "only a demand for another censorship, which would be worse in direct proportion as the censors were better," and he had advised Dorothy not to waste her time on it. She decided that he was indulging in his "hopelessly incorrigible naughtiness" and went on collecting signatures.

At the moment she was trying to enlist the aid of another old friend, Josiah Wedgwood, to get the petition before the House as a Question. Although Wedgwood had asked her for a copy of it, she thought she detected in his letter a "delicate criticism" of the methods they had pursued thus far. It had never occurred either to her or to any of the *Close Up* staff to approach certain M.P.s for their signatures. Apparently Wedgwood was hinting that if they had done this, there would be more of a chance now for the petition. At any rate, he said he would do his best to pave the way for a deputation. Dorothy, in reporting all this to Bryher, said she thought they might be excused for "not knowing that Parliament can present petitions to itself." For the time being, once they had decided how the Question was to be put, they could do nothing but wait to hear from Wedgwood.

For the rest of the year Dorothy concentrated on small translations she had begun to do for *Argosy* magazine, which Alan's brother Vincent was editing. These translations were a quick, relatively easy source of income, and during the autumn of 1929 very little income came in from any other source. Bryher sent a check, which Dorothy accepted apologetically, for work she had done on the petition. She said she would have liked not to take any money for work like that, but she had to.

Alan was drawing solely for Fan Frolico Press and had gotten absolutely nothing so far. Lindsay had not drawn up the third contract as he had promised, but Alan was determined to believe it would be as good as Lindsay had claimed. When the new year began and the contract still dangled in the distance, Dorothy was grateful when John Austen recommended an American publisher he thought might be interested in Alan's work.

Austen also devised a scheme that involved her. He wanted to produce a book about the art of the illustrator that would contain, in addition to his text, several samples of his own work drawn specifically for the purpose, and he asked Dorothy if she would contribute a foreword. Both of them, he said, would be published by William Jackson, under the imprint of Joiner and Steele, an imprint used for a series known as Furnival books.

The Furnival books were fine editions of new stories by both established and beginning writers. Each book carried a foreword and a full-page woodcut or drawing. Austen himself had done an illustration for a story by H. E. Bates, and Alan Odle—whether at Austen's suggestion or on Jackson's own initiative—would illustrate the fifth volume in the series, which would appear in 1931. The volume, entitled *The Last Voyage,* would be the work of James Hanley, one of the youngest of the Furnival authors. His tales about Irish life and the sea, in which misery and horror prevail, were then just beginning to appear and were very much to Alan's taste.

In January 1930 Dorothy agreed to write the foreword to John Austen's book. She planned to use her old notes for the exhibition catalog and the data Austen would provide her about himself. She ventured to hope that Jackson would consent to pay her fifteen guineas. She allowed Austen to make the fee arrangement and said she would accept whatever fee was negotiated, so long as it did not fall below five guineas. When Austen reported that an agreement had been reached for £15, Dorothy responded that she was the "grasping" kind and that she had meant *guineas.* She got guineas.

By then, however, the book had been quite altered, apparently at its publisher's suggestion, and Dorothy's insistence on fifteen guineas was understandable, for she was now writing the book herself and Austen was contributing the foreword. Austen would still be the illustrator, and the limited edition would be embellished with a signed Austen wood-engraving and would be autographed by both of them. The text by Dorothy Richardson became a 2,000-word essay on the art of the illustrator entitled *John Austen and the Inseparables.* In it Dorothy argued that illustration is a primary rather than secondary form of "fine art" when, of course, the author and artist are "worthy of each other" and when the illustrations have a beauty of their own as well as in relation to the words on the page. Under these conditions, the text of a book and its illustrations are

Facsimile page from a letter written to Claude Houghton by Alan Odle at Hillside during the mid-1940s. Courtesy of the Humanities Research Center of The University of Texas at Austin.

"inseparables." This was the case, Dorothy said, with John Austen's drawings for Norman Douglas's *South Wind* and for *Madame Bovary, Tristram Shandy,* and *Manon Lescaut.*

Dorothy finished her essay by the end of February 1930, and during March she helped Austen with his foreword. He sent her the first draft. Though brief, it showed the difficulty he had in arranging his thoughts into word designs. Dorothy was familiar with his problem from her experience with Alan, who might spend anywhere from a day to an entire year on an ordinary letter, although this was largely because he printed rather than wrote. Dorothy tried to explain to Austen as delicately and gingerly as she could that he had only to apply the principles of his own art and keep his sentences "direct and simple, like an outline drawing." But for Austen this was easier said than done. When the second draft arrived, Dorothy saw that she could not hold to her good intentions. She had not wanted to interfere with the way he expressed himself, but in the end she recast his foreword, taking care at the same time to assure him of her respect for his individuality. The finished product, however, bears the unfortunate marks of her respectful editing. It reads as a poorly woven garment would look, its original stitches, uneven and too tight, merely straightened and loosened when they should have been dropped altogether.

Nevertheless, the book was handsome in its slim, ivory-colored binding. One of its reviewers was the American poet Marianne Moore, who commented on its beautiful appearance and on John Austen's "powerful" illustrations, which "stay in the mind." As satisfying as this was to both author and artist, the book served Dorothy in yet another, quite unexpected way. Several months before its publication in the early fall of 1930, the Jackson firm began to take a more extensive interest in her as a novelist. In the capacity of "export booksellers," they decided to buy from Duckworth fifty copies of each of five volumes of *Pilgrimage.* They asked her to sign some of these to be sold at special prices, and they agreed to pay her a royalty on them. She was surprised, to say the least. Trying to fathom the offer, she decided that Jackson was hoping to sell the books on the American market, since they wanted only early volumes which were out of print in the United States. But in April, while in Trevone Cottage for the spring, Dorothy received another explanation from a young visitor named Rupert Clive-Cook, who claimed to know the book world. He told her that first editions of *Pilgrimage* had become collector's items. "It seems grotesque," she said.

She was just as confounded by Clive-Cook's purpose in calling on her. He wanted to buy the manuscripts of her novels. She had kept only one, however, that of *Pointed Roofs,* which Alan did not want her to sell. But if manuscripts were a possible source of income, she would begin to preserve them. Even though she now sometimes used the typewriter, finding that it helped "pull things together," she resolved to write and revise the current volume entirely by hand. She would probably get more for the manuscript than for the finished book, she said.

When Jackson first divulged its scheme, she had hoped it would induce Duckworth to pay her a larger sum for volume ten than he had for *Oberland.* She thought he might even be persuaded again to make her an advance, since he was now getting rid of most of his remaindered stock. But she did not take into account her considerable debt to Duckworth, who, in his turn, saw this new development as a way to reduce her debt appreciably. He proposed that the royalties Jackson offered to pay be given to him rather than to her. She grumbled in disappointment, but could not help seeing the justice of the arrangement—from the point of view of Duckworth, that is. Perhaps, under the circumstances, he would pay her £20 for volume ten.

2

William Jackson had still another surprise in store for her. They now wanted to publicize her work and felt that this could be better achieved if Dorothy were to write a paragraph about each of her books, telling how it came to be written and describing its story. Dorothy was sure that John Austen was behind this plan. She wrote to him, expressing her gratitude and explaining her refusal. Each of her volumes, she said, was a single chapter of an unfinished whole and, properly speaking, had no "story." But she did not tell him of the countersuggestion she had made to Jackson. If they wished to do something, she had told them, they might consider the possibility of approaching a person who liked her work for a short article that could be printed as a book resembling the one on Austen. When

241

they asked her to recommend someone, she offered the name of John Cowper Powys. Powys agreed at once and even set aside his new novel to work on the essay.

While he wrote about her, Dorothy tried to devote herself to her tenth volume, performing what she called an "ostrich act-of-faith." She claimed it could be finished within the year if she were certain of getting a decent sum for it. Given the number of other projects she had in mind, she could not really have expected either to get the money or to finish the novel by the end of the year. One of the projects was the completion of the translation of Proust's novel, which had been left undone at the death of Scott-Moncrieff in February. Almost at once she had written to Knopf, who was then printing *Albertine Disparue* as *The Sweet Cheat Gone*, the volume finished by Scott-Moncrieff before he died. Knopf replied that he did not yet know how much of Proust's work remained to be translated. Dorothy waited to hear from him again. She had also suggested herself to Victor Gollancz as the translator of Giraudoux's *Caligula* and had asked the Cayne Press if they were interested in English versions of Panaït Istrati, the Romanian novelist who wrote in French. It is hard to imagine what she would have done if all these projects had materialized, but she knew there was little chance of that. In fact, they all fell through, almost all at the same time, when she and Alan came up to London in early June of 1930.

They were also greeted by the most serious news of all. After a year's work, Alan had sent in from Cornwall the finished drawings for the mimes of Herondas. He was expecting to receive the first installment of the finally agreed-upon sum of £200. But neither money nor word had arrived. In London they learned that Fan Frolico Press was nearly bankrupt and did not know whether it could publish Herondas, much less pay for the illustrations. Dorothy decided to do something at once, rather than wait to find out what would happen. She applied to the bank for a £200 overdraft on the Australian securities she had bought with the Treasury Grant that Wells had helped her to get a few years earlier and with the remains of Alan's legacy from his brother Sidney. The bank agreed, and Dorothy felt they were safe for the moment.

Now, for a new quarterly called the *Window*, Dorothy wrote "Ordeal," her first short story in six years. As one might expect, its mood and substance were intimately tied to the circumstances of the moment, even though Dorothy drew upon an earlier experience for its setting. The woman in the story, Mrs. Fan Peele, comes to a nursing home to undergo surgery (as Dorothy had done in 1925, just before the opening of the *Golden Hind* exhibition), but this may be a much more serious operation than the one performed on Dorothy. She is brought there by another woman whose relationship to her is indeterminate but whose anxiety and agitation suggest Alan's behavior during even the most minor of Dorothy's illnesses. Once the other woman leaves, however, Fan finds herself no longer able to sympathize with the feeling of "those others out in life." She is now totally absorbed in her own existence and occupied in minutely examining her own feelings. Some of these have to do with her "sense of personal life," which she had thought would cease in a place like this but which, instead, she finds intensified. Indeed, its "vivid palpitation" causes her embarrassment. She finds it strange that, just as she had been surprisingly composed for the last two days, she now feels cheerful, and she wonders why. Conceivably she is hanging up her clothes in the wardrobe for the last time. Why, then, is she smiling as she does it? Perhaps she has an "unconscious organic certainty of getting through." But the only certainty she is *conscious* of is the "life-risk" she is running. Whatever the answers to these questions, Fan Peele decides that her "intensity of being" in the present makes "the possible future look like a shallow expanse," and she is perfectly willing to sacrifice the future if she can now attend exclusively to herself.

She proceeds to do just that—to consider only herself—as she settles down to wait for the "summons." She has taken care of her husband. In a book she has brought along (*Green Mansions,* which Dorothy had just read in Trevone) is a note she had decided not to leave for him. He does not know she is here. If he *had* known, "his suffering presence would have been in the room with her." She rejoices in her decision not to tell him, in being completely alone, "severed even from Tom." "With a deep, blissful sigh she felt all the tensions of her life relax. She was back again in the freedom of her own identity, in pre-marriage freedom, in more than childhood's freedom, with all the strength of her maturity to savor its joy. In bright daylight the afternoon lay before her, endless—*the first holiday of her adult life.*"

As Dorothy herself wanted, she gave to her fictional character a "holiday from responsibility and from the tension of human relationships." But expressed in the story were dangerous feelings that she had to guard from consciousness—for example, the relief she felt in a severance from her husband. The use of the word "sever" suggests an umbilical relationship, she the mother and Alan the child. Moreover, she knew that the cord between them would never be cut until the death of one or the other. Thus the woman in her story has a "holiday" that "only the chance of death had had the power to give her." Only with the threat of extinction hovering about her can she regain "the freedom of her own identity." For just a moment Dorothy permits Fan to contemplate the attractiveness not of death but of dying, if in dying one could achieve "the sense of being in its perfect fullness," released as one might then be from everything and everybody except the self.

This attractiveness has disappeared by the time Fan Peele looks up from the book she is reading—the book containing her note to her husband—and sees that only half an hour remains to her. At five o'clock they will come to take her to the operating "theatre" ("absurd unsuitable word for the reality . . . near at hand"). Before that, however, she is given a hypodermic, which she bitterly resents: " 'I'd have gone quietly,' she said." Once in the theater, the real drama begins, the fight to preserve her sense of self that had flowered anew on this hard-won afternoon. The anesthesia is administered.

> Her heart answered, her blood answered; but not herself. Desperately and quite independently her threatened heart fought against this power that was bearing her down. She raised her hands to still it.
> "Clasp your hands."
> All of herself was in her clasped hands, beating, throbbing. Less, and less, and . . . less. . . .

Thus the story ends, without revealing whether Fan Peele survived, whether her cheerfulness and composure had indeed stemmed from an "unconscious organic certainty of getting through." Dorothy Richardson did not tell, perhaps because she herself did not know or did not dare to guess. It was her own situation she had momentarily escaped in writing the story, and the survival she predicted would have been her own. The hands alone in the final paragraph testify to this. To Dorothy Richardson they were a central symbol of the strength of the self. She had given her own large masculine hands to the heroine of *Pilgrimage,* too, and they were the mark of Miriam's identity as well. They failed Miriam only once, in the crisis of her mother's suicide. At the end of *Honeycomb* (written while Dorothy was deciding whether or not to marry Alan Odle), Miriam sat in the house where her mother lay dead of the wound inflicted by her own hand and "clasped her hands together. [But] she could not feel them." Her strength, her identity had been annihilated by the act committed by her mother, and the woman in the story written thirteen years later struggles against such annihilation, against the fading sense of *her* self in her similarly clasped hands. What Dorothy seems to have produced in "Ordeal" is an inner dialogue between despair and determination. She had married Alan Odle as a means of preserving her identity, and her marriage had meant assuming the care of him. She would keep her part of the bargain, but she would struggle all the while to keep her responsibility to that part and not the whole.

3

While writing "Ordeal," Dorothy received from John Cowper Powys the manuscript of his essay about her. She was stunned by it. He had produced 8,000 words, which she had committed herself to type, knowing that he always wrote in longhand. She had also agreed to edit the manuscript at his urgent request. He gave her *carte blanche.* "Imagine," he had said, "that you and I are both together composing an appreciation of another person altogether, a *third* person." You have the power, he told her, of "becoming invisible and hovering over the projected 'eidolon' of your own image as a writer, as you do [in *Pilgrimage*] over your own image as a person." The more she pruned and revised, Powys said, the more pleased he would be. But his essay was so filled with extravagant praise that Dorothy feared her critics would use it against her.

In describing the manuscript to Bryher, and telling her that she was "embarrassedly engaged in toning down & cutting [it]," Dorothy could not bring herself to admit the true nature of its origin. She said that the idea of it had come from Powys, "the generous great creature," who had thought of writing a 1,000-word leaflet for Duckworth, to be issued with his catalog. Powys might well have suggested such a leaflet at some point or other, but Dorothy does not explain how the leaflet for Duckworth had been transformed into a booklet for Jackson. She apparently preferred that her own part in the scheme not be known. There was a difference, in her eyes,

245

between a spontaneous, irresistible flamboyance on her behalf that she modestly tried to curb, and one that she herself had set into motion. The fact remains that Dorothy must have known what Powys would produce when she recommended him to Jackson, and Powys gave her, unstintingly and quite naturally, what he sensed she really wanted. He compared her heroine to Faust and Hamlet in her "female quest for the essence of human experience," and he likened Dorothy Richardson herself to Dostoyevski as an "original philosopher *and* artist." Finally, in stentorian tones, as though in a lecture from a platform, Powys addressed to his audience the ringing line, "I tell you this woman is a Pythian soothsayer."

With good reason (though she knew that Powys had not been immoderate throughout his essay, that he was often just and accurate in what he said about her novel), Dorothy was to fret over the essay until, after being held up to serve as advertisement for volume ten, it finally appeared in 1931. She deplored it, defended it, apologized for it, and sent a copy to Bryher for reassurance, which Bryher promptly gave.

During the summer of 1930, while she worked over the essay in her spare moments, Dorothy followed a schedule she had outlined for herself. Most afternoons were spent in the Reading Room of the British Museum, gathering material to translate for her brother-in-law's *Argosy*. It was an unusually hot summer for London, the temperature occasionally rising to nearly 90 degrees, turning the city into a "furnace." With St. John's Wood and Queen's Terrace nearly half an hour's journey from the Museum, Dorothy would have suffered even if she had been doing something she liked. But for Dorothy this hunting in French and German magazines for "translatable" bits was work against the grain: the sort, she said, that grew not only harder but more and more destructive. In three years she had managed to write only half a novel, and she blamed her lack of progress on all the other work she had done instead.

For the present, there seemed little chance of her finishing the novel and a good deal of evidence that she was not yet ready to finish it. Duckworth had offered her £25 if he could have the volume in autumn. Dorothy claimed such a deadline was impossible to meet: too many other things had come up. A Chicago publisher (Argus Press) had opened negotiations with Alan for drawings. A New Jersey press was applying for the American rights to his illustrated *Candide* and was offering what Dorothy described as "decent terms." With Fan Frolico still in the throes of bankruptcy, these proposals were heaven-sent (although Dorothy suspected John Austen of having had a hand in them). Austen was certainly responsible for an inquiry from Grant Richards. He had introduced the work of Alan Odle to a man named Kean, who was in Richards's new publishing firm, Toronto Ltd. Kean asked Alan for samples of his work to show Richards and for suggestions as to books they might publish with illustrations by him. Alan sent Kean the Fan Frolico drawings, and according to Dorothy, Grant Richards was "scared to death" by them. She may have been right; years before, he had been afraid to publish Joyce's *Dubliners*. In any case, he seems to have decided that it would be safer to bring out Dorothy Richardson than Alan Odle, and he asked to see her sales statements. This time, Dorothy said, he had "heart-failure." He wrote a charming letter and backed out altogether.

Instead of growing skeptical about American firms after Grant Richards's retreat, Dorothy pinned her hopes on them, completely ignoring the economic turmoil of the States. She and Alan had already settled in Cornwall (at Constantine Bay) for the winter, and she had resumed work on her novel when the final letter from Richards came. But in December blow followed blow. The Argus Press canceled negotiations because of "trade depression." Julian, the New Jersey press, decided that prospects of the American book trade had changed and that a new edition of *Candide* was no longer an attractive venture. Then the bank informed Dorothy that the value of her stock had fallen from £300 to £230, with the result that her overdraft had nearly run out. They advised her to sell immediately, in order—she presumed—to make sure of recovering their outlay. When she demurred, they agreed to wait, in the hope that Australian 5 percents would rise. The final blow came just before Christmas, when their tenant in the rooms at Queen's Terrace died, having paid only two months' rent.

About this time, toward the end of December, Dorothy received a letter from a Harley Street surgeon, Dr. Wilfrid Trotter. The letter, a model of its kind, asked with the utmost delicacy when another "segment" in the "intense life" of Miriam Henderson could be expected. He had become accustomed, he said, to the appearance of a new volume as a "biennial event" of such importance to him that he did not quite trust himself to describe it. He hoped the "rather disturbing delay" since the publication of *Oberland* in 1927 meant only that the next chapter would be "bigger and richer than the others." In any case, he wanted to convey his gratitude for the pleasure Dorothy Richardson had already given him with *Pilgrimage* as it stood. In January 1931, Dorothy wrote Dr. Trotter, "Alas, or hallelujah as the case may be, the circumstances that for so long have kept chapter X at less than a snail's pace are livelier than ever they were & the prolonged labour will have resulted, sometime this year I hope, in something more akin to a mouse than to a mountain." She added that a letter such as his kept her from "total discouragement" and was "a ray of sunlight across a prospect uniformly bleak."

The prospect she described to Dr. Trotter had driven her to write to Bryher at about the same time, though in much more explicit detail. Given the circumstances, Dorothy felt she had no alternative but to appeal to Bryher for a loan and, in the process, to break her strange promise to Prime Minister Baldwin not to divulge the Treasury Grant with which she had bought the Australian 5 percents. She asked for £100, to finish volume ten. It would see them through the rest of their stay in Constantine Bay and through part of the spring in Trevone. If she could also manage to get a contract for translation and finish the job by May, she could earn enough to support them until they went to London. Once there, she would "hawk round" a series of articles on feminism she had in mind to produce. By then her stock should have recovered and she would sell it to repay Bryher; but if it should improve before this, she would sell at once, repay to Bryher the portion of the loan already spent, and carry on with the balance remaining after the sale. Her calculations were minutely unrealistic. Even if Australian 5 percents behaved as she wished them to, the amount of work she had projected for herself in the space of five months was in the realm of fantasy. Bryher seems to have understood the nature of the pride that lay behind all this. She urged Dorothy not to sell the stock (since it brought in a small income), and made her a gift of the £100. "You won't let me borrow?" Dorothy wrote back. "So be it."

4

By the end of January 1931, in the strange way events have of defying what would seem to be logic, London publisher George Harrap invited Dorothy to translate a German monograph on the life

Alan Odle in the 1920s.

of Madame DuBarry. When Dorothy first received a copy of the work, it struck her as being "decidedly vulgar," but by the beginning of March it had become "a really good book" and the first to do the lady justice. Dorothy worked on it constantly, even during meals, developing eyestrain but thoroughly enjoying it all.

As strange as it may seem, Dorothy found in her subject a kindred spirit. Madame DuBarry, who had been born the illegitimate daughter of a cook, had grown up to succeed the famous Madame Pompadour as the mistress of the aging Louis XV. When Louis died, he willed that she be confined in a convent, but DuBarry instead established herself as the beautiful chatelaine of Louveciennes. Lover followed lover, and from each affair, however disastrously ended, she seemed to emerge with but one concern: for her health. She was accused of being heartless, of being incapable of genuine love, and of being a peasant masquerading as an aristocrat. Dorothy Richardson admired her unquenchable desire to live on any terms at all. To DuBarry the sheer fact of life was as marvelous as it had always been to Dorothy, for whom indeed nothing was more important or astonishing than life itself. As Dorothy believed this, so also did the heroine of *Pilgrimage*.

Yet the price Dorothy had to pay for discovering Madame DuBarry was high. The translation work was unquestionably a boon. It established her in a field she had been trying to enter for years. Several other books came her way as a result of the praise received by her translation of *The DuBarry*. Four of these she would take on during a period when she could least afford to be diverted from *Pilgrimage*. Just when it was most important that volume ten be followed by volume eleven as soon as possible, she could not resist the lure of translation. It brought in quick money, and the books were challenging. But while she worked on the translations, the tide of her reputation as a novelist came in unexpectedly and went out. As if this were not enough, four years of the pressures of translation and publisher's deadlines subverted her health. She seemed not to have absorbed one of the primary lessons DuBarry had taught; but then, in spite of DuBarry's concern for her health, she had ultimately lost her head.

CHAPTER SEVENTEEN

Fiction and Fact

As Dorothy translated the DuBarry book, she was troubled with headaches, dizziness, and nausea. She blamed these on having plunged "too frenziedly" into the work, which had brought on nearly all the symptoms of "sea-sickness." She laid the blame specifically on the constant eye-shifting she was forced to do, from text to manuscript and from manuscript to "crabbed" German dictionary. When she slowed down, the symptoms abated. She cut out work at mealtimes, devoted evenings to her novel, and still managed to finish the translation by the end of May.

In June 1931 they went up to London, where she was determined to finish volume ten, now entitled "Earthenware" instead of "Amabel." Dorothy wanted to give it to Duckworth (for the £20 they had finally agreed upon) no later than the beginning of August. But as it neared completion, her anxieties seemed to grow. Duckworth was planning to publish in the fall, which meant she would soon be faced with reviews, and she "flinched in advance."

Also to be considered was Powys's essay, which had already appeared in two spring issues of Murry's *Adelphi*. Dorothy nervously explained to her friends that although Murry had published the essay in two issues, he had cut it somewhat, with the result that certain qualifying remarks had been omitted. The remarks would be restored when the essay appeared in book form, she said, and would serve to tone it down. She was trying to disarm criticism by anticipating and agreeing with it. Yet when her old acquaintance Hugh Walpole wrote to her about the essay, commenting on its aggressive manner, she agreed with him reluctantly but tried to defend Powys. Powys had written his essay, she said, "in a mood of furious indignation" over the state of her sales and the "tone" of her American press, which she described as a "who-reads-this-deadly-bore-now tone." Walpole, who believed in gentlemanliness, might well have had in mind the harsh way in which Powys referred to her critics. He called them "superficial" and "banal," and at one point had even named G. B. Stern as presumably one of the harshest. But Dorothy herself might have stirred him up with her own complaint, during their talk together, about Miss Stern's "malicious" (as she had called it) review of *Oberland*. Dorothy knew how "noble" Powys's intentions were, yet she could not come to his defense without ambivalence, for, as she herself confessed, her own emotions *were* mixed. Having always insisted, too, on her fundamental cowardice, she could not help hoping in her heart (which she opened to Peggy Kirkaldy) that when the book appeared, they would "leave me alone & go for John."

1

Dorothy spent the last days of July and the early part of August trying not to think about the fall and working on the typescript of her novel, which still had its second title, "Earthenware." She was revising the novel and at the same time writing the last section. She knew there were "bad bits in it," and she could account for each one. But she claimed to feel satisfied with the whole. A month later, with the publication date and the reviews that much closer, she was not sure at all. It looked in proof "like the shadow of a book," thin, brief, and bearing the marks of a thousand interruptions. It would probably appear, she estimated, at the beginning of November, with the title she had finally settled on, *Dawn's Left Hand*. She might as well have been reporting the date of an execution. So vulnerable did the novel now seem, that when she learned Powys's book was scheduled for publication earlier than planned and in advance of *Dawn's Left Hand*, she treated the news as if it were a lifeline thrown out.

Once the proofs had been sent in and there was nothing more to do but wait for the worst, Dorothy and Alan set off for Sussex to join his brother Vincent and his family on a camping holiday. During their stay, to Dorothy's delight, an early play of Noel Coward's (*The Vortex*, his first success) was being revived, and she leaped at the chance to see it. She and Alan stayed up nearly all night afterward, discussing Coward's technique with Vincent and Rose, though Dorothy confessed that what she liked best was his *Weltschmerz*. From Sussex they went to Essex for a week, to visit with Peggy; then they went to the Austens' new home near Canterbury, where Dorothy said she found such peace and leisure that the plan of her next volume was "then & there set down."

The peace, as might be expected, was short-lived. It vanished in London, and taking its place was a "hornet-brood, rising from within . . . of worries about being worried by incessantly worrying worries." To begin with, she paid Duckworth her second visit in sixteen years, with the aim of convincing them that a successor to *Dawn's Left Hand* should follow very soon. When they agreed with her, she asked point-blank for a promise of £100 during the coming year to write the book, and she offered them "an Olde Wrapper" for it. Although they did not commit themselves, she admittedly was flattered by their reception. It was "a red-letter day" for them, she reported they had said. (Miss Edith Sitwell had come to see them that morning too.) Dorothy went home feeling hopeful. Alan was at the point of signing a contract with the publishing house of John Lane. But the next morning Duckworth wrote to say that because of the loss they had sustained with *Oberland,* they could give her only £25 on the new volume. Furthermore, since it was no longer the custom to provide a "decorative" jacket to what Dorothy said they described as the "superior, intellectual(!) type of novel," they would not need a wrapper by Alan. Enraged by what she interpreted as a game of "cat and mouse" and wounded by the failure of a personal effort that had been difficult for her to make, she then observed with dismay the breakdown of Alan's contract with Lane. They claimed that there was too much uncertainty both in England and America, so for the present they had to abandon Mr. Odle's book. Even Alan became worried and went out to look for advertisement work; but it had been years since he had even thought about such work, and by 1931 most of it was done by photography rather than by hand.

With the next year looking more and more unpromising, Dorothy was scarcely in the mood to be interviewed as though she were a highly successful novelist. Her friend Louise Morgan (Theis), who had been writing a series of articles on current authors for the weekly paper *Everyman,* wanted Dorothy to be the subject of one of them. In response, Dorothy claimed that she and Alan were preparing to leave for Cornwall, so there simply was no time for an interview. Furthermore, the conditions under which she worked (a standard question asked by Louise Morgan), Dorothy said, would not "bear description," and she had "no neat opinions." But she sent a few general statements and invited Louise to tea, merely, she said, to see her before they left London.

On the morning of October 9, when Louise Morgan was coming to tea, Dorothy received the corrected manuscript of the DuBarry translation, and she promptly flew into a rage. Every instance of the historical present had been cut out, it seemed, because it "worried the American publisher." But Dorothy had deliberately retained the present tense of the original because it seemed to her that Von Schumacher had exercised discrimination in its use and had gained a good deal dramatically by it. She also thought the historical present applied perfectly in representing universal emotions. Harrap's reader apparently did not agree with her. He seemed also to have felt that in certain places the meaning of her text needed sharpening and simplifying, for he had made a good many alterations. To these she responded with contemptuous fury. Some of them deserved contempt, others did not, but Dorothy had no desire to be reasonable. She promptly rang up Harrap to withdraw her signature from the book. Harrap begged her to indicate on the manuscript all her objections. She refused to do this, except in one chapter, and returned the book that morning.

When Louise Morgan arrived in the afternoon, Dorothy's wrath was spent. She had played her scene with a publisher, acting out with Harrap the resentment she had felt toward Duckworth. She enjoyed a four-hour chat with Louise, who was determined to interview her in spite of her protests. She assumed they were token objections, but Dorothy insisted afterward that she had not been aware that an interview was taking place. When Louise showed her a draft of the interview, Dorothy begged to be allowed to modify and cut it, and she continued to have second and third thoughts about what she had said.

She was particularly concerned about the references she had made to the Cornish. The night before leaving London she remembered having used the word "peasants"; it had to come out, she wrote Louise. And would Louise please correct the statement about the absence of wireless and gramophone; this was true only during the first few years they had gone to Cornwall. In Cornwall three days later, on October 17, with *Everyman* due to appear on the twenty-first, Dorothy suddenly realized she had committed yet another "enormity": she had spoken of the shopowners as "tradespeople." She wrote at once, imploring Louise to substitute "pur-veyors." Her hair had turned white over it, she said. It would spread through the parish. The local shop carried *Everyman,* and the news was sure to go round that they, the "eccentric harmless foreigners," were in a paper. She was right about the news circulating, but whether "trade" bore quite the stigma in 1931 that it had had in her youth, and that her father had conditioned her to feel, is open to question.

Meanwhile, the DuBarry affair continued. She refused to accept the elimination of the historical present from her translation. In the course of a long conversation with Harrap (who agreed that most of the other changes were uncalled-for but insisted on retaining the alteration of tense), it was decided that the book would be issued under a name other than hers. Advance notices, however, had already appeared, citing her as the translator; and she was sure that "scores of ineptitudes," as well as a style that "clashed" with hers, would be "credited" to her. On this certainty, the ultimate and inevitable compromise with Harrap rested. After weeks of argument, letter-writing, and telephoning, with "curses, deep & bitter" on Dorothy's side and "immensely detailed revelations of *what,* in *every* kind of way, it is, *dear* Miss Richardson, to be a Publisher" on Harrap's, she "persuaded" him to send her the entire manuscript so that she could "alter the worst cases of bad sentence-rhythms." By late December, proofs of the corrected book began to arrive, and though she entered immediately into another conflict over Harrap's "house-rules" governing punctuation, *The DuBarry*—under her name as the translator—finally appeared in February 1932.

Back in October 1931, Dorothy had picked at Louise Morgan's interview with her even after its publication. It was "much too heavy on the pathetic note," she complained. Louise had "mud-dled" what she had said about women. Alan, who never missed a day's work, had emerged as working only when there were commis-sions and seemed to spend the rest of his time in the Café Royal. She might have thought this impression was conveyed by the portrait of Alan reproduced in *Everyman,* the one Adrian Allinson had painted twenty years before, which hung in the Café Royal, but it was *not* conveyed by anything in the text. She was also unhappy with Louise's pointed declaration that of the "two innovators in English prose of this century—James Joyce and Dorothy Richardson"— Joyce was "acclaimed on two continents, and Dorothy

Richardson . . . 'entirely forgotten.' " But as the text shows, the phrase 'entirely forgotten' was Dorothy's rather than Louise Morgan's. Yet her printed statements, combined with an account of her extremely modest circumstances, struck what she heard as a "pathetic note" that she did not appreciate. She did not comment on the tribute Louise had paid to the color, richness, and force of her personality.

However, she did not complain to the author. On the contrary, she told Louise that Alan, as well as she, liked the interview, and they "prostrated" themselves "before [her] ability to make bricks with almost no straw." Indeed, if the interview became a booklet (as the others had), she would welcome the opportunity to make just a few alterations. In any case, if there were any copies left over, she would like them "for relatives who adore such things."

In a month or two, the insufficiencies of the article paled before the evidence of its favorable reception. She got "*masses* of letters" about it and decided that everyone she had ever spoken two words to had read *Everyman*. Among the most amazing letters was one from the school in North London where she had taught in the early 1890s, which she had fictionalized in *Backwater*. Dorothy reported that she had received "a wonderful letter" from the headmistress, whom she had renamed Deborah Perne in her novel. Miss Perne, she said, was now nearly a hundred years old and had commented that Alan had "a nice, pleasant kind of face." This description of the artist whose drawings could scarcely be sent through the mails at first startled Dorothy; then she began to see what Deborah Perne saw: Alan's face belonged to her own period, and in recalling her youth, she could not help but find it agreeable.

Louise Morgan's article had practical consequences as well. The Jackson firm arranged to print it as a pamphlet and to distribute 10,000 copies free of charge. At the time that she heard from Jackson (in November), the *Times Literary Supplement* carried a review of John Cowper Powys's book. Dorothy was expecting the worst, for *TLS* had never treated her delicately (and she assumed that Powys's subject would call for rough handling even of him), so she read the piece with astonishment. The reviewer noted that Powys wrote "with the fury of the enthusiast," and then went on to say that "coming from a lecturer, critic and novelist of such ripe experience, this remarkable panegyric can be treated only with respect." She could scarcely believe it. John had performed a miracle, and he had paved the way for *Dawn's Left Hand,* which was just about to appear.

At the very last moment, as though it were as inevitable as the tides, Dorothy's heart sank again when she learned that Duckworth had raised the price of the volume from the usual 6s. to 7s. 6d. But he was advertising it, and indications were from the first that it would sell better than usual. She waited for the reviews, which began to appear toward the end of November. One praised her "artistry" as "certain and direct." Another asked why Dorothy Richardson was "so neglected" and Proust "trumpeted" when she was "at once quintessentially English and exquisitely individual." A third found *Dawn's Left Hand* "an adventure in thought." Dorothy breathed a sigh of relief and pleasure. After the "miseries of apprehension" she had suffered beforehand, these were sweet words indeed.

2

Dawn's Left Hand is about events that took place in 1906. Dorothy verified the date for Bryher, who had surmised as much. In the novel Miriam contemplates the ten years she has known Hypo Wilson. Dorothy herself had met Wells in 1896. This, then, was the year following her return from the Oberland, the year of her affair with Wells and of her meeting with Veronica Leslie-Jones. By 1907 (which Dorothy said she was sorry she had not reached in the novel and which could have been reached with the addition of a brief section), these two relationships had so altered her life that she had left London in a precarious mental and physical state. It may very well be that Dorothy had ended *Dawn's Left Hand* where she did in unknowing self-defense, for when she finally picked up the threads of 1907 in the eleventh volume, she broke down again as she had years before, and the new book would not be published until 1935, after another delay of four years (like the one after *Oberland*). By then the enthusiastic reviews of *Dawn's Left Hand* had been virtually forgotten and in a real sense had gone to waste: the great—and successful—effort she had made to transmute fact into fiction seemed to have exhausted her.

In *Dawn's Left Hand,* however, Miriam comes back to London refreshed by her Swiss holiday (as Dorothy herself had been) and feeling strong enough even for the persistent Hypo Wilson. She finds a note from him awaiting her: "Welcome back to your London, my dear. I'm more in love with you than ever." Yet for Miriam, his signature, formed by the "small interwoven capitals" (presumably HGW), weakens the effect of his words. "He was 'in love' in his way; once again. But behind the magic words was nothing for her individually, for any one individually." He would already have forgotten precisely what he had said. *She* would go further than this, and forget *him* for a while, realizing at the same time that she can neither "wish him away" nor really "avert" him. She knows it will not be long before he becomes her lover. In this confident, self-possessed mood, her eyes fall upon a letter—from Hypo's wife—that she had missed at first. The Wilsons were coming to London to treat her to dinner and then to Wagner at Covent Garden. Miriam would not be able to forget him, it seems, even for a while. But she does manage to thwart his lovemaking on three separate occasions, and to transform his success on the fourth into a triumph of her own.

The evening at the opera had been planned by Wilson as a prelude to seduction. In spite of several mistakes of judgment and Miriam's full awareness of his motives, the event, on the whole, serves his purpose: "to catch her in the full after-glow of her successful holiday, and submit her, in the best possible circumstances, to the emotional solvent of music." Hypo makes his first error at dinner: without her knowledge he orders lark pie. When the waiter tells Miriam what it is, she nearly dissolves into tears. Otherwise he is careful during the meal to refrain from striking the "wrong note," the note of "didactic speculations." He loses control only once, but with a glance at Miriam's face checks himself. She had just said there was probably "no such thing as travel . . . nothing but a Voyage autour de ma Chambre, meaning de tout ce que je suis, even in a tour du monde." Hypo begins to retort in Wellsian fashion, "We are going to travel, Miriam, *everywhere*. This small planet is a misfit. . . ." He stops, and Miriam knows with deep satisfaction that she can have the last word: "There's more space within than without." This is the theme of her opposition to him, for he refuses to recognize an inner world of the self, as Dorothy was convinced also was true of Wells.

Wilson's choice of music for a pointed evening strikes Miriam as typical. Instead of offering Beethoven or Bach—experiences of the "solitary human soul"—he gives her Wagner—"a huge, exciting world-party . . . everybody speaking at once." And to her utter dismay he had taken a box, in her opinion the worst possible place to sit for both opera and theater, far too near the stage and the music. Poor Hypo. He defends his choice with reasons normally dear to Miriam's heart: "Privacy, and freedom to come and go without assault and battery." He has a point, she admits, but she then goes on to ask him effectively, "But when you visit a picture gallery do you prefer to look at the pictures from one side?" It doesn't really matter, she adds, "I shall imagine the stage. Sit with my back to it." Furthermore, "no one can see and hear to perfection at the same moment. And the wonder of Wagner is that through your ears he makes you see so hugely."

She does sit with her back to the stage throughout *The Flying Dutchman,* turning only once to see "Senta at her wheel" and the "good *German* effect" of all the long-haired maidens. And in spite of her inner and outer resistance, Hypo's plan works, though "the emotions rising in her . . . were not those he intended." Listening to the "massed music roll by," to the "tremendous ado" not "having its full chance" because of the box they are in, Miriam feels everything this music is not saying and that the music of Bach does say. The opera produces in her precisely those feelings Wagner leaves out (except from the ballad of Senta) and what Hypo calls "turnip-emotion"—the "deep, quiet sense of *being.*" This was emphatically *not* Hypo's purpose.

Sure of his eventual success, however, he follows up the evening at the opera with a more direct approach a few weeks later. They have dinner in the small private room of a London restaurant, alone together for the first time. The episode is not dramatized. In still another room not long afterward, Miriam remembers it as a total failure. The fault, she admits, had been hers. Undaunted, Hypo tries again, and so does Miriam. But a new barrier has grown between them. It is the young French girl Amabel, whom Miriam had recently met at the women's club near Flaxman's Court. As she explains to Hypo after the strange, awkward, comic collapse of their second evening alone, "I'm preoccupied. . . . Perpetually, just now, with one person."

Amabel does indeed dominate her thoughts. Even in the moment of their first encounter, when she came toward her as she was leaving the club, Miriam heard a "warning voice within." What, she had wondered, did this unknown person want? During the next few days she finds out. The beautiful, dark-haired girl with the oval-shaped face (to which Miriam has always been partial) had decided that Miriam is wise and pure, hence worthy of adoration. To Miriam, Amabel begins to seem an artist, perpetually creating a single work of art—herself; and Amabel believes that only Miriam can read her. Although Amabel is involved with a man named Basil, she pursues Miriam, gains access to her room and scrawls "I love you" across the mirror, invades the dental office with a long letter in the most expressive and pictorial handwriting Miriam has ever seen, and in every other way virtually surrounds her. Once again, as she had been with that other artist, Eleanor Dear, Miriam is "isolated with this girl." No one else seems real, and "all the visible circumstances of her life had retreated to inaccessible distance."

Amabel's siege is meant to parallel Hypo Wilson's. Her success underscores his failure, perhaps even causes it. Amabel's presence in Miriam's mind blots out Hypo during the evening they spend together in the room he has rented for the purpose of making love to her. As she sees it, he does not succeed in bringing her to life as a woman, because he is incapable of "homage," of recognizing her for what she is and for what she represents. Furthermore, she does not find his body beautiful. It was "interesting as partner and foil, but not desirable." It did not have the power to stir her as his clothed figure walking in a garden or entering a room had so often stirred her. Along with the familiar clothes, "something of his essential self seemed to have departed. Leaving him pathetic." What follows is at once ludicrous and revealing. Miriam clasps this pathetic body to her breast, maternally, and is shocked to feel him, when she lets go, responding in kind, and one wonders why she is shocked by an answering tenderness. Clearly she wants him to resume his role as the male, as the leader, a role from which tenderness is presumably excluded and which she has just abrogated. In truth, he had seemed unmanned; and faced with the unexpected fulfillment of her unconscious desire, Miriam draws back in fear.

Yet through the rest of the evening and in scenes that follow during a weekend at the Wilson home, the unacknowledged wish hovers beneath the surface of feeling and act. It is she who restores him to leadership, soothes his ruffled pride, agrees with his salvaging comment, "Your reputation's in shreds, Miriam, virginal though you be," and suggests they go to her favorite London haunt. In Donizetti's, fully recovered, he plans her future. She will write sketches, then criticism, and, after having a child, she will produce the inevitable novel in the "green solitude" that he would provide. Miriam objects to his concrete talk of money and support. "No economics," she cannot help insisting. "Whatever I do, no economics. They shut things off." They would make her dependent and put her into a circumscribed position. Moreover, when she shifts the conversation to Amabel and launches into a description of the girl preoccupying her mind to his disadvantage, it is to present Hypo with a humiliatingly triumphant rival.

The masked struggle continues during the weekend that follows at Bonnycliff (modeled on H. G. Wells's Spade House in Kent). On the first evening, a few hours after retiring early with a heavy cold, Miriam is half-dreaming of a visit she had once made to a sweet little village in Yorkshire when Hypo enters the room— through the window. " 'I'm not here,' she said, searching the dreamy void for something beyond mere indignation over this adroit arrival." It is not the mere fact of his coming in that she cannot abide. Once there, he cannot help but begin to exert control, standing over her "like a short doctor: flattering, warning, trying to edit her mind." She refuses to utter a word except to repeat, "I'm not here," accentuating the dreamlike mood she refuses to allow him to break. Hypo leaves, with the equally insistent assertion that she (as well as he) will "come back." But he also says, "*Don't* attach importance to these inevitable preliminaries." And once he is gone, she is fully awake, sitting in judgment on her behavior. In terms of the past, of her feeling for him and her own consent to the direction their relationship has been taking, she ought to have yielded to him. But as certain as she is of this, another kind of certainty is even more powerful—that her unconscious will was *not* to yield—and it was this she had obeyed. She feels that she has won another round.

The next day, however, Hypo changes strategy. He pays no attention to her at all and after breakfast goes off to work in his study without even asking her how she intends to occupy herself. He deserves to find her gone, she thinks, returned to town, when he emerges from his study. But she does not leave. She decides that she owes to *him* the sureness and strength with which she had wakened this morning; she would repay him by remaining and amusing him with lively talk. Hypo surprises her once again by not standing still, as her mind would have him. At lunch he is thoroughly happy, "a neatly plump Silenus with intelligent brow," basking in the attentions of his radiant wife, who knows his morning's work has gone well. Afterward he disappears again, without a word about the afternoon walk they have always taken together on her visits. When Alma tells her that she will spend her afternoon with a dressmaker and says that she hopes Miriam will "be happy, playing alone, until tea-time," she finally understands Hypo's tactic. "Methodically, deliberately, he was leaving her to herself. To demonstrate a principle: elimination of the personal." For the sake of that principle, on which he wanted their sexual relationship to be based, he was cutting her off from both "the resources of her far-away London life and . . . the life down here that he knew was centered, throughout its brevity, upon himself."

In the manuscript of *Dawn's Left Hand,* Miriam's response to Hypo's "demonstration" was not "anger" as it appeared in the printed text, but "hurt" that "ranged out over the world, out into space, seeking relief." With the substitution of "anger," the world became "too small to contain it," and the "relief" was sought "vainly." The primary change of feeling suggests that Dorothy Richardson wanted her heroine to respond more positively and less passively than perhaps she herself had. Though in neither version does Miriam confront Hypo with her feeling, the subsequent play of her mind seems to stem from anger and to match her earlier thoughts about him. She imagines, for example, how he would behave if she were to seek him out. He would first listen attentively to her, and then he would "protest against her failure to recognize the compliment he was paying" her. Next he would launch into a discussion of his abiding theme: "the right, intelligent way of managing life's incompatibilities" by eliminating the personal and the subjective. Finally, "he would become affectionate, with reservations," that is, he would move toward her as a sexual being. And when she rebuffed him, he would really wish she were not there, wanting instead Alma and the "screened inaccessibility" his wife allows him. By contrast, Miriam would try to get too close to the self she believes his wife does not attempt to penetrate. He could never understand, she decides, that what she herself wanted was "something far beyond sympathetic affection . . . something as detached and impersonal as even he could wish: a sharing . . . of intimations he refused to recognize." In truth, "he was an alien. To Alma, to any woman ever born."

Miriam works off her "anger" in this way, as Dorothy must have soothed her "hurt," by analyzing Hypo and concluding that he is foreign, that *no* woman can hope to "naturalize" him. During the evening of this embattled day, it becomes clear that Miriam will not so much yield to Hypo as accept his challenge—the challenge to the feminine consciousness he does not even know he has made. By morning Miriam has met it successfully. She goes back to London no longer at a "disadvantage" among women, with the "burden" of her virginity removed, "leaving a calm delightful sense of power." Indeed, "she was full of inward song and wishing for congratulations." There is no doubt that in her mind—and in Dorothy Richardson's—the victory does not belong to Hypo Wilson.

Whether victory had actually belonged to Dorothy in 1906 cannot be known. What is more important is the evidence, provided by her novel, that she wanted it to be hers and in retrospect saw that it had been. She built this novel, which had been so difficult to write, around the two persons, Wilson and Amabel, whose living counterparts had taken possession of her younger self in such different ways. But the fictional account cannot be accepted as fact without careful qualification, for it emerged not only from the consciousness of an older person but also from certain imperious, unconscious needs. One of them was to minimize the degree of control and power wielded by H. G. Wells in their relationship. Miriam is more in command and less in love than it would seem Dorothy had been. Then, too, some of Miriam's ironic comments about Wilson are echoes of Dorothy's about Wells years after they were lovers, when she saw him through the eyes of a married woman whose husband was not her adversary. Wells had been a formidable opponent, as Wilson is through most of *Pilgrimage*. But in *Dawn's Left Hand* he becomes alternately ludicrous and formidable.

Having reached in fiction the point of her actual affair with Wells, Dorothy seems to have turned it into a series of foiled maneuvers on his part and a final "surrender" on hers that is really a triumph. It is always possible that in 1906 Wells was as clumsy a seducer as Hypo Wilson, but the greater likelihood is that years later Dorothy heightened and adorned his awkwardness. Indeed, she could have hit on no better means by which to conceal the identity of Wilson as the experienced, if not notorious, seducer, H. G. Wells. Such at least was Wells's reputation. So in this case Dorothy had achieved unwittingly the "collaboration between the conscious and the unconscious" which she valued so highly.

With the creation of Amabel, Dorothy fulfilled yet another strong need, the need for atonement. She had sacrificed Veronica—influenced her to marry Benjamin Grad (as Miriam was yet to influence Amabel to marry Michael Shatov)—so that she might regain her freedom from an intensely personal and complicating relationship, an involvement that spelled danger for the future. As it was, Veronica would love Dorothy for the rest of her life and would demand that Dorothy share her life. But as a wife and mother, her passionate and appropriative nature would be dispersed rather than concentrated upon Dorothy alone. Dorothy herself did not marry until ten years later, and then she chose a man whose only passion was his art. In providing him with the means of satisfying that passion, she might well have been making amends indirectly to Veronica Grad. She made more direct amends in *Dawn's Left Hand*, by enslaving Miriam to Amabel and by making Amabel a greater threat to her own intense need for independence than Hypo Wilson.

Given the frustrating circumstances of her life during the composition of this volume, which alone among her novels had three separate titles (the first of which was "Amabel"), and given the current crisis in the Grad household and the death of Jane Wells, the novel seems to have been an exercise in self-determination and self-acquittal. No wonder it is a novel in which talk prevails. (It even contains a disquisition on speech sounds.) Yet its inner and outer dialogues do not work at cross-purposes. *Dawn's Left Hand* holds together astonishingly well (as most of the reviewers saw), perhaps because its surface could not help but reflect its intricate depths.

CHAPTER EIGHTEEN

Breaking Down

WHEN the translation of *The DuBarry* appeared in February 1932, Dorothy's feeling was largely one of relief. Her struggle with Harrap over the editorial changes had nearly ruined the pleasure she had experienced in the book itself. But by March she was proudly reporting to Bryher that the reviewers were hailing her translation as "excellent," "magnificent," "perfect." These were words she was not accustomed to. "I blow out my fur & purr," she announced.

Soon afterward she received an inquiry from a German writer for which she thought the favorable press reviews were responsible. Would she translate a book he was just finishing? Apparently he had been in touch with an English publisher who had left him free to choose his own translator. Dorothy wondered at such liberality, especially toward someone who seemed to her a virtual unknown.

The name Brecht meant nothing to Dorothy Richardson, but this thirty-four-year-old author was no by means unknown in Germany. There he had already achieved considerable success with his plays, both adaptations and originals, and he had been offered the Schiffbauerdam Theater of Berlin for use in staging his productions. In the late '20s his *Dreigoschenoper,* based on John Gay's *The Beggar's Opera,* with music by Kurt Weill, had played for more than a year. In 1933 that play would be staged in New York as *The Three-Penny Opera,* but by that time Brecht would already be exiled from a Germany rapidly falling under Hitler's control.

The book that Brecht asked Dorothy to translate in 1932 was probably *A Penny for the Poor,* a novel that he did not complete until 1934, the year after he left Germany. For some months the manuscript seemed on the verge of arriving, but Dorothy never saw it, and when an English version did appear in 1937, it was the work of another hand.

Dorothy was hoping the translation would materialize as a job for the summer of 1932, and while she waited she undertook to translate an essay on the work of a writer she scarcely knew, the Swiss philosopher and novelist C. F. Ramuz. The essay was to be published as part of a series the following year. From the first she did not feel comfortable in the task, frankly admitting she had agreed to do it only for the money. Though the sum was only £25, she had been promised immediate payment, as an advance on royalties, whereas in the usual case of translations she had to wait for payment until the work was finished. However, the essay made her so uneasy that she mentioned the name of her subject only to Hugh Walpole, to whom she turned for advice about books that might be helpful as background reading. Wanting to trouble Hugh as little as possible, she wrote the author's name on an enclosed card that he could fill in and mail back to her. But her uneasiness won out, and after doing some preparatory reading for the essay during their spring stay at Trevone Cottage, in the early summer she abandoned it. A few years later, with the sense of having wasted time that she should have spent on the new volume of *Pilgrimage,* she would write a small piece about Ramuz. Her only gain had been an excuse for not reading Powys's new novel, *A Glastonbury Romance.* Alan, she claimed, had spent five weeks reading it and was just about to begin again on the "nearly two thousand pages of small print, & . . . forty-three leading characters." She promised Powys she would try to read it during the summer.

By that time, as if with poetic justice, she was engaged in translating a German novel almost as monumental in size as Powys's. Its author, Robert Neumann, and the publisher Peter Davies had proposed that she not only translate *Die Macht* but also condense it for the English reading public. The double labor did not especially appeal to her. It would bring in more money, however, than the essay she had abandoned, and she felt qualified to do it. The agreement she made with Davies was to shorten *Die Macht* by 50,000 words, and she set to work at once on the sprawling naturalistic novel, hoping to be finished with it by mid-September. All through the summer she carried it about, on their annual visits to her sister, to Vincent and Rose, and to Peggy Kirkaldy, until *Mammon* (the title of her English version) became a millstone around her neck. Prolix, exclamatory, discursive, with a narrative technique the opposite of her own (with Neumann announcing to his readers where he was going and why, and shifting clumsily from scene to scene and from character to character), the novel began to weigh more and more heavily upon her. Yet its cumbrous text had a certain power, and though its theme (the conflict between innocence and the corrupting force of money) was outlandishly dramatized, Dorothy found herself actually growing fond of the book. She took to speaking of it as her "beloved-hated job."

Toward the end of August, within a few weeks of finishing, she could no longer ignore the physical toll the book was taking. A London heat wave during that month had made everything almost impossible, she said, and when it was over she felt utterly drained, as though she could not react to anything or anybody except "silently very far away inside." Nevertheless, she pushed on and turned over the manuscript to Davies in September, at which point Alan fell ill with the flu and she caught it. By then they were about to leave London for Cornwall. On the day before their departure, Peter Davies called to say that her cutting of *Die Macht* had been too drastic, so the next morning Dorothy carried with her to the train the seemingly inescapable manuscript of *Mammon.*

She revised it at Lynx, restoring some of the omitted passages. She tried also to get another translation to work on during the winter. But when Neumann's novel was finished, and no new job came through, the need to go on as though nothing were wrong seemed somehow less imperative. She admitted that she could scarcely drag herself through each day, but neither could she help feeling guilty. If there was no translation to do, then she ought to be writing her novel, and this—as she would *not* admit—was what she felt quite incapable of doing.

2

Self-recrimination ebbed and flowed as 1932 came to an end and a new year began. A letter she wrote to John Cowper Powys struck him as being charged with meanings he could not fathom. Her sentences were gnomic, he said, each one weighted "with more riddles than Oedipus ever coped with." Though he did not know what it was, he sensed that something was radically wrong, that indeed a storm was brewing.

For the moment, it seemed to subside. Dorothy prepared herself for the proofs of *Mammon,* which had been delayed and were now likely to come in February. Here, after all, was something she had actually done. And once the proofs arrived and were sent back in March, her attention was turned outward, to the events taking place in Germany. The Reichstag had been burned down at the end of February 1933, and a few weeks later, with the passage of the "enabling bill," Hitler had gained the full powers he wanted. Discussing the situation with Bryher, Dorothy said she thought that "no one on earth [could] arrest the process going forward in Germany," that "political & racial passions [were being] unchained" and the victims of them were helpless. It seemed to her that all the Jews and the "intelligentsia of the Left" ought to be evacuated as soon as possible. But how was one to do that, she asked. Most people, she rightly sensed, would argue that Hitler was doing his best to restrain his armies and that he could not, after all, allow the opposition a perfectly free hand. Nevertheless, she had written letters, she said, to the people she knew who might be able to use their influence.

At the beginning of April she and Alan shifted as usual from Constantine Bay to Trevone. In May advance copies of *Mammon* were circulated. Then the axe fell. Neumann took offense at the printed version of his book. Despite Dorothy's expansion of the original abridgement, the novel had been shortened more than Neumann had anticipated, and his complaint to Davies resulted in the scrapping of the entire edition. Years afterward, Dorothy would speak of it as "a sad story. Of human frailty." At the time, she was strangely unmoved. When Neumann visited London a few months later, she met him and found him a most "delightful creature." Not only was he gigantic and a past swimming champion of Austria, she said, he was also a sailor, like Conrad. Both she and Alan "fell in love with him."

Her reaction to the disappearance of *Mammon* may well have been part of an extended calm before the storm. During the spring in Trevone, she had felt revived, even able to work on her novel again, and to think of finishing it within the year. All the reasons for not delaying this volume took a fresh hold on her, the most pointed of them being Duckworth's March statement, which had shown a distinct increase in sales. In fact, for the last six months of 1932, he actually owed *her* £8. But somehow when she talked about finishing the novel, she was not convincing. Something else had a stronger hold on her, something that drove her to seek other work. She had already written to Alfred Knopf, applying for the translation of Léon Pierre-Quint's study of André Gide.

Meanwhile, Bryher, perhaps trying to read between the lines of Dorothy's letters as Powys was, told her that she had made an arrangement whereby Dorothy would have an annual income of £120, tax-free, for the next seven years. Dorothy wrote back to say that there were "no plain terms" to describe what Bryher was really giving her. On the same day she wrote to Powys (in French, as if a personal revelation were easier in another tongue), to tell him that one of the most horrible of her demons had just been curbed. A good many of them, she knew, were "heraldic," but this did not make them any less "redoubtable." The identity of the curbed demon was clear, and she was quite right to speak of this fear of not having enough money as bridled rather than conquered. She also sensed that a great many of her fears were wriggling out of their halters at once and that it would not be long before she gave herself up to them.

3

For the time being, Dorothy took on the Gide book, which would pay about as much as she would get from Bryher for the year. She planned to work on it in June, at Queen's Terrace, after devoting nearly the entire spring to her novel. But she could not keep her mind off translation, and she wrote letter after letter to various publishers suggesting any number of books, knowing perfectly well that if any of her suggestions were agreed to, she would have to do the work immediately.

Once in London, she worked on Gide most of the time. It seemed to go well. French was less of a strain to her than German. She did not depend as much on the dictionary. And the subject was congenial. Only a few years before, she had read Gide's *Voyages au Congo* and had found him "incomparable." There is no way to determine what other Gide work she knew before undertaking Pierre-Quint's study, but she appeared to be as interested in the man as in his work. He saw himself in terms that were familiar to her, as a man whose nature was compounded of contradictory elements at war with each other and stemming from his dual inheritance.

Gide was both puritan and sensualist by virtue of his strict Huguenot father and the wealthy, mixed Protestant-and-Catholic background of his mother. He claimed that nothing could be more different than the influences of these two families and the provinces in which they lived, "harsh Languedoc and lush green Normandy."

Dorothy, too, felt conflicting elements within her, and to the heroine of *Pilgrimage* had given, on her father's side, a Puritan background in the south of England that militated against the West country artistic strain derived from her mother. She constantly showed duty vying with pleasure in Miriam's life, until she finally achieved the hard-won insight that the obligation to self is moral, though in the eyes of others it might wear the look of selfishness. So, too, did André Gide's "religion of the senses" appear to many to be corruption, and his confessions of homosexuality seem like "subtly mendacious art."

If Gide the man bore marks of kinship to Dorothy Richardson, the novelist was closely related too. Whether she knew *Les Faux-Monnayeurs* or not, simply to have read about it would have told her that the methods of Gide were similar to her own. Here, in the form of a diary kept by Edouard, the central character, who is writing the novel into which Gide has put him, was fiction interwoven with autobiography. Planning and discussing the novel that shows him planning and discussing, Gide-Edouard resembles Dorothy Richardson's heroine, who moves toward the writing of *Pilgrimage* while she is acting in it. Both novels also have a curious blend of past and present. At one point Edouard reads aloud from his work-in-progress the very scene he is in, and carries it further than Gide did, almost as if to ask who is the better writer, the character or the author, or, indeed, to ask which of them *is* the author. Though in *Pilgrimage* the materials blended are rather different, the tongue-in-cheek quality is similar. Dorothy sent Miriam to the Wagner opera with the Wilsons in *Dawn's Left Hand,* had her refute Hypo Wilson's belief in music drama as "an admirable solvent," and at the same time wrote an essay for *Close Up* in which she took Wells to task for having given the name "music-drama" to the art of cinematography.

With so many points of sympathy between them, Dorothy did not grumble about her translation of the Gide book in quite the way she had spoken of the Neumann. She described the work as that of a "coolie," but a note of pride crept in with her mention of Gide. Pierre-Quint, however, was another matter. She did not communicate with him until the end of the summer, when she was nearly finished, ostensibly because he had been traveling about. She seemed to feel remiss, nevertheless, about getting in touch with him so "late in the day," and with uncharacteristic meekness agreed to the conditions he now set forth to her: that she respect all his "idiosyncrasies" of punctuation and spacing, and also the distinction he had made between quotations of written and spoken words. This meant that she had to revise her manuscript, but the only sign of annoyance she permitted herself was the remark that his book was "a compositor's nightmare."

She might have said more if she had known what was to come. Not only the fall but most of the winter in Cornwall had to be spent working on the manuscript. After completion of her revisions, she learned from Knopf that he expected her to translate the bibliography as well, which she had originally understood would not be required. Furthermore, he expected all the quotations from French poetry to be rendered into English, "so that," she no longer meekly remarked, "the dear Americans shan't be puzzled, & shall be instructed, as they love to be." Along with these "extras" went a mass of correspondence: letters to and from Pierre-Quint, Knopf, the English publisher Jonathan Cape, and even Gide himself, who declined to settle a point she was arguing with Pierre-Quint. Gide politely—and sensibly—wrote back that he left it to her judgment. Years later she remembered the episode as Gide's diplomatic way of telling her she was right. But at the moment, in the midst of disputes and last-minute alterations, all she cared about was being rid of the manuscript. The French language, so pleasant a change the spring before, by January 1934 had become a source of extreme irritation. She railed and fumed against "the goings on of the corps de ballet of prepositions, the *d'ailleurses & aincis & au contraires* posturing, in soul-racking superfluity, up & down the page."

By then, too, she had still another translation on her hands, a German one again, having agreed in December to translate Josef Kastein's *Jews in Germany*. She called it a "learned treatise," and to her Kastein seemed bent on avoiding direction and simplicity, his sentences averaging half a page in length. Nevertheless, she plunged into the job of dismantling and reassembling those sentences while still occupied with the final details of the Gide book, so that it looked as though she dared not stop for a moment—and dared not think of the consequences. She insisted that the constant dizziness and nausea she was suffering from were merely the result of eyestrain.

Then, on New Year's Eve, an incident occurred that was a kind of grotesque enactment of the madness of her life. At nine in the

271

evening, hearing a tap on their window and a shout, she and Alan stepped out into the black Cornish night with their torches to find Adrian Allinson and a lady. Allinson was standing upright, but his friend, whom they had never seen before, was "elegantly and elongatedly and complicatedly entangled" in their high barbed-wire fence, "with the moon composed just above and behind her and the darkness below." They had come for a visit, bringing with them their own food, for they ate everything "raw."

When the startling guests left after a few days, Dorothy felt utterly desperate over the lost time, and she promptly entangled herself further by agreeing to translate a short story. As a result, she had not finished the Kastein book when they moved to Trevone at the end of March. It still needed two weeks' work, which brought her to the point of correcting a double set of Gide proofs, for both the American and English editions. Once these were read, and before the Kastein proofs arrived, she managed to squeeze in a bit of work on her novel. At least Kastein raised no problems. She had been careful to get in touch with him early, but his book must have opened large veins of memory. He was a Zionist, and the Zionist movement had become familiar to her in the days of her youthful involvement with Benjamin Grad, the period of her life she was trying to bring to a fictional close in volume eleven.

Mingling with work on the Kastein book were thoughts not only of Benjamin Grad and Michael Shatov but of Wells and Wilson as well. In June Dorothy had stayed on at Trevone Cottage a week longer than usual, to continue work on volume eleven after reading the Kastein proofs. Upon her return to London on June 15, she devoted the last two weeks of the month to the novel and actually finished half of it. This meant she had reached the point in the novel at which Miriam, walking with Hypo Wilson, had "braced herself against the truth of their relationship, the essential separation and mutual dislike of their two ways of being," and had said goodbye to him. A few days later Wells asked Dorothy to read his forthcoming autobiography, which, she said, consisted of "two hundred thousand Wellsian words." She agreed, for a fee of £50, to make corrections, comments, and suggestions, despite the fact that she had also undertaken and had promised to finish in two months another translation, a small French book entitled *Les Heures de Silence,* about a sanatorium for tuberculars.

She spent a month working on the autobiography, while Wells went off to Russia and mailed back "bits" he was still writing. Thus she had moved from her own "biographical" portrait of him in *Pilgrimage* to his "gigantic" self-portrait, as she put it, and found it "rather fascinating" as well as "very instructive." In it she discovered that Wells had identified himself as the original for Hypo Wilson in Dorothy Richardson's "curious essay in autobiography," and that he had singled out for mention only *The Tunnel,* the fourth volume published fifteen years before, in which Hypo Wilson appeared for the first time and cast his charming spell over the young Miriam Henderson. Now, in the eleventh volume, Dorothy was engaged in demonstrating that the spell had finally been broken. But did she not remember, or was she trying hard to forget, that in parting from Wells she had paid a high price?

At the moment she clung to the theory that the exhaustion she felt nearly all the time was purely physical, due not only to eyestrain but perhaps also to "old age." She claimed to be "quite definitely antique" and told Alan he would have to grow a beard or wear a gray wig. She herself had taken to "cap & shawl," she said. Antiquity notwithstanding, she had a deadline to meet for her translation of *Les Heures de Silence.* After seeing Wells's autobiography through the press, she had but a month left in which to work on this quiet little book by Robert de Traz. In making this change, it seemed as if she were duplicating the sequence of her earlier life, when she had left London and the articulate Wells—whom silence made uneasy—to live with a Quaker family. De Traz was no Quaker, but the experience he records, of his visit to a mountain sanatorium in a world apart, among human beings whose illness has given them a heightened consciousness of self, resembled her own experience among people who knew how to get in touch with themselves.

The patients on the mountain, according to de Traz, must confront themselves in order to face the solitary task of regaining their health; to turn away from themselves is to meet death. Their cures are largely the result of their own care and a constant examination of self. Thus the world outside becomes completely irrelevant, and people who are well—thick-skinned and active—have no relation to them any longer. To reinforce their solitude and emphasize by rule what ought to be self-imposed, the hours between two and four in

273

the afternoon are consecrated to utter silence everywhere on the mountain. Nothing moves. No one speaks. All turn inward. Such a perfect stillness of the body in combination with a life of the mind Dorothy had observed among the Quakers and had tried to achieve as a way of bringing herself back to health. Years, ago she had succeeded, by separating herself on the farm in Sussex from the active world. Now it was that very world for which she was translating *Les Heures de Silence,* and she had to meet the deadline it imposed. At 5:55 P.M. on September 12, Alan raced down the Strand to the publisher's office with the manuscript. Dorothy, her eye on the clock of St. Mary-le-Strand, followed panting far behind. Alan burst into the office just as they were closing.

4

As though she had done them for that purpose alone, Dorothy claimed that with her five completed translations she had earned five months "clear" to finish her novel. But three years had already passed since publication of *Dawn's Left Hand,* and she was now feeling an antique sixty-one. As a matter of fact, in an unguarded moment, she had revealed to herself how much more than that she was feeling. Toward the end of the summer, when she was still translating de Traz, Jack Beresford had unexpectedly appeared at Queen's Terrace. She had not seen him for ten years, since his move to Switzerland and then to France. To her he seemed unchanged, though his hair was white and his face was lined. The sight of him made her feel, just as she used to feel during her long visits with him in Cornwall and Buckinghamshire, that the responsibility for everything was on *his* shoulders, not on hers, that she could count on him to take care of her. But now of course her life was changed, and her needs were more complicated than ever. She might have told him, however, that a man named Koteliansky wanted to assume something of the burden he had borne an age earlier and to find her a new publisher. Perhaps she even told him of the confession she had recently made to Koteliansky, that she had no idea whether she could do any more of her own work.

S. S. Koteliansky (whom nearly everyone called Kot) had come into Dorothy's life during the summer of 1933. Although he lived near Queen's Terrace, in Acacia Road, and was a friend of Barbara Low, whom Dorothy had often seen, it seems that she had never met him until he began to take an interest in *Pilgrimage*. Even then, they communicated first by letter. Finally, in September 1934, Kot called on her. He was a strange personage, dark-complexioned, at one and the same time sensitive- yet fierce-looking, with a "big booming voice" in which he pronounced intellectual dogma. Dorothy found him a little overwhelming. After he had left, both she and Alan felt as though they had been "passed several times through a powerful mangle." But Dorothy liked him. He expressed determination to find her a better publisher than Duckworth, in his opinion, had been; and she had the sense that somehow he would. After only a few months in a new job as reader-adviser for the newly formed Cresset Press, he appeared to have learned everything about both it and the publishing world. He could tell her, she reported, the "methods, bank balances & future prospects" of every firm in England and America. He also knew, she claimed, "the name & disposition, & moral value, & taste in hats of the second cousin of the junior partner's sister-in-law's half-sister, by marriage."

Kot had come to England from Kiev in 1911, though under what circumstances and for what original purpose, it is difficult to know. His decision to stay, however, appears to have been political; he may have been a so-called student radical in the eyes of the Czarist secret police and hence an object of suspicion. In any case, he got a job in London with the Russian Law Bureau (a much less official establishment than its name suggests), and soon began to carve for himself what would be an unusual and semi-literary life, eventually translating (among others) the works of Bunin, Chekov, Gorky, and Tolstoy, sometimes in collaboration with others such as D. H. Lawrence, Katherine Mansfield, Middleton Murry, and Leonard Woolf.

By 1914 Kot had met Lawrence, whom he found "ingenuous" and who in turn thought him "a bit Jehovah-ish," and had become part of the circle surrounding that young collector of "disciples." In 1924 he was present at the ill-famed "Last Supper" Lawrence gave at the Café Royal. When Lawrence invited all his guests—the Carswells, Murry, Dorothy Brett, Mary Cannan, Mark Gertler, and Kot—to be founders with him of a colony on the slopes of the Rockies, most of them tried to evade commitment. Kot reportedly began to smash the wine glasses, shouting, "No woman here or anywhere else can possibly understand the greatness of Lawrence."

Ten years later, nonetheless, he had become the champion of Dorothy Richardson.

His first plan was to persuade the Cresset Press to publish a compact edition of her ten novels, two or three of them together in four volumes. Dorothy explained to Kot why such a plan had a special appeal to her. It would allow her, first of all, to make corrections. There were printer's errors, she claimed, and inconsistent punctuation, the latter due to an "orthodox reader" at Duckworth who had "corrected" her punctuation, which she herself had then unsystematically re-corrected. Then, too, even Duckworth agreed that such an edition would "pay its way," but he said he could not afford the venture. It would require new plates, because the books had been set originally in a variety of typefaces. He was willing to release her, however, provided that the firm taking over would buy out his stock and settle her debt to him. She thought the debt amounted to about £60.

Faced with more than he had bargained for, Kot came back with another idea. How would she feel about the Cresset Press publishing her next novel? Dorothy balked, on several grounds. She could not leave Duckworth, after so many years, in a way that would not benefit him. Though she did not think he had managed her affairs brilliantly, she was grateful to him. He had been good to her, she felt, and he had "risked publishing what other publishers scorned." Furthermore, it seemed to her that the "little public" she had, associated her with the Duckworth house. "How many would follow me if I were lost & strayed?" It was a curious note in an otherwise sensible argument.

She played the note even louder in her next letters. To leave Duckworth, she said, without an assurance from the new publisher that he would take over all her books would mean "the total disappearance at one fell swoop" (if, that is, the plates were destroyed) "of the whole of an unfinished book" and leave only a "small unsupported, shivering fragment," the volume as yet unpublished. Koteliansky did not respond. She wrote again, repeating her objection, to ensure that he understood. Once more there was no answer.

A couple of weeks later (it was by now April), she learned from Duckworth that an American named Peter Smith wanted to handle his edition of *Pilgrimage*. Since Knopf had refused *Dawn's Left Hand* and had allowed several of the earlier volumes to go out of print, she felt that Smith represented a chance for her books to circulate again in the United States. Moreover, an arrangement with him would in no way interfere with a publisher who wished to start a fresh edition, for Smith intended to purchase volumes, and the American rights would remain in her hands. Accordingly, she told Duckworth to go ahead, and she approved of his suggestion that he sell the books to Smith for 2s. 6d. each and give her a 10 percent royalty on net returns. She now wrote Kot that she had to stay with Duckworth because the "only chance" for *Pilgrimage* to "remain in existence" rested with him. Apparently she felt that she was fighting for survival.

At this point Kot began to write to her about literature and philosophy. Did she not agree that Rozanov was a "scoundrel"? If so, she replied, then she "must be a scoundreline" because she saw herself in him again and again. She was just as unreliable as he was. Having opened yet another Pandora's box, Kot apparently took issue with her self-deprecations. Not to be deterred, she "confessed" to him in July, not only that she was "a very quiet, simple sort of person . . . always afraid, & extremely often quite sure, of boring people," but also that when it came to her work she could no longer "bank" on herself.

Kot switched back to business. He asked for precise figures regarding her situation with Duckworth, and exactly what she wanted. She told him in no uncertain terms that an interested publisher would have to pay Duckworth £59 19s. 3d. (the amount of her debt to him) and £242 for his stock, plates, and molds. Then he would have to issue a "definitive, corrected, unlimited edition of *Pilgrimage* in four volumes, beginning either at once or almost immediately after the publication of the new volume." Finally, she wanted £30 in advance of royalties on that new volume. Nothing short of this would do, she said, and she thanked him for having tried to "pull [her] out of a blind alley."

Three weeks later, at the end of August, when her translation of de Traz was nearly finished, she told Kot that merely to think of the "chaotic business side" of her work sent her temperature up and made her feel faint. Kot strategically withdrew for the time being, and Dorothy met her deadline for *Les Heures de Silence*.

5

Between the middle of September and the second week of October, when Dorothy and Alan usually left for Cornwall, she tried to steady the balance that for months had been wavering like an uncertain pendulum. During their last week in town, Barbara Low came to lunch; but with Alan present, Dorothy would not have introduced the subject of her health even if she had wished to. Thus he remained unaware until the last possible moment that she was suffering from anything more than she claimed, the translator's "seasickness." He accepted, also without any question, her decision to indulge in the "restful extravagance" of boarding with Mrs. Tippett at Towan Veals for the three weeks of October instead of going directly to the Lynx.

Her scheme simply delayed the inevitable. She struggled along, feeling that all her senses were exposed nerves. Yet she managed to respond overtly with calm even to a new idea of Kot's which required her to write letters. He had begun to talk to J. M. Dent about the possibility of publishing a new edition of *Pilgrimage* as a joint venture with the Cresset Press. To advertise it, he proposed a brochure containing tributes to Dorothy Richardson's work by well-known people. She reluctantly agreed to write to Wells and Shaw, and after she sent the notes, she informed Kot that if the plan turned on her writing any more, it would have to fall through. She could not do it. A personal appeal to these people struck her as being an "attempt to exploit them" and, perhaps, an indignity to herself, which she could not endure. It would be "useless," she told Kot, for him to "boom" at her.

As she had half expected, Shaw declined, excusing himself on the ground of being ill from overwork. Wells, however, agreed, informing her by return post that he would prepare a statement at once. His willingness pleased Dorothy immensely. But a few weeks later, she bitterly advised Kot to abandon the entire project. She could not "afford" the new edition: she was ill, and doctors' bills and wages for an extra servant had to be paid.

Ten days before Christmas it became clear that something was radically wrong. She could neither sleep nor eat. She winced at every sound and shrank from the slightest task. Her head pounded. Alan telephoned for the local doctor, who came and diagnosed "acute neurasthenia." She pounced on these magic words that enabled her to go straight to bed. "It is a relief to give way," she was able to write Peggy on December 29. But by January she had to face the fact that simply remaining "docile" for a while would not bring her around. She saw then quite plainly that the magic words had a real significance, and that her entire being was out of order.

278

CHAPTER NINETEEN

The Healer

THROUGH most of January and February 1935, Dorothy could do little more than write an occasional letter, sometimes businesslike and sometimes tragic in tone. On one hand, she spoke of her illness resignedly to Owen Wadsworth, as if it were a debt she finally had to pay; on the other, she described her situation to Bryher as a net which her own nature and the thumb of fate had mercilessly drawn about her. No matter what suggestion Bryher made, Dorothy countered it with an obstacle that could not be overcome. A trip to town to talk to a psychoanalyst was impossible: where on earth would she "park Alan"? Besides, how could she travel in her neurasthenic state? True, "a brief analysis" interested her "immensely," but no, it was unmanageable, and then, too, she ought not to need such help. At her age, with even just "a moderate amount of insight and reflectiveness," psychoanalysis should be supplied by "life itself." For the present, however, she wanted no "stimulus" from outside; it would only aggravate the trouble. And the trouble was, she said, that "nervous tension" had built up over a prolonged period of time, to the point where the "nervous system" was forced to break down.

But what was she going to *do*? Bryher kept asking. Dorothy did not know. She might of course have to move into rooms, with attendance, though at the moment she claimed she was too weak even to arrange this. It meant going into Trevone and finding someone who could handle both her and Alan, with their two diets, "& not be electrocuted by Alan's drawings." For Alan to engineer such a move was out of the question; it was all too uncertain and complicated and pitiful. But in spite of the fact that Alan could do nothing for her at the moment, she consoled herself with the realization of what she had managed to do for him. The last three years, as far as her own work was concerned, might well be "cancelled." Nonetheless, they would have played their part in the "slow & serene" production of "the one & only illustrated Rabelais." It would be "Alan's achievement & contribution to the world's store." How ironic, she said, that "I have always been prejudiced against satire."

Self-pity ran like a winding stream through the letters she wrote in March. Yet she was also reporting to Bryher that she was feeling better and was beginning to sleep through the night. To work was still impossible. Kot had written to her several times in February about his negotiations with Dent. Apparently Dent wanted to publish a new single volume first, and then follow it a year later with a reissue of all the books. Dorothy warned Kot that she did not know when her half-finished volume would be ready. In her present state, she was not to be counted upon. Kot seemed unperturbed. As a matter of fact, he did not take her very seriously, and went on making arrangements for her release from Duckworth and a contract with Dent, assuming in all of this that volume eleven would be finished. She did not object strongly, even when it became clear that Kot had not breathed a word to Dent about her illness. Furthermore, he asked her not to mention delay in her own communications with Dent. She agreed, with the proviso that if a direct question about the date of completion were put to her, the answer would have to be that she would do her best but could make no promises. She also assured Kot that if Dent reproached her, she would not reveal that he had known of her "inability to work." It would seem, then, that in a small corner of her consciousness Dorothy, too, was convinced of her powers of recovery.

She did not, after all, find it necessary to move from the Lynx. They stayed through March as usual and then made the short trek across the fields to Trevone. By mid-April she had picked up volume eleven, to go on with it and to prepare the completed portion for a typist. She was proud of this typist: it was Wells's "secretary-daughter-in-law" (Marjorie Wells, the wife of G. P. Wells), who had offered her services when she learned of Dorothy's illness. Wells himself had sent £50, not in the least meaning to be "generous," she said, and *not* having heard of her condition from her. The money would allow her to take a brief holiday after finishing the book, an event she now appeared to be taking for granted. But the quality of the book was quite another matter. It was rather frightening, she claimed, as if it were something written by someone else before her breakdown. She was afraid that what she wrote now would be entirely different; indeed, it might be bad. Nonetheless, in May 1935 she signed the contract with Dent that Kot had achieved at last, promising to deliver her manuscript by the first of July. She reported this to Powys, also telling him for the first time of her illness and immediately begging him never to refer to it again. He ought not to write her at all, she suggested, as insurance against his making an accidental allusion which Alan might see. Her greatest fear, he must understand, was "failing" Alan, who was "so helpless in all the affairs of life." But when her book came out, he would have to write, of course, to tell her, if he honestly could, whether it was really all of a piece. She was worried not only about the "split personality" of volume eleven but also about the health of the mind that was producing it. She had asked the local doctor for an opinion, and he had said that though her heart and nerves were rather "sickly," her "mental condition," unlike the rest of her, showed no signs of age.

If she had prepared herself for total disintegration, it gradually became clear that this was not to take place. During the month of June, still in Trevone, Dorothy worked at her book almost exclusively, choosing at last as its title *Clear Horizon,* and she paid a good deal of attention to the announcement Dent planned to insert in its forthcoming catalog. But the quality of the book itself was a nagging worry: it was brief, it was thin, and it might even be dead. Dent might send it back to her, she warned Powys (who had disregarded her injunction not to write), and ask her to enlarge it, which would mean postponing publication from autumn to spring. To Kot she was equally cautious and guarded. To Peggy Kirkaldy she announced, "My old bk. is finished & so, nearly, am I."

At the end of June Dorothy and Alan went up to London with the completed manuscript, but only to deposit their belongings before paying a visit to Dorothy's sister Kate in Long Ditton. From there they shifted to Peggy's house in Essex, and then rounded out July with a stay on the seafront, in the little village of Walton-on-the-Naze. Dorothy seemed relaxed and contented as she gazed at the "yacht-dotted sea" and watched—from the little café where she and Alan spent most of the day—the ceaseless "processions of proletarians" in their bathing suits. But as soon as she returned to London, *Clear Horizon* nagged at her once again. There was no word about it from Dent, and she asked Kot if they were "stupefied."

She soon learned that its publication was scheduled for late October. The news was comforting to some extent: the day of judgment had been put off for a while. But the inexorable reviews would come, and she was sure that after an absence of four years *Pilgrimage* would not be greeted with joy. It would probably even turn out that she herself had dug its grave. Then this sequence of depressing thoughts was interrupted by a strange young man whose unorthodox life took hold of Dorothy's floating imagination.

2

The man was an American named William Macmillan, whom she had met the summer before, when he came to live near her in St. John's Wood. To many people he might have been (and probably was) merely a curiosity, if not a charlatan. To Dorothy he seemed to represent the limitless power of the unconscious, for Macmillan had recently discovered that he was a "healer."

It had all begun for him one evening in the spring of 1933, the year before he moved into St. John's Wood. He was visiting London with an eye to taking up residence there while he decided what to do with his life. He had been training for the priesthood at an Episcopal seminary in America when he suddenly realized that he could not continue. It seemed to him that in England he might be able to find a new direction. On this particular evening, though, he anticipated nothing more than good food and conversation at the home of a friend and countrywoman. As it happened, his life was to be utterly transformed.

Among the guests at the fateful dinner party was a well-known medium. To Macmillan, not yet thirty, raised in that part of upper New York State where both hedges and minds were well trimmed and tended (though elsewhere, in the vicinity of Rochester, the state was the birthplace of modern American spiritualism), the subject of spiritualism had no place in a serious discussion. It was not even a matter for disapproval as far as he was concerned, and it certainly was not one to be talked of at dinner. He therefore decided to ignore the profession of the man seated opposite him and to enjoy the food. But during the meal the medium leaned across the table toward him and said firmly and decisively, "You are a healer." Macmillan could only laugh, but he saw that no one else was amused. All the other guests had fallen into a hushed silence and were scrutinizing him.

The dinner ended at last and the ladies rose to retire. Before the hostess left the dining room, she took Macmillan aside to insist upon the authority of the medium. Whatever he suggested, she wanted "Mac" to do. There was no doubt in her mind that if he said so, Mac did have the power to heal. He in turn could not dispute with his hostess; that would have been unmannerly. Neither did he feel he could refuse to cooperate, since she went on to tell him of her own sufferings from sinus and antrum infection. She was in pain even then, she said, but was doing her best to carry on through the evening. He might have guessed she would play a part in the proceedings to follow.

The guests gathered in the drawing room and sipped their coffee, while their hostess, who was to be the patient, sat in a chair at the center. It seemed to Mac, watching, that no one but he thought this was an odd and tasteless parlor game. But he had agreed to it, and he stood there—a large, gentle, soft-mannered man, his face a curious mixture of fleshiness and crags—quietly waiting for instructions. The medium told him to rub the "patient's" affected areas for ten minutes. As he did so, the congestion appeared to be relieved. When he had finished, he was shown how to do "passes" for another five minutes, waving his hands with controlled movements a few inches above the patient's face and with a downward movement away from the head. During the longest five minutes he had ever spent, Mac followed the directions. Afterward everyone congratulated him and settled down to enjoy the remainder of an apparently normal evening. For the bewildered Mac, the episode had no reality; yet his hostess was obviously free of pain. He began to wonder whether perhaps the others were less peculiar than he. But his common sense reasserted itself: the "cure" must have been the result of "auto-suggestion." Discovery of that word comforted him. He relaxed and shrugged his shoulders. If people wished to entertain themselves in this way, it was their concern and not his.

The next weekend Mac was in the country as a guest of a clergyman friend to whom he told the story. "Don't worry about it," his friend advised. Later in the day, however, he remarked to Mac that it was a pity he could not use his recently discovered gifts on the cook, Mrs. Small, who was suffering from a painful bunion. Without understanding why, Mac went to the kitchen to seek out Mrs. Small. She agreed to be treated and did not even wince when he rubbed her toe. At the end of ten minutes the inflammation and most of the swelling had vanished. The joint itself had loosened enough to be movable. Disturbed and frightened, Mac fled to his room, flung himself on the bed, and tried to control his shaking body. What he had done had been successful, but he vowed never again to yield to such a temptation.

An emergency was a different matter. A while later Mac spent another weekend with friends who already knew of the original incident. When the wife spilled hot grease down her left leg, they called on Mac to help. He knew nothing about burns, though anyone could see that these were serious. Forgetting his fright, feeling only that he must do something, he knelt and touched the raw flesh. She felt no more than a slight discomfort, and by the time he had finished his treatment new skin had begun to form. In a few days the burns healed without leaving a trace of a scar.

Mac pondered the complete faith in him that this woman had shown, and he began to think differently of the perplexing power he seemed to have. He decided that it had to be "divinely inspired." As much as he disliked doing so, he would treat people when forced to, and he hoped the occasions would be rare. But even if they were, he would have to learn what to do with his ability, how to keep it "tame and safe," and how to accept it as an unknown force within him.

Some months later, still determined not to heal except under extraordinary circumstances, Mac met the well-known social worker and preacher Dr. Maud Royden. She tried to persuade him to make healing his life's work. Mac argued that he could not do this as a "passive agent" because he might injure someone. Furthermore, it was inconceivable to him that he practice without legal recognition. If the source of his power was divine, it could not be exercised in secrecy and behind anything like beaded curtains.

Dr. Royden was convinced of Mac's uniqueness. She set out to help him gain legal sanction. Together they assembled a list of "sponsors" and sent it, along with an application, to the office of the Secretary of State for Home Affairs. In due course, Mac was granted permission to practice for a year as a psychotherapeutist: the Home Office did not know what else to call him. Then Dr. Royden offered him the use of her vestry at the Guildhall as an office. He bought a treatment table, and his work as a healer began.

The vestry soon proved inadequate to his needs. He discovered, among other things, that his early experience of immediate or rapid "cure" was not to be the rule. Many of his patients suffered from more "complex" ailments and required daily treatment over a period of several weeks. Some of them found it difficult, if not impossible, to make the trip to his office each day. As the number of patients continued to increase, he moved into a maisonette in St. John's Wood to accomodate them, but to his surprise this was not large enough either. Now it occurred to him that if he were to move again, he ought to venture into the professional area rather than remain in a residential district. He "owed" it to his work, he felt, to use "the most dignified and professional setting" that he could. Such a setting, in London, could only be in the Harley Street area. But would such a move seem "a direct challenge to orthodoxy"? He had no desire to challenge any group. On the other hand, he was firmly convinced that his "mission" had to "override personal considerations." Accordingly he moved into Devonshire Place. Scores of people flocked to him, but the medical profession showed no sign of feeling threatened.

By the summer of 1935 his practice had flourished to such an extent that he hired a staff of assistants; and when he learned that Ibornden Hall in Kent was available for summer rental, he took it, installing there both his patients and his sizeable staff. It was toward the end of this summer, in August, that Dorothy and Alan Odle came to Biddenden, a mile away from Mac and his entourage. They had been summoned to a family conference; and, knowing of Mac's presence in the area, Dorothy went, as soon as she could, to see his establishment. One of the patients there, she reported to Peggy Kirkaldy with total conviction, was recovering from a disease that, according to medical science, was "absolutely incurable." The woman had been treated for six years, Dorothy said, by thirteen successive Scottish doctors, eleven Harley Street specialists, and at the last moment by Lord Horder, but had grown progressively worse. When Mac first saw her, she was almost completely paralyzed. Within a week, Dorothy claimed, "Mac had her on her feet." Now, "for the good of her soul," she was helping him conduct his business affairs and was walking, with help, a few yards farther every day. Dorothy also told Peggy rather casually that Mac insisted upon treating her, too; she said he thought he could do something for her eyes.

During all of September and part of October she saw him every day, presumably in St. John's Wood, where he had continued to live. Afterward, without identifying him, she wrote to Bryher that

285

six weeks of treatment by "a man, *inter alia*, who [was] both psychologist & psychiatrist" had done her "an immeasurable amount of good"; she believed he had "put [her] in the way of keeping going." Despite Bryher's plea at the beginning of the year that she consult a psychoanalyst, even for a short period, Dorothy had waited seven months before consulting anyone—and then, when her recovery seemed assured, she chose an unorthodox healer. Mac was not only young but unworldly as well. Indeed, some years later, when he was forty-five, Dorothy would describe him as "still a virgin."

Whether it was his innocence and youth or his "magical" power that appealed to her we cannot know, for she never spoke directly about his treatment of her. The likelihood is that William Macmillan did not challenge her self-image as a psychoanalyst might have done, and that he deprived her of none of her own power. She could extol his gifts, praise his modesty, and take him under her wing. He was nearly as childlike as Alan.

3

The astonishing Macmillan, the "reluctant healer"—as he called himself—remained part of Dorothy's life until he died. (He came to know Veronica Grad as well.) This very Christmas, he would visit them at Cornwall as her "beloved American friend." At the moment, however, the end of October was nearing, and her book was scheduled to appear. Imagining the worst from the reviews, she was glad that she and Alan would be in Cornwall when *Clear Horizon* came out. They were not returning to the Lynx. Dorothy had rented Rose Cottage in Trevone instead, as a more sheltered and manageable abode. They had stayed in it eighteen years before, when it was a genuine laborer's cottage with "one squint window" in the front room and "a huge kitchener for warmth & cooking (& smoke!)." It belonged now to the young niece of the Ponder sisters, Norah Hickey, and her husband Edward, and was considerably altered in appearance. It had a new, wide bay window, a glazed door that let in light, and a large skylight in the scullery. It had plumbing, too, instead of the pump in the road and a privy. It was so convenient that Dorothy claimed to feel "surrounded" and "almost suburban," with "gloves growing on [their] hands & veils on [their] minds." She missed the turmoil of the elements in Constantine Bay.

By contrast, Trevone seemed civilized and tame. Here in Rose Cottage, on November 1, 1935, she began to write the twelfth volume of *Pilgrimage*.

The calm did not last very long. By mid-December the Atlantic gales had come; so had the reviews of *Clear Horizon*. She did not know what to make of their "shrewishness," as she called it. It seemed to her that a reviewer ought to pass on to someone else "an author who bores him to shrieks." Alan's timeless comment was that most of her male reviewers "snarl[ed] because they imagine[d] M. a feminist." Dorothy told Kot that a wood-louse could see that she was not.

A wood-louse might indeed have seen more than many of the reviewers of *Clear Horizon*, and Dorothy scribbled dry little rejoinders on her press clippings. On one from the *London Mercury* entitled "Quintessential Feminism," for example, she flatly denied that in typical feminine fashion she had followed "the least line of resistance" by "recording the unordered flow of impressions as they pass through the mind." But she did not waste any effort on the most obvious "critical blunder" in the piece, the remark that World War I had "had no noticeable effect whatever upon the mind of the author." Such an effect would be rather strangely felt in a novel in which the action takes place in 1907.

There were other blunders and lapses in reading. Dorothy was "dismayed" to discover that some of the reviewers had completely missed the point of the dinner scene between Miriam and Hypo Wilson. Hypo himself had failed to understand that Miriam was *not* pregnant as she had thought, and that therefore the need to make plans no longer existed. Dorothy rightfully termed it a "comic interlude," but certain reviewers had missed the tone entirely. Perhaps what had thrown them off was the vanity Dorothy had shown operating in both Miriam and Hypo. Hypo could not believe that he had not fathered a child, and Miriam was wrapped up in her equally vain desire to be independent of her lover. She wanted independence on principle, despite the fact that, as Hypo kept pointing out, it meant always going without enough food—except when he took her to dinner. What it did not mean to Miriam was "equality" in the feminists' sense.

Once, in a discussion with Michael Shatov, she had called the feminists "a libel on the universe" and "an insult to womanhood," because it had seemed to her that the basic assumption in the rights campaign—that women had been "subject" in the past—was entirely false. In her view, women had never been subject and never could be. The "disabilities, imposed by law, [were] a stupid insult to women, but [had] never touched them as individuals." Whether this was true or not, it was Miriam's personal individuality that Hypo Wilson threatened, largely because he did not really believe in it. To him she was a "biological contrivance" whose functioning in pregnancy was most "proper" and constituted "the sole justification for her continued existence." Miriam, rebelling in thought against this "reduction" of her, seemed in 1935 to have struck many of the reviewers as an insufferable bore. But in 1907 her attitudes had been fresh and vital; indeed, they had had to be flung in the face of tradition, which mirrored Hypo Wilson's view of women.

The fact remains, however, that the passage of nearly thirty years had rendered much of Miriam's "thought-life" rather "commonplace," as Dorothy Richardson herself realized. This was one explanation for the hostility of the critics. Another, which she hinted to Kot, was the difficulty of dealing with *Clear Horizon* as a separate entity. More than any novel she had published thus far, it was a "chapter" in a series, and she complained to Kot that the "lads who read & review a thousand books a day . . . are content with remarking that C. H. is either the fourteenth or fortieth of the series, they don't know which, & don't care." But those who knew *Pilgrimage* and were familiar with Miriam's entanglements, preoccupations, and obsessions could read *Clear Horizon* for what it was: the culminating chapter in the London adventures of its heroine. They were able to see that all events in the novel were ruptures or partings—a breaking away from involvements.

In the opening pages of *Clear Horizon,* Dorothy Richardson strikes this determined note of freedom from involvement. There is a new boarder in Mrs. Bailey's house, a young poet who once would have attracted Miriam immediately. In early days she would have involved herself with the well-bred, blond-haired boy who wanted to "live by disseminating poetry." Only after lengthy exchanges, rather than with her now quick and penetrating glances, would she have recognized him as the utterly social being that he is, with merely a courteous relationship to life. Although she would like to see how the future dealt with him, he represents to her another fruitless entanglement, and in her mind she bids him farewell. She will bid actual farewells throughout the novel.

The sitting room at 140 Harley Street, London, where Dorothy Richardson
worked as a dental assistant.

The most dramatic assertion of freedom from involvement in the novel is the parting of Miriam from her lover, Hypo Wilson. This takes place after a long scene, at the beginning of which Amabel too is present. Miriam will also disentangle herself from the intense relationship with her by introducing her to Michael Shatov, another person from whose dependence she wants to be free. There are breaks of a less dramatic sort as well: with the Lycurgan Society, with Dr. Hancock and the dental office, and even with the city of London, which in all the novels set against its background had very nearly played the role of a human being. It is toward "a vista . . . swept clean of all impediments" that Dorothy Richardson has Miriam move. Whether her own departure from London about the same time was executed as neatly as Miriam's is impossible to ascertain, but in all likelihood the reality had rougher edges.

Dorothy's parting from Wells, for example, was not attended by a false pregnancy but by a miscarriage, and she took leave from her Harley Street job to recover. In *Clear Horizon* Miriam bids goodbye to Hypo Wilson as he walks with her to Tansley Street after he has learned there will be no child and she has realized the "truth of their relationship," how separate they are in their essential selves. Her decision is largely an intellectual one, uncluttered in fiction by the strain that accompanied it in fact. Dorothy Richardson cleaned up the fact, removed from it the virtual breakdown she had suffered, but did not dispose of it entirely. The breakdown became, instead of an actual event, a threatening possibility foreseen by Miriam's friend Dr. Densley. When she visits him on behalf of her sister Sarah, in the course of making arrangements for her, he gives Miriam an unassailable reason for leaving the dental office—that in his professional opinion she is on the verge of a collapse. When Dorothy was writing this portion of *Clear Horizon,* transposing and adjusting her earlier experience to the fictional shape she wanted it to have, the threat of another real collapse materialized. Did she perhaps hope that by denying the old one in fiction she might disarm the new one in fact?

Whatever it was that unconsciously drove her, the novel she eked out during the years of the big translations and in the months following her illness took the form of a series of wishes fulfilled. Her own life had held substantially the same complications as her heroine's, and in extricating Miriam from situation after situation, Dorothy was smoothing out her past and rendering it less painful to relive. In this more pleasing version of a difficult and trying time, her surrogate self did not flounder. Miriam acts resolutely, resisting the efforts of Hypo Wilson to hold on to her and deciding—in spite of her fear that her motives may be impure—to introduce Michael and Amabel to each other. If they should get along, she might well be relieved not only of the burden of Michael's dependence upon her but also of Amabel's grasping and appropriative love.

The meeting between her two friends is more successful than she even dared to expect. When Amabel tells her afterward that she thinks Miriam ought to marry Michael, that he is "wonderful" and "beautiful," Miriam's "spirit leap[s] to the touch of an incredible hope. . . . 'Then marry him, my dear, yourself,'" she blurts out, scarcely aware of what she is saying. Amabel replies that she would; she would marry him tomorrow. Thus begins the solution to one of Miriam's (as it had been Dorothy's) most delicate problems.

The fictional marriage would not take place until the next volume of *Pilgrimage;* and there it would be pictured as having come about without any further move by Miriam. But Dorothy had had more to do with the marriage of the originals of Michael and Amabel than she was willing to admit in fiction, and even there a disagreeable trace of manipulation had crept into her careful handling of the material. The thoughts she gave to Miriam concerning the two people who are being brought together seem to turn not on their suitability to each other but instead on the freedom a relationship between them would allow her. At the same time, she did not permit Miriam to probe deeply into her own motives. Once the idea of the introduction occurs to her, Miriam finds it "impossible to imagine the occasion as not taking place." The decision had been made in her unconscious, and whatever its motives, good or bad, it was "irrevocable."

The section dealing with Amabel and Michael forms the bulk of the first chapter of *Clear Horizon*. The second contains the dramatized evening spent with Hypo Wilson, at the end of which Miriam parts from him. In the third, she breaks with the Lycurgans, realizing that she cannot "experience the emotions that kept Lycurgan socialism on its feet." Each of these chapters is rather long, and together they comprise two-thirds of the novel, that is, 84 pages in a total of 132.

These chapters are followed by eight more, which seem to be those Dorothy wrote after her illness—the final third of the novel that she had feared would be "scrappy and dim." Her fears were justified. The book is weak structurally. The eight chapters are brief, like the flickering of an unsteady light or a light being turned on and off too quickly for complete illumination to occur. What fails to be illuminated is Miriam's mind—the atmosphere of it—which remains, as Dorothy herself admitted, "imperfectly realized." Take one of those chapters, the fourth, for example. It describes Miriam writing a book review (recognizably the review of Gabriel Tarde's *Underground Man* that Dorothy had written in 1907) and reaching certain conclusions that strike one as having a bearing on the direction of the novel. But because the emotional tone is uncertain, it is difficult to tell just what the author intended. What, for example, is Dorothy suggesting when she writes that Miriam's decision to read a book with a view to writing about it means to be "shut up and turned away from life?" That Miriam's ultimate decision to write *Pilgrimage* (and by inference her own decision as well) would have a similar meaning? For one might argue that to embark on an autobiographical novel is tantamount to reading the book of one's life and writing about it. If this is true, does Dorothy intend to convey by means of this chapter another step in Miriam's movement toward freedom from the emotional involvements that spell life? Though the book seems to be moving in this general direction, the tone of the words ("shut up and turned away from life") is not positive.

The volume to follow *Clear Horizon* appears to provide an affirmative answer to the question, since it shows Miriam living among the Quakers, trying to read herself, and beginning to write an autobiographical novel. Plausible as the pattern may be, it emerges in *Clear Horizon* only as a blurred outline. The presence of thoughts about Amabel in chapter four of *Clear Horizon* might be meant to serve as connective tissue, for she is one of the people from whom Miriam will cut herself off, one of the representatives of life, one of the human claims she is deciding not to meet any longer. The ground here becomes shakier than ever, largely because of Dorothy's weak hold on the last third of her novel. Although she wanted desperately to be told that the weakness did not exist, in her heart she knew that it did. What its effect would be on the plans of her new publisher for a collected edition she tried to avoid thinking about.

4

Even before reviews of *Clear Horizon* had begun to appear, she had written, at Bryher's request, a short story entitled "Nook on Parnassus," and into it she had interwoven ironic speculation and realistic assessment. Sometime during the autumn months of 1935, Bryher had asked Dorothy for a story to publish in *Life and Letters To-day,* the magazine she and the novelist Margaret Kennedy had recently taken over. In response, Dorothy drew as usual on one of her own experiences, this time on something that had happened to her in Cornwall. The result, with its intriguing title, appeared in the December issue.

As Dorothy put it, "Nook on Parnassus" was "a scribble . . . improvised upon an urgent demand, founded on fact, but fictional as to the number of Van Gogh's." On a shopping expedition to Padstow, she had suddenly seen in a stationer's shop window the perfect solution to her annual Christmas-card problem. There, so unobtrusively placed that she nearly missed seeing them, as she probably had missed them for months, were five reproductions of French masters "comfortably larger than postcards and, no doubt, conspicuously thicker." She went inside not only to look at them but also to try to discover how these copies, which seemed so newly done, had come to be in unlikely Padstow. The mystery was solved when, in answer to her question as to whether there were any more, the fawning, elderly shopkeeper, whom Dorothy "ached to be rid of," turned away muttering and entered a frosted door at the back of the shop to summon a young "red-gold" girl, who appeared wearing a smock the color of "a ripe orange." Dorothy recognized in her at once an art student who was enduring this "lamentable sequel" to the art school she had entered with such high hopes. She realized too that the girl, by introducing her copies—"these radiant aliens"—among "the detested wares of a sceptical employer," was desperately trying to "redeem" her fate.

She came slowly toward Dorothy, moving just a little too elegantly, "as if fastidiously picking her way through an unworthy universe," and then stood in silence in the face of her "miniature exhibition." She knew it deserved tribute; there was no point in saying anything. But Dorothy, as she stood with the girl "confronted by her gods," wanted to share them with her, "to take her by the arm and say, quietly and chummily, 'Aren't they heavenly?'" She felt "checked," however, by the girl's "chill aloofness," and said instead that she wanted some of them for Christmas cards but found it almost impossible to make a choice. The girl uttered the single word "Yes" in a manner of "faintly supercilious detachment."

The problem was a matter of indifference to her. What had she to do with the difficulties of a country woman dressed in a weather-stained mackintosh carrying an ancient shopping bag? In that moment the "country woman" had decided to assume that identity. "Quite a number of D'yawrers," she remarked, and waited for the reply she expected and wanted. It came. "The Dürers are nice," the girl breathed, giving the name a slight prominence. The game continued—"Toolooze-Lowtreck . . . Gogang . . . van Go . . . Mannay . . ."—until finally one "van Go" was chosen, and the girl accepted an order for a handsome quantity of the "van Goch," to be called for in due course. Dorothy left, pleased at having helped the young woman score "her first triumph over her employer's incredulity."

Such was the experience Dorothy recalled when Bryher asked her for a story. Why? The answer is contained within "Nook on Parnassus." Both the first-person narrator *and* the girl are Dorothy. The art student arouses her sympathies, but she also calls forth a critical irony that is directed in part at herself. One begins to detect the presence of these elements when, on the third page of the story, the young girl is perceived by the narrator as having been "weighed in the balance and found wanting." In consequence, she suffers not only that "torment" but also the indignity of a stationer's shop in Padstow, where all her delicate instincts are suspiciously scrutinized by a pair of "rapacious" commercial eyes. Yet the understanding eyes of her first customer judge her too, noting the defensive lack of humility and the offensively patronizing air.

Dorothy's own position as a novelist was uncomfortably close to that of this proud young art student with the fine sensibilities and the consciousness that they were not enough to win for her a place on Parnassus. She has but a dubious nook in remote Cornwall. Putting her there, Dorothy might well have been wondering whether, after all the sacrifices she had made, the "scrappy and dim" novel she had just published would deny her even this little corner. She might have been wondering, too, whether her own friends were concealing their "perfect pronunciations," even as she had concealed hers in the face of the girl's pathetic need to be superior where such a distinction was almost meaningless. For in 1935 James Joyce was flamboyantly writing *Finnegans Wake*. In such a context, Dorothy Richardson was indeed the art student in a Padstow stationer's shop, but without the youth and beauty that would capture the heart of an aged crone like herself.

Who could heal the wounds of such a consciousness as this? Not the gushing Powys, or the booming Kot, or the gentle Bryher, or the virginal Mac. That remained to be seen.

CHAPTER TWENTY

Culminations

IN 1936 much more than the outcome of Dorothy Richardson's personal crisis remained to be seen. This was the year of the Italian threat to Ethiopia and of Haile Selassie's poignant but unsuccessful appeal to the League of Nations. It was also a year of mounting uneasiness about the situation of Jews in Hitler's Germany. Dorothy had been getting somber letters from Owen Wadsworth, who was then with the *News Chronicle* in Berlin. But not even Owen's observations could bring home to her what was happening in the same way as did a letter that arrived at Rose Cottage early in March.

The letter came from a German painter named Paul Gangolf, who had visited Alan five years earlier at Queen's Terrace. Gangolf had brought some of his drawings and etchings for Alan to see, and Alan had found them very good indeed. At the time of his visit Gangolf was independent, had a small family property in Germany, and was engaged in a study of British art. Now he wrote to the Odles from Lisbon to beg for help. He had lost everything and, during a six-month imprisonment in Germany, had been so badly treated that an arm and leg were permanently damaged. After his release he had fled to Lisbon, where he had sold newspapers as long as he could, but now he was ill and broken. Could they help him with a little money and put him in touch with the English Zionists? The Odles had not known that Gangolf was a Jew.

They sent whatever money they could spare, as well as the names and addresses he requested. Then Dorothy wrote to Bryher in the hope of enlisting her aid too. But the specter of all the others like Gangolf was more troubling than either of them cared to admit.

Dorothy herself felt plagued just then. She had slipped and fallen in the wet garden of Rose Cottage and had badly wrenched a tendon and the muscles of her right foot. Not long before, they had received the news that Alan's brother had suffered a heart attack. Although

his brother Vincent was his closest remaining relative, Alan did not
go to see him, apparently because Vincent had not been told how ill
he really was, and a visit from Alan would have given everything
away. They waited for further news, expecting to hear the worst.
But Vincent seemed to pull through, and Dorothy's attention turned
again to the ominous world scene.

Someone sent her two issues of the French paper *Vendredi*. One
contained a warning piece by Romain Rolland about the nations of
the world going up in flames, in a fire set by Germany and her vast
unsuspected store of arms. In the other, an international "expert"
pointed out that airplanes could be neither made nor tried out in
secret, and that even if Germany had been making planes for years,
most of them would by now be obsolete. Along with nearly
everyone else, Dorothy wanted to believe the "expert," but there
was fascist Italy annexing Ethiopia and Nazi Germany trampling on
the Jews. The whole world seemed precariously unbalanced.
Dorothy's own life was not much steadier. Against this backdrop of
international affairs, such a thing as *Pilgrimage* was small indeed,
yet it held what amounted to her identity, and it seemed in danger
not of going up in flames but of disappearing into oblivion.

Early in March, Richard Church of Dent wrote a letter to Dorothy
that she could not bring herself to answer for a month. He made it
clear, as delicately as he could, that Dent counted on publishing a
collected edition of *Pilgrimage* that would be the finished work. It
would be advertised as such and would bring about (in Church's
words) the secure establishment of her fame. But he thought a
politic handling of the affair was very important: everything had to
be ripe before Dent could make what Dorothy understood Church to
be saying would be the final bid for establishing her work. She
understood only too well the message that he wanted to convey, and
it left her speechless. It would be better to delay the new edition than
risk publishing an unfinished *Pilgrimage*.

A misconception about the volume she was writing had arisen and
had never been cleared up. She could not remember suggesting at
any time that this twelfth "chapter" would conclude her novel; but
Dent had apparently assumed as much and had made plans accordingly. Now that they suspected the error, it seemed to her that
Church was saying, "Let us wait until you *can* give us the whole
work." The trouble was that she herself did not know when that
would be. If the new edition were delayed, perhaps for an indefinite

period, what would happen to all the Duckworth volumes? Would Dent allow them to lapse? One of them, *Deadlock,* was already out of print. And what about chapter twelve, *Dimple Hill?* Would Dent publish it, or would she again have to beg Duckworth to take her back? The uncertainty and the fear of her books sinking out of sight were almost more than she could bear.

When she finally brought herself to answer Church's letter in mid-April, she and Alan had moved from Rose Cottage to Trevone Cottage, a few yards up the hill. Here she worked out a letter that was a combination of persuasion, appeal, and demand. If Dent were to postpone indefinitely the carrying out of their agreement with her, what exactly did they propose to do in the meantime? Would they keep all the volumes of the series in print and listed in the catalog? There were good, practical reasons for Dent to follow this course. For one thing, although the quantities were small, each of the volumes continued to sell and appeared on every biennial statement Duckworth sent her. Furthermore, she was sure that combinations of volumes (a feature of the proposed new edition) would sell even better and would, in the long run, justify what seemed now a large and immediately unprofitable undertaking. After persuasion, she tried appeal. She said she had been counting on income from the sale of the new sets to help her produce the concluding volumes more quickly than the earlier ones. Now she feared that she might not be able to finish *Pilgrimage* at all.

Having made an effort to stave off postponement, she wrote to Kot a few days later to tell him that she thought postponement was inevitable. She could not compel Dent to fulfill the contract "against their own judgment"; that would help nobody, she said. Nor could Dent be forced to accept the reasoning in or to act along the lines suggested in her letter. But this did not prevent her from hoping that Richard Church, as the gentleman she knew him to be, would rise to the occasion and prevail upon Dent to carry out, if only in a modified form, its publishing agreement.

Toward the end of May a letter arrived from Church. Dent *would* issue sets of volumes at periodic intervals, but to allow time for rousing public interest a decision had been made not to issue the first set until 1938. They were hoping, moreover, that by the time all the sets had come out the book would be complete, although they would continue to publish even if it was not. Under the circumstances, Dorothy saw that she could do nothing but indicate that the delay would not help her write the final volumes. At the same time, she admitted (though not to Church) feeling some relief that the matter had been settled. To Church she expressed the hope that Dent would keep all the Duckworth editions in print, both for what they would bring in to her and as a means of reconciling her to some extent to the change in plans.

Here matters stood for a while, with Dent remaining noncommittal about the Duckworth volumes. After all, most of them were still in print. Furthermore, sales of the latest volume, *Clear Horizon,* which they had published, did not lend very much weight to Dorothy's concern about keeping her books in print. Until Christmas only about 500 copies had been sold. It must have seemed to everyone at Dent that Dorothy Richardson was manufacturing problems, and there were quite enough to deal with as it was.

2

The real problem, which Dorothy only hinted at even to herself, was the question of her ability to go on with *Pilgrimage.* She was having trouble getting into *Dimple Hill* for two reasons. First, now that Miriam had left London, she had to move against an entirely new background. *Dimple Hill* required the buildup of much new atmosphere, in contrast with that which had accumulated in the old volumes. Second, Dorothy had begun to feel an increasing distance between her self of the present and the past. Though she had apparently recovered from her illness, she had suffered a genuine breakdown nevertheless, and she found that her restored self seemed not quite the same as the original.

Dorothy only dimly sensed the break that had somehow taken place in the continuity of the self she had always believed in. This would account for the eagerness with which she welcomed letters from people in her past. One of them, from Miss Ayre or, as Dorothy called her, Miss Deborah Perne, who now was 100 years old, invited her to tea when she came up again to London. Dorothy went as soon as she could, and spent an entire afternoon reliving the years at Edgeworth House, the school in North London that Miss Ayre had run with her sisters. Also present was one of the pupils with whom she had made friends, whom she had called Grace Broom in her novel and whom she included in the opening scene of . *Dimple Hill.* The visit was just what she wanted, an orgy of girlhood memories, a plunge back into her young self, the self that an older Miriam was about to come to terms with in *Dimple Hill.*

But during the summer of 1936 Dorothy seemed compelled to move about, and *Dimple Hill* got very little attention. Dorothy made two separate visits to her sister in Surrey, one to Peggy in Essex, another to the Austens in Kent; and she spent a few days at Walton, which would have been positively blissful had it not been for torrents of rain and a plague of mosquitoes. At home at Queen's Terrace, the knocker was always sounding, or invitations that Dorothy had no desire to refuse were arriving in the post. For the first time, also, they had their own telephone, which had been installed by their winter tenant. Alan paid not the slightest attention to it and even refused to acknowledge its existence, but Dorothy thought it convenient. She proudly listed its Primrose number at the head of her letters and liked to be surprised by its ring.

Beneath the surface, the summer was a mixed one. Dorothy had decided it was time to draw up a will and had realized that a literary executor would be needed, for Alan could not be expected to cope with even the small burden of her literary estate. The most likely person, in her eyes, was Owen Wadsworth. She broached the subject to him in a letter, emphasizing the slightness of the duties that would devolve upon him. Actually he would be joint executor with Alan, and she illustrated for him one of the problems they might have to face. If Dent were one day to propose a fresh edition in a purple binding with yellow spots, he and Alan could object and demand a yellow binding with purple spots. Owen hesitated nonetheless. He did not actually refuse, but he did not enthusiastically agree either, and Dorothy's attack of anxiety began to subside. She stopped talking about herself as "the defunct" and did not make a will. It was clear, however, that she expected Owen eventually to do as she wished.

These days she found the people who did not do as she wished more and more trying. The less she felt in touch with herself, the more imperious she became with others. Always sensitive to manipulation, she discerned it now with lightning quickness; and feeling played upon herself, she could give advice to Peggy Kirkaldy, who she thought was being subjected to a kind of emotional blackmail by the man she loved. In consequence, her letters to Peggy were filled with a delicate, refined awareness of the wounded heart and with a tactfulness she had rarely had in her youth. Then she had been too busy protecting herself to cultivate tact, and she was reminded of this all through the summer, while she thought about reviving the graceless Miriam in *Dimple Hill.*

At the end of the summer, she once again came face to face with the "arch-manipulator" of her young life. Just before she and Alan left London for Cornwall, they spent an evening at H. G. Wells's home in Regent's Park. Also present were the Baroness Budberg, who was introduced as Moura, and Wells's son Anthony West. Wells must have remarked during the evening that he could not persuade Moura to marry him, for Dorothy told Bryher afterward that she thought Moura was very wise to resist. But Anthony was something of a shock, she said, looking "tense & glowering far away at the back of himself," where she was sure he had withdrawn to "escape coercion of one sort or another." She hoped his young wife would help to draw him out. At the moment, however, it seemed to Dorothy that he could hardly speak—in her opinion, because of the "attempts" that must have been made on his life. She felt she knew at first hand what such attempts were like.

3

A few days after the party at Wells's, Dorothy and Alan once again settled in Cornwall. They had not gone back to Rose Cottage, preferring instead the rigors of the tin-roofed bungalow at Constantine Bay now that she was well enough to cope with them. Her task for the winter was *Dimple Hill,* which she had actually promised to Dent for the following June. They had come around, she claimed, to her view of things and were beginning preparations to bring out sets of volumes. She had worked her will with them, it seemed, but she could not work her will with the novel. She had "written & scrapped & scrapped & written" until it seemed utterly hopeless. Now that Dent was proceeding with the new edition, she tried to convince herself that the book could be written, if only she put her mind to it. It ought to help her, she kept saying, that Dent was so much more "complex & orderly" than Duckworth, which gave her a sense of security. And, in fact, by November she had made enough progress on the novel to feel encouraged. It went more easily than at any time in the past two years, though very slowly and differently. A changed focus, she thought, might account for the difference. The focus struck her as older and wider, but she feared that it might also be less vital or, if vital at all, differently so. She confessed that she could not really tell. In any case, the writing seemed to her like that of a "somewhat ponderously-moving stout old dame."

This was the way she looked, after all, whereas Alan at forty-eight was scarcely altered in appearance. He worked serenely on, day after day adding to the growing pile of drawings for his illustrated edition of Rabelais. Occasionally there was a chance to publish something, which inevitably petered out. He interrupted Rabelais, for instance, to submit drawings for an edition of Cellini's *Autobiography,* but they were turned down. Dorothy claimed that publishers nearly always admired his work but that it made them very nervous. They were apt to accept at first, then to back out after consultations in committee. There was no doubt that such scatological and irreverent drawings as Alan's were difficult to publish above ground, so to speak, and he seemed resigned to this fact. When someone showed an interest in his work, he was grateful—and surprised. Anything more than interest was totally unexpected.

Alan was stunned when, in February 1937, H. G. Wells told him that one of Theodore Roosevelt's sons wanted to see some of his drawings. One evening while Wells was entertaining Colonel Roosevelt and his wife, he showed them the two drawings by Alan that he had owned for years. The Colonel was greatly impressed and asked where he could see others. Alan sent Wells a few samples, a selection of the milder Rabelais drawings, guaranteed, Dorothy said, "not to burn holes in walls or endanger the stability of roofs." Wells acknowledged their receipt and gave his own opinion that neither the Colonel nor Mrs. Roosevelt would object to a measure of indelicacy. He forwarded them to the hotel where the Roosevelts were staying and where, shortly afterward, they featured the drawings at a small dinner party. Wells, who was present, reported that the entire company had "crowed with delight . . . at the rich decor." Alan was content with the unexpected bonus when the Roosevelts bought four drawings, but Dorothy had already begun to weave an elaborate fantasy of wealth and fame. The Roosevelts would return to their country and their vast social circles, and Odle drawings would soon be the rage in America. Needless to say, Alan never heard another word from the Roosevelts, and he never said another word about them. It was to Dorothy and not Alan that such things as praise and reward mattered. It was she who needed friends and encouragement, and to her the equanimity (or was it passiveness?) of artists was a marvel.

That summer she had a glimpse of another artist very like Alan, obscure and content. Peggy Kirkaldy had taken them to call on Cedric Morris, who lived with an artist named Lett-Haynes in a beautiful Elizabethan house in Essex. All around the house, which had been left to the artist by his aunt, were sculptures and paintings by Haynes that had scarcely been seen except by visitors. He occasionally got a commission, but he made his living by running a nearby school of art with some thirty to forty pupils. Dorothy recognized that Alan and Haynes were a certain type of artist.

Alan's friend Adrian Allinson, however, was entirely different. Dorothy was convinced that he came to visit them in Cornwall every now and then to lecture them on the inferiority of their taste. But his visit during the spring of 1937 was different. This was his first visit while they were staying with Mrs. Pope in Trevone Cottage. The moment he stepped into the parlor—a Cornish cottage parlor that had been untouched since the eighties—he fell "prostrate" before it and immediately asked the incredulous old lady for permission to make sketches of it at teatime, with all the tea things, including saffron buns, still on the table. Eventually Dorothy and Alan appeared seated at the table in a brilliantly stylized painting destined for the Royal Academy. On this visit Allinson stayed for five weeks. While he sketched feverishly, Alan was laboring next door on a frontispiece, which the publisher turned down, for John Cowper Powys's new book.

At this time John Austen, Alan's other artist friend, was engaged in producing a book on the art of "black-and-white," in which he planned to include a series of sketches by Alan representing the various stages of one of his drawings. Austen firmly believed that Alan had no peer in graphic art, that he was a supreme master of the pen; and he said this in his book. It was Dorothy, however, who made sure that Alan and Austen saw each other at least once a year. Most of the time it merely required keeping up the correspondence, and an invitation would duly come to visit with the Austens in Kent. This year (1937) there had been few letters, and none at all in spring and early summer. By the end of July, when they had been in London for a month, Dorothy began to consider what might be done to guarantee the annual visit, which she particularly wanted to take place this year. The first step was to assume that everything was as usual. On July 29 she wrote to Peggy saying she could not promise to visit her on September 3 (as Peggy had asked), because the exact date of their visit to the Austens early in the month (when they

Preliminary sketches and painting of Alan Odle and Dorothy Richardson at tea in Mrs. Pope's parlor in Trevone, Padstow, by Adrian Allinson, 1936–37. Courtesy of Miss Mary Mitchell-Smith.

usually went) had not yet been fixed. On August 16 Dorothy penned a note to the Austens, asking whether all was well with them. "We feel a little disquieted," she went on, "& though to put the question just at this time seems like saying aren't we coming down to see you this year, it has no such intention." But it had no other intention, and Dorothy and Alan made their journey to Kent as she had wished.

4

By the time of the visit to the Austens, *Dimple Hill* had been sent in and read. It had gone to Dent later than expected—in August instead of June—and Dorothy's own feelings about it were still very mixed. She had delayed sending it as long as she could, and now, while she waited to hear from Richard Church, she complained bitterly about all the external things beyond her control. Dent was "playing for time," she was sure, and counted on holding up publication. No doubt they thought that if they stood firm and withheld the new edition, she would wind up the series "in despair." She had a few words to say about the Cresset Press as well. They had put down the money to pay Duckworth; now, in view of the sales of *Clear Horizon* (she herself had received not quite £36 in two years), their chief was furious with Koteliansky, who had argued him into the purchase. She even maintained that Kot had been fired. But he had fallen ill, and she had to admit that the Cresset Press was being good enough to pay him his full salary and to keep his dismissal suspended. A good deal of this came from her overactive—and hostile—imagination.

She kept it up until word came from Richard Church that he liked *Dimple Hill* even better than *Clear Horizon*. He reported, as well, that preparations had begun for the publication of a four-volume edition of all her books. The entire edition would appear sometime in 1938, each of the volumes to sell for 7s. 6d., just the price she wanted. The volumes would be published on thin paper, with good print, and between simple board covers. The only change was the cancellation of the separate appearance of *Dimple Hill*. Instead, it would form the last chapter of volume four, and its presence there would be heavily stressed in the advance publicity. Dorothy conceded that this was something of an inspiration, "supplying," as she saw it, "a cunning bait for sales." At the same time, Dent was candid enough to point out that such a plan would also cancel the advance she was to have received upon acceptance of *Dimple Hill,* and that it would cut down her royalty on it to the 10 percent already agreed upon for the omnibus edition. There was not much Dorothy could do except complain—and she did—that they were adding insult to injury by asking her for "an almighty amount of collaboration." To begin with, they wanted a preface or foreword to the entire edition; this struck her at once as something she would find very troublesome. Then they wanted excerpts from the press through all the years *Pilgrimage* had been appearing. Finally, though this was by her own choice, she would have to correct all the errors that she claimed the Duckworth volumes contained. Indeed, it suddenly occurred to her that this must be why she had an "obstructive reputation for unreadable prose." Once she had formulated an idea, she would not let it go. To the end of her days she insisted that the chaotic state of her commas was responsible for her reputation.

However convinced she seemed to be about any number of things, fear and diffidence lay beneath the skin. The visit to the Austens is a case in point. Until it actually took place, she behaved as though it were quite settled save for the precise date. Yet in her heart she knew it was not, and she feared that John Austen would prove too strong and independent for her. She also learned that this year he really *was* too busy to entertain them. He had only hinted at this, but Dorothy would not allow herself to take the hint. Feeling thwarted on every other side, she was determined that the visit would take place. After all, she was not far wrong to think of herself as being at the mercy of Dent and the Cresset Press. Being told that the edition they were haggling over and constantly changing their minds about was her "last chance" did not serve to calm her nerves. If she could not manage Dent and the Cresset Press, she could at least try to bend John Austen to her frustrated will. It was of no account that he and his wife had just moved into a new house; she and Alan would come later in the month. It did not matter that John had to go to Oxford then, to sign copies of his book; she and Alan could come as late as August 17. On that date, finally, they went down to Kent, with Alan ignorant of everything that had gone before and the Austens presumably resigned.

When they arrived back in London, Dorothy took up her battle with Dent. She wanted a date set for the publication of the omnibus edition, but Dent continued to hold off, pleading for time to lay their plans with care. Dorothy, bent on fathoming the reasons for delay, decided it was partly their wish to sell additional copies of the Duckworth edition, which was to be scrapped when the new one appeared. Now, instead of worrying that the Duckworth volumes would disappear before the new edition came out, she claimed they were only selling "in driblets." As a matter of fact, Kot (who was apparently back at work) told her that the difficulties were being made by the Cresset Press and not by Dent. It was not easy to wage a war against shifting opponents, or indeed against someone like Richard Church, who kept saying he wanted to do as she wished but could do nothing without Cresset. But Dorothy seemed unwilling, or felt unable, to tackle Dennis Cohen of Cresset, who everyone insisted was the real villain. She studiously avoided corresponding with him, probably because she knew how powerless she would be to deal with anyone supposedly engaged in publishing her books solely as a business venture. Even she would have had to admit that such a purpose was ludicrous; and to argue with Cohen on this basis would have been to indulge in pure fantasy. In any case, Dorothy resorted to the only threat she felt qualified to make, which had its own ironic undertone, but she made it to Richard Church, whose sympathies were assured. She would have to put aside the successor to *Dimple Hill* "in favour of other work."

She may not have thought she was winning the battle, but Church was feeling the strain. He wrote to her in Cornwall that autumn, almost with tears, to explain that no sort of settlement could be made without Dennis Cohen—and he had stayed away on holiday, it would seem, for three months. The tone of his letter placated her; and as it turned out, she wrote a portion of the new chapter, already entitled *March Moonlight,* during the winter in Cornwall.

She also struggled with the foreword to *Pilgrimage* that Dent had asked her to supply. It was, she said, " the most horrible job" she had ever attempted. To introduce one's own work would not be pleasant under any circumstances, but in this case there was urgency as well, which her publishers seemed to feel and she could not help but absorb. What was she to say about *Pilgrimage* that the novel itself did not express? A work of art must be its own justification.

But Dent and the Cresset Press were afraid to trust *Pilgrimage,* so they were making their nervous arrangements for its "proper" reception. Church was writing an "Essay in Estimation," to appear as a brochure beforehand. For this Dorothy had to collect critical comments, which he wanted to weave into his essay. He had also asked several contemporary writers who knew her novel to contribute remarks he could include. One of them, the poet Ralph Hodgson, found himself forced to be "ungracious," as he put it, and to refuse. Much as he disliked saying no to a man like Church, he thought the idea of the brochure "a bit absurd," and he preferred to be "left out." Dorothy Richardson's readers, he said, could find her for themselves. It seemed to him that "good printing and binding . . . and the ordinary announcement in the Press [were] the proper homage that should be offered to such a writer and in keeping with her own qualities." He even dreaded a foreword. His comments were words of sense in the midst of madness, but Dorothy never heard them, and she never saw his letter.

She worked against the grain, through the winter months of 1937–38, to produce some sort of preface. No matter how hard she tried or how many drafts she scrapped, the result refused to be anything better than labored and heavy prose. The right note simply would not sound in her ears, and when she finally surrendered the piece to Church, she had decided that everyone would "shriek with laughter" over it.

While she wrestled with the foreword, Dent came through at last with a date of publication—autumn 1938—and proofs came next. She began to believe the edition would actually appear. There was still haggling about royalties (whether she would get them on sets or on volumes), but the great machinery had been put into gear, and she knew that now nothing short of an explosion would stop it. This did not mean her mind was at ease, for she never learned precisely how Dent's plans were being executed, and something told her that they too were striking the wrong note. In March 1938, when she sent the critical extracts she had chosen to Church from Constantine Bay, it seemed clearer than ever to her that she did not really understand what he was doing. By the beginning of April she had still not heard from him, although the office had sent her a printed form of acknowledgment, and his silence bothered her. At the same time, she hesitated to write him yet another nagging letter. Instead she wrote to Kot, asking him if perhaps *he* knew how Church had reacted to the things she had sent. Was it the kind of thing he had in mind, or was it so far off that it had "stricken [him] into a disgusted silence"? She would "hate him to feel," moreover, that he must put together a letter he did not want to write. A few days later she had a letter from Church himself, "a nice little letter," which she told Kot indicated that he "must have boomed gently & with discretion." For the moment she felt relieved.

But it was a brief moment. Everything in her own small world and in the world at large seemed so uncertain and fragile that without the wand of a magician there could be nothing like real contentment for anyone. The Austrian situation was sheer anguish. Like so many others, Dorothy clung to the belief that no immediate developments would come, that Hitler would busy himself "solidifying his empire." But this did not help the Jews, and their fate seemed to her the worst and saddest thing in the whole world. One's personal affairs were minute by comparison, yet one carried on with them as usual. Dorothy solved her small problem of where to go for the spring, since old Mrs. Pope had confessed to being unable to take them any longer. They went next door to the cottage named Bloomfield, where for a while Dorothy was calm enough to note the blooming of the hawthorn in Trevone and its nutty scent in the rain-washed air. She even continued to write *March Moonlight*. But when the page proofs did not come from Dent, she began to suspect a "deliberate delay."

The proofs arrived in June, along with an advance copy of the brochure. Her reaction to the brochure amounted to a failure in perception. Dent had announced the new edition as "the complete work of twelve parts, including one not hitherto published." In other words, they were subtly representing it, and Dorothy saw this perfectly well, as the whole of *Pilgrimage*. But her only comment was that she did not "enjoy" it. Her hands were neatly tied, and the fact of her utter helplessness sank in gradually. By August she was filled with "dismay and disgust." But even then she did not realize what effects the misrepresentation would have.

Perhaps no one could have realized those effects or would have been equal to them. Certainly Dorothy's attention was distracted during the summer of 1938. First of all, when she and Alan went to London in June, they discovered that nearly all their books of value, including illustrated editions, John Austens, signed Wellses, old first editions, and the books Alan himself had illustrated, were gone. So were many of Alan's drawings. He was left without a single example of his illustrated work. They knew that everything had been sold, piece by piece, by the young man who had rented their rooms for the winter, as he grew more and more desperate for money. He confessed to everything, and there was nothing Dorothy and Alan could do except tramp up and down Charing Cross Road trying to find any of the books in the shops that had bought them. They had no success.

June slipped into July, and early in the month Dorothy's brother-in-law, Kate's husband, died. He was eighty-two and had been ill for about two years, so "nothing was there for tears," but one felt the brush of it nonetheless. She again picked up the matter of her will, with Owen Wadsworth as her literary executor. He was back in England, fortunate, everyone thought, to have gotten out of Berlin after his forthright dispatches about the Nazi regime, and he reluctantly agreed to do as she wished.

The rest of the summer of 1938 was uneventful, but it was destined not to close quietly. At the end of September war seemed imminent; and Dorothy, who had been focusing on the October 13 publication date of the omnibus edition, felt her own history repeating itself. In 1914, when *Pointed Roofs* was yet to appear, the World War had struck. Was it really going to happen again? Was her novel so ill-fated as this? It was a paralyzing thought. She knew she ought to be thinking instead about getting out of London. Everyone seemed to expect the bombs to fall at any moment, and streams of people were leaving the city daily, many of them headed, Dorothy learned, for the West country. They felt it would be the safest place in England, not realizing that Cornwall's Falmouth had become an important naval base and that Devon's Plymouth would also be a prime target.

When Dorothy finally rang up Waterloo to inquire about train conditions, she was advised that if she intended to make for Cornwall at all, she ought to get away before mobilization made civilians "of no account." In other words, she ought to leave at once. But this she could not do. Then it occurred to her that they might go by road. She rang up various garages to ask the price and discovered that £20 would be the lowest (since the rationing of petrol was expected any minute, and the returning car might take days to get back). She could not decide whether to pay the price.

While she weighed the situation, the crisis evaporated. By October 9 London breathed freely again, for the time being at least. The Odles went down to Constantine Bay on October 18. A friend of theirs who was on the train staff congratulated them for waiting He would never forget, he said, the three worst days of the scare.

His train had been packed to the limit, including the last inch of the luggage vans.

Amid the international panic and the seesaw alternations between wild fear and willful hope, the omnibus edition of *Pilgrimage* was published at last. In Cornwall, where ARP (Air Raid Precautions) had already been fully organized and arrangements had been made for constructing shelters in the dunes, Dorothy waited for news about her book and about the war, expecting the worst in both cases. All she had seen so far was a notice in the *Telegraph* by a man who admitted he had only dipped in and wondered what the fuss on the wrapper was about. The news that came first was of the loss of their London home. The building at 32 Queen's Terrace was to be torn down, the site to be taken over by the War Office. They would have to remove all their belongings. It was a hard blow. For a quarter of a century Queen's Terrace had belonged to them, had contained their London selves, had guaranteed them their London summers. They were only glad they had not known when they left that they were crossing the threshold for the last time.

Then in November 1938 the reviews of *Pilgrimage* began to arrive, and Dorothy began to realize "the horrid fruit" of Dent's plan. The implication that *Pilgrimage* was finished was already having disastrous results. Friendly critics were frankly puzzled, and they passed over *Dimple Hill* in silence. It could only seem to them, Dorothy decided, "a *cul de sac* rather than a conclusion." The rest were delighted to announce, she said, that they had been right all along: the endless chronicle had simply petered out. This was only the beginning, but Dorothy saw it rightly as the end. Save with two or three reviewers, the misrepresented *Pilgrimage* had not the ghost of a chance. After all her years of struggle to remain alive, she was to feel not simply overwhelmed but virtually buried.

Part Four
1938-57

CHAPTER TWENTY-ONE

Storms and Shadows

To a careful reader who has no prior expectation that *Dimple Hill* is the end of *Pilgrimage,* the absence of any conclusion can clearly be seen. The last pages, in fact, explicitly suggest future development, and throughout the novel additional evidence can be found that Miriam had not yet reached the point of turning back to recreate her own "pilgrimage," the point Dorothy Richardson clearly aimed to reach. At the same time, *Dimple Hill* contains traces of the circumstances that prevailed when it was written: the misunderstanding on the part of Richard Church and Dent that Dorothy had become aware of only a few months after she began work on the novel, and her own unarticulated wish that Dent and the Cresset Press could publish a completed *Pilgrimage.*

One can see certain summarizing touches all through the novel—links made between Miriam's present experience and moments in the distant past that seem to serve (as primarily intended) not only as means by which Dorothy overcame the problem of an entirely new setting in *Dimple Hill* (the continuity is, as it always had been, in Miriam's consciousness), but also as suggestions of comprehensiveness that in turn suggest something like an approaching end. Dorothy's feelings were complicated indeed as she wrote *Dimple Hill,* but, surprisingly enough, the novel did not suffer. It has both moral and artistic integrity, and Richard Church's preference for it over *Clear Horizon* was sound.

Dimple Hill begins in a cathedral town to which Miriam has come with the Broom sisters, her friends since the days of Banbury Park. (The town is identified as Chichester in the manuscript, but is unnamed in the published text.) When their shared holiday comes to an end, Miriam remains in Sussex, to stay ultimately with a family of Quakers as a paying guest on their farm. Her reasons for remaining are fairly clear: she has had something like a breakdown (though it is barely referred to); she has taken a six-months leave from her job; and she wants a quiet place to try to write something more than brief essays and reviews. She is interested in trying her hand at a long narrative, possibly a novel, but not—she has decided—"the confessions of a modern woman," an idea put into her head long ago and keeping her until now "on the wrong track." The right track would lead, she thinks, to the "reality" that precedes, accompanies, and survives the "drama of human relationships"—the track most people move away from as soon as they get close to each other because they "expect each other to be all in all." It is this reality she wants to try to approximate in her own writing.

Dimple Hill is then a reworking of and an adjustment to the stage Dorothy Richardson had reached in 1907 (Miriam seems more advanced in some respects and less so in others than Dorothy had been), when she went to Sussex, then to Switzerland, and then returned to stay with the Quakers on the Penrose farm on Windmill Hill in Sussex. Miriam will not go to Switzerland, however, until the end of *Dimple Hill,* and the Swiss sojourn will provide the material for the novel to follow—the thirteenth volume, never to be completed.

In this twelfth volume Dorothy keeps Miriam entirely in Sussex (except for a visit to London), so she does not reach the point of writing the "middles" for the *Saturday Review* that she herself had begun to write during the winter of 1907–8 in Vaud. Yet several of those middles are virtually "rewritten" in *Dimple Hill;* that is, the material of them is sometimes also the material of the novel. The first one, "A Sussex Auction," is compressed into a paragraph describing Richard Roscorla's determined purchase of a used chain-harrow for the family farm. Others, such as "Lodge Night," "A Sussex Carrier," and "The Wind," reappear in the novel as descriptive passages and scenes here and there; and one can see, by means of them, Dorothy Richardson's fidelity not so much to fact as to the sense of the fact, and her ability to retrieve the consciousness that had experienced Sussex and the Quakers nearly thirty years before. From this ability the wholeness of the novel stems, for Miriam's consciousness embraces and absorbs all.

Her relationship with the Quakers seems in general like Dorothy's own, if one is to judge by the nonfictional book, *The Quakers Past and Present,* that Dorothy wrote about them in 1914. They had certain qualities that set them apart and made them particularly attractive to a person like Miriam, who was bent on discovering and following the direction in which the inmost self, rather than another individual or group, would lead. The Quakers seemed able to approach themselves through the medium of contemplative silence, to descend to an "impersonality where past and future, vanished from their places, lay powerless to nudge and jostle, far away within the depths of a perfect present," an impersonality that Miriam felt would provide her with a way to mediate between the demands of an importunate self and the desire to relate to others. It seemed to her that in learning from the Quakers the meaning of distance, she would also learn something about the nature of "human association."

By the end of *Dimple Hill,* after yet another of her strange romances, an involvement with the eldest Roscorla brother, Miriam is ready once again (as she had been at the end of *The Trap*) for a trip to the mountains of Switzerland. In the last chapter she writes to Amabel (who has just married Michael Shatov) of her desire to leave the farm and of her equal reluctance to consider life going on at Dimple Hill without her observing eye. Nonetheless, she has shaped her plans for the immediate future, and the thirteenth volume of *Pilgrimage* would open with another letter describing the journey to Vaud, an opening implicit in the last pages of the twelfth. But *March Moonlight* was destined to have no end.

2

At the Lynx in Cornwall in 1938, where the tin roof had been replaced with slates so that for the first time they were not bombarded by the wind, Dorothy watched the working out of fate in her own life and in the world. Their Queen's Terrace rooms were dismantled for them by young David Grad, and all their things were placed in a repository in Willesden. Dorothy and Alan had no idea where else to go in London this coming summer, that is, if they could manage to get there at all. They did not even know whether any lodgings would be available in Cornwall for the spring. They might have to stay at the Lynx, if that were possible. In other words, everything was problematical, except perhaps the course the reviews of *Pilgrimage* were taking.

Dorothy said that her poor *Pilgrimage* felt like the man in Poe's *Cask of Amontillado.* The reviewers were walling it up, she claimed, brick by brick, and closing it off from those who might have liked to read it. Apparently (or so Dorothy believed) Dent had made the further mistake of sending out for review only the last volume, which would certainly have made the reading of it a problem for someone unfamiliar with the others. Her guess was that Dent had done this out of fear that her foreword would "put up the backs of reviewers." She did not elaborate.

The foreword was certainly indirect and ponderous, even badly written, and its tone was vaguely hostile. She had been obliged, after all, to explain who she was and why her life's work ought to be read. Under such circumstances it seemed too much to expect either friendliness or expansiveness from her. She was annoyed and she showed it, though in a cryptic way. She referred to Joyce and Virginia Woolf, for example, without naming them. They were two of the writers who needed none of the explanation she apparently required and who had, in effect, superseded her. They had originally joined her, she said, on a "lonely track," which had then become a "populous highway," the woman mounted on a charger ("magnificently caparisoned") and the man walking, with his eyes "devoutly closed" and "weaving as he went a rich garment of new words wherewith to clothe the antique dark material of his engrossment." It was perfectly clear, of course, whom she was thus describing, yet she took the trouble to name Proust, another of her highly regarded contemporaries. But he (along with Balzac and Henry James, whom she also named) was safely dead.

Virginia Woolf posed more of a problem to Dorothy than Joyce. It was not only that as women writers they were often compared (usually to Dorothy Richardson's disadvantage) but also that Mrs. Woolf's gentility irked the granddaughter of a "chapel" tradesman. Though Dorothy had always made much of her father's intellectual pursuits and his self-styled "connections" with Oxford, she liked to maintain that the upbringing of the daughter of Sir Leslie Stephen in academic circles had burdened her with a heritage she could not overcome. Virginia Woolf (she thought) could not escape from what Dorothy called a "docility . . . to certain kinds of generalisations" that troubled even those who admired her work. She had a "specialist angle of vision," "all her avenues" had but "brief perspectives," and in the end her "wonder-working talents show[ed] . . . like peacocks in prison." Dorothy harped on the word *peacocks*. Sometimes, she said, "they strut and strike attitudes. But always with drooping wings.'' Her way of dealing with the elegance of Mrs. Woolf's prose was to reduce it to a stylistic show. When she was asked in 1937 to review Virginia Woolf's new novel, *The Years,* she refused on the grounds that none of the preceding books had moved her deeply, and said that, in spite of her admiration for the work, she felt the *London Mercury* ought to put the book in the hands of someone to whom she meant a great deal. Dorothy thought she was being admirably just to Virginia Woolf (in taking a stand with the *London Mercury* that she no doubt felt they themselves should have taken with the reviewers of her own work), but in the process she misspelled Virginia Woolf's name, and she confessed a few days later that she never had been sure of the correct spelling.

James Joyce was quite another matter. For one thing, critics could not refer to him as the ''leader'' of the current women novelists. For another, Joyce had left all his fellow novelists behind, and with *Finnegans Wake* had ventured into a realm virtually no other writer could even approach. So although she refused to deal with Virginia Woolf's new novel, Dorothy agreed to review *Finnegans Wake* for *Life and Letters To-day.* Complaining while she read—or struggled through—Joyce's massive work, describing her blood as alternately curdling and freezing in her veins, she nonetheless produced a remarkably intelligent piece about it.

In May 1939 there was no help with *Finnegan* to be found either in Cornwall or anywhere else. Yet Dorothy plunged in and emerged aware of what she had been through. There was plenty of justification for weariness, she said, as one struggled from ''thicket to thicket'' without a clue, surrounded by abstruse references and pelleted with languages both ancient and modern, with regional and class dialects, with slang and catchwords and slogans. And there was plenty of reason to be incensed, she said, when you gradually realized that all these diverse elements were linked largely through their sound rather than their meaning. Indeed, they were interspersed with the sort of ''spontaneous creations'' that bored children were wont to produce, shouting as they sometimes did a single word, repeating it with a change of vowel, with another change and yet another, until they were silenced by an interfering adult who had had enough. *Finnegans Wake* was just as maddening as this, Dorothy claimed, and she pointed out that the author had no doubt known it would be, had foreseen that even the most faithful Joycean would break down ''in the neighborhood of the hundredth page.''

319

Here, then, he had come to the rescue with a chapter that seemed to her "exceptionally, and most mercifully, explicit." She understood as the "high purpose" of this chapter the demand that the novel be poetry; and she extracted from it the following directive, that "to concentrate solely on the literal sense or even the psychological content of any document... is... hurtful to sound sense." Did Joyce mean, she asked, that one ought to "*listen* to *Finnegans Wake*?" Apparently she thought he did mean just that. If one listened not so much to what Joyce said as to the way he said it, one would hear the "rhythms and undulating cadences of the Irish voice." She, for one, was prepared to "take the author at his word," and she advised all his readers to do the same—to release themselves from "literary preoccupations and prejudices, from the self-imposed task of searching for superficial sequences," and simply plunge into the text—enter it, she said, and "look innocently about." The reward, Dorothy claimed, would be sheer delight.

She did not see *Finnegans Wake* only as "inexhaustible entertainment," however. She also made an attempt—quite courageous for its time—to get at the feeling that pervaded the book. To her, though Finnegan and his wife and their friends might "symbolize life or literature or what you will that occasionally call for mourning," they provided Joyce with food for "incessant ironic laughter" that was also very possibly a "screen for love and solicitude." Moreover, to her the laughter seemed mitigated by touches of "wistfulness" that reached "a full note" by the end of the book. To have caught this note was to have listened to the human voice in *Finnegans Wake* as it celebrated, with a sadly comic longing, the triumph of fantasy and the unconscious in life.

3

Dorothy worked her way through *Finnegans Wake* during May and June. In March she and Alan had left the Lynx in Constantine Bay and had gone into lodgings in Trevone, which they were lucky to have found. They were staying at Hillside, a house not far from Trevone Bay, owned by people she understood to be spiritualists. The family consisted of an uncle of seventy-nine, his spinster niece of sixty, and a grandniece of twenty-one. Dorothy found them friendly and sensible, and there was no trace of communications with the spirit world in the way they ran their household. Intrigued, however, by the possibility of such communications, she kept a watchful eye for signs of them.

Otherwise, life around her held little that was unexpected. By now she knew the actual sales figures for the new edition. In the first few months, only 699 volumes (individual volumes, not complete sets) had been sold. This meant that nothing more was due her; the £30 paid her on publication had been deducted from the royalties on the sales. She might get a small amount in the autumn, she thought, from the few hundred unbound sheets that Knopf had bought. And that was that, as Dorothy herself put it. The fate of the volume she was still working on seemed clear. Dent would have to be deranged to bring it out. They were right, after all, she said, to have claimed that *Pilgrimage* was finished.

It was finished in her own heart most of all. The life of her novel had run its course, but the course had ended too soon, and she was left, it seemed, with a pathless pilgrimage. She would suffer from the intangible loss through all her remaining years. It was as if she had been deprived of ballast. In the past there had always been the fixed goal, the completion of another volume of *Pilgrimage*, on which she could count. It provided her with justification—for doing this and not doing that, for feeling and not feeling what her conscience rendered problematical. But now *Pilgrimage* was failing her. She knew only too well that to turn out one more "chapter"— even if it finished the book at last—would make no real difference to anyone, not even to her. Though she claimed she would produce the volume anyway, and "leave it to take its posthumous chance," the words had no will behind them. In the next fifteen years she wrote only two-thirds of a volume.

For the moment, the sense of loss that she felt could be traced to several different sources. Queen's Terrace was one of them; and when it seemed likely they could get to London that summer after all, she set about finding a substitute. From an advertisement in a London paper, she booked a flat she was sure would be disastrous, but it was quite the opposite. They arrived in town toward the end of June 1939 to discover themselves in a house of the Regency period, like the one in Queen's Terrace but even larger, and just as charmingly "dilapidated." They had a good room, the use of a garden, and (until it was let) another room with French windows that opened into the garden. Most pleasing of all, they were still in St. John's Wood. The house was at 58 Boundary Road, northwest of Queen's

Terrace, between the Abbey and Finchley roads. From this base she and Alan would, unknowingly, see London for the last time.

They led their usual summer lives of bus rides, cinemas, visits, and a short stay in seaside Walton. But London was visibly on edge, full of refugee Jews and without its customary complement of traveling Americans. The English could do little more than wait for Hitler's next move. They had known since March what would happen if he were to attack Poland; at any rate, they thought they knew. Through most of the summer, until mid-August, while the British government negotiated with Russia in its attempt to gain an ally against Germany, many feared that Chamberlain would resort once again to appeasement. A confused and anxious Parliament adjourned at the beginning of August for its summer holiday, but not without assurance from the Prime Minister that, in the event of another crisis such as the one of the year before, Parliament would be reconvened.

The first three weeks of August passed in relative quiet. Dorothy and Alan planned to return to Cornwall on September 15. She had arranged with the family at Hillside to stay there until the Lynx at Constantine was available, probably in October. Then on August 22 the storm clouds gathered. The Germans and Russians announced their intent to sign a nonaggression pact. On the twenty-third the House of Commons was notified to convene the next day. On the twenty-sixth, according to Hitler, Poland would be invaded. At the last moment he postponed the attack until September 1. During the frenzied days between, while Britain's Nevile Henderson went back and forth from Chamberlain to Hitler, hope alternated with despair, and sandbags were heaped on the basement windows of Parliament. Dorothy and Alan decided to try to leave London on Saturday, September 2. But on Friday, September 1, when the German army marched into Poland, the evacuation of 3 million mothers and children from the threatened areas of England began, and it was clearly impossible for Dorothy and Alan to get away. They managed to spend the first with her sister Kate in Ealing, and they returned to London in total darkness—"a pall of black velvet" as Harold Nicolson described it.

The gloom that descended upon the city was mixed, for some, with outrage. The English were not keeping their promise to help the Poles. In the House, on the evening of September 2, Prime Minister Chamberlain nearly set off a riot with his phlegmatic report of the sequence of diplomatic moves and his intimation that no decision had yet been reached. Challenged, he insisted that he meant to stand firm but that England had to work with France, make no declaration without her. He was delaying, in other words, because of Georges Bonnet, in whom he claimed to have full confidence. But many members of the House distrusted Bonnet and felt, too, that Chamberlain was aware that they had sufficient grounds. The House adjourned in uncertainty and moral indignation, and Londoners slept through another black night.

When they woke in the morning, it was to hear of the ultimatum delivered to the Germans, which would expire at 11:00 A.M. Dorothy, rising late from breakfast on this sunlit Sunday to learn of the ultimatum, felt hope renewed—and then heard ''all the syrens of the vast city... shrieking up & up... and dropping down & down....'' It was already 11:45, the ultimatum had gone unanswered, and England was at war.

The sirens shrieked again in the small hours of Monday morning. Dorothy and Alan listened to the sound of people stumbling in the darkness toward candles and gas masks, but they did not get up. Alan would not take refuge in the basement; he refused even to leave his bed. ''*Let* them,'' he said, ''I'm not going to stir.'' Though this, like the first, was a false alarm, Londoners had been warned that the worst bombardments would take place during the early weeks of the war. For Dorothy the noise of sirens (and of bombs, if they should fall) was a more difficult prospect to bear than injury and even death. The sirens ''shrieking in chorus,'' she said, were ''horrible beyond belief.''

During the four days of the evacuation, while the Odles waited to be able to leave, the sirens continued to sound, but no bombs fell. On September 5 they left London with no idea that, in effect, they were going into exile and that, at the war's end six years hence, the city would have lost its compelling lure and they would feel that the last remnant of their youth had gone. For the present, however, they wanted only to reach Cornwall, a trip they would have to make in stages.

A friend who had an ARP car drove them to Salisbury, where they planned to spend the night. They found that in the ancient cathedral town only the cathedral itself, its close and precincts, remained serene and beautiful. The rest of the town had been transformed, as if by black magic, into a seething mass of soldiers, equipment, and displaced London children. Once in Salisbury, it took them two days to get out again. They did not want to stand all the way to Padstow, so they followed the advice of the railway people and waited until it seemed safe to venture on the regular Cornish Express. In the meantime, they stayed at a small, stuffy "Commercial Inn" frequented by members of a business "Order," as Dorothy described it, with "sacred laws" that would have warmed the heart of Alan's father. But the irony of it escaped Dorothy, who was busy trying to ward off the din.

The train they finally took was nearly empty. They found that Padstow and Trevone still had no evacuees, although some were said to be coming from Bristol and Plymouth. All but the prices that were fixed by the government had begun to soar, and Dorothy observed with dismay that the housing situation was as tight as it could be. They could stay at Hillside until October 18. On that date they had planned to move into the Lynx, but it was no longer available. Mrs. Dawson-Scott's son needed it as a refuge for London relatives. Dorothy feared at first that this change might leave them homeless, but she was even more concerned that her sister Kate, who was seventy-three, was in the thick of things at Ealing. She had been left tired and strained by her husband's long illness and recent death, but was nonetheless talking about getting work as a domestic.

Dorothy spoke of the growing problems with the utmost seriousness, but in spite of her own words and the evidence of her senses, she did not yet believe in the reality of war. She clung to the feeble hope still held by many that after Hitler had conquered Poland he would make overtures of peace to England. In Cornwall especially, with only the gulls cawing overhead, one could indeed grasp at straws.

4

In less than a month the Polish resistance had been broken down, unable to withstand not only the Germans but also the Russians, who had attacked from the opposite direction on September 17. On the twenty-seventh, Warsaw, which had held out the longest, surrendered, and Poland was partitioned by Germany and Russia. With Poland out of existence, the conquerors issued a joint statement on the twenty-eighth calling for an end to the fighting. So the "peace-offer" had come after all, but what on earth did it mean? Could Hitler be trusted? What did he *really* want? Was it still possible to take a pacifist stand?

To this last question Dorothy, for one, answered no. Peace was not an end in itself, she felt, but "a by-product of the balance of dynamic forces." She did not believe in planning and agreeing to avoid conflict—or "strife," as she put it—simply because strife was "destructive & uncomfortable." No wonders would be worked in this way, it seemed to her, if only because "every contrivance system" had a "compulsive element" somewhere. Every system had its "bosses," and they compelled in one way or another and inevitably competed too. By this time (the latter part of October), Dorothy shared fully in the general awareness of the need to fight.

For the rest of the year, however, though the British prepared themselves, and it seemed more and more likely that Winston Churchill would be their war leader, there was no actual fighting. The expected aerial attack on Britain did not materialize, but the uncertainty and inactivity imposed a great strain on the nation. Hitler's threats against Holland and Belgium hung in the air, and when at the end of November the Russians began to bomb Finland, the waiting British watched the Finnish resistance with amazement. Even Alan wanted to rush to their aid. He had gone, Dorothy said, "all militarist."

She, in turn, was engaging in finding a place to live. With war conditions already prevailing, Dorothy knew she had waited too long. She should have secured something for them to fall back on, but it had been difficult to believe that there would be absolutely nowhere to go. Yet by the end of September this appeared to be the case. What she really wanted was a place that promised some degree of permanence, but one needed money for that. Then during the early part of October a solution offered itself in the form of a tiny cottage. It was the property of an invalid lady who lived in Wadebridge and had not been near the place, Dorothy said, for ages. The woman preferred to sell the cottage, but Dorothy prevailed upon her to rent it for the winter by agreeing to take it just as it was— begrimed, musty, and not yet blacked out according to wartime regulations.

After scrubbing and blacking out their new quarters, the Odles moved in during the last week of October, while a northeast gale screamed. Sea View, as the little cottage was named, stood in

325

Dobbin Lane, off the main Trevone road. Actually, it was one-half of an ex-golf-links shanty that had been moved from its native heath and separated from its other half by a wooden partition. It had four cramped rooms all opening into each other, with two of them leading directly outdoors. The smallest room was not lived in, but was used instead as storage space for luggage, various odd belongings, and—in the absence of a larder—for food. Dorothy claimed that the kitchen was too small, got too hot when she cooked, and was too warm for meat or milk to be kept in it safely. The other rooms, however, were cold, with "inches of gap above & below" the doors, with window frames that did not fit, and without fireplaces. Finally, every sound could be heard through the partition. The only virtue of Sea View was its splendid view of the sea, of foamy surf and jagged rock, from a wide casement window in their sitting room.

They could stay in Sea View until April, when its owner planned to sell it; after that they would be stranded again. Dorothy weighed the merits of committing themselves to settle in Cornwall or trying to find somewhere else. Having lost both Queen's Terrace and the Lynx, they were no longer in a position to move about; they simply could not afford it. This meant they had to decide where to stay put. In many ways Cornwall seemed the most sensible place, but this decision would cut them off from friends and relatives in or near London, and indeed from London itself. Even though from all reports the city seemed to have retreated into the eighteenth century, to become again "a group of scattered villages joined, at night, by dark & dangerous highways," it still represented life in the world to Dorothy and Alan. For them to give that up would mean a kind of death.

That Dorothy spoke, and apparently thought, as if a choice could be made was characteristic of her. But the truth seemed to be that she had no options. She herself admitted, in fact, that to leave Cornwall without being able to come back was almost as blood-curdling a prospect as having to give up London. More to the immediate point, they were already in Cornwall, and with every week of war—even this "pretended war," as Churchill called it—movement of any kind became less and less feasible. Petrol was already scarce, not only for private use but for commercial use as well. It would be difficult and expensive to move any distance just as they were, leaving aside their stored belongings (which Dorothy realized, after making a few inquiries, had best remain in Willesden for the time being). The cost of transporting them would be prohibitive. So any but furnished quarters were out of the question, and finding these outside of Cornwall under the prevailing circumstances would be most unlikely.

So when Bryher offered to lend Dorothy the money for the Sea View alterations, she leaped at the chance to buy one of the most uncomfortable homes they had ever experienced. She could only manage the purchase with a full mortgage though, and it turned out that only a private investor—should such be found—would undertake anything like that. Dorothy went through the motions of looking for a private investor during most of January and Feburary 1940, but clearly—after her initial enthusiasm—the whole affair struck her as being much too troublesome. What she really wanted was to be taken care of, whereas Bryher's help required that she put forth considerable effort. It would be nice to own Sea View once it had been altered and made reasonably comfortable—if, that is, she herself did not have to take care of it all and arrange for everything. Then, toward the end of February, just the kind of help she hoped for seemed miraculously to be in the offing.

Richard Church wrote to tell her that he was trying to get her on the Civil List for a small grant or an allowance. He had already seen Chamberlain and had found him sympathetic. Dorothy would be informed one way or the other sometime in March, but Church felt confident. Although she was afraid to count on it, Dorothy allowed herself to say to Bryher that however small the award might be, it would "make just all the difference" at this juncture. She went on to speak of the difference it would make in economic terms: she and Alan would be able to "keep their heads above water locally," especially if the purchase of Sea View turned out to be impossible, as it seemed.

Early in March Dorothy heard from Whitehall that she had been granted a Civil List pension of £100. What the award meant most of all was recognition of her as Dorothy Richardson the novelist. No one expected her to prove anything with another book; what she had done already was acknowledged and deemed sufficient. This gave Dorothy "inexpressible heartsease and relief," she said. She was also gratified to learn, as she gradually did, that a group of people had worked in her behalf. Church had asked several others to write to Chamberlain. One of them was Hugh Walpole, who had felt troubled about "bothering" the Prime Minister at such a "bad time" but had written anyway. Walpole himself would receive the Order of Merit, and would wonder whether in accepting it—as he wanted very much to do—he was not confirming his suspected conventionality. No such soul-searching went on in Dorothy; besides, her situation was quite different. She had made no money from her novels, whereas Walpole had made a great deal from his. As an eminently successful writer, he was obscurely rankled by his very popularity, which he feared might mean that he was not an artist. When Dorothy wrote to him in March to praise his newly published book, *Roman Fountain,* he was "delighted" and "relieved." She also told him that she had suspected the part he had played in her Civil List pension and that for this she was touched and grateful. Walpole admitted nothing, saying only how glad he was and reminding her of their early days in Cornwall with Jack Beresford. The three of them, he mused, had "all in [their] different ways gone along the same road." At another time Dorothy might have winced more than a little to think of the vast difference between her career and Walpole's. As for Beresford, he had never made a bid to posterity as she had; he had merely, by dint of very hard work, supported his family. But now the pension of £100 was balm to old wounds; she felt momentarily pacified, if not mellow.

5

Her first act after hearing of the pension was to arrange for temporary lodgings at Hillside (which they could now afford) when their tenancy at Sea View expired in April. They even moved out of Sea View a week early, "plutocratically," Dorothy said. Each day she and Alan walked over from Hillside to put a few more things together—and in supreme justification of this "expensive" procedure, Dorothy typed up the "scraps" of the new volume of *Pilgrimage* she had "wrested from [herself] during the past year." There was no more than a mere suggestion that she might go on with the volume. The only commitments she spoke of were to edit a book that her friend Macmillan was writing and to write a short story for a new monthly being brought out by Woodrow Wyatt.

The promise to edit Mac's book had been made in March, when he had stayed at Hillside for three weeks and had tried to persuade Dorothy to write about his work. She could not agree to do this

Owen Wadsworth in Prague, 1922.

because, as she put it, there was "still a stop in [her] mind." However much she claimed to admire and believe in him, it was quite another thing to announce her endorsement of his healing to the world at large, and that far she could not bring herself to go. But when Mac wrote the book himself, much of it while there at Hillside, Dorothy provisionally consented to look it over and supply a preface. She found the book "entirely, incredibly, unreadable," but instead of throwing up her hands and backing down, she spent two months editing what eventually, in 1948, would be published as *This Is My Heaven, Two Treatises on Healing and other Essential Matters*. But she never wrote the preface.

Mac's book occupied her during April and May, and even into June. That it kept her from her own writing was perhaps what she wanted. She was too distracted anyway by events in the "real world." Germany had invaded Norway and Denmark in April, Holland and Belgium in May, and then France. The news received toward the end of May, that the German armored attack through the Ardennes had reached the Channel coast and had cut off the British Expeditionary Force from the main French armies to the south, was strongly felt in Trevone. Since September many B.E.F. wives and their children had been quartered there. Dorothy saw them now as "wraiths" of what they had been when they came. She watched the change with fascination, and in the present crisis joined with other residents of Trevone in trying to distract them from their preoccupations. She also thought it necessary to dissuade Alan from volunteering for night patrol. He agreed not to join up unless there was a shortage of men, which seemed to her unlikely. But he chafed under her restraining hand.

They both listened to daily news bulletins of the battle of France with sinking hearts, as did everyone around them. They had a radio of their own, sent to them by Owen Wadsworth, who was back from Berlin and had come to Trevone for a visit at the end of May. Nothing he actually said about his experience in Germany was more vivid and convincing than the way he could not help glancing over his shoulder and at doors and windows, and lowering his voice to a murmur. Dorothy was shocked. Alan stared with comprehending eyes at the specter of Nazi Germany that Owen's behavior conjured up.

On June 18, a few days after Owen's radio arrived and, to Dorothy's joy, began its "career" with a Beethoven trio, Marshall

Pétain announced that the French army could fight no longer. *"Il faut cesser la lutte,"* he said; and the fate of England hung by a thread held, many people thought, in the pudgy hand of Winston Churchill. He had been Prime Minister for more than a month and had already delivered his first great speech of the war, vowing that the English would fight on their very beaches. Now, in the sickening first moments after the fall of France, he proclaimed that his country's "finest hour" had come. In speech after speech during the months that followed, he filled his listeners with resolution and admiration; but he could not prevent invasion scares such as the one that swept through Cornwall during the summer. It was rumored that Hitler had decided to land on this southwestern coast in a surprise maneuver. The Cornish themselves had remained calm for the most part, and on the alert. They watched the sea night and day, patrolling the beaches, manning the outlooks (at Steppe Point, for example, on the cliffs above Padstow), and quietly scolding anyone who spread demoralizing rumors. Nonetheless, more than just a few scattered people seem to have firmly resolved, in the event of a successful invasion, to kill themselves. Mothers of young children were determined to kill them, too. These civilized beings refused to endure barbarism, even if their hatred of violence drove them to commit it upon themselves.

Whether or not Dorothy Richardson and Alan Odle had so resolved, or had even entertained the thought of defeat, they certainly had braced themselves for a mighty battle. But when the sirens sounded in Trevone, Dorothy retired into a corner and held her hands over her ears. She fulminated against the BBC, and in fact wrote them, about the chords and pauses used in introducing news bulletins. She found the "niminy-piminy chords" expressive of utterly hopeless resignation and claimed that during the "awful pauses" between the chords the listener hoped against hope that the chord would not recur—but it always did. She suggested various alternatives that were gay and lilting, and at least continuous. If none of these were satisfactory, she begged of them, why not restore the World War I procedure: the gentle thud of quiet footsteps, popularly described as "The Ghost in Galoshes." Was this an irrelevant and frivolous protest? Or was it a thoroughly English focus on manner?

There was no doubt that she was being her thoroughly English self in this war. Back in February, when the rationing of sugar and butter and the rise in the price of milk had become distinct realities, she had contributed a piece entitled "Needless Worry" to *Life and Letters To-Day*. In it she had pointed out that children, as well as adults, would be better off without so much of these foodstuffs. If, as the dentist had long been maintaining, sugar proved itself "a demon in the mouth," how could it "become, in the stomach, a beneficient angel?" As for butter, there were quite enough "trustworthy substitutes," and milk (which was one of the "spoiled foods" anyway) had been "intended by 'Nature' only for the toothless mammals." In other words, there was no cause for anxiety. Be sensible, she exhorted mildly.

It was not with mildness, however, that she engaged in a defense of England to the critical Bryher, who contended that after dragging its feet for so long, the country would find itself beaten roundly. By October London was under full siege, and Bryher had managed, with a great deal of difficulty, to leave Switzerland and get to her adopted daughter and H. D. in London. She was angry and bitter at the persistent disregard in the thirties of Churchill's warnings and Anthony Eden's advice about Spain. Her condemnation of England gave Dorothy "an almighty shock" and tore a protest from her. She agreed that Churchill and Eden should have been listened to, but she was absolutely convinced that English "deliberation (call it slowness & stupidity)," the "refusal . . . to face what are sometimes called *facts* & to have (in the Wellsian sense) *plans* is the defect of something supremely good." It was what made the English socially "go about less armed than any but the Americans, & sceptical of nuisance until it is under our noses." She felt it was something "utterly lacking in the logical French," who thought "solely with the intelligence, as distinct from the reason, which included feeling." The French, she insisted, had "floundered because they were the prey of competing logics." They had not been able to unite, and they were at the mercy of "treacheries." And "*nothing,*" she rang out, "rots more swiftly than logic."

A month later she took up the cudgel again, exultantly. Bryher had mentioned John Milton in one of her letters, and Dorothy reminded her that though the first load of bombs falling on the city had flung his statue from its base, it had failed to break it. "There it lies," she said, "in calm repose amongst the debris." The survival meant, to her, that English liberty would not crack under the strain.

But the strain was by now terrific. The raids on London had begun on August 16. From September 7 to November 3, the city was bombed every night, and for a time it seemed destined for utter demolition. Piles of masonry were everywhere. A pall of smoke often hung in the lower sky. A smell of burning was always in the air. One never knew, moreover, from day to day or moment to moment, what strange and horrible vision might appear—a huge plane, for instance, had come down outside a pub near Victoria, and a complete airman's boot, ripped up both sides, lay bizarrely in the street. Dorothy heard both the facts and rumors of what was happening in and around London, and she felt that to be in Cornwall was to be relatively safe, though at the mercy of imaginings. But she feared, with a sense of rising panic, for the survival of her sister Kate, who was exposed to everything in Ealing. It was not the war that would take Kate's life, however, in spite of Dorothy's fears— fears that she now sought refuge from in the battered haven of writing her book. In the face of unbearable possibilities, she suddenly became more engrossed than ever in the projection of her self as Miriam Henderson, as someone who lived in a known and controllable past.

6

Dorothy seems to have turned again to *Pilgrimage* once she had solved the problem of where they would live after their stay at Hillside ended. She came upon the solution in a totally unexpected way. In September the village of Trevone was diverted from its wartime anxieties by the news of an impending marriage. The prospective bride was a sixty-five-year-old spinster, whom Dorothy knew and who until then had been the tenant in a house called Zansizzey. When Dorothy learned that the bride and her groom did not plan to live in the house, which stood on the winding hill of the main road of Trevone, she asked that she and Alan be recommended to the owner as possible new tenants. But, with the village uncharacteristically crowded at this time and an empty house a great rarity, she did not have high hopes. It turned out, however, that the owner was the cousin of a woman Dorothy had met in Château d'Oex nearly forty years earlier. They got the house not only at pre-war winter rates but also for an indefinite period of time.

Dorothy worked hard at trying to justify this stroke of good fortune. She argued that the landlady was not Cornish and did not need the rent, having bought the place only for holidays. Besides, the house had disadvantages: it had a great deal of floor space, which would mean a lot of housekeeping, and its location would mean climbing halfway up a steep hill to get home from trips to the post office and the general store.

Nevertheless, Zansizzey had things to praise as well. Dorothy called it a "villa," using the term rather loosely. She claimed that her landlady's husband was "a sort of squire" in the neighboring village of St. Issey, where his family had owned land for "hundreds of years"; and, in fact, when he had bought the house in Trevone, he had named it Zansizzey, the medieval name of his ancestral seat. But the house was simply a bungalow of decent size, with three bedrooms, a sitting room, a kitchen, and a bath. It had been completely wired for electricity, but Dorothy preferred to use candles as much as possible because they were cheaper, and she continued to cook on her own portable "Beatrice" rather than use the electric stove. The house had a fairly large garden, that, by the end of the war and of the Odles' tenancy, would become a wilderness. Once in their "villa" they learned that it could be quite damp, with beads of moisture often showing on the walls. But Zansizzey was securely theirs, a refuge and a home in the uncertain world of 1940—one that had, moreover, if only in its name, a touch of the unusual.

The way Zansizzey was situated had distinct charms, too. Because it was on the hill, one could look down and see Trevone Bay. Across the road was an immense sweep of view, from the coast to Bodmin Moor, with the two highest points in Cornwall—Ro'tor and Brown Willy—visible against the horizon. Dawn and sunrise were ravishing sights. Alan and Dorothy took to standing on the steps every morning to watch the light move across the entire expanse until it reached the sea. Alan set up his drawing table beneath the front windows of the sitting room so that he would have the whole living scene before him all the time, with the local farmer's cows grazing in the foreground and the tips of the two mountains in the background, pressing lightly against the sky. In this setting, the most spacious and aesthetically gratifying of their lives, both Dorothy and Alan settled down with evident relief and pleasure. They could scarcely believe their good fortune.

334

Now, too, they were more in touch with the daily life of Trevone than ever before, perhaps because things were quite different. The population of the village had swelled nearly to the bursting point, with retired people seeking shelter from the assault on the rest of England, with evacuees, families of servicemen, and relatives and friends of the residents. The assortment was colorful and varied, and common concern over the war created a unity that everyone felt and acknowledged. Alan, for example, had become less and less awkward in his encounters with other human beings in Trevone. He had something to talk about that was of passionate interest to him and to any person he might meet, and though he continued to stride up and down the hill with a look of remote frenzy, he began to respond with more equanimity when someone crossed his path.

The Odles liked to visit the local café next door to Rose Cottage. It was the gathering place for the young airmen stationed at St. Eval; they seemed to prefer the café to the pubs near the aerodrome. When these young men flew overhead on practice flights, they would greet their friends in Trevone by "knocking" the roofs and chimneys of their houses. One Trevoner complained about the low flying, but the rest of the village—Dorothy and Alan included—responded by signing a statement that they liked it, to prevent the young men from being punished. But they could do nothing about the bombing raid on the airfield that killed twenty-three of the young flyers, who had been in a shelter that stood between two hangars.

Such was the note on which 1940 ended in Trevone, and there was no reason to expect anything better in 1941. London had survived the German bombers, but even the provincial cities were under constant attack, and civilian morale was low. The threat of invasion still hung over the country. While the campaign against the Italians in northeast Africa was going well, Britian as yet had no ally except Greece. To make matters worse for Trevone, Cornwall was plunged into an unbelievably cold winter. Snow fell several times; pipes froze, cutting off the water supply; and flu raged. During normal winters Dorothy had invariably come down with flu. This season she began with a "vile cold" in the middle of January, and by February she had passed this on to Alan as flu, the tiresomely real thing. Preoccupied with nursing each other, they kept to themselves again for a while, reading some of the books Bryher and Owen Wadsworth were always sending them—Mann's *Lotte in Weimar,*

Symons's *The Quest for Corvo,* Compton Mackenzie's *The Red Tapeworm*, and Edwin Muir's *Autobiography*.

Dorothy also got a copy of the latest Wells, *Babes in the Darkling Wood*, "duly signed and messaged," which she assumed meant that he had returned from his controversial trip to the United States. Apparently a few government figures did not trust Wells's discretion in the least and feared he would go about saying things that would prejudice the cause of England in the States. There had even been what Dorothy called a "comic-opera parliamentary debate about our Mr. Wells & his goings-on in New York" that seemed to have come to nothing. At any rate, Dorothy read the new Wells book and had to admit that the writing was "amazingly vigorous & good." He was after all, she reported, nearly seventy-five. But the "milieu," she went on to insist, "was the same old humanistic concentration camp complete with Gestapo of Intellectuals." Still, "as a Protestantism," she conceded that it had perhaps some value. It was the "same old" mixed tone in Dorothy's voice, too. Her ambivalent feelings toward Wells had not been resolved, though she herself was sixty-seven. Perhaps they could never be resolved, in part because Wells would never settle down as one or the other of the many people he seemed to be.

For Dorothy, to think of Wells was to conjure up a past that she had by now rigorously intellectualized; and this intellectualization, with its separation of ideas from feelings, was what gave her the trouble she was having with *Pilgrimage*. The novel had become more of a conception than an emotional reality—a book to finish instead of a life to order and relive. Thus, in now going back to it, her approach had changed. Instead of coming up from the depths of herself and her past, she was trying to climb in from the outside—a method that would not work, that could not give her the complete satisfaction of the original involuntary one. One cannot know whether she understood the nature of the frustration she felt, but in the midst of her current illness and retreat, when she was exercising her mind on other people's books and finding her own sealed up, the sudden death of her sister Kate brought about the kind of emotional plunge that was no longer possible with *Pilgrimage*.

Early in March 1941, Kate's son wrote to Dorothy and informed her that Kate was seriously ill with a case of bronchitis that was developing into pneumonia. Almost immediately afterward, a telegram arrived announcing her death. Despite Dorothy's fears for

Kate, their realization was a stunning blow. "Incredulous & absurd though it seems," she said, she felt "much more desolately *young* than in losing a parent." But this was what Kate had largely been to her. The seven-year gap in their ages had never really closed, and her eldest sister had always represented to Dorothy the authority that their mother had wielded for such a relatively short time. With Kate gone, "the very look of things had changed."

Then, before Dorothy could adjust to this altered universe, letters began to arrive from all of the childhood and girlhood friends who had kept in touch with her sister. Some of them, Dorothy realized, must have been "amazing ages." They belonged to Abingdon days and to Putney, and their memories remained astonishingly sharp. They reminded her of details, events, and people she found she had not forgotten, that sprang into being out of "an everlasting present" within her. It was "wrapped about [her]," she said, "the whole of [her] life, fold upon fold," as it had been years before when she first began to write *Pilgrimage,* that is, to perform the creative act of unfolding. Not for a long time had she felt so in touch with the world that had nurtured art.

CHAPTER TWENTY-TWO

War and Obscurity

LETTERS from Kate's friends continued to come, along with replies from relatives to whom Dorothy had written the news of Kate's death. She read the letters avidly. Each one seemed to open new doors and windows in her mind, and the phrase *so long ago,* which occurred so often in them, grew more and more meaningless. Dorothy was struck by the similar tone of these letters received from people who still lived within what seemed to her the "serene Victorian tradition." This was why, she thought, they had survived and remained "so youthful & so keen"—and "tolerant" as well. She envied them their firm roots in that old, safe world, while she hung awkwardly between the old and the new.

It was a familiar position for her. She had always somehow been caught in between: two worlds (the Victorian and the modern), two social classes (trade and the professional middle class), two styles of life (the bohemian and the conventional). Most of the time she saw herself as poised or balanced, rather than dangling, but she rarely considered herself, or even projected herself in fiction, as fully committed to one or the other of the endless alternatives operating for her in reality. She liked to imagine secret reservations, concealed inner lives, or undisclosed judgments, especially in her occasional short stories. She wrote one of these early in 1941, a small example of the characteristic position—a delicate balance of the internal life and the external pressure—that she could not help dramatizing.

"Tryst," published in *English Story* (1941), describes ten minutes of freedom from emotional responsibility that are enjoyed almost drunkenly by a woman whose husband and visiting grown-up children have gone for a walk. By the time she finishes her chores, only ten minutes remain until their scheduled return for tea. She had hoped for more, and even thinks—when she sees how little time there is—of giving it up. But the sacrifice would be too great. She slips out of her cottage (evidently Sea View in Dobbin Lane) to go down to the sea nearby. There, with the entire natural scene—the "high sky," the "rich, moist air" and "rain-sodden moss," the "deep dense waveless grey" of the sea—and her essential self in relation to it all, she holds her tryst. Because she lingers on her way back to the house, her family gets there before she does, depriving her of the little extra time she needs to squeeze herself into shape, "to dispose of her elastically expanded being." As she opens the door, her husband bears down upon her. He can't find his spectacles. She murmurs a few words "meditatively, as though trying to think where they might be, and [feels], with the sounding of her own voice, the door of her inward life close against her as surely as the house-door clicked into its latch."

Here, then, is Dorothy's characteristic view of the secret inner life at odds with the emotional claims of another person, even though in this case that person stands in one of the closest relationships possible between two people. Furthermore, she describes the woman in her story as struggling to regain her balance, which can only be achieved by closing herself off. Otherwise she cannot relate to her husband, and she realizes that he is vaguely aware of her "absence," that he is uneasy, beginning to be troubled while she "hover[s] between two worlds." What she must do is "cover the tracks" of a brief excursion into her own free and private world, and return to the public, domestic, maternal world in which her husband is sure he knows who she is.

Dorothy would never cease to find this question of identity at the center of everything. It was the continuing crisis of her life, both as a woman and as an artist; and at the present moment, when not only the identity but the very survival of England was threatened, the question occupied her more than ever. It became a haunting theme with variations, particularly during the months from March to June 1941. Kate's death was followed by that of a cousin who did not mean nearly as much to her but who had nonetheless been part of a distinctive phase of her life—the Bloomsbury years, when she had often spent weekends at Cambridge with her cousin and his family.

When her cousin's widow died in March, Dorothy became involved once again in correspondence with people she had not heard from for half a lifetime. It surprised her to find how easily she could talk to them now and "how well, during the years of silence, [she had] grown to know them,'' as if to say that no experience ever really came to an end, that it continued to work within, whether one was aware of it or not. She was, in truth, resisting the idea of extinction, which seemed then to dominate everyone's thoughts. She believed that one had to fight against the possibility of ''giving in,'' no matter how much evidence there was of finality, no matter how much destruction and annihilation went on.

It was a hard fight and Dorothy moved these days from death to death. At the end of March she heard of the suicide of Virginia Woolf. It was ''understandable,'' she said, ''in view of the particular slant of her weltanschauung,'' by which Dorothy meant that in her opinion Virginia Woolf had despaired of the world, had ended her life because its cultivated mode seemed doomed by the barbaric German hordes. But she did not know that Mrs. Woolf had been more afraid of the loss of her own sanity than that of the world. Dorothy's view of her, therefore, as simply ''giving in'' was very partial. She took the view so readily because at the first sign of anything resembling it, surrender sprang into her mind, as it did into nearly everyone's at the time. Moreover, she had always thought of Virginia Woolf as weak, the victim of paralyzing generalizations about people and life that she had been brought up to believe but had never really found satisfying.

Dorothy saw Virginia Woolf respond to a world in chaos— defying clear statement—by leaving it, whereas she herself wanted to stay, to witness the shape that would ultimately come forth. Indeed, she claimed to have even more faith than this, for she believed in the social revolution the war was bringing about and in the generation then growing up, which she felt would be ''less malleable to pundits than [her] own.'' ''I can't feel gloomy,'' she said, ''for this dark moment is pierced right & left.'' There was no doubt of the sustaining strength of her will, nor of her sense of identification with the country Hitler was seeking to bring to its knees. Though she would not have been one of the old ladies who fed pigeons in Trafalgar Square while bombs fell and AA guns roared—because she hated noise—she would have said of them: they are England. And like those old ladies, neither *her* knees nor *her* spirit ever bent.

She was shaken, nevertheless, at the news of yet another death, Hugh Walpole's, on June 1. When the BBC made an announcement that belittled his work ''before he was cold'' and made no mention at all of his "lifelong devoted labour on behalf of his beloved Littratscher [i. e. literature]," Dorothy pronounced it "a scandal." This was anger for both her friend's sake and her own. If the popular Hugh Walpole was treated thus, what would be meted out to Dorothy Richardson? Fortunately, she could not know that few people would even be able to identify her when she died—after she had devoted a lifetime to the labor of identifying herself.

2

The veil of obscurity was beginning to thicken. Settled in Zansizzey for at least the duration of the war, Dorothy found herself more and more inclined to live from day to day like everyone else around her. It was easier to cope with the shortages of food, the difficulty in getting cigarettes, socks, and toothbrushes—problems that were not hers alone—than to grapple in isolation with a book that seemed increasingly irrelevant. When one of her friends—Bryher, Pauline Marrian, Peggy Kirkaldy, or John Cowper Powys—asked about the progress of *Pilgrimage,* she said there were occasional half-hours she could devote to writing. The truth was that after a brief attempt, early in the war, to escape from the present, she was now immersed in it. Under no circumstances would she miss hearing the broadcast of one of Churchill's speeches. Besides, the war kept grinding out drama: Hitler invaded Russia in June, Churchill and Roosevelt met in early August to draft what would come to be known as the Atlantic Charter, the French poet and novelist Jules Romains was suspected of having "gone entirely Vichy," and the English novelist Norman Douglas, old and ill, was stranded in Portugal.

Dorothy heard about Douglas's plight from Bryher and threw herself immediately into the effort to rescue him. She wrote to Wells (who replied peevishly that no one at the Foreign Office would listen to him) and to Josiah Wedgwood (who was in the United States). She suggested an appeal to the P.E.N. Club or a "round robin" to the Lisbon Legation, and bemoaned the indifference of people to an aging writer whose novels had given them so much pleasure. Such ingratitude, she lamented; such heartlessness was "monstrous."

Douglas managed eventually (by the end of 1941) to get to Scotland. Before then Dorothy had taken up another cause—finding someone to hire her friend Pauline Marrian as a lecturer on Hun-

341

gary, which was *her* passionate cause. Pauline wanted to describe what she had seen the Germans do to the country and the people she had met and loved during her brief visit there. She had poured it out to Dorothy, and Dorothy responded by pouring it out again to nearly everyone she knew in the letters that were gradually becoming almost the only writing she was doing. She might well have said, in her own defense, that life is short and war is long.

But no one would have asked her anything that required this sort of defense. And to the delicate questions that were in fact asked, she continued to offer the half-hour or the "fagged evening-ends" as the time she could wrest for her novel. She claimed that her days were entirely filled with the necessities of life. Cooking, housework, and "masses of correspondence of all sorts" had to be seen to. She was also helping the local farmer with his clerical work, records that the government required him to keep, which confused him because he had never before had to do anything of the kind. Patiently and painstakingly Dorothy systematized the task and taught him how to proceed from day to day so that periodically she could handle the summing up. The farmer, sweet-natured, blue-eyed, pink-cheeked, and intelligent, regarded her with a mixture of awe and curiosity that Dorothy did not mind at all. In addition, to make sure it was quite clear how little time she had for writing, Dorothy even insisted that, because Alan's hands were not suited to such work, she was trying to trim their wild garden, which never seemed to show the slightest sign of these attempts. Sometimes, though, she would confess that there were "shorts" she felt she had to write rather than going on with *Pilgrimage*. "They attract me," she said. Four of them were written during the next four years. Why these stories attracted her is evident, for in the substance of each is a current preoccupation.

The first, "Haven," did not appear until 1944, in *Life and Letters To-Day*. Exactly when Dorothy wrote it cannot be determined, but the central (and only) character's problem of finding the perfect conditions for writing was unmistakably her own—indeed always had been; and now, in the early 1940s, it seemed to have become a compulsive refrain in her letters. In her story she treated the problem ironically, by having the writer discover, to his deep chagrin, that when he finally hits upon what he had always thought would be the ideal surroundings for his work, they turn out to be the very opposite of what he needs.

The story opens with Mr. Purling, a bachelor, just moved into new living quarters and wondering once again, after a series of disappointments, whether this landlady and these rooms will provide the "haven" he has been looking for. To satisfy Purling she must be able to supply all his wants as if by magic, without ever obtruding on his consciousness; and, in like fashion, the rooms must be so bland that he never sees or thinks about them. To his astonishment, the landlady and the rooms *are* absolutely perfect, and for a few days he revels in his good fortune.

Then Purling begins to harbor a secret wish that the landlady would make a sound, for he realizes with dismay that her silence is intrusive. He is now fatally aware of her, "concentrated upon him and his needs, creeping about, muting, on his behalf, the sound of all her doings." This is unnatural, unlifelike; he cannot bear it. But what is the alternative? "To ask her, beg her, to go about her work and her recreation as if he were not there." She would understand, he knows. But he also knows that then he would suffer from the awareness of her awareness, "conscious of himself as its object," and he would not be able to immerse himself in his work. What it comes down to, he finally decides, is that "the surest security is in the lion's mouth." The rooms he had left, in a house where storms rage all the time, were infinitely preferable. There "the life of the household, wrapped nourishingly about him, had yet left him untouched. *Had never come between him and himself.*" He decides to go back there to find, paradoxically, "peace at the heart of a storm."

In the midst of the storm of war and the demands of her married life as she saw them, Dorothy wrote this story about a bachelor whose needs must have seemed, in contrast with her own, fairly simple. His concern was not, after all, with what he himself had to do but with the activities of those around him. When he was not satisfied, he moved. Dorothy was tied to Alan, and as a woman (it is by no means accidental that for the first time her fictional point of view is a man's) she felt that her responsibilities were inescapable. She had always talked a great deal about the time it took to take care of Alan and to organize their life together. Whether she actually spent as much time as she claimed to spend is beside the point, for even if she only *thought* about her obligations, they distracted her. When, in 1941, she was entering the twenty-fifth year of her marriage, she let fall the cryptic remark, "If anyone had told me [in 1917] that we'd live, both of us, to see our silver wedding, I might have hesitated even more than I did." In those words she might have been saying that she had counted on bearing the burden of Alan for a much shorter period, or that she had thought her life would take quite a different route than it had. Whichever—or whatever—it was, the story about Purling expressed some of her abiding hostility toward Alan and the role she had assumed in marrying him. Usually dormant, her resentment seemed to flare up during these years of war when housekeeping was especially difficult and when Alan (who was eager to help but very nearly incompetent) worked steadily at his illustrations of Rabelais, which he did not really expect ever to publish. Dorothy was incapable of such purity, and she knew it.

She also knew that what engaged her creative faculties most at this time was not the middle-aged image of herself that Miriam Henderson had become in the volume she was writing, but her somewhat "antique" (as she put it) present self on the one hand and, on the other, the small child she had been in the far past, long before Miriam appeared on the scene. Both of these selves—the old and the young—get into another of the pressing "shorts" she wrote at about this time, in which she conveyed her belief that the distance between the two was a mere hair's breadth. Such was the lesson she had learned from her experience after Kate's death. All those letters had resurrected Dorothy the little girl, who was remembered by Kate's friends, and the mature Dorothy's imagination was caught by her.

How easily this younger Dorothy could come into being is shown in the story entitled "Excursion." Its focus is on Grannie, who is advanced in age. Her consciousness is the story. The other characters, two apparently young women and an obviously young man in service, who is spending the last night of his embarkation leave, are not defined in their relationship to the old woman. They are simply there, but whether as the grandchildren they would seem to be, given her name "Gran," one cannot really tell. Nor does it matter, since the important relationship in the story is between Grannie and herself. If, moreover, Grannie is Dorothy—as seems most likely—she would have been inclined, quite naturally, to leave such details vague. The four of them have been on holiday in a rented cottage at a seaside resort. The three women intend to remain a while, after the young man's departure, and are therefore concerned that the noisy people across the road have not gone home yet, as they had seemed to be getting ready to do in the morning. Gran realizes they are still there when she hears the bark of their dog, a sound that none of the others catches. It has the instantaneous effect of plunging her back sixty years into the past, to a morning in Weymouth when a dog had also barked and she and her three sisters had learned that their holiday had been extended for a week. The two sounds suddenly merge in the old woman's mind, and she becomes again the small, passionate child in pigtails, with one sister close to her in age and two older sisters: Dorothy's own family on one of their seaside holidays.

What Dorothy has Gran realize, as she herself had come to believe, is that this is not memory. The dog across the road barked many times before and nothing happened. Other dogs, on other occasions, had barked just as suddenly and abruptly and wildly, with no effect on her. But this time the conditions and her state of being are exactly right, producing, instead of an experience remembered, the experience itself, seen no longer chronologically but composed, "after the manner of a picture, with all the parts in true perspective and relationship." Age has made this possible. When one is old, Dorothy's character concludes (and, as the saying goes, "wandering in mind"), the accumulated "wealth" of the mind can finally be discovered—the "immortal, inexhaustible" moments that all of us possess, that we mourned when they passed, only to find them opening out in old age, "reveal[ing] fresh contents every time we go back into them, grouping and regrouping themselves as we advance." She even thinks it possible that "one of these days, perhaps before long, as I sit listening to the talk of others, a chance phrase, or some sudden evocative sound, will so deeply involve me in experience that I shall be unaware of speaking from the midst of it, irrelevantly, into a current occasion. Perhaps, even worse, I shall produce the sound known as a senile giggle."

What Dorothy has Grannie describe in "Excursion" she had been working out for herself since the death of her sister, and had been hinting at in letters. In her story she achieved the full expression she was trying for; it left her free to go on with the new projection of herself as a very young child, and to experience further the "opening-out" of certain rich moments that her mind possessed. These were contained in the two stories that followed "Excursion." Again it is difficult to tell just when they were written, but the little

345

girl of "Excursion" and her sisters reappear in both. At the time of the publication of the stories in 1945, Dorothy wrote to her younger sister Jessie, who was in Texas, to let her know that the two of them appeared in the stories as Berry and Pug, and that the circumstances—as Jessie would remember—were the visit of their crippled aunt to their house and the subsequent visit they made to their aunt's house in Blewbury. All the circumstances, details, and characters would be familiar to Jessie, and would give her pleasure, Dorothy was sure; but her own real interest lay in the apprehensions and insights of the child she had been, and in the shape the experiences of long ago now took.

Both stories proceed as if from the child's consciousness, and the burden in each is the effort on the part of the child to find something beautiful in what strikes her as ugly. In "Visitor" it is the deformed, pain-ridden body and homely face of crippled and "chapel" Aunt Bertha that Berry is determined to transform. She succeeds at this by deciding, after sustained and careful observation, that the most repulsive aspect of Aunt Bertha, her "chapel-ness," is precisely what brings her peace and renders her whole. Therefore one does not need to pity her. Having reached this comforting (and desired) conclusion, the child is filled with rage at her "stupid, stupid Mother" whom she hears murmur, "Poor *Ber*tha!" To Berry this means that her mother "only knows Aunt Bertha is a cripple"; she has seen nothing more, thus ruining the birthday gift that Berry gave her, the embroidered text, "I Know that my Redeemer liveth," done under the watchful eye of Aunt Bertha and, in the mind of the child, *containing* her. Her mother "is spoiling the text, because she can't *see*" Aunt Bertha there, within it, beyond either compassion or pity.

The strong-willed child of "Visitor" is much the same in "Visit." She and her younger sister (who has to be under constant surveillance or she will blurt out an embarrassing "truth") find Aunt Bertha's country cottage, to which they have come for three days on a return visit, quite common. The cottage is cramped and musty, not at all like the spacious home they have left; and though Berry shares Pug's feelings, she kicks her little sister's foot under the table whenever she makes an invidious comparison. To Berry, moreover, Aunt Bertha is not so easily transformed in her own setting. She smiles less, for example, than when she was a visitor, and she often snaps at her brother Albert, who seems to have the task of helping her move about. In turn, he strikes Berry as being a pathetically frightened man, more of a child than she. Of the remaining members of the household (another brother and the old, blind, partially deaf mother), only her Uncle Henry appeals to Berry; he at least is playful. But he also appears to be something of a rebel, and to Berry's disappointment he vanishes just when she wants him most—on Sunday, when Aunt Bertha will not allow the children into the garden. The grimness of a chapel Sunday finally stirs Berry herself to rebel, by taking Pug and slipping out to find "the country" that they had thought they were coming to see and that so far had been nowhere in sight. In this way Berry manages to escape from the ugliness of the cottage and the sadness of Uncle Albert playing "at a crooked harmonium, . . . in a bare room with no carpet, . . . all out of tune and out of time, the only Sunday music he knows."

From one point of view, these stories of childhood are curious productions, coming as they do during the most intensely anxious years of the war. But from another, more personal point of view, they are completely understandable. Not only were they means by which Dorothy Richardson held on to herself in a time of loss and disintegration, but they also allowed her to escape from Miriam with a certain measure of impunity. To feel dogged by one's own creation is, to say the least, an uncomfortable state of mind; and when that creation bears as many of the earmarks of a self-portrayal as Miriam did, the urge to get away from it is bound to cause trouble. Dorothy took care of the trouble very neatly, by turning to her childhood self as a substitute for Miriam, whose image she no longer felt the old imperative need to call up. The fading of middle-aged Miriam was no small event in Dorothy Richardson's life, but, like many such significant psychic changes, it produced hardly a ripple in the surface of existence.

3

This is not to say that the surface of wartime existence was smooth. While for most people the war meant dislocation, often in its most extreme forms, for Dorothy and Alan Odle it meant quite the reverse. By the end of August 1941 they had been in Cornwall for two years, the longest time by far, as Dorothy noted, that they had ever spent without a move. The two years, moreover, would stretch to six. Not until the autumn of 1945 would the Odles leave Zansizzey, and then only to move a short distance farther down the hill in Trevone.

Although they spoke during this time of perhaps finding a niche in London after the war, it became increasingly clear to Dorothy that her days of moving about were over. She was too tired, too weak, too stout to begin again those rounds of packing their goods and transporting everything, including themselves, to a series of temporary dwellings. Life itself was by now temporary and precarious enough. She was approaching seventy. Her blood pressure was high, her heart fluttery, her old susceptibility to flu more apparent than ever (in May 1942 she had not only flu but bronchitis as well, and she suffered with a bout of lumbago that went on intermittently for months). How could she manage anything like the transportations of the past—and Alan, too? So, when she heard Alan remark one day to the visiting Adrian Allinson that he did not care if he never saw London again, Dorothy felt an immense relief.

Dorothy herself thought it would be delightful to spend a few days in London again when it was accessible, but in her heart she knew even that was unlikely. The longer they "stayed put" in Zansizzey, the more unlikely it became. The new experience of being stationary and secure gradually worked itself into her, and she began to realize how vital this kind of security was. Whether she also realized that it had certain negative effects is not entirely clear. How much awareness was there in the comment she made in 1943, that at one and the same time she wanted to do nothing but write and did not care whether she ever wrote another word? Both feelings stemmed in large part from the sense of security that enveloped and enchanted her, lulled her into passivity. She had never been passive before.

Nor was old age responsible, for although her body grew sluggish and feeble, her mind and senses were as alive as they had ever been. When a detachment of Spanish soldiers from French Morocco was quartered in Trevone, she could not take her eyes off them. Their slenderness and grace were "a joy to see"; every one of their movements was "music." She was by no means dull. Her letters were full of sharpness and tempered acerbity. She wrote them constantly (125,000 words a year, she estimated in 1944, the equivalent of nearly three of her books), and she read whenever she could, including a good deal of contemporary writing, which prompted her to remark, "We are indeed in the age of intercommunications. Almost every cat is out of its bag at last." This was not feebleness of mind.

Yet something was definitely happening to the author of *Pilgrimage*. As she herself admitted, the present seemed more important and richer to her than it had ever been. *Pilgrimage*—that is, Miriam—represented the past, her own past, and the struggles with ideas, ideologies, and points of view that people—especially men like H. G. Wells—had tried to force upon her. The Miriam of those days, the person she had been, who had engaged in the fight for selfhood, was now more distant than the small child whose links to her aging body and timeless memory were far stronger. The rapport with little Berry was effortlessly established; to get into contact with Miriam required an exhausting exertion of will. Moreover, the reward for the exertion was slight, if there was any at all. Practically speaking, to finish the "chapter" of *Pilgrimage* she was writing would be to accomplish very little, for Dent had indicated in no uncertain terms that another volume would be worth considering for publication only if it had three or four chapters. Given the returns on the omnibus edition, their attitude was understandable. That attitude, along with the personal difficulty she was experiencing, served to relegate *Pilgrimage* to the background of her consciousness.

In the foreground was "current existence," which she described as "the ultimate astonisher" in the book that it prevented her from finishing. It offered, for breathless watching and suspense in the fall of 1941, the siege of Moscow and Leningrad. Then on December 7 all eyes were riveted on that distant point in the Pacific, the scene of "the Japanese folly." A few days later the distance closed up. The world shrank. Hitler and Mussolini declared war on America.

In the face of all the madness that seemed to her and to millions of people to have been spawned by Hitler, she brooded about her "nostalgic affection" for Germany. Did it have anything to do, really, with the Germans, she asked herself? There was the music they had produced—but Beethoven was Dutch and Mozart was Austrian. And their philosophy? Kant's father had been a Scot, Hegel was Austrian. Science? Produced, she claimed, by Jews. What remained was their language, with its "convolutions & involutions," its "massed inflections" and "stodgy obstructiveness." These were harsh words for the writer of *Pointed Roofs,* and

349

harsher still was the conclusion that seemed to her inevitable: "a people bathed from birth in the influence of the strutting & goose-stepping of [such a] speech-form [as theirs had to] develop a corresponding spiritual attitude."

Wrenching herself from a fifty-year love affair was one of the by-products of living almost entirely in the present. Instead of associating Germany with her personal and romantic past, she now began to view the country in terms of the future. Indeed, she would come to see it as a perpetual threat, against which Europe had forever to be on guard—an immensely conceited and solemn country, with "an in-turned, shapeless, transcendental mysticism" that led to the dreaming of "monstrous dreams." No other people in the world, she would claim, was as dangerous as this one.

Hers was not a solitary opinion, especially among the English. Alan, too, looked upon the behavior of Germany with a mixture of loathing and contempt. Early in January 1942, despite Dorothy's attempts to dissuade him, he joined the ARP—and promptly had a dream in which he drew, as he described it the next morning, one of his most brilliantly expressive pictures. It was of a grotesque ballet performed by the intricate parts of a German incendiary. The dream had come after one of his first lessons as a new volunteer of ARP, examining the parts of an incendiary as they were passed around the group that met one cold evening at the Women's Institute in Trevone. Alan came home to report that everyone's hands had been so numb they kept dropping the smaller bits and "grovelling" for them in the darkness of the blacked-out room. Dorothy saw that, although Alan's satiric eye was at work at the ARP meeting, he felt proud to be doing something. It amounted to no more, perhaps, than blowing a whistle during an alert, to signal that enemy planes were either approaching or already overhead, or making sure that blackout regulations were being followed; but still it meant he had a measure of responsibility, however small, which other people thought him capable of carrying out. As time and the war went on, Dorothy noticed that Alan's sphere of activity became considerably enlarged. She watched the process with great interest—and with mixed feelings.

That Alan needed to be taken care of had been, since 1917, one of the cardinal operating principles of her life. That is to say, practically speaking, he was a helpless babe. But in every other respect he was an independent, self-contained being, with an absolutely firm grasp of his moral, aesthetic, intellectual identity. This Dorothy knew, and she had always known it. Five minutes spent with Alan Odle were long enough to reveal to any attentive person the solidity and depth of his anchored self. Dorothy may not have known, however, that Alan's physical dependence upon her contributed to her own identity. When he began to show unprecedented signs of competence in the realm of the material and the ordinary, Dorothy began to feel her own dissolution.

Between March and May 1942 (with her sixty-ninth birthday occurring on May 17) she suffered through an unusually long siege of flu. She did not go to bed, though, because, she said, Alan was incapable of running the household. He took over many of her chores nonetheless, and as a result felt, in her words, "frightfully important." But he could not cook, so she felt she had to keep about all the time. She was up and about, then, although manifestly unwell, when Alan received word that his brother was seriously ill. Vincent lay dying just a day's journey from Cornwall, but Alan did not go to him. "He could not leave me," Dorothy explained; "we have no domestic help." Yet, as she put it, Vincent was Alan's "favourite and only surviving brother."

Vincent's death left Alan without a regular correspondent, without anyone to talk to except Dorothy. Although Alan seemed not in the least bit troubled by this, Dorothy thought it an unhealthy situation. So when Vincent died, she considered even more important than at first a letter that had come from an old friend of Alan's about a month earlier. If a steady correspondence could be established, Alan would feel the loss of his brother less sharply. The friend who had written after a long silence was the novelist Claude Houghton. He and Alan had met during their bohemian days, when they both had made their way with some regularity to the South Kensington salon of Madame de Verley. At that time Claude Houghton (who derived his pen name by simply dropping his surname, Oldfield) had been trying his hand at poetry.

But Houghton, unlike Alan, had not entrusted his entire life to art. He had become a chartered accountant and had held a civil-service position in the Admiralty for many years. He did resemble Alan in other ways, however: in the quiet, orderly tenor of the outward life he had led after his marriage in 1920; and in his discrepantly unquiet, intense, and original imagination. The stories and novels he began to write in the 1920s, filled with the mysterious, the eccentric, the bizarre, and the grotesque, suited Alan Odle's taste, and he had read most of Houghton's fiction as it appeared.

Alan Odle's letter from Claude Houghton, written in February 1942, seems to have been the first direct communication between them in about twenty years. With that letter Houghton had sent a copy of his latest novel, and he had asked rather timidly whether Dorothy and Alan knew of his other books and liked them. Dorothy answered with a long, friendly letter and, within a few months, had managed to ease Alan into the role of Claude's correspondent. She was delighted to see how often he sat bent over a sheet of foolscap, printing a letter to Claude, responding with the utmost seriousness and sometimes at great length to Claude's questions. In their letters they discussed philosophy, art, literature, and of course the war. Alan was thus drawn out to express his most cherished views, and Dorothy clapped her hands with glee. She contributed to the correspondence by inserting clarifications in the margins.

Alan's letters confirm her claim that he took immense pride in carrying out domestic responsibilities. When he remarked to Claude, for example, that he was closing a letter because he had to "foot-slog into Padstow to buy fish for dinner," his pleasure was evident. It was the pleasure in performing the ordinary, banal act that a person will have who knows he has always been regarded as quite strange, if not perverse and perhaps even slightly mad. Indeed, he described himself to Claude as looking like one of the Sibyls by day and Cardinal Newman by night. He was well aware of the effect of his unusual physical appearance and of his difficulty in talking about the practical affairs of everyday life, with which it was usually assumed he had no experience at all.

Now that Dorothy found herself less and less able to move around easily, Alan began to do all the shopping. In wartime this was an exacting chore, requiring both ingenuity and zeal. It was also very much a communal activity, so day after day Alan found himself among groups of people and engaged in face-to-face encounters with shopkeepers. To his own surprise as well as theirs, conversation actually occurred. He began to report casually to Dorothy that "Mr. Buckingham said . . ." or "Someone in the greengrocer's told [me] . . . ," and Dorothy's eyes widened. Then he began to come home triumphantly brandishing an egg or some other delicacy that a shopkeeper had slipped into his basket. The truth was, as Dorothy had rightly perceived, the shopkeepers rapidly grew fond of the gentle, warm-eyed, skeleton-like apparition that glided into their shops every day and would stand waiting patiently, if allowed, for an hour, rather than seem to intrude his presence. In other words, they discovered that he was more—instead of less—than human. Alan was discovering this too.

Dorothy took careful note of it all, and she understood that more than anything else it meant growth. Her child-husband at fifty-four years of age was beginning to reach his full stature as a human being. His daily contact with people whose lives lay entirely outside the world of art, which for him had always been the only world, and the new relationships he was forming on the level of feeling rather than intellect virtually revolutionized his attitude toward such people—that is, toward most people. He had never thought they mattered in the least, that any one of them could say anything to him that was worth hearing. For, in Alan's view, to be ignorant of art had meant to be ignorant of everything, and to be, therefore, totally negligible. Now, without being altogether aware of it, he was revising his opinion and, in the process, was providing Dorothy with a good deal of food for thought.

She began to talk about the likelihood of Alan surviving her. No longer did she feel certain that he would die first. Could he manage, alone there in Cornwall, out of reach of relatives, with most of his belongings in storage? She felt she ought to "establish him in some manageable corner, near to relatives & surrounded by his own goods and chattels." But nothing was available in London except for the duration of the war, and that would be of no use at all. Well, then, if he were to be left in Cornwall, she would have to teach him how to handle his financial affairs. This would be no easy matter if Dorothy was right in claiming that he could neither do compound addition nor even write a check.

It is not clear whether she tried to instruct him in compound addition, but she did give him lessons in writing checks. To make out a check, she said, took him nearly as long as a small drawing. He would need, also, to understand about rebates, tax vouchers, and income-tax returns. Dorothy said she had done her best to explain these things, but she felt much more relief in setting down all this information in a notebook labeled "Data for Alan" and in telling Peggy Kirkaldy of its existence. One can imagine an aging mother putting together such a notebook for the benefit of her feeble-minded child. No doubt Dorothy would have maintained, despite all the recent evidence to the contrary, that for all practical purposes Alan—"poor lamb"—was indeed feeble-minded. The "poor lamb," meanwhile, with no interest in money whatsoever and with all the interest in the world in behaving as though Dorothy were eternal, would not have dreamed of depriving her of his helpless-ness.

4

The charade went on: Dorothy needing every so often to write a letter about the possibility of her dying at any moment, and Alan playing dumb. Neither of them ever alluded to her age. Alan proba-bly never knew it; at any rate, Dorothy believed he did not. As for the precariousness of her health, she said he knew only that the doctor had placed certain restrictions on her activities. She could not lift heavy objects or go out in strong winds, and there were numer-ous minor prohibitions. She did admit once to Peggy that the doctor had also said that if she were very careful there was "a good chance of evading a real smash for years." As one might expect, this was what Dorothy really thought too. Under the circumstances, Alan behaved quite sensibly: he was a quietly wise innocent.

Sometimes, however, he was allowed a show of authority and a degree of awareness. In the fall of 1942, when Bryher invited them to spend a few days in London at her expense during a quiet period of the war, Dorothy wrote back to say that Alan was sure the Russian campaign would take a new turn and free the Luftwaffe again for raids on London, and he refused to allow her to go. Alan's premonition about the Russians proved to be wrong, but it is clear that, despite the general impression of him she wished to convey, occasionally she found it convenient—as married persons often do—to avoid saying no directly by placing the burden of refusal on her spouse. On these rare occasions Alan became a normal husband, in a different version of the charade. But most of the time it was more to Dorothy's advantage that he be other than normal, requiring enough care and attention to justify her not writing the thirteenth volume of *Pilgrimage*.

With the problems of war, housekeeping, and her health added to the problem of Alan, she had sufficient justification, in her opinion, ·

not to continue writing *Pilgrimage*. But any other problem that happened to come along was all right as an excuse too. In February 1943 she received word that a Spanish publisher had inquired of Dent about the translation rights to *Pilgrimage*. A long process of negotiations began, during which Dorothy discussed the possibilities, speculated about the outcome, and complained to her heart's content. She offered to help the translator—that is, when he or she was finally chosen. She railed against Duckworth for having lost so many opportunities in the past by asking too much for translation rights; Dent was behaving sensibly.

She was surprised to learn that the Barcelona firm wanted all twelve volumes translated. It would be a large venture—and a great compliment. Then she was asked, through Dent, to supply some biographical information that would introduce her to Spanish readers. She winced at this but agreed. She settled down to work and spent months torturing it out of herself. Dent warned her from the start that foreign publishers were apt, even after lengthy negotiations and full settlement of all the details, to drop their scheme without a word. She toiled on the biographical sketch nonetheless; and the more time she spent on it, the more convinced she became that the entire project would fizzle out. Through May, June, July, and into August 1943, while Dent kept her informed of the "snail's pace" at which things were proceeding (via the British Council, acting as intermediary with Spain), she tried to put together a few facts about herself. She was doing it against the grain, she said. It was being "screwed out" of her "under third degree." And in the midst of this agony she agreed to revise the manuscript of Adrian Allinson's autobiography, which he had brought down with him on a visit and dropped into her lap.

By the middle of August she had managed to finish the autobiographical sketch, and she immediately began to explain it away. It was "really very jog-trot & simple," she claimed, "in cliché" because it had to be; Señor José Janés's English was "of the oddest" sort. Toward the end of September a contract was actually signed, but Dent warned her that the last word would be the censor's. Now she decided that for Franco's Spain the early volumes of *Pilgrimage* would be anticlerical and socially subversive; they would not pass. She was right. Word came in mid-January 1944 that her books had been banned and that the censorship regulations did not permit the purchase of the rights with an eye to a possible lifting of the ban later on. Señor Janés sent her a sad letter in which he hoped

355

Dent would consider the rights to be his, so that when he succeeded in getting the ban lifted, he could go right ahead with the translation. At this point Dorothy stopped speculating. She declined to venture a prediction. It was all too maddening, except that she rather enjoyed having been banned.

In the biographical sketch she came to entitle "Data for Spanish Publisher," Dorothy offered few facts about herself. She focused instead on the emotional tone of her childhood and upbringing. She confessed to a "deep-rooted suspicion" not only of facts but also of "ordered knowledge," which she claimed had been "unconsciously fostered" by her mother. She described her mother as a "semi-invalid" during the greater part of her life and a "saint"; her father as "an amateur of most of the arts," a "gentleman," and an "epicurean" who because of his "puritan forbears" was "both fastidious and firmly disciplined"; and herself as a happy, sensuous child who hated being told "this and that" about things, especially about the things she loved, like the garden, the woods, the sky, and sunlight. In truth she had wrapped her childhood round with the soft veils of a golden past. Not even the troubles of her father's financial reverses (he had speculated disastrously, she said, and "lost the greater part of his resources," but she did not so much as hint at bankruptcy) and her mother's death (there was not a scrap of detail) were enough to darken the tone of her memories.

She made light of her London years in the Bloomsbury attic, living on a pound a week; they were much more years of exploration and discovery than of struggle. She also glossed over her beginnings as a writer, determined to present everything in the most favorable light. She ended with her marriage to Alan in 1917, entered into "in spite of misgivings," she said, "on both sides. These have been falsified," she concluded, "and we are still married."

It was indeed a simplified account that could safely be seen by anyone. It revealed almost nothing personal, not even the year of her birth—which is not surprising, since Dorothy made it clear when she spoke of the piece that Alan had read it. (He seems even to have been especially fond of it, and when she sent off her copy to Peggy Kirkaldy, he insisted that she make certain it would be returned.) She could not, even now, let Alan know how old she was, and she phrased the information in a most clever way: "My birth, towards the end of last century. . . ." Years afterward, when it was safe to do so, she added "(in May 1873)."

There is no doubt of the seriousness with which she took the matter of age, especially in relation to Alan. But again, characteristically, the subject was of much more significance to her than to him. He was simply not interested in such things, and it is difficult to believe Dorothy did not know this. This suggests that here was a piece of reality—the difference of fifteen years between her and Alan—which it annoyed her not to be able to adjust at will and out of need, as she had already adjusted her background both in *Pilgrimage* and in the "Data for Spanish Publisher." There was nothing she could do, however, about being seventy when Alan was fifty-five.

5

In 1943, when Dorothy reluctantly became a septuagenarian, "the war which won the war" was being fought in Russia. The battles waged during the summer months—at Kursk, Orel, and Kharkov—made it clear that Hitler had been beaten. By September the German armies on the central and southern fronts were in full retreat. Then came news of the Italian surrender. But joy over the news from Italy was short-lived. German troops within that country continued to fight furiously. They seized Rome, and the Italian armies seemed to be surrendering to them everywhere. As did everyone else, Dorothy and Alan kept tuned in to the news on their radio, trying to understand what was going on, waiting to hear the outcome of the battle of Salerno. Although the Allies won that battle, the fighting in Italy went on for months, and Anzio and Cassino were yet to come.

Nonetheless, toward the end of the year, attention began to shift to the first meeting of Churchill and Roosevelt with Stalin, at Teheran; and at this time, too, the argument about the trustworthiness of Russia seems to have begun in earnest. There was deep suspicion among the English that the Russians were not quite civilized, and Dorothy took up the Russian cause. In a letter to her sister Jessie, she maintained with her usual decisiveness that, whereas Germany could not be trusted for a moment, there was nothing to fear from Russia, and she suggested that Jessie go around repeating this. Trotsky may have wanted to "Bolshevise" Europe, she said; but now Russia wanted nothing—indeed, she had everything within her own vast borders in Europe and Asia.

Dorothy was convinced that what Russia needed, and would need for a long time, was "security to restore her ravaged country." She also thought that, among the European powers, England was the best choice of an ally for Russia. The Russians and the English had a certain "spiritual attitude" in common; an ethnologist from the Moscow Academy of Science had once told her that. Her own experience, moreover, was that she had always felt immediately more at home with Russians than with any other continentals.

Dorothy had plenty of opportunity to indulge her fondness for generalization these days, with Trevone oozing soldiers of various nationalities. (Cornwall was one of the concentration centers for troops.) After the beautiful Spaniards left, a detachment of Americans took their place, and Dorothy found them surprisingly small in size. She also noted with great interest that the Negro soldiers were scarcely ever to be seen, that they must have kept to themselves. One day, however, she caught a revealing glimpse of a member of this invisible group. As she was walking down the road, approaching a bend, she saw a file of cows ambling leisurely across to a meadow, and heard a huge truck coming rather fast. She stopped, waited for the truck, and raised her hand as it came into sight. She expected to see the familiar American grin in the cab and to hear the familiar "good mornin' ma'aaaam." This time the driver, who was black, would not even look her way. Dorothy kept talking about this episode, not least to the American soldiers she had the chance to meet.

One of the favorite gathering places of everybody in Trevone—soldiers and residents alike—was the little tearoom called The Cot, next to Rose Cottage. Dorothy and Alan took to spending nearly every afternoon here. Sometimes they arrived early, before anyone else, so that Dorothy could have a go at billiards without being observed. Alan would sit smoking while she bent over the table, stiff, portly, absorbed, trying to recover the deftness she had once had. But most of the time they got there a little before five and stayed till seven. Dorothy watched faces, listened to talk, greeted friends, chatted with people who stopped at their table, and felt sublimely happy in this buzzing room that was the closest approximation to a London atmosphere that one could find in Cornwall. For if the flesh was unwilling and unable to travel, the spirit was eager to recapture something of the old life.

When one of their friends came on a visit, even more of that exciting old life came back, especially when the visitor was Adrian Allinson. He never failed to discover something new, and would invariably return from a walk howling with pleasure. Once he found a herd of goats in a distant meadow and, in Dorothy's word, went "mad" over them. He was going to do an enormous picture, but he needed sketches. He borrowed a bicycle to get to and from the scene and began to make sketches. That took too long, though, so in a typical Allinson operation he unearthed the secretary of a Siamese prince who was "in residence" across the estuary from Padstow and owned a first-rate camera, a Leica. The Odles watched Allinson with their customary attitude toward him—half-indulgent, half-admiring. He had come to Cornwall to recover from an illness and from the death of his wife, and he managed to do both with his usual elasticity. Although Allinson was always amusing, he was also predictable and quite exhausting. "We like our Adrian," Dorothy once said when he was about to descend upon them, "but still ora pro nobis."

Moreover, little Trevone and Padstow were packed with so many people who provided not only fresh experiences but surprises as well. One marketing day in February 1944, Dorothy joined Alan in his weekly expedition to Padstow, and instead of returning home immediately, they decided to have their tea in the waterfront café. They shared a table with a young British airman who, in spite of his obvious shyness, seemed to want to talk and did not mind being questioned. When Dorothy asked him whether he had been born in London, he said that indeed he had—in Brentwood—and he was proud of it. At this, Dorothy remarked to Alan that Brentwood was where Charles and Florence (Daniel—the publisher and his wife) used to live. Her mind had moved back instantly to the beginning of her London years, to the day- and night-long talks with the Daniels, to the endless weekends, to the meetings of the Tolstoyan Society.

The next moment the young man seated opposite her in the Padstow café was telling her that the Daniels were his parents. Dorothy stared at him incredulously. She had known of his birth, which had taken place after she had left London, and of the name (Henry George) that had been given him because they were all then ardent land-reformers and single-taxers. She even had a few youthful photographs of him. But she had never met him, and here he was in Cornwall. Furthermore, this was his last day there. He was about to leave for—of all places—Calne in Wiltshire, where Dorothy, when she had first met his parents, had been making "flying visits" to stay with her sister Richie. As long ago as that was, she could still give Henry George some introductions to people in Calne, the children of her sister's friends.

By the time she and Alan left the café, Dorothy was feeling dizzy. Fifty years had shrunk to nothing and she had the sense of being young again. But as they walked to the bus, her breath was incongruously short, her pace was annoyingly slow, and her old body could not be denied.

There were, however, certain compensations for advancing age and for what she sometimes thought of as galloping decay. Her status in the village, for example, was special. While the local population felt obliged to entertain as many servicemen in their homes as they could, only a few selected ones were sent up to the Odles, and then only for morning coffee, since Mrs. Odle could not be expected to prepare meals. The selection was usually made by a young woman named Ann Jackson, who helped to run The Cot and who seemed to choose by some sort of divine instinct just the right soldiers.

In this way Dorothy and Alan met an American boy named John Fontaine, from Rhode Island, who was actually related to the author of the fables. It was a case of adoption at first sight on both sides. John Fontaine wanted to be a painter and even carried a few canvases about with him. He also had a Daumier lithograph that he had picked up in Europe and brought triumphantly to Zansizzey for Alan to examine. He took to dropping in at Zansizzey whenever he could, and as the friendship deepened, he confided in the Odles more and more. He was terrified of dying. If something happened to him, as he fully expected it to, what would become of all his possessions? No one at home was really capable of appreciating them. Could he leave his things with Dorothy and Alan, and come back to claim them if he survived?

John Fontaine's regiment was quartered in Trevone for more than a month. By the time he left, with his belongings safely stored at Zansizzey, Dorothy and Alan felt they were losing a son. It was much more unusual for Alan than for Dorothy to have grown so attached to the boy. Alan had always kept a certain distance from the young people who came to see Dorothy and who invariably grew

Winifred Bryher, 1920s. Courtesy of Mrs. Perdita Schaffner.

into friends; somehow they never really engaged him. But this open-hearted, affectionate youth (who called him "Uncle") had reached him. This marked yet another stage in Alan's development. As for Dorothy, she was pleased to be called "Aunt"; after all, she might have been John Fontaine's grandmother. She referred to him constantly. It was clear that he had touched a responsive chord in both of them. Perhaps at this point in the war, if not in their lives, they needed just such a personal relationship: with someone who was a part of the vast operation going on in the world, someone who knew them only as they were then.

They worried about him, waited for his letters, and were overjoyed to hear finally that he was safe. This is not to say that they were unconcerned about their friends in the thick of things in London: Allinson, Bryher (who was running *Life and Letters* almost singlehandedly now), Kot, and Barbara Low (the psychoanalyst). They were also concerned about Pauline Marrian, who was firewatching, and about Owen Wadsworth, who was reporting for the Kemsley newspapers—not to mention H. G. Wells, who obstinately refused to leave his Regent's Park house, even though nearly all its windows had been smashed in raids. Wells had been seriously ill during the spring and summer of 1944 not long after John Fontaine had gone off with his regiment. The fate of the young man, so painfully uncertain, contrasted sharply with that of the old man, which seemed ordained. Everyone believed Wells was dying.

His daughter-in-law kept Dorothy informed. When she reported that Wells had grown used to the ministrations of two nurses who were in constant attendance, Dorothy, knowing how he hated being taken care of, felt sure the end had come. Her heart turned toward him in confusion and sadness. His death would be in the nature of "a major landslide." But when Bryher suggested that Dorothy come to London to see him, she said no. She doubted whether he was able to see people; besides, she could not count on herself, she said, from day to day. Furthermore, Alan "went up in flames" at the idea, she said: how could she think of traveling in her state, with conditions what they were. The truth is, Dorothy did not want to go, for she did not want to see a helpless Wells. It was more than enough to contemplate his disappearance, to know that when she thought about him he would no longer exist. Indeed, the more she thought about this, the less able she was to accept it.

362

In the midst of her troubled reflections came news of the Allied landing in Normandy. She could not help imagining what Wells must have been feeling, knowing as she did how "100% British and pugnacious" he was, and wishing he could "see things through." At the same time, she could not resist falling into her old habit of criticizing him for not understanding the nature of patriotism. How could he realize what mattered to a whole nation when he could not understand individuals? But then the pendulum swung back. Wells had to survive; the world was inconceivable without him. Dorothy reminded Alan of the "terrific Wells vitality." His father and grandfather had had a long, vital old age. It was just possible that even now he might "pull round." Alan shook his head, and Dorothy agreed that this was wishful thinking.

The next morning a note arrived from Marjorie Wells announcing that the patient was making a remarkable recovery. He had come downstairs, was slowly but steadily gaining strength—confounding his doctors. Dorothy reported it all to Bryher, and when a few days later Wells himself sent her a note—"in his own paw," she said, only a little shaky—she quoted from it to everyone she wrote. It was pure Wellsiana. He had recovered, he said, by "disobeying [his] doctors & nurses in every possible way." His only "afflictions" now were "gout (well deserved, thank God!) & bores." The irreverence was music to Dorothy's ears. Within a few months, when he began to publish again, she could once more jab at him with perfect ease of mind.

6

D-Day had signified that the tide was turning at last, though this did not provide much comfort to the people of London, who suffered through the weeks of bombing that followed. The German V-1's (pilotless planes carrying tons of explosives) wreaked havoc on the city, causing 10,000 casualties during the first week. But by the end of July 1944 only one out of seven of the so-called doodlebugs was getting through; and in late August the Allied armies succeeded in overrunning the bases.

Dorothy heard about the bombardment from Bryher, who was finally driven to leave London after having stood up to the worst of the blitz. But Wells stayed on. To him the V-1's were simply a nuisance. Even when a bomb fell directly opposite his house one night, he merely emerged from his bedroom (which had shutters instead of windows and was therefore the only room in the house not strewn with shattered glass), asked what the noise was about, and then went back to sleep. Dorothy, who would have been writhing at far less noise than that, considered Wells superhuman. She admired Kot, too. He was living alone in St. John's Wood, in a house that had had all its windows smashed for the third time during this latest siege, and he still refused to leave. Dorothy knew that Alan would have been equally firm and brave, while she would have done everything in her power to get away. But there was no likelihood of her having to be cowardly. Trevone had escaped virtually unscathed, and by the end of the summer of 1944 the worst really did seem to be over for all of England.

CHAPTER TWENTY-THREE

Hillside

AT the beginning of 1945, with the war in its final phase, certain changes had already begun to take place in Dorothy's quiet life. After nearly five years of publishing nothing but a poem in the *Spectator*, her story "Haven" had appeared in the August 1944 issue of *Life and Letters*, and "Excursion" was scheduled for publication in the 1945 issue of *English Story*. Later in the year she sent "Visitor" and "Visit" to *Life and Letters;* they would be published together in the September 1945 issue. At the same time, Dorothy found herself faced again with the problem of where to live: the owner of Zansizzey wanted to move into it at the end of the summer.

Despite her concern about Alan's being left alone in Cornwall in the event of her death, Dorothy decided to remain there. It came to her attention that a former landlady of theirs, Miss Lina Symons, was planning to convert her two-story house called Hillside into separate flats. Dorothy and Alan had stayed in the house once before, early in the war. It was nearer to the bay and the shops than was Zansizzey, and it was on a much smaller hill. When Dorothy offered to contribute toward the cost of the alterations if she and Alan could rent the downstairs flat, Miss Symons agreed; she would live upstairs, with her niece Gwen and an infant. The work of conversion was scheduled to be finished in October.

Hillside was still not ready in November, but the owner of Zansizzey could not wait any longer, so on November 23 the Odles moved into utter chaos. The workmen were still there. They had no kitchen, no hot water, no lavatory. All of their kitchen and larder materials were in the sitting room; the Beatrice stove sat there, too, on a packing case. Piles of belongings choked up two other rooms. Their meat ration, vegetables, oil cans, milk, beer bottles, and a variety of other oddments crowded the front porch, leaving only a narrow path into the hallway of the flat, where some of Miss Symons's furniture stood waiting to be stored in the garage after the workmen had finally cleared out.

Dorothy took the chaos with a light heart. It amused her to imagine the look on the faces of certain local folk when, as she knew would happen, they dropped in after a week to see the Odles settled in their new home and had to make their way through the debris. She herself had not been able to do much of the actual moving, because she had felt shaky and out of sorts. She had let Alan take care of nearly everything. He had run up and down the hill between Zansizzey and Hillside for days on end, had gone into Padstow, had devised little schemes to ease the difficulties, and had been "grand, from first to last."

In spite of the disorder, which lasted more than a month, and the audible six-month-old child upstairs, Dorothy liked living at Hillside. Though they both missed the miles and miles of unobstructed view, Dorothy was glad to be rid of the steep hill and to have other people in the house to call upon in an emergency. Alan, however, was temperamentally unable to think along such lines, and he found it difficult to work with the various noises upstairs. These ranged, he told Claude Houghton, "from thumping footsteps to a perpetually bawling baby"; and he hoped that "familiarity [would] breed a merciful form of deafness." Otherwise he had no complaints, and once the flat was in reasonable order, Alan settled down as though he had always been there. As long as a fairly regular routine operated (one of the few needs of his austere life), he was content. Then he could draw freely, wildly, scatologically, secure in the knowledge that breakfast, dinner, his walk, tea, and supper would all take place about the same time every day.

Even variations of routine had to be regularized. Thus, when a guest house opened across the road from Hillside, at which midday meals were served to the public as well as to its residents, Dorothy wove into Alan's life the habit of lunching at Bowen House on certain days of the week. Before this, she had accustomed him to having a meal in Padstow on the days when he did the weekly shopping, a practice that Alan rapidly ritualized. When Bowen House opened, its nearness struck Dorothy as being positively heaven-sent but, at the same time, as being an indulgence she could not afford. She alluded to it as a tempting luxury in a letter to Bryher, who promptly offered her a small allowance to cover a main meal at Bowen House every week. She wanted Dorothy to be able to write, above all to finish the volume of *Pilgrimage* she knew had been in progress now for six years; and Bryher was determined to help in any way that could not be construed as charity.

Much less certain, however, was the extent of Dorothy's own determination. Again and again she assured Bryher she wanted to finish *March Moonlight*. Whether Dent would publish it was quite another matter, which she said was of no real significance to her. She knew, though, that if they were to insist on two additional "chapters" to make a volume the size of the others in the omnibus edition, she could not produce them. *March Moonlight* itself, even in its present unfinished state, needed a "grand overhaul," she said. Merely to accomplish this would be for Dorothy nothing short of miraculous, or so it seemed to her.

Yet under the "right" conditions, she could still work well, it seemed, and these conditions were not necessarily the ones she repeatedly set forth, especially to Bryher—those having to do with an unattainable and almost mystically longed-for freedom from domestic responsibilities that she had been talking about during her entire married life. What she actually needed was attention to her writing and praise of it, which she got when her pair of stories, "Visitor" and "Visit," appeared in *Life and Letters* in September 1945. The magazine's editor, Robert Herring, seems to have received such a number of extra orders because of her stories that he was eager to follow them up with more contributions from Dorothy Richardson.

Herring asked Bryher to see what she could do, and she began to press Dorothy, who was then preparing for the move to Hillside. One would have thought the time singularly unpropitious, yet Dorothy responded with alacrity to Bryher's and Herring's suggestion that perhaps part of *March Moonlight* could be published as "Work in Progress." This is not to say that she raised no objections at all. She thought the opening chapter, about 14,000 words, would be too long. Although a later one might be conceivable, she had only "a faint & faded typescript" that she would copy if she could find the time and the strength. But a few days after moving into Hillside, with the workmen about, the flat in turmoil, and Alan in charge, Dorothy sent Bryher the long first chapter of *March Moonlight*. If Herring did not wish to print all of it, a break could be made at a point she indicated, which would still leave him with a

10,000-word piece; if he wanted something still shorter, she would type the other revised chapter, which ran to a little more than 3,000 words.

Herring decided that he would divide the long chapter, but for the purpose of publishing the whole in two issues. Furthermore, he paid Dorothy more, she claimed, than she had ever earned from an entire volume, and in gratitude she offered him the other, smaller section for nothing. He took it but insisted on paying her for that too. Herring's treatment of her (no doubt influenced by Bryher) was just what Dorothy needed to make her feel alive again as a writer. For a year, from the fall of 1945 (when the stories had appeared, and she had begun to work on *March Moonlight* for Herring) to the fall of 1946 (when the third issue of *Life and Letters* carrying a section of "Work in Progress" came out), Dorothy had the old sense of being someone noteworthy in the world of letters.

Even before Herring had appeared on the scene, Dorothy had had gratifying bits of news. First had come the report from Dent that the Spanish publisher had actually paid for the rights to *Pilgrimage* and that her share was £120, the largest sum she claimed the book had ever brought her at one time. Ironically, despite the fact that Janés had succeeded in getting the censor's ban lifted, the translation never appeared. But Dorothy got the money and found herself faced with the unusual and surprising problem of having perhaps moved into a higher tax bracket. Unwilling to risk having such a thing happen, she held up a check that Bryher had given her until after the end of the financial year.

Then, a few months later, Dent sent word that a French publishing firm was interested in translating *Pilgrimage*. Dorothy had learned enough from the Spanish experience to react more calmly this time and to wait for specific details instead of speculating about possibilities. Even when one of her friends reported that she had seen the French edition advertised, Dorothy was merely puzzled; the advance publicity, if that was what it was, seemed advance indeed. Moreover, she had other things to think and talk about that diverted her attention. A Paris literary agent wrote to her, asking to handle either her books or any short pieces she might have, and her friend Kot wrote to tell her that he had been approached by an English critic (whose name he could not remember) who wanted to do a BBC broadcast on her work. The critic had been told that Kot could provide him with "personal data," but Kot advised him to write directly to Dorothy. Though she never heard from the critic, the proposal itself was a feather in her long-unplumed cap.

From her friend Macmillan came even more pleasing news. He had recently come back to England after a long stay in America. In the London hotel he went to when he arrived, he turned on a radio and heard a French voice holding forth on *Pilgrimage*. The discussion, just begun, lasted half an hour, during which two people, a man and a woman, both of them intelligent and appreciative, Mac said, talked about Dorothy's novel. One of them even analyzed the leading characters. Flattered beyond words, but at the same time aware that only very relatively speaking could all this be construed as fame, Dorothy said, "Dear me!"

The attention she was getting might seem to us negligible—and justly so. It was scattered, in part secondhand, and none of it solid. But in 1946, to Dorothy at seventy-three, it signified the possibility of survival. If she could only believe that her books would endure, that they were not destined for total oblivion, that, even though she herself had described *Pilgrimage* as a wartime casualty, it really was not so. She wanted to believe that something of significance was finally taking place. Look at what was happening to Henry James. Someone had told her that suddenly his books were "selling by the carload"—to people who had just now heard of him. The shops were reportedly sold out, she said, and quantities of reprints were in the offing. Was it absolutely impossible that something of that sort might one day happen to her?

2

When the three sections of *March Moonlight* appeared in *Life and Letters* in April, May, and November 1946, few people understood that they continued *Pilgrimage*. The sections were entitled "Work in Progress"; they had no commentary of any sort accompanying them; and, curiously enough, the text itself seemed to obscure its own identity. First, the opening chapter, which constituted the selection published in the April issue, contains the name of Miriam only once—and it was misspelled in print as Mirian (an error that was especially confusing because the name Marian occurred in the next chapter). Second, and even more significant, is the fact that the letter to Miriam that opens *March Moonlight* is addressed to "Dick." The name Dick or Dickie, it turns out, was given to

Miriam by a new friend she had met in Vaud; but this is not easy for the reader to grasp. This means that throughout the first chapter or selection the only name that recurs is the totally unfamiliar "Dick." It would seem that Dorothy herself was not especially eager to have it widely known that Miriam had cropped up again and *Pilgrimage* had resumed its course.

After the first three chapters were published in *Life and Letters,* nothing more of the novel appeared in print until the omnibus edition was reissued in 1967, with the last volume containing the whole of *March Moonlight* as Dorothy had finally left it. There were ten typescript chapters, totaling 162 pages and an estimated 40,000 words. The average length of her last three novels had been 55,000 words. Statistically, it is probable that her thirteenth volume was more than two-thirds complete; but on her own testimony, only the first three chapters had undergone revision. The remaining seven, though vivid and accomplished in some passages, have a thin and hurried quality. The movement and action are extremely condensed. New and important characters appear almost as if they had been pressed into being by the button of a jack-in-the-box. At the same time, Dorothy dated events in the novel more explicitly than she had ever done before, having them pointedly occur between 1908 and 1912, but the last two years pass virtually in a single phrase. Apparently she was straining to reach the year 1913, when *Pointed Roofs* had been finished.

She seemed also to want to record her meeting with Alan Odle, even though it had not taken place until much later. At the end of *March Moonlight,* Miriam rents a room in a Regency house in St. John's Wood, and the door of the house is opened for her by "a tall skeleton in tattered garments." This is Mr. Noble, Miriam learns, who is a "weird artist," with an elegant bearing and a satirical voice. It all happens too fast, and the fairy-tale quality that Dorothy gives these last years of her fictive existence is disconcerting, to say the least.

The fragment, even at the very end, still has touches of the old comic life of *Pilgrimage.* (For instance, the episode in which Miriam asks Hypo Wilson whether he thinks she ought to tell a new young male friend of her affair with him. Hypo answers, "Yes, by all means, if Miriam felt she ought to," and adds that she could also tell him that if he, Hypo, "were compelled to settle, for life, with just one woman, it would have to be [Miriam]." Miriam decides, after her initial pleasure, that Hypo had merely given her "a first-class 'reference.'") However, the last seven chapters are, for the most part, written as though from a great psychic distance. They seem more remote than anything Dorothy Richardson had ever produced.

On the other hand, the first three chapters are more successful. In them there is complete control in the way in which Dorothy caught the intricate movement of Miriam's mind, interweaving at the same time three physical places: Vaud of the recent past, Dimple Hill and Sussex of the more distant past, and her sister Sarah's home of the present, where she has come to recover from the flu. The effect is of a symphonic orchestration of different times and places and experiences. The girl Jean in Vaud may or may not be a successor to Amabel, but the entire dramatic experience with Amabel is conjured up again as Miriam recalls her encounters with Jean, whose voice runs through the first two chapters of *March Moonlight*. In the third chapter Miriam spends a weekend with the newly married Amabel and Michael Shatov, who are not happy and from whose unhappiness Miriam seeks to escape with as little responsibility as possible. Here the novel really ends.

After this Dorothy has spun out a fairy tale, even solving the Shatovs' marital problems with the birth of a son. With the sentimental and superficial taking over, *Pilgrimage* is nearly reduced to a quest for a husband for Miriam. But in truth Dorothy herself had by now come to think of herself and of *Pilgrimage* as one and the same. What she cared about most was the survival of *Pilgrimage* in the future, thereby ensuring her own survival. *March Moonlight* had in her mind but a problematical relation to the novel that posterity would judge as *Pilgrimage,* and it suffered accordingly. After 1946 she could no longer take this fragment seriously.

3

During the summer of 1946 Dorothy reached the high point of what she felt was her return to the world. In June the shadow of war was at last completely lifted. Even little Padstow carried on a victory celebration from one morning to the small hours of the next. Alan described to her what was going on when he tried to get through the town to the library, and for a while she listened to a radio account of the "doings" in London. She would have liked, she confessed, to have seen the mascot leading one of the marching Air Force contingents. The mascot—a goat—had evidently been trained not only to lead but also to know that he was leading, poised and unruffled in spite of the din around him. Dorothy thought the role was an enviable one to play, goat or not.

In July she and Alan had a private celebration. The occasion was the arrival, after months of delay, of all their possessions that had been stored in the Willesden repository since the beginning of the war. They had grown increasingly anxious about the condition of their things, after hearing from various people that a moth-eaten and mildewed state—not to mention breakage—was fairly common to belongings stored for such a long time. Convinced that their belongings had been moldering all these years, Dorothy thought it fortunate that bonfires were now permitted again. But there was no need to burn anything. To their immense relief nothing was broken, and only two pieces had fallen victim to moths, though of course the furniture (little as there was) had turned black from the London grime that had seeped in.

Dorothy and Alan spent days looking through and at everything, almost as if they were renewing old friendships. When they finally crawled out from beneath it all, it was with "broken limbs," Dorothy said, "& delightedly broken hearts." Then they had to decide where to place the familiar objects that had filled their Queen's Terrace rooms, for what they really wanted was to reproduce the look of those rooms. They had given up London, but something of the sense of living there could be retrieved in the Hillside sitting room. The books went into the shelves, the reproductions of Manet, van Gogh, Gauguin, Cézanne, Renoir came out to "gleam all around," the plaster copy of Houdon's Voltaire stood in profile toward their painted wooden copy of a limestone Nefertiti, who looked down at sharp-nosed Voltaire from her perch upon a carved and painted Russian casket. They felt at home at last, in their strange new edition of Queen's Terrace, with the light of Cornwall conferring "stateliness" on all their possessions. Dorothy saw them as the visible signs of their special tastes and of their moneyless yet cultivated lives. For Alan all of this was just as it should be; he had never seen or tried to see either himself or his life through anyone else's eyes. Dorothy could not help standing back and contemplating the effect she had produced.

Nor could she help noting, during this wonderful summer, that on their "visiting list" were four retired colonels and their ladies. They were all regulars, she said, not amateurs, and not one of them called to mind either Kipling or any colonel met in fiction. It was she, not Alan, who took pleasure in thinking they were part of the Trevone elite of retired colonels and doctors. Yet the small circle that met regularly on Sunday evenings *was* rather special. Colonel Morrison, for one, had been publishing fiction since 1903. He wrote stories and novels, some of them exciting mystery thrillers. But he was also interested in religion and philosophy, and talk with him sometimes took an esoteric turn. Dr. Cobbledick, for another, was a friend of the painter Walter Sickert and a student of contemporary literature as well as of art.

Dorothy's pride was justified. But she also had a way of describing ordinary activities so as to transform them into unusual and noteworthy events. The social life in Trevone during this first war-free summer underwent such a transformation through Dorothy's account of it. She was having "a riotous time," she reported, with people coming in and going out at all hours, little parties to attend at the local tearoom, luncheons with friends here and there, and evening coffees out. It sounded like one of the whirlwind summers of the past in London, except for the absence of names.

The memory of those summers of heat and dust and joy was surely sharpened in mid-August with the news of the death of H. G. Wells. It had come as an "immense surprise," she said, because only a short while before she had heard from Wells's daughter-in-law that he was better again after another illness and was even planning to attend a meeting of the British Association. To her friend Pauline, who had written a letter of sympathy at once, she said, "it goes deep." To her sister Jessie she described it as "a landslide," and to Bryher, a week and a half later, she confessed to only beginning to take in the "fact." But after this she took to repeating the account of his death sent to her by Marjorie Wells, which allowed her to correct the erroneous statement in some of the press reports that Wells had died in his sleep. On the contrary, she said, he had been fully awake (it was the middle of the afternoon) and had sent his nurse out of the room. When the nurse looked in ten minutes later, he was dead. Dorothy was certain that he had known what was coming upon him and that he had wanted to be alone, "without onlookers." It seemed to her a commendable wish and a desirable way to die.

She was impressed by the tributes the newspapers paid to him. They were "endless," she remarked to her sister, and apparently she was reading them all, for Owen Wadsworth had undertaken to send them all to her. She made no comment about them, however. One would like to know what her feelings were as she read through the thousands of words that testified to the impact made upon the world by the little man she had met in 1896 who, as she had said long ago, looked like "a grocer's assistant," and to whose "dicta" she had claimed, only a few months before (when he was reportedly ill again), that she could no longer attach any importance.

But Dorothy did not say of Wells's death what she had said bitterly of Conrad's: that his last illness had not even been announced and his death had gone almost unnoticed in the daily press. Dorothy had made the remark in a letter to John Cowper Powys, who was wondering why nothing was appearing in the newspapers about Wells's condition (after the announcement of his illness). Dorothy explained that during his illness in 1945, when he was believed on the verge of death, Marjorie Wells had objected to daily bulletins, and the press had complied. Dorothy assumed the press was being considerate again. But she could not refrain from suggesting to Powys, by alluding to Conrad, that he (Powys) lacked perspective: why should Wells get so much attention when Joseph Conrad had gotten almost none? Yet nine months later, in the face of Wells's death and the flood of tributes she was reading, Dorothy said nothing at all about Conrad. At that moment Conrad was beside the point.

It was one thing to jab at a live Wells, quite another to deal emotionally with his "disappearance." He had been a part of her consciousness for half a century. That he had also been one of her targets a good deal of the time did not matter now. He would be a target again, once the sense of loss had faded. But in the days immediately following the news of his death, the sense of loss was strong, and it showed in a remark she made to her sister, that the last eighteen months had removed three of her old friends: Hugh Walpole, Josiah Wedgwood, and now H. G. Wells. But Walpole had died in 1940, six years rather than eighteen months earlier. Dorothy did not often err in matters of time, so the link between Wells, Walpole, and Wedgewood was perhaps an effort to neutralize her feelings.

That she was trying to achieve neutrality might explain her reaction to another death that occurred a week after Wells's. Old Dr. Salt, who had treated her for many years before his retirement, died in Padstow. With every mention of him in her letters came a mention of Wells too, as if again to put the subject of Wells on safe ground, to connect him with someone she was uncomplicatedly fond of. She herself explained that she spoke of the two men in the same breath because both had died swiftly, in a few minutes, without anyone watching, and Dorothy thought it "quite the best plan." She might well have described her manner of diffusing emotion as also quite the best plan.

4

The summer of 1946, which had begun by capping a jubilant year, had ended on the chastening note of death. Dorothy seemed deflated. By autumn, the exuberance of the past year had all but disappeared. Even though the third selection from "Work in Progress" was published in the November issue of *Life and Letters* and the editor clamored for more, even though she got an extraordinary letter of appreciation in November from one of her readers who was also a writer, Dorothy scarcely made a sound. She did not even allude to the letter; but she preserved it.

The letter came from a woman Dorothy knew, whose Christian name she had used in *Pilgrimage:* Amabel Williams-Ellis. They had met, as she reminded Dorothy in her letter, at H. G.'s; and she went on to praise the portrait of Wells in *Pilgrimage.* She had never seen one, she said, "which brought so much of a man into print." It seemed to her that Dorothy had drawn him vividly as a human being, but she also had to admit that she probably felt more respect than Dorothy "for his realisation of what the scientific attitude [meant]." In any case, she had just reread *Pilgrimage,* straight through, in about a fortnight or so, and was "immensely impressed." Although she did not agree with all that Dorothy said ("heaven forbid" that she should, she said), she found herself in the most complete accord with the things in the book that seemed "main" to her. One of these was the stress laid upon the savoring of the present, which it struck her one found only in children and painters, besides Dorothy.

Coming from a fellow writer (Amabel Williams-Ellis had published novels, a biography of Ruskin, and books for children), the letter—with its genuine admiration and its appealing modesty—must have impressed Dorothy, but she seems to have said nothing about it. A few days after receiving it, she mentioned another she had gotten from someone else, and a few months later she disclosed that one had come from the American poet Babette Deutsch. But she kept silent about Mrs. Williams-Ellis, who perhaps, in the last part of her letter, had talked about herself in too painfully emotional a way for Dorothy. She told her that she had lost her son in the war and found it hard to live. For a long time she had been unable to write, but now she wanted to tell Dorothy that *Pilgrimage* had "helped to reconcile [her] to the world a little." Though Dorothy must have answered this letter (she always did), it would also seem that the feelings expressed were too raw for her.

Dorothy did not retreat from strong feeling; rather, she disliked having a response to it expected (or demanded) of her. When, at this same time, her friend Peggy wrote to her about her own agonizing sense of helplessness and despair while she watched the slow decline of an incurably ill sister, Dorothy answered with compassion and empathy. Neither did she turn away from the personal confidences of her friend Pauline. But with both Peggy and Pauline she had maintained a steady, continuous relationship that she both wanted and needed and in which she felt perfectly at ease.

During this period, the kind of relationship that seemed to satisfy her most was one in which she could expound her theories, express her opinions, and make her judgments without having to trouble herself about the sensibilities of an unknown or unfamiliar person. These are the conditions that apparently prevailed in the correspondence she undertook at this time with an old friend of Alan's, Henry Savage. He had been the literary editor of *The Gypsy* while Alan was the art editor. Why he wrote letters to Dorothy instead of to Alan is not completely clear (unless Alan preferred it that way), but he did claim some years afterward that he had deliberately asked her leading questions—about God and religion, about art and literature, about certain books in particular and life in general—in order to have her answers on record. He would have known that Dorothy did not need to be coaxed to answer such questions, and he might have thought there was little to be gained from asking them of Alan. For though Savage believed it possible that those who pronounced Alan a genius as a draftsman were right, it was Dorothy's intelligence he respected, her mind he wished to tap—and her irascible, dogmatic temper he enjoyed stirring up. It amused him to annoy her for the sake of the swift retort. She would address him as "Harry boy," or tell him to "be [his] age" (he was five years younger than she, but she did not let him know her exact age, only that she was "quite a bit older"—and she warned him not to tell Alan), or inform him that she was "administering a smack."

No such responses were to be gotten from Alan. Savage knew that one did not tease Alan, that to ask him any but the most trivial question was to get a reply from his whole being—and sometimes a violent expression of it. Savage asked him about this time if he would consent to illustrate a volume of new poems he had written. Alan declined, because, he said, if he were to produce the illustrations the poems should have, no publisher would dare to print them, and he refused to draw in any other way but as he saw fit. The atom had been harnessed, he went on to say, but not he, *ever*.

So Henry Savage devoted himself to Dorothy, who could never resist tossing off an opinion or a pronouncement that he would disagree with and argue about. True, it disappointed him that she was rarely personal. He liked the confidences of women because he liked women—intelligent women, that is—but if Dorothy shied away from intimacies, he had to content himself with an exchange of minds. And he thought of her as quite a remarkable woman.

On her side, the correspondence was more than satisfying. It was an outlet, and there were few of them available to her in those days. After the year in which everything had called up images of fame and triumph, she was fading into a meek and domestic life like that of the war period. She described herself as a "servantless housewife," coping with the postwar food shortage, trying to scrape together the ingredients for a few cakes and buns this Christmas that were "less austere," shivering through Cornwall's coldest winter in sixty years, and relishing village life, with something happening in "the huge family" every day. Sometimes, as an afterthought, she claimed to be engaged in "work in progress." It was indeed visible to guests: a pile of white paper that during the next five years turned yellow—without Dorothy noticing, it would seem. But she also claimed to have "more ideas and impulses" for writing than she had ever had, and they were forced to "stay buzzing round & round within" because whatever time there was each evening found her "too done-up" for much more than sitting about or reading, if her "lame eyes" allowed it. She had sclerosis of the lenses, and her friend Dr. Cobbledick had fitted her with a green shade for reading.

There was not a sign, however, of the aging of the mind that Dorothy seemed to fear most of all. As another spring and her

377

seventy-fourth birthday approached, she told Henry Savage, who had been writing to her about his own old age, that he was stepping out of an old suit into a new one that was ageless. He would come into possession, she said, of something "vainly sought" throughout one's life, and only the "simple cynics" would cry "too late!" But the finder would have lost his sense of time altogether, and his spirit would dance its jig with a gaiety of which youth knew nothing. Did not Harry see that? Harry wrote back to suggest that when Dorothy was as old as he, she might have something different to say. Dorothy answered, "Harry boy, I'm quite a bit older than you," and seemed to mean that she was not as much of a fool as he.

Ironically enough, in the midst of her paeans to old age, Dorothy discovered how susceptible she still was to youth and beauty. Since the spring she had been anticipating a visit from Well's daughter-in-law Marjorie and her two children, whom she had last seen in their nursery days. She alluded to the visit for months before it materialized; and at the last moment it very nearly did not take place. Marjorie felt obliged to stay in London because a neighbor and friend of hers was ill and alone, with no one to take care of him. But her son and daughter insisted upon making the strip to Cornwall anyway. She agreed, provided her daughter was accompanied by the young woman who had recently tutored her, successfully, for the Oxford scholarship examination. So it was that, in the late summer of 1947, the eighteen-year-old Catherine Wells arrived in Trevone with her not much older companion, Sylvia Miller. (Her brother Oliver came separately a few days afterward.)

Dorothy found all three young people surprisingly mature and perceptive. They were not materialistic in any sense, nor did they seem to her "imprisoned in any one of the psychological 'isms'" of the day. They had escaped, she noted, "both a misrepresented Darwinism & a dogmatic Freudianism." In short, they were thoroughly admirable. But Miss Miller, the young science mistress of Sherbourne School, had struck Dorothy at once as a special being. She was not only beautiful to look at, Dorothy said, with delicate features and what Dorothy described as "perfect little bones" that would "keep her lovely . . . in extremest old age," but also beautiful to stand near and to experience her presence. Dorothy said she felt, whenever she stood near this girl or met her direct gaze, that she was losing her balance from the edge of a cliff. She

378

lost as well, she claimed, all sense of space and time. She said she understood for the first time what Mariolatry might mean. It was an amazing experience, she remarked, and one that a person did not quite get over, ever.

She went on thinking, talking, marveling about Sylvia Miller, trying to explain what she felt, insisting that Alan felt the same way (which is doubtful), and discovering that Miss Miller lived near John Cowper Powys's brother, which for some reason opened up in her conscious mind the possibility of a correspondence with Sylvia. There might indeed have been letters exchanged, if the early part of 1948 had not dealt Dorothy a staggering blow.

5

When the year opened, Dorothy was answering questions about Sylvia from John Cowper Powys. Though she did not neglect to note it, the more recent visit of William Macmillan was taking a distinctly secondary place in her thoughts. Mac had arrived in Trevone during the middle of December and stayed for three weeks, spending most of his time with Dorothy and Alan. He was not a happy man these days. His mother, with whom he had always lived, had just died. He hated "healing," Dorothy said, but felt compelled to go on with it, besieged by people who heard of his seemingly miraculous cures. Only a short time before, according to Dorothy, he had removed a child from an iron lung and cured it of infantile paralysis. But apparently he was sick of himself, weary of clamorous and weak-willed people ("Why don't they cure themselves?" Dorothy reported him as asking), and longed to escape to a Chinese monastery. Of this strange, tormented being, Dorothy spoke with equanimity. She was fond of him, admired the "opulent" style of his life, and believed in him to some extent at least (she had suggested him to Peggy for her dying sister), but her deep feelings had never been engaged, not even when Mac had administered to her twenty years before.

When Mac left, feeling somewhat better than when he had arrived, a flu epidemic hit Trevone. Dorothy and Alan were caught in it, and both were ill on Alan's sixtieth birthday, January 12, 1948. They were just beginning to emerge late in the month, and by February Dorothy seems to have recovered fully, but Alan could not shake off his cold and cough. Nonetheless, they settled back, quiet and organized, into their winter lives.

One of Alan's rites was a trip to the Padstow library each Saturday. On the morning of February 14 he prepared to go as usual, collecting the books and consulting with Dorothy about the weather. It had rained earlier, and the mid-morning sky was still overcast and vaguely threatening. For a brief moment Dorothy thought perhaps she should try to dissuade him from going, but she knew it would be next to impossible. When he eventually left by the front door, Dorothy went into the kitchen at the back of the flat. A few minutes later she heard him returning. He stood in the doorway, looking at her so penetratingly that she ceased what she was doing and gazed back at him. Then he smiled, and spoke. "Do you think it's cold?" A banal yet mysterious question: it was he who had been out of doors. She responded, though rather lamely, still lost in that first look, and they agreed that the sky was lifting. He left once again.

About fifteen minutes later, a friend of theirs appeared at the door. Alan had fainted, he said, at the top of the hill, so he had come to drive her to him. On the way up, he told her that a young hedger (a boy she knew, who always exchanged greetings with Alan) had seen him striding up the hill as usual and then had seen him stagger and fall when nearly at the top. The boy had rushed to him, and in the same moment the district nurse had appeared on her bicycle. He himself had come up in his hired car, and two other men had materialized, one from a side road, the other from a house. One of them was telephoning for the doctor.

Alan was lying in grass, on the hedger's coat, at the side of the hill where he had been moved. Dorothy knelt down. Someone told her the doctor was on his way, although he had not wanted to come. He was busy and was not feeling well himself, but he had been persuaded. Alan did not stir. The others stood waiting silently. When the doctor came, Dorothy rose to make way for him. He put his hand inside Alan's opened shirt, turned to her, and said indignantly: "He's dead. *I* can't do anything."

The police arrived. When Dorothy wanted to bring Alan's body home in spite of the law of mortuary, they agreed to ignore the law. The law of inquest was taken care of by Dr. Shirvell—who had regretted his abruptness at once; he declared that he had seen Alan two days previously and would certify that his death was from heart failure. Dorothy felt sure he was inventing this (although he might possibly have seen Alan walking about), but his action was just what she wanted.

The body was brought back down to Hillside, and she had it put in a little back room that was used for storage. It had not been opened since autumn, so it was musty and airless. The windows, which were high and difficult at best, now could not even be reached because of the clutter. The district nurse had come along at her own request to attend to the body, even though the task belonged to a local woman. She was unprepared, so she simply washed the body with soap and water, while Miss Symons and her niece Gwen helped Dorothy to bed. Alan's body lay there for the rest of the day, all night, and well into Sunday.

Early Sunday morning, when Dorothy went into the room, it seemed as fresh as a summer garden at dawn. There was, she claimed, "a strange pure air centred most strangely about that shrouded form." It was unaccountable, but it was not, she insisted later, her imagination. In the afternoon she noticed the same smell in a cupboard that was probably the dampest spot of all in that neglected room; and the pure air lingered for a while after Alan's remains had been removed. Dorothy only wanted to record it, she said, not explain it, just as she wanted to record the peacefulness and the "stern beauty" of his face.

She recorded nothing but the bare fact, however, for nearly two weeks. A postcard went to Peggy, and one to Powys, almost at once, with the news of Alan's death, "quite suddenly & peacefully," of heart failure. That was all. Dorothy did not attend the funeral service. Those who did told her that the church was full and that the minister had avoided orthodoxy. Alan's body was buried in the cemetery between Trevone and Padstow, off the road he had taken thousands of times to the library and the shops, under the wide and incessantly moving Cornish sky that his eyes were always lifted to when he walked. His simple grave was marked with the date of his death, February 14, 1948, and the words "In Loving Memory of Alan Elsden Odle."

In the long days that followed, Dorothy was mostly silent. Miss Symons and Gwen took care of her. She spent the time—suddenly empty and yet seeming to hang about her full of meaning—reading letters of sympathy from people of all sorts and conditions in and around Trevone. They startled her, testifying as they did to the impression Alan had made. He had somehow become a part of their lives, not only as a familiar figure on the roads and the cliffs, but also as a presence they now struggled to define. The word many of them found, to Dorothy's intense interest, was "luminous."

She had been so used to thinking of him as her responsibility, as her child, that the discovery of his separate influence and effect amounted to a revelation. Still clinging to the image of him that presided in her mind, she concluded that here in Cornwall he had "completed his growth." She also confessed that a burden had fallen from her heart: now she would never have to leave him to face life alone. At the same time, she knew that the people who wrote to her had sensed him not as a child but as a man with a special quality of being, whose shyness and disinclination to talk had not concealed his awareness of them and his deeply sympathetic nature.

Dorothy herself knew little beyond what Alan had chosen to tell her of the encounters that took place without her. He never told her what he had said one day to Colonel Morrison's young daughter Evelyn, who had shown Dorothy something she had written. Dorothy had been critical, and Alan had been conscious of what to the young girl might seem to be harshness. Shortly afterward, when he met Evelyn walking on the cliffs, he stopped to tell her she should not mind, that Dorothy would have had plenty to say to Shakespeare.

Given the habits of mind developed over a period of thirty-one years, Dorothy alternated between the helpless-child theme and the rare being, between desolation and joy. In the letters she began to write at the end of February, she veered back and forth—in a strophe of pain, antistrophe of relief. The pattern became fixed; the account of Alan's death took an almost unvarying form; and her feelings, reduced to words, were more manageable. To write letters, to say all the things expected of a bereaved woman, was to screen herself. But during the first ten days, before the words began to flow, a silent, shocked Dorothy stared at the fact of Alan's death. Who would have thought it? He had left *her* alone.

The loneliness was what her friends thought of at once. Peggy wanted her to come to Colchester to stay for a while. Bryher suggested Switzerland. Dorothy said no. If she could be spirited to Colchester, she would agree, but to get herself physically there was impossible. And Switzerland was out of the question. Besides, she would not be alone: Mac had written, as soon as he heard the news, to say he was coming down again. Even if he were not, she preferred to remain in Hillside, at least for the time being.

Hillside was not only where everyone knew her to be, but also where so many things had to be done. All of Alan's drawings, for example, had to be sorted and packaged. They would be sent to his nephew John, his brother Vincent's eldest son. Then, too, there was a wish of Alan's to carry out: he had always wanted the Padstow library to have a complete set of *Pilgrimage,* in place of a single battered copy of *Pointed Roofs.* Dorothy decided to go through the volumes to eliminate printer's errors, and by the end of March she had begun a task which amounted to a reading of *Pilgrimage*—as a new and detached reader, she said, realizing for the first time what had made quite a number of readers "sit up and attend." She kept on reading and did not turn to Alan's drawings for months. That would be a painful task. This one brought home the fact of a newly untrammeled life by putting her into touch again with the old one. On the eve of her seventy-fifth birthday, to read the book that contained her self made her feel slightly giddy.

6

Dorothy's sense of freedom grew sharper and stronger as the weeks following Alan's death turned into months. Having only herself to take into account was so novel and so pleasant that sometimes she forgot what had brought it about. But even when she spoke of Alan, it was to say more and more definitively that in dying as he had, suddenly and without pain, cared for to the last moment, he had had the most desirable end, and she was at peace.

She was free, then, to feel that she had earned the modest income intended for a surviving Alan, and she could now reassure the friends who asked her that she was not in need of money. As a matter of fact, she reported, her former Harley Street employer, with whom she had always kept in touch and who was now well into his eighties, had decided, when he heard about Alan's death, to send her directly the £100 he had bequeathed to her in his will. Like her former employer, most of the people she knew were accustomed to thinking of her as being one step away from indigence. But for the first time in nearly sixty years, since her father's bankruptcy, she had quite enough money for herself, and she could even help someone else—her sister Jessie, for instance, who happened to be in financial trouble at the moment. It was a new and gratifying experience for her. She also took to sending certain of her friends the money for the train fare to Cornwall. Why not, when she could easily spare it?

Her friends came, in any case, one by one. As spring approached, Dorothy anticipated a special visitor. "Amabel" (she rarely used Veronica's real name) had written to say she would come alone. They had not seen each other for years. When she arrived at the beginning of June, Dorothy found her unchanged, except that her hair had turned white. She would try to keep her, she said, as long as she could—a few weeks, as it turned out—for the link between them was nearly as strong as ever. In the early years of the century, young and adventurous, they had slipped in and out of a multitude of identities, and Amabel had never quite settled into any one of them, despite her husband and her children. She had always engaged in the kind of activity that would involve her with people. During the war (while Benjamin had been interned because he was not a British subject) she had taken in young persons who had been "bombed-out" and who were in need of temporary shelter. At the moment, deputizing for Land Army hostel wardens on leave, she was still vibrant and beautiful; and to Dorothy's joy, as old, stout, and cronish as she herself was, Amabel still loved her.

When she left, Dorothy actually felt able to work. For some time the editor of *English Story* had been asking her to give him something. Now, at the end of June 1948, shortly after Amabel's visit, she remarked to Powys that she was writing a short story "being plagued out of [her] by Woodrow Wyatt." It was the first since her pair of childhood stories produced in the early forties, and it seems so different not only from them but also from any she had ever written that one is inclined to take a hard look at it. Here is a story in which Dorothy does not appear to be present, as she always had been in some form or other.

The setting of "A Stranger About" is a village in Cornwall, and its source, an episode in the life of a Cornish family, had been stored in her memory for nearly twenty years. Back in 1930 she had described to Peggy Kirkaldy the experience of the woman who came once a week to clean for her. The woman, Mrs. Stanley Bennett, was then living in Harlyn Cottage on a lonely, unfrequented road. When a strange man, who looked like a tramp, had been seen loitering about the dunes, Mrs. Bennett reported that fact, as well as her fright, to her husband, who refused to take either of them seriously. He went off on an errand, leaving her and her two little girls alone in the approaching dusk. While he was gone, a farmhand, who was trying to deliver a message to the Bennett house, was taken by the three occupants for the tramp, so he found the house locked and dark, while everyone cowered and trembled inside. Bewildered, he turned away. In the lane he met Mr. Bennett, who was coming home and understood everything after a few moments. He managed to convince his wife that it was safe to open the door; then he sank into the nearest chair in a fit of laughter.

Why did Dorothy remember this particular episode after so many years? Could it be Mrs. Bennett's outraged indignation at being laughed at by her husband, which Dorothy had focused upon in retelling the story to Peggy? As a matter of fact, the one alteration in the written story has to do with that indignation, giving it a firmer basis than actually existed for Mrs. Bennett. For the farmhand with the message, Dorothy substituted a young friend of Mr. Bennett's, who comes to borrow a scythe under an arrangement made earlier in the day but which he had neglected to mention to his wife. Thus the woman in her story can justifiably feel mistreated and made light of by her husband: he thought so little of her fear that it did not even occur to him to tell her someone would be stopping by. Dorothy's change does more than sharpen the focus in the story; it also serves to suggest why she happened to write the story.

The key fact is, surely, that she began to write it after Amabel's visit. Amabel would have talked about her husband and their life together. Indeed, it is difficult to imagine her *not* talking about these things to Dorothy. Though Stanley Bennett of Harlyn bears no discernible resemblance to Benjamin Grad, what Mr. Bennett saw as his wife's laughable silliness corresponded in tone to Grad's abiding conviction of the superiority of men. Mrs. Bennett's story had struck that note when Dorothy had first heard it, and the note would have sounded again nearly two decades later when Veronica, who had come to comfort a widowed Dorothy, had called up again in her memory the years she had spent as companion to Benjamin Grad. The result was a simple story with a buried life that Dorothy had kept her distance from, and the matter-of-fact form in which she told the story, the objective manner of it, reflects the distance achieved. In this, the last story she ever wrote, she removed herself entirely, as though she had finished with fiction altogether.

Not long after she completed the story—suggesting an interlocking chain—Dorothy began to work on an essay about the Russian philosopher Nicolas Berdyaev (which was finished early in 1949 and typed for her then, but which never appeared in print). Berdyaev, who was not a recent discovery, had been praised by Dorothy and had been recommended by her to her friends for years; but her essay is not an altogether friendly one, for she takes him to task for what seemed to her his contradictory pronouncements on the subject of women. Her point was that Berdyaev had ''fixed [himself] upon the horns of a dilemma'' by denying women spiritual natures on the one hand, and by admitting on the other that the prophetic spirit so vital to the life of Christianity had been represented in Catholicism entirely by women. If Berdyaev were to plead, moreover, that these women were exceptions, then Dorothy would like to remind him that ''spiritually gifted males'' were also exceptions. Berdyaev, Benjamin Grad, Veronica: the links are strong, and Dorothy strengthened them further by spending the rainy summer of 1948 reading novels by gifted women—Jane Austen and the Brontës.

In the fall, after visits from Mac, Marjorie Wells, and Adrian Allinson, Dorothy began at last to go through the drawings Alan had left behind. She spent October and November sorting them out bit by bit. Not until the following spring did she finish, for the task was overwhelming. Alan had never destroyed anything he had done; so, except for work stolen from him and work he had sold, his entire artistic life—from the days of his first art school in Canterbury—was contained in that mass of drawings, and because it was, the gaps made by the several thefts were all the more visible.

Dorothy claimed that most of the missing drawings were of his best period: from 1914 to the early 1930s. The ones he had exhibited at the Bruton Galleries in 1920 were missing. The Herondas illustrations had disappeared; and some of the Rabelais had been sold by the desperate young tenant of their Queen's Terrace rooms. The gaps meant there could never be a fully representative showing, and Dorothy claimed that anything else would be a ''travesty.'' No wonder it had taken her so long to get down to the job of sorting, and once begun, she dragged it out for months. Her own work, by contrast, was famous. Alan's work seemed to have met the obscurest of dead ends. This was dramatized a few months later when Henry Savage wrote Dorothy to tell her he was sure that an unfinished drawing on silk he had come upon in Flanagan's Junk Shop was Alan's.

By the beginning of December Dorothy had had quite enough, for the time being, of Alan's career. Besides, Veronica and Benjamin

Grad were coming to spend Christmas with her. The weather was mild and sunny at the end of December, and Dorothy looked forward to 1949 without any of the old fears for Alan. Whatever might happen to her would have little real effect upon anyone else. She had no money problems. She had quite enough to satisfy all her wants: to have an afternoon meal at the hotel at least once a week, and to take a cab to and from Padstow and have the driver wait for her while she shopped and had tea in the café on the quay. Owen Wadsworth had agreed to be her literary executor, and it had been decided that everything that pertained to Alan would go to the Odle family.

Dorothy now knew that nothing grand would come of *Pilgrimage;* and that knowledge, strangely enough, brought with it a kind of balance and a sense of proportion. She could savor the small surprises without feeling compelled to magnify them, to see them as signs of approaching greatness—surprises such as the inquiries she got during the next few years from students writing theses on *Pilgrimage* and from a professor compiling a checklist, or the reference to her as an "abominably unknown" writer that she had come upon in Ford Madox Ford's *March of Literature*. These were small pleasures indeed, but they spiced up an old lady's quiet life.

Occasionally there were larger surprises too. One was when Owen Wadsworth told her of an annotated catalog he had seen at a book show. In it she was named as one of the best current short-story writers, and it called attention to her "Cornish yarn," "A Stranger About." This, she said, caused her to go about with her nose in the air. What had pleased her most was the word *current*. But how ironic that a story she herself did not think of as a story should bring her to life, while as the author of *Pilgrimage* she remained practically buried except to thesis-writing students.

Even more ironic and astonishing to her than this unexpected consequence of her last story was the resurrection of her early one, "Christmas Eve," by the BBC. By whatever means it was unearthed, the old story (written in 1919) was read on Christmas Eve and was rebroadcast a few days later. Dorothy was paid for the reading at the rate of £1 per minute, a total of £23. She thought it wonderfully bizarre, with the crowning touch supplied by a reviewer named Giles Romilly, who called it a "perfect story." He remarked in the *Observer* that it was the only item in all the BBC programs that had made the presence of Christmas actually felt.

The BBC broadcasts took place in 1951, when Dorothy had had three full years alone at Hillside. Those years had been what she wanted: unencumbered, undemanding, placid, but not entirely uneventful; and she had been, as she wanted most of all, in complete control of the circumstances and the style of her life. Though the world at large could not be counted upon (it was far away), her own small world paid her homage and deferred to her will. Only during certain hours of the day was she available to friends: for tea, and then again between eight and ten in the evening. Otherwise both she and Hillside were closed off, her solitude and privacy nearly inviolable. Furthermore, if these few hours were all she gave and her guests received, the time was too precious to be wasted, and Dorothy insisted imperiously on the flow of talk. "Get on, get on," she would say to a hesitant or timid visitor, who might sometimes gather the courage to retort, "I can't get on if you press me like that." Then Dorothy might half relent and point out, "But there's so little time," referring both to that particular day and to her own life. Yet within herself she did not seem to feel either pressure or anxiety. Her impatience seemed both personal and philosophical.

The truth was that she felt more free than ever to express and impose her personality, the strong personality that had dominated *Pilgrimage* and had even come to stand for it. Indeed, in an essay written before Alan died, she had insisted that every novel was "a conducted tour" into the personality of the author, and that this personality, most of all, ultimately either attracted or repelled the reader. In a real sense, Dorothy was now acting out *Pilgrimage* rather than writing it. Most of her friends, who seemed to know this without realizing that they did, came to Cornwall to see both the person they loved and the embodiment of *Pilgrimage*.

Her friends stayed near Hillside (as they always had), in a guesthouse or the hotel, and spent the allotted hours with her. They came, during these years, in a steady stream: Veronica, Macmillan, Peggy, Pauline, Owen, and—after fifteen years without any communication at all—her sister-in-law Rose, Vincent's widow, who had written to her when she had learned of Alan's death. Her nephew Philip Batchelor was an occasional visitor; so was Barbara Low. Adrian Allinson came at least once. Bernice Elliot arrived from the States. Rose's younger son Francis appeared one day, and came again after that; Dorothy noted at once that his walk was very

388

like Alan's. And one afternoon she answered a gentle knock on her porch door to find standing there a middle-aged man of delicate appearance, who introduced himself modestly as the son-in-law of "Peyton Baly" (the character in *Pilgrimage* whose original was Hancock's dental partner, Leyton Orly). Even Louise Morgan, whom Dorothy had not seen in twenty years, made the journey of homage to Cornwall. The friends who could not come in person— Bryher, John Cowper Powys, Henry Savage—wrote letters regularly. It was in her answers to these letters that Dorothy carried on her intellectual life.

She always had something interesting to say; this was what Wells had seen in her from the start and was what Savage relished. Savage wrote her once of a curious dream he had had about unity with his ancestors. Knowing of his various relationships with women, Dorothy wrote back to suggest that the dream may actually have been his "first thorough-going love affair, dawning in the ageless, permanent part of [his] being, independent of time and space." She found herself, indeed, contemplating more and more the way "words, the names of people and things," seemed to "move away from their belongings until, [she imagined,] one must make an effort to remember one's own name." And it occurred to her that this demonstrated the "insufficiency of labels and the way, in the end, things flow together." One of her constant themes was: there is no past. Another theme was love, especially love of the self. She did not think of self-love as self-admiration or narcissism. The narcissist, she said, loved neither himself nor others.

Despite her troublesome eyes, she read the *Spectator* and the *Times Literary Supplement* every week, making out her library list from them. In this way she found a book called *The English Mystics,* by Gerald Bullitt, which she recommended to everyone for months. Impressive as the book was, she decided nonetheless that Housman should have been included, because he had declared that "eternity was too short for the contemplation of apple-blossoms." She had no reservations about another book, Mark Rutherford's *Revolution in Tanner's Lane,* which she reread and found "as fresh and relevant" as it had ever been. But Henry Miller's "over-elaboration and reiteration" were too much for her. She found his style like John Cowper Powys's and was not surprised to hear that the two admired each other. The poet Auden was another matter altogether. She saw him as "adult and awake," with "something to say, even to preach." And in her opinion E. M. Forster knew a good deal more about women than did D. H. Lawrence.

So the weeks and months passed at Hillside. Bryher invited her to come to London or Switzerland for a visit. Dorothy declined. The dates Bryher had named were full, she had said, and she felt no need to travel. All the places she had ever been were in her mind, intact and current. Cornwall, moreover, was more precious than ever. She would speak sometimes with a Cornish accent, and talk of "they days" when she and Alan had first come there together. When she walked slowly and heavily down to Trevone Bay, it took courage for anyone who saw her to break into her reverie. But the villagers who walked by Hillside might have heard her as she sang inside with the radio, "Keep right on to the end of the road," an old music-hall song that was her favorite. They might even have known she was giving music lessons to the little boy upstairs, with the help of whistling and singing—the same child whose infant cries had punctuated Alan's days and nights in 1945. He had a perfect ear, Dorothy said.

7

Early in 1951, when Owen Wadsworth told her he was thinking of emigrating to Australia, Dorothy decided at once that not even her uncomplicated literary estate could be handled from so great a distance, so she asked Rose Odle to take his place. She drew up a new will in October, transferring the executorship, and she informed Owen of what she had done, telling him at the same time that the sales of *Pilgrimage* during the first six months of the year had netted her the sum of £2 19s. 2d.

When 1952 opened, Dorothy was already looking forward to a visit from Bryher in the spring, the first in many years. She had several essays in progress which might, she thought, get themselves finished. She was working mornings on *March Moonlight,* she said. But there was no sense of urgency about any of these things. She felt relaxed for the most part, her affairs legally settled and her family obligations fulfilled. Yet, when 1952 closed, she had withdrawn into a silence that would never be broken.

Early in the year, according to Dorothy herself, she had an irritated throat that led her to decide to give up her lifelong habit of heavy smoking but caused, she remarked, a tiresome gain in weight. She made no mention of any other consequence (such as nervous irritability) and gave no evidence of any in her letters. All one can see on the surface is that she had made up her mind to stop smoking—a decision she appeared to think laudable—and that she did. But her friends in Cornwall thought she was engaged in something like a test of the power of her will, and they feared she would harm herself. The only other reason she gave for relinquishing cigarettes, besides the condition of her throat (which soon cleared up), was that they cost too much money. This did not convince her friends.

Through the winter, spring, and summer, she was apparently passing the test. Without the habitual cigarettes she carried on her life much the same as she always had. In the spring Owen Wadsworth unexpectedly returned to England from Australia, and he came down to Cornwall for a visit. In July the eagerly awaited visit from Bryher took place; and a few days after she left, Mac appeared. He had come on an impulse, he said, and did not seem to notice anything wrong. In August Dorothy wrote a letter to an Indian doctoral student who had asked questions about the influence of Bergson upon her; she denied being conscious of any. In September she was noting with delight that the unusually warm weather had produced a second crop of honeysuckle. In October she remarked, almost in the same breath, that her royalties from the sales of *Pilgrimage* had mysteriously doubled and that she had taken to playing the piano again—a piano that belonged to Miss Symons. She wrote two letters to Bryher, on November 6 and 7, telling her that the second half of *March Moonlight* went much more slowly than the first and that the mild weather had turned suddenly into a bitter and buffeting wind. She sent an undistinguished postcard to John Cowper Powys on November 9 and November 14. These contain the last words she ever wrote to anyone.

Then, in the latter part of November, she came down with the painful nerve infection called shingles. Miss Symons and Gwen looked after her for as long as they could, well into the new year. Veronica would have come down to do this, but she had developed a case of shingles herself. Instead, Rose Odle stayed with Dorothy for a few weeks, and she recovered gradually. But eventually Miss Symons, Gwen, and Rose realized that Dorothy had lost interest in the business of living and that she could not be left alone.

With another winter in prospect, Rose arranged to move Dorothy into a room at the Dunrovan Hotel, which was not far from Hillside and was run by Major Edgar Andrew and his wife, both of whom Dorothy knew. She seemed content there and kept to herself, but she required attendance. When the Easter season approached, Major Andrew tried to explain to her that he needed the room, and he begged her to leave. She alternately begged and demanded to be allowed to stay. In anguish he appealed to Rose, who decided that Dorothy would have to be moved not only from Dunrovan but from Cornwall itself. Neither she nor Dorothy's nephew Philip Batchelor could be of help to her that far from London.

Dorothy knew quite well what Rose was planning, but Rose did not know the extent of Dorothy's stubbornness or her attachment to Cornwall. Philip Batchelor, called in to help, proved as helpless as Rose. Dorothy refused to leave. The only person who managed to gain Dorothy's attention to persuade her of the need to leave was Norah Hickey of Rose Cottage. So, in the spring of 1954, after thirty-six winters, Dorothy found herself taken from Cornwall. For the residents of Trevone, it marked the end of an era. For Dorothy Richardson, it was the end of everything.

Epilogue

DOROTHY RICHARDSON'S last journey, from Cornwall to a private nursing home in southeast London, took two days. Since Dorothy was scarcely cooperating, Rose Odle felt it would be less of a strain on both of them if they made the trip in stages. They got off the train at Exeter, and Rose checked in at the Great Western Hotel opposite the station, planning to have dinner and spend the night there. It was an ordinary hotel (though its gray stone exterior made it look bare and prison-like), but Dorothy resented having been torn from Dunrovan, and she did not want to hear the Great Western Hotel praised at all. She decided not to go down for dinner. Rose argued, pleaded, cajoled, but Dorothy was adamant. When Rose was at her wit's end, Dorothy gave in and allowed herself to be led downstairs. As she entered the dining room, looking somewhat disheveled and haughty, she announced in her fortissimo voice that she did not approve of the decor.

She did not approve of the nursing home in Sydenham, either, when she saw it the next afternoon. It was a tight-looking, stiff, tan-brick house built in painfully Victorian style, which stood in the very shadow of the Crystal Palace. It was located at No. 2 on Thicket Road, a cramped little street that ran along the base of the hill that was crowned by the Palace. Dorothy disliked the place at once. She was intractable and unhappy during the two months she was there, and she communicated little more than hostile misery until Rose made other arrangements.

At the second nursing home, which was on Albemarle Road in Beckenham and was run by the same people who ran the first, Dorothy would live out the three years left to her. The second home was larger and more pretentious than the one on Thicket Road. It had an imitation Tudor facade and a circular driveway, and it simulated the air of a country house. Albemarle Road itself was a de-

393

cided improvement over Thicket Road: it was graded and was more expansive than the narrow, paved city street had been. The Albemarle house even had a small rectangular garden, in which the less difficult guests were allowed to sit.

Dorothy at first was one of the more difficult guests, despite her improved surroundings. She objected to regimentation, to sharing a room, and, in short, to nearly everything. She did so merely because she wanted to, and quite simply because she did not want to be there. No one there knew or cared who she was. In fact, it was believed at first that she had delusions. When the matron told one of Dorothy's visiting friends that she thought she was a writer, the startled friend exclaimed, "But she *is* a writer!"

Nevertheless, Dorothy had a practical need to be there. With Beckenham just a stone's throw from the heart of London, Rose could visit her easily, as could her many friends. Owen, Veronica, Pauline, Evelyn Morrison, and Mac (until his sudden death in January 1955) came as often as possible. They found Dorothy at one and the same time aware and oblivious, vague and sharp, regal and pathetic. They were never sure whether she was paying attention to them, whether they were in touch with her or not, whether when she talked about the past she knew it was the past, or whether she had forgotten the present. Sometimes, after remarking (as she often did) that Wells was coming to see her, she would then announce, with some surprise but no sadness, that H. G. was dead. Most of the time she was impenetrable, but she was rarely obscure except at the very end.

Her friends accepted the impenetrable veil as an effect of extreme old age, and the impatience, querulousness, and dogmatism as an intensification of Dorothy's nature. If they had known her father, they would have recognized him breaking through at last. They would have seen him in her scorn for the other residents of the house, in her contempt for the governing ideal of equality, in her pride at being able to speak with authority of such people as Shaw and Wells. Here, writ large, was the autocratic, domineering, condescending Charles Richardson, who had delighted in and boasted of his associations with the leading scientists of his day. Now his favorite daughter was his true reflection.

When Dorothy died on June 17, 1957, there was neither a burial nor a ceremony. One of her last acts had been to donate her body to the Royal College of Physicians and Surgeons. Veronica Grad, who

knew nothing of this arrangement until the last moment, was inconsolable until she got the wedding band from Dorothy's finger, which
she and Benjamin had bought. More than two years later, Dorothy's
body was returned to the family and interred in Streatham Park
Cemetery. Her tombstone was inscribed "To the Memory of
Dorothy Miriam Odle, Authoress D. M. Richardson." The substitution of Miriam for Miller seems to have been an error made without
anyone's actual awareness of it until after the fact. Nearly as ironic
as this, the location of her grave cannot be determined by the date of
her death, for in the cemetery records her name appears (quite
properly) in the later period of time when Streatham Park received
her. This confusion of the two identities (Miriam and Miller) and of
the two periods of time (of death and interment) seems a curiously
fitting coda to the life of a writer who had had separate but merging
identities (in fact and fiction) in an equally merging past and
present.

The inscription goes on to describe her as a "pioneer among
novelists," a place that no one would deny Dorothy Richardson but
that now seems of less importance than it did at a time when the
century was little more than half over and innovativeness still
ranked high. Deserving as she is to be among the pioneering
novelists of the early years of the century, her most enduring qualities are those she shared with the great fiction writers of all time: a
sense of the drama and comedy of human relationships, an ear for
tone, an eye for place, a distinctive character and style, an attitude
toward life and the world that was her very own. But in spite of her
great gifts, she did not achieve greatness, and perhaps the time has
come for an accounting of this that would also provide a new
perspective on Dorothy Richardson and *Pilgrimage*.

It may well be that Dorothy Richardson did not achieve greatness
because she was never able to choose between art and life, to give
herself up with her whole heart to the creative imagination that
shapes and fashions art out of life—and leaves life behind. In this
she bears a closer resemblance to D. H. Lawrence than to any of her
other literary contemporaries. Lawrence, too, could not always
bring himself to cut the cord, to separate himself from Life the
Parent, or for that matter from the world that seemed to stand *in loco
parentis* to him, a separation needed to create such independent
entities as the also contemporary James Joyce and Virginia Woolf
were engaged in producing. They had no trouble, it would seem, in

395

making their choice—of art over life, of art as distinct from and infinitely superior and preferable to life, and of art as a private world in which the imagination reigns supreme and inviolable—unless, indeed, it were more accurate to say that the choice was made for them by the special nature of their psychic selves. While Dorothy Richardson and D. H. Lawrence were always tilting with life and the world—and with themselves in it—in one way or another, the others, in varying degrees, turned their backs on the world or thumbed their noses at life or treated it as though it were art, each of them driven to do so, no doubt, by a powerful urge to express their visions in a complete form and thus to preserve them as autonomous and unique.

It is of no small significance that Dorothy Richardson's *Pilgrimage* was never consciously directed toward a shrine or toward an intellectual structure that would be discernible at the last. The integrity of her novel lies elsewhere—in the insistence upon physical and emotional details as meaningful in their own right. Indeed, such a vision of reality, made up of the particular and the concrete, confers wholeness on a work that remains unfinished in the usual sense of the word. Lawrence, too, many critics have remarked, had trouble with conventional endings. He found it hard not to be ambiguous, or at best inconclusive, about his endings, thus affecting his readers in opposite ways. In this regard, one has only to think of the final paragraphs of *Sons and Lovers* and the fundamental question they raise: will Paul live or die? But *The Rainbow, Women in Love*—and even perhaps *Lady Chatterly's Lover*—seem to come to a stop rather than an end. In any event, it can be argued that they lack the aesthetic integrity of James Joyce's *Ulysses* and *Finnegans Wake* or Virginia Woolf's *Jacob's Room, To the Lighthouse,* and *Between the Acts*.

The difference between Dorothy Richardson and D. H. Lawrence and the more creative James Joyce and Virginia Woolf may be in the latter's confidence, as well as their need and will, to risk detaching themselves and their visions from life, treating fragments as though they were wholes, and taking their chances with posterity. Dorothy Richardson and D. H. Lawrence were too wrapped up in the interplay between themselves and the world to be able to take such risks, and they could not remove their eyes from their own reflections mirrored in the world. It is true that Lawrence had much stronger designs on the world than Dorothy Richardson had, but her readers did not always seem to know this. They quite often felt as harangued by

Miriam Henderson as some of Lawrence's readers felt harangued by him. In contrast, the Joyce and Woolf novels have an almost classical calm, despite their intimate connections with the physical world of London, Cornwall, and Dublin, because they have an independent existence as finished works of art.

Yet *Pilgrimage*—in spite of its unfinished state—bears a stamp of completeness in the unity and philosophic integrity of its vision. It is an extraordinary mixture of art and life, at once autonomous and dependent, self-sustaining and tied to its creator. The bond between the work and its author is made up of the very threads that connect Dorothy Richardson with that ordinary life in the world which Joyce and Woolf somehow had the courage and genius—indeed, also the madness—to transform and transcend. Dorothy Richardson is, then, a brilliant example of the disservice life can do to art when the claims of both are given equal measure, when the artist sees herself as much a mediator as a creator. The result is a novel like *Pilgrimage:* many-layered but single-voiced, flawed as art when judged by its highest standards but a creation rare and distinctive nevertheless.

Notes and Sources

THE source materials of this biography fall into six categories: (1) the various historical records and directories, (2) the unpublished letters and papers in various public institutions (enumerated below) and private hands, (3) the memories and impressions of Dorothy Richardson's relatives and friends, (4) Dorothy Richardson's own writings, (5) writings about Dorothy Richardson, and (6) other writings.

The public institutions and their holdings are as follows:

1. Yale University (the Beinecke Library) holds the Dorothy Richardson Papers, which, in addition to miscellaneous matter (notes, drafts, newspaper clippings, magazine articles, typescripts) and the manuscript of *Pointed Roofs,* consist mainly of Dorothy Richardson's letters to John Austen and his wife Tommy, to Peggy Kirkaldy, to John Cowper Powys, and to Henry Savage. There are also a few letters from Dorothy Richardson (hereafter referred to as DMR) to Bernice Elliott, E. B. C. Jones, Ruth Suckow, Pauline Marrian, and others, as well as some to DMR, many of these from John Cowper Powys.

Separate from the Dorothy Richardson Papers are some 400 letters to Bryher and H. D. (mostly to Bryher) in the collection of the late Professor Norman Holmes Pearson.

2. The New York Public Library (the Henry W. and Albert A. Berg Collection) holds about 300 letters of DMR to P. Beaumont Wadsworth, and a few miscellaneous items.

3. The University of Texas at Austin (the Humanities Research Center) holds a storehouse of materials related to DMR. There are, to begin with, the journals of Hugh Walpole (fifteen volumes) and letters to Walpole from various people such as Richard Church, J. D. Beresford, Claude Houghton, and May Sinclair. There is a good deal of Houghton material (among which are Alan Odle's letters to

398

Claude Houghton), Edward Garnett material (including letters from Beresford and John Cowper Powys), and miscellaneous Wells items. Finally, there are a few letters from DMR to Middleton Murry, among others, and the partial manuscript of *Dimple Hill*.

4. Princeton University (the Firestone Library) holds the Sylvia Beach Papers, among which are various clippings and reviews of DMR kept by Sylvia Beach, two letters from J. M. Dent & Sons to Miss Beach, and seven letters from DMR.

5. Rice University holds twelve letters from DMR to Curtis Brown and/or his office.

6. The British Museum contains the Koteliansky Papers, which include sixty-five letters and postcards from DMR.

Most of the material in private hands has already been described in my acknowledgments and is cited in the appropriate places in the notes. (The whereabouts of the letters of DMR to her sister, the late Jessie Abbot Hale, which Mrs. Hale allowed me to photograph before her death in 1962, are unknown to me.)

DMR's own writings, and published writings about her, are listed in the bibliography.

For the sake of readability, and because so much of the material out of which this book comes is unpublished, diverse, and not readily available for perusal, I have decided to avoid conventional footnoting altogether and to indicate my sources, as well as provide additional information, chapter by chapter in the pages that follow.

I have used the following abbreviations for the most frequently cited sources:

RP	Richardson Papers
Beg	"Beginnings: A Brief Sketch," DMR's autobiographical sketch published in *Ten Contemporaries: Notes Toward Their Definitive Bibliography,* 1933
Data	"Data for Spanish Publisher," autobiographical sketch published in the *London Magazine,* June 1959
Walne	Peter Walne, M.A., former County Archivist of Berkshire
Som	Somerset House records
PI	Personal information
JA	John Austen
Bryher	Winifred Bryher
HD	H. D. [Hilda Doolittle]
BE	Bernice Elliott

VG   Veronica Grad
JAH   Jessie Abbot Hale
EBCJ   E. B. C. Jones
PK   Peggy Kirkaldy
Kot   S. S. Koteliansky
PM   Pauline Marrian
RIO   Rose Isserlis Odle
JCP   John Cowper Powys
HS   Henry Savage
PBW   P. Beaumont Wadsworth
HGW   H. G. Wells

The correspondence between DMR and her friends and associates forms a large part of the resources used in composing this biography. Since most of this correspondence was informal and personal, the dating was haphazard, but in many instances dates could be determined by the postmark or the contents of individual letters and by the collation of letters written to different people. In this section, references to letters not specifically dated by DMR are identified by the following system:

n.d. indicates an undated letter not identifiable as to time

[Season, e.g. Spring '41] indicates a letter undated but identifiable as to season and year

[Month, e.g. Nov. '39] indicates a letter undated but identifiable as to month and year

The published materials cited in the notes in abbreviated form are listed in full in the bibliography.

The references to *Pilgrimage* are to the four-volume edition published in 1967 by J. M. Dent & Sons Ltd.

PART ONE

Prologue

The information about Abingdon comes from the *Handbook for Travellers in Berks, Bucks, and Oxfordshire, Guide to Abingdon, A History of Abingdon,* and *The Fourteenth Century Decorated Ceiling in St. Helen's, Abingdon.*

Albert Park was laid out by Christ's Hospital in 1864–65, and the *Illustrated London News* of July 1, 1865, has an illustration of the inauguration of the monument to Albert in the Park. Houses were built on the Park estate within a few years.

A great modern restoration of St. Helen's took place in 1873, at the cost of about £7,000.

The information about the Richardson business comes from Walne, Som, Mrs. Rant, and Mrs. Tombs. The inventory of the sale of the business to George Rant, a sixty-four-page document dated May 18, 1874, gives the exact sale figure as £5,173 16s. 2d.

The Nonconformism of the Richardson family is not easily described. There is no doubt that a branch of the family was Baptist; certainly the Blewbury and some of the Abingdon Richardsons were. On January 20, 1874, for example, a child of one week, Bessie Richardson, born to William and Mary Ann Richardson of East Street, Abingdon, was buried. The child's burial record was signed with the initials of Seth V. Lewis as the officiating minister. Lewis was a well-known Baptist preacher. (He died in 1893 at the age of eighty-one and was honored with a memorial tablet in the Cothill Baptist Chapel.) Thomas Richardson, Dorothy Richardson's grandfather, was also buried in Abingdon on January 20. In his case, however, the record does not show any signature at all. It is at least conceivable that Lewis may have officiated at both burials that day but signed only the child's record.

The only indirect evidence of the Richardsons as Wesleyan Methodists (as they are described by John Rosenberg in his recent book, *Dorothy Richardson, The Genius They Forgot*) is the marriage of Charles Richardson's only sister, Elizabeth, in the Wesleyan Methodist Chapel in Ock Street (Som); but it may well have been the man she married, Henry French, who was the Wesleyan Methodist, since according to Kelley's Post Office Directory of Somerset of 1875 he later taught at the Wesleyan College in Taunton, Somerset. (At the time of the marriage, in 1861, French was a tutor with a B.A., but Kelley's Directory for that year does not give him a commercial listing as it does in the later.) The fact that in *Pilgrimage* DMR made her heroine's paternal grandparents Wesleyan Methodists is far from conclusive. There is not enough evidence to take *any* position, as I see it.

Charles Richardson's connection with the Junior Constitutional and his abhorrence of the reformer Stead are revealed by DMR in a letter to JCP, March 31, 1939. I am grateful to Mrs. Marjorie Watts for information about the Constitutional and Junior Constitutional

Clubs as founded in the nineteenth century by Lords Salisbury, Rosebery, and others for the new businessmen and merchants who were traditionally excluded from the great clubs but who were a vast potential support for the Conservative party.

I have also made use here of Data.

CHAPTER ONE
Alternations

Information about the Taylors and East Coker comes from the church records, the Rev. Malcolm Thomson, and a letter to HD (Nov. 4, '31). I have drawn upon Data, Beg, JAH (PI), Walne, and a letter to Bryher (Mar. 1, '35) for my account of DMR's childhood in Abingdon; for the trips to Dawlish, upon JAH (PI), DMR's "Journey to Paradise," *Devon, Cradle of Our Seamen,* and the official guide to Dawlish; for the visit to Blewbury, on DMR's "Visit" and letters to JAH; for the stay in Worthing, on JAH (PI), Data, DMR's "What's in a Name?"

My account of the Putney years comes from Data, Beg, Walne, Miss A. L. Reeve, JAH (PI), letters to JAH (June 7, Sept. 20, '45), to PK (Aug. 22, '43), to Bryher ([Spring '24]).

My account of Hanover is drawn from *Guide to Hanover,* Mr. Mundhenke, directories of Hanover, Data, Beg, RP; and of the Finsbury Park years from Data, Beg, letters to PBW (Aug. 18, '36), to JAH (July 5, '47), to Bryher (Dec. 22, ['31]; Aug. 26, Nov. 23, '36), and from Mr. Philip Batchelor to the author (Mar. 24, '61).

The question of DMR's brief employment as a governess is problematical. The only evidence that she worked for Horace Avory (as John Rosenberg claims in his recent book) would seem to be the statement in the London *Times* obituary of June 18, 1957, which singles out this "early employment" but also gives the inaccurate information that the Richardson family lived in Barnes. I do not know who or what the *Times* source was. But since DMR herself never referred to Avory in any of her letters (though she often alluded to that period in her life, and must also have known that Mr. Justice Avory heard the alleged libel suit in 1913 against Violet Hunt by Mrs. Ford Madox Hueffer [see the *Times,* Feb. 7, 1913] which might in later years have led her to mention him when she spoke of Violet Hunt, whom she already knew in 1913); since JAH could not remember whom her sister had worked for as a governess; and finally since DMR could also have drawn upon her visits with her sister Richie in Wiltshire for the novel *Honeycomb* (in which Miriam is a governess in the country home of Felix Corrie, Q.C.), I would hesitate to accept her employment with Horace Avory as fact until further evidence can be adduced.

My account of Mary Richardson's suicide comes from JAH (PI), Som, *Times* (Nov. 29, 30, 1895).

CHAPTER TWO
London and H. G. Wells

My account of the months following the suicide is drawn from JAH (PI), and letters to JAH (Jan. 10, '45) and to PK (June 22, '45).

According to JAH, her older sister Alice, or Richie, left the employ of the Harris family after a few years, married a French citizen, and moved to his country. She died in her early forties.

My account of London in the 1890s is drawn from *Highways & Byways in London, A Social and Economic History of Britain 1760–1950, English Social History, The Anarchist Prince, The Secret Agent* (Author's Note).

My description of Bloomsbury and of Harley Street is derived from DMR's "Yeats of Bloomsbury," *New York Times,* May 20, '69; Kelley's P.O. London Directory (1896–1910), *Dental Record* (1912–25); letter to Bryher (Dec. 30, '38). The Omega Workshops were opened in 1913 by Roger Fry, with the help of Vanessa Bell and Duncan Grant, with a view to giving young artists a chance at both design and production (of furniture, pottery, etc.). See Quentin Bell's *Bloomsbury.*

I have drawn details about Maude Beaton and Arthur French from JAH (PI), and letters to JAH (May 31, Aug. 8, '43; Apr. 29, June 17, '45). Arthur was the son of Henry and Elizabeth (Richardson) French; he had, besides his brother Charles, two sisters named Alice and Louie. Years later DMR remembered (to JAH, Aug. 18, '45) that on one of her visits to Cambridge, her Uncle Henry, by then a widower, was paying a visit to Charles and his wife Emmie, and proved a great trial to Emmie by going to chapel and inviting home for tea "a grocer in the town!"

403

For my account of Wells, I have used his own *Experiment in Autobiography*, Lovat Dickson's *H. G. Wells: His Turbulent Life and Times*, Norman and Jeanne Mackenzie's *The Time Traveller: The Life of H. G. Wells*, RP, and a letter to HS (Apr. '50).

CHAPTER THREE
An Affair of the Will

For McTaggart and Wilberforce, see *J. McT. E. McTaggart* by G. Lowes Dickinson and *Basil Wilberforce: A Memoir* by George W. E. Russell.

For DMR's weekends in Cambridge and her attendance at Westminster, I have used RP, letters to JAH (Jan. 10, Aug. 18, '45) and to PK ([1943]); and for her letters to Wells and attitudes, I have used RP, letters to PK (June 16, ['49]), to Bryher (June 20, '49), to HS (Apr. '50), to Vincent Brome (Jan. 16, '50).

For Wells's quarrel with the Fabians, see Dickson, the Mackenzies, and *A History of the Fabian Society* by Edward Pease; and for his relationship with James, see *Henry James and H. G. Wells*, ed. Leon Edel and Gordon N. Ray. (John Rosenberg would seem to be in error when he cites Dickson as one of the sources of his account of DMR's affair with Wells and the "scandal" he claims it caused in the Fabian Society. Dickson makes it quite clear that the "scandal" had to do with Rosamund Bland and Amber Reeves, about whom the Mackenzies provide an even fuller account; indeed, Dickson names them [see pp. 130–33], but nowhere does he even allude to DMR.) DMR's remarks about James occur throughout her letters, for example to HS (Sept. 18, '49).

For the Daniels (who were not yet married when DMR first met them), I have drawn upon a letter to PK (Feb. 21, '44) and *The Truth about a Publisher. An Autobiographical Record* by Sir Stanley Unwin. (Sir Stanley recalled that in 1916 or 1917 his own firm had rejected the manuscript of a novel which dealt with homosexuality and conscientious objectors. The author of the novel was advised that Charles Daniel would probably be the only publisher who might consider handling the work.)

For Benjamin Grad, I have drawn upon RP, the letters of VG to RIO, and DMR's portrayal of him as Michael Shatov in *Pilgrimage*. For the Arachne Club, Miss Moffat, Woburn Walk, and the trip to the Oberland, I have drawn upon VG to RIO (n.d.), VG to DMR (n.d.), DMR to Bryher (Feb. 15, '38), DMR's "Yeats of Bloomsbury," Frederick Sinclair's "A Poet's World in Woburn Walk," *St. Pancras Journal,* and Joseph Hone's *W. B. Yeats 1865–1939.*

Wells published the very different novel *Kipps* between *A Modern Utopia* and *In the Days of the Comet,* with Artie Kipps a first cousin to Mr. Lewisham.

DMR's reviews for Daniel are listed in the bibliography.

For my account of Veronica Leslie-Jones I have drawn on VG to RIO and DMR (n.d.), on RIO (PI) and PM (PI).

CHAPTER FOUR

Downs and Alps

For DMR's movements during 1907–8, I have drawn upon letters to JAH (June 7, '45), to Bryher (Oct. 4, '40), to PK (Oct. 5, '40), and her own essays and reviews.

Veronica and Benjamin Grad had two children, David and Rachel. Years later, when Rachel was Mrs. Edwin Ayre and needed help for a seriously ill son of her own, DMR appealed to Bryher on her behalf (Aug. 20, Sept, 8, '49).

For the *Saturday Review* sketches, see the bibliography. In my account of them, I have used RP, letter to Bryher (Oct. 28, '38), and "Seven Letters from Dorothy M. Richardson," ed. Joseph Prescott.

For my account of the Sussex years, I have drawn upon letters to Bryher ([1924]; Feb., Oct. 28, Nov. '38); to JAH (June 7, '45); to HS (Feb. 19, '39); to HGW (1910). Curiously enough, Bryher seems to have been at school in Eastbourne during the years when DMR was staying at Windmill Hill.

For DMR's friendship with the Beresfords, I have drawn upon my talk with the late Mrs. Beatrice Beresford, RP, J. D. Beresford to Hugh Walpole (Aug. 1, '20), DMR to Bryher (Aug. 11, '42), *Twentieth Century Authors,* eds. Stanley J. Kunitz and Howard Haycraft, *Hugh Walpole* by Rupert Hart-Davis.

For my account of the writing of *Pointed Roofs,* I have drawn upon RP, Louise Morgan's "How Writers Work," Mrs. Beresford (PI), and the information supplied to me by Mrs. Mabel Parsons (née Geach).

CHAPTER FIVE
"An Original Book"

For DMR's movements from 1913–15, I have used RP, information from Mrs. Beresford, C. V. Wedgwood's *The Last of the
Radicals: Josiah Wedgwood M.P.*, J. D. Beresford to Hugh Walpole (Jan. 22, Apr. 19, '15), J. D. Beresford to Edward Garnett
(Apr. 22, '15).

Charles Richardson died on March 28, 1915, in Kingston, Surrey
(Som).

The correspondence with Edward Garnett about *Pointed Roofs* is
among RP. (For an interesting view of Garnett, see Richard Church,
The Voyage Home.) The novel entitled *Pilgrimage* was probably by
C. E. Lawrence (London, 1907), a historical fiction set in the Middle Ages.

The reviews of *Pointed Roofs* are listed in the bibliography. See
also Rachel Trickett's essay "Dorothy Richardson" in the *London
Magazine* (June 1959), and Leon Edel's chapter on DMR in *The
Modern Psychological Novel*.

Pointed Roofs was dedicated to a friend of DMR's, Winifred
Ray, whose identity remains obscure. Though it is not clear exactly
when they met, they continued to be friends for years without seeing
each other very much (DMR's letters contain occasional references
to her). Apparently Winifred Ray had certain linguistic gifts and
engaged in translation, as well as various forms of journalism.

PART TWO

CHAPTER SIX
The Artist

See the bibliography for columns in the *Dental Record*.

For the events of this chapter, I have drawn upon RP, Som,
Kelley's P.O. London Directory (1910–39); letters to PBW (Dec. 8,
'38); to BE (Feb. 26, '39); to PK (Aug. 22, '43); to HS (Oct. 29,
'49); to RIO (Oct. 31, Nov. 27, '49); from RIO to the author (Mar.
31, '64); Alan Odle to Claude Houghton (n.d.); Alan Odle to DMR
([1917]); DMR to Alan Odle ([1917]); RIO's *Salt of Our Youth;
Colour* (May and July, 1915); *The Gypsy* (May 1915 and May
1916); *Café Royal: Ninety Years of Bohemia* by Guy Deghy and

Keith Waterhouse; unpublished diaries of Henry Savage; "Promenade Picaresque" (unpublished memoir by Henry Savage); Houghton and Walpole material at U. of Texas; *The Golden Echo* by David Garnett; *The Receding Shore* by Henry Savage; *The Life and Genius of T. W. H. Crosland* by W. Sorley Brown; "Julian Grant Loses His Way" by Sylva Norman (essay on Claude Houghton in *TLS,* Jan. 30, '69); *Mark Gertler: Biography of a Painter 1891–1939* by John Woodeson; *Carrington Letters & Extracts from Her Diaries,* ed. David Garnett; *The ABC of Pen and Ink Rendering* by John Austen.

Alan Odle and Aubrey Beardsley would be linked again years later as the result of a curious error. In 1966 a Beardsley exhibition was held at the Victoria and Albert Museum. Among the paintings was one of Alan by Adrian Allinson, lent by its owner and labeled by him "Mr. Watkins," who was described in the exhibition catalog as "reputed to be a natural son of Aubrey Beardsley." After protests by Rose Odle, her two sons, Allinson's brother, and his executrix, and evidence supplied in the form of photographs of Alan Odle, the Trustees of the Museum corrected the error. For correspondence about it, see *TLS,* Aug. 25, '66, p. 770; Oct. 6, '66, p. 919; Oct. 13, '66, p. 939; and Oct. 20, '66, p. 959.

CHAPTER SEVEN
The New Life

For the autobiographical material in *Backwater,* I have used RP, JAH (PI), and letter to Bryher (Sept. 25, '37).

For my account of the months following the marriage, I have drawn upon RP, RIO (PI), letters to Curtis Brown (Aug. 31, Sept. 22, Oct. 17, Oct. 27, '17) and to HS (May 1, '51).

Catherine Amy Dawson-Scott had begun her literary career in the 1880s, at the age of twenty-one, with a long poem entitled "Sappho," which was followed a few years later by a second book of poems and then by a series of novels full of the Cornish lore she never tired of collecting.

I am grateful to Mrs. Dawson-Scott's daughter, Marjorie Watts, for leading me to Levorna and providing me with information about it, and to Norah Hickey for information about her aunts, Nellie and Beulah Ponder, and their cottages.

CHAPTER EIGHT
The Edge of Fame

See the *Little Review* (1918–20) and *James Joyce* by Richard Ellmann.

I have drawn, for the years 1918–20, on RP and letters to Hugh Walpole (Oct. 24, '18); to Edward Garnett ([Spring] '19; Feb. 7, '20; Mar. 7, 12, 14, ['21]); to Curtis Brown (May 1, June 2, July 28, '19; Jan. 1, '20); to PBW (May 1, July 31, [Summer], Aug. 15, Sept. 15, 25, [Winter], '19); to HGW (Dec. 1, '19); Lady Desborough to DMR (Apr. 16, '19); Alfred Knopf to William Heinemann (unpublished letter of Feb. 17, '20, owned by Marjorie Watts). The novel of Mrs. Dawson-Scott under discussion was *Headland*.

See the bibliography for reviews of *The Tunnel* and *Interim*.

Lady Desborough was a well-known hostess to literary personalities in her mansion overlooking the Thames, Taplow Court, in Bucks. See Michael Holroyd, *Lytton Strachey*.

I am grateful to Mr. Jack Ingry, grandson of Mrs. Beatrice Carne, for information about her cottage in Trehemborne and his memories of the Odles.

It is interesting to note the resemblance between Mrs. Bailey's hopes for her daughters and the bitter little story in Joyce's *Dubliners* ("The Boarding House") about the helpless boarder trapped by the lady of the house into marrying her daughter Polly. Though this must have been a common situation, the intriguing fact remains that one of Mrs. Bailey's daughters is also named Polly.

DMR would refer to the Canadian doctors of *Interim* in a letter to PK (Aug. '36), saying that the "nicest" of them had just come to visit her in Queen's Terrace, but she never alluded to an original for either Mendizabal or Eleanor Dear.

CHAPTER NINE
Past and Present

For the events of this chapter, I have drawn upon RP and letters to PBW (May 3, Dec. 5, '20; Jan. 9, Mar., Nov. '21; [Spring], May 4, [Summer], Oct. 31, Nov. 11, [Nov.–Dec.], Dec. '22); to EBCJ (Apr. 21, May 12, Sept., Sept. 26, '22).

See *Deadlock* (3:68) for the reference to Voltaire.

E. B. C. Jones was the first wife of F. L. Lucas of Cambridge, and DMR addressed her in various ways, as "Jones," as "Mrs. Lucas," and as "Topsy Lucas."

Horace Gregory says, in *Dorothy Richardson: An Adventure in Self-Discovery*, that *Pilgrimage* "sustains its resemblance to the movement, storms, digressions, relapses, and recoveries of life itself" (pp. 107–8).

See the bibliography for reviews of *Deadlock* and *Revolving Lights*.

The interviews with novelists printed in the *Pall Mall Gazette* were collected in a volume published in 1921 as *The Future of the Novel: Famous Authors on Their Methods: A Series of Interviews with Renowned Authors,* ed. Meredith Starr.

Between 1918 and 1922, DMR's debt to Duckworth grew to the daunting sum of £300.

It was Henry Savage, who stayed with Mrs. Pope in Trevone Cottage in 1922–23, who recorded her description of seagulls' eggs in "A Cockney in Cornwall," published in *Book News*.

Pauline Marrian had discovered DMR's novels through the book by S. P. B. Mais entitled *Books and Their Writers,* and then met Mabel Koopman, dramatic critic for the *Era,* who had known DMR for some years and introduced Pauline to her.

The Muirs lived in a flat above one occupied by Barbara Low before they went to Prague (to PBW, July 26, '40).

DMR's first short story, "Sunday," appeared in *Art & Letters,* n.s., in the issue of Summer 1919.

The Whitman book that DMR had reviewed was *Days with Walt Whitman* by Edward Carpenter, and the review published in May 1907 was of *Book of Lords* by Morrison Davidson.

CHAPTER TEN

A Borrowed Year

Proust died on November 18, 1922.

Lawrence's remarks occurred in "Surgery for the Novel—or a Bomb," published in the *International Book Review.*

See the bibliography for reviews of *Revolving Lights.*

Priestley reviewed three other novels along with *Revolving Lights,* one of them by J. D. Beresford (*Love's Pilgrim*), and another by Alan's brother E. V. Odle (*The Clockwork Man*). DMR said of

Vincent's book (to PBW, Apr. 30, '23) that it had "been received with a vast unanimous roar of applause," that it was "a huge lark and something more."

For the events of 1923–24, I have drawn upon letters to EBCJ (Mar., Aug. '23); to PBW (Apr. 30, July [1], Sept., [Oct.], Nov. 20, Dec. 20, '23; Feb., Mar., Aug. '24); to Bryher (June, [Summer], [Sept.–Oct.], [Oct.], Dec. '23; [Jan.], Jan. 12, Feb., Mar., Mar. 31, [Apr.], May '24); to HD (Sept. '23; [Jan.–Feb.], [Mar.], Apr. 14, Apr. 28, '24); to Clement Shorter (Sept. '23); to Edward Garnett (Oct. 26, '23); to Ruth Pollard (Jan. '24); to JA (Jan. '24); to Middleton Murry ([Feb.–Mar.], Apr. '24); Ernest Hemingway to DMR (June 8, '24); to PK (Oct. 23, '29; Nov. 1, '43); to HS (Oct. '49); Bryher's *Heart to Artemis;* Ellmann's *James Joyce;* Robert McAlmon's *Being Geniuses Together* (which in DMR's opinion contained an inaccurate description of herself and Alan); Douglas Goldring's *South Lodge;* Henry Savage's "Promenade Picaresque."

The American Dorothy Richardson's book was called *The Book of Blanche,* and in the Autumn-Winter (1924–25) issue of the *Little Review,* a letter from Robert McAlmon would appear, protesting the failure of the American writer or her publisher to distinguish her from the English Dorothy Richardson.

Mary Butts died in 1937 at the age of forty-four.

Owen's friend was Roger Pippett.

See the bibliography for DMR's poems and the Swiss articles in Shorter's *Sphere.*

CHAPTER ELEVEN
Ironies and Ambiguities

For the return to England and the stay with Mrs. Pope, I have drawn upon letters to Bryher ([Apr., May '24]).

See the bibliography for DMR's essays and reviews. The two biographies of Wordsworth that she reviewed in 1930 were by C. H. Herford and Herbert Read, and she would suggest that both portraits were "true," even though Herford saw Wordsworth as a "progressive pilgrim" and Read as a "self-deceived egoist."

For DMR's return to London in June, I have used letters to Bryher and PBW (June, July, Aug., Sept. '24), and to Clement Shorter (June 7, '24). As for Conrad, references to him crop up again and again in her letters; and in 1929, in her first talk with JCP (see Chapter Fifteen), she would allude to Edward Garnett's "discovery" of herself as well as of Conrad (RP).

CHAPTER TWELVE
The Trap

For the quarrel with Wells, the dinner party at May Sinclair's, and the winter in Harlyn, I have drawn upon letters to Bryher (Oct., Nov., Dec. '24; Jan., Feb., Mar. '25). Samuel Odle, Alan's father, died on March 12, 1923.

For the spring with Mrs. Pope, the exhibition, and the summer in London, I have used letters to Bryher and PBW (Apr., May '25).

For reviews of *The Trap,* see the bibliography.

Arnold Englehart may well have been modeled after Leslie Haden Guest, who in 1905–6 had been one of Wells's radical supporters in the Fabian Society (see Mackenzie).

The young society doctor in *The Trap* may have been modeled after Dr. Robert Murray Leslie, who delivered DMR's younger sister's only child, now Mrs. Natalie Bushee (JAH [PI]).

CHAPTER THIRTEEN
"A Life in Duplicate"

My account of the summer of 1925 draws upon letters to PBW (Oct. 4, [Winter] '25) and to Bryher (Aug. '25, Nov.–Dec. '25; Jan., Feb., Mar. '26). See also the London *Observer,* Sept. '66 (for articles and letters about HGW on the hundredth anniversary of his birth); Brigit Patmore's memoirs *My Friends When Young,* ed. and intro. Derek Patmore; HGW's *Experiment in Autobiography,* Dickson, Mackenzie, HGW's *Mr. Britling Sees It Through.* Mackenzie gives an account of HGW's relationship with Rebecca West, which had begun late in 1912. Their affair lasted roughly until late in 1923. See also Gordon N. Ray's *H. G. Wells & Rebecca West.*

For the spring and summer of 1926, I have used letters to Bryher (Apr., May, June, July, Aug. '26), and to Louise Morgan Theis (Sept. '26). See also *Experiment in Autobiography,* Mackenzie, Vincent Brome's *H. G. Wells: A Biography,* and *The World of William Clissold: A Novel at a New Angle,* dedicated to Odette Keun.

The Treasury Grant came from Prime Minister Stanley Baldwin (see notes to Chapter Sixteen below).

CHAPTER FOURTEEN
A Matter of Identity

For my account of the late summer, fall, and winter of 1926, I have drawn upon letters to Bryher and PBW (Aug., Sept., Oct., Nov., Dec. '26; Jan., Feb., Mar. '27), and to Louise Morgan Theis (n.d.) and Mrs. Stanley Bennett (PI). The essay in the *Atlantic Monthly* was by Ethel Wallace Hawkins (see bibliography).

For the spring and summer of 1927, I have drawn upon letters to Bryher and PBW (May, June, July '27), and for the account of the publication of *Oberland,* on letters to Bryher and PBW (Nov., Dec. '27; Jan., Feb., Mar., Apr., May '28).

PART THREE

CHAPTER FIFTEEN
"The Shock of July"

Jane Wells died on Oct. 6, '27 (see Mackenzie). HGW wrote to DMR about it.

Mrs. Dawson-Scott's Lynx is now owned by her son (she died on Nov. 4, 1934). For the founding of the P.E.N. Club, see Marjorie Watts's *P.E.N.: The Early Years, 1921–1926.*

For the winter in Constantine Bay and the spring in Trevone Cottage, I have drawn upon the letters to Bryher and PBW cited above, as well as to EBCJ ([Spring '28]).

For the summer of 1928, I have drawn upon letters to PBW (June, July, Aug., Sept. '28); to PK (June, Aug., Sept., Oct. '28); to JA (Aug. '28); and RP. See also *Twentieth Century Authors.*

Later on Peggy Kirkaldy would try her hand at writing short fiction, and DMR gave her advice.

See the bibliography for the articles by Storm Jameson and DMR in the *Evening News.*

For my account of the winter and spring of 1928–29, I have used letters to PK (Nov., Dec. '28; Feb., May '29); to Tommy Austen

(Dec. '28); to Bryher (Dec. '28; Mar., Apr., May '29); to PBW (June '29).

See the bibliography for DMR's periodical writings during 1929.

For the account of the meeting with John Cowper Powys, I have drawn upon RP; letters to JCP (June 24, '29; n.d.); to PK (June, July, Aug. '29); to BE (July 3, '29); *New York Times,* June 18, '63 (obituary article on JCP, who was ninety when he died); JCP's *Autobiography.*

CHAPTER SIXTEEN

Openings and Closings

My account of the fall and winter of 1929 is drawn from letters to PK (Sept., Oct., Nov., Dec. '29; Jan., Feb., Mar. '30); to JCP (n.d., Sept., Dec. '29; Mar. '30); JCP to DMR (Jan. '30); to Bryher (Nov. '29; Feb., Mar. '30); to JA (Jan., Mar. 15, 30, '30); to PBW (Jan. 21, '30).

According to a letter to PK (Feb. 5, '45), DMR had looked up Violet Hunt at this time (because Peggy Kirkaldy wanted to meet her) after not having seen her since the days early in the century when they had met at the Wells home in Kent. In 1930 Violet Hunt, who was sixty-nine, was already old and difficult, but she would live until January 1942 (see notes to Chapter Twenty-two below).

For my account of the spring and summer of 1930, I have used letters to Bryher (Apr., May, June '30); to JA (Apr., May, June, July, Aug., Sept. '30); to PK (May 30, June, July 24, 28, Aug. 15, 24, 28, '30); to PBW (May 19, July, Aug. 22, Sept. '30); JCP to DMR (May 8, '30); to EBCJ (May 20, June '30).

DMR had bought the Australian securities (Australian 5 percents, they were called) with her £250 Treasury Grant from Baldwin and £50 left over from Alan's legacy.

Fan Frolico *did* bring out a limited edition of 300 copies of the Herondas book in 1930, but DMR never revealed how much Alan was finally paid.

For the winter of 1930, I have used letters to JA (Oct. '30; Jan. 14, Mar. 7, '31); to PK (Dec. 10, 19, '30; Mar. 5, '31); to Bryher (Jan., Feb. '31); Wilfrid Trotter to DMR (Dec. 16, '30); to Wilfrid Trotter (Jan. '31); to PBW (Feb. 12, '31); to BE (Mar. 29, '31).

CHAPTER SEVENTEEN
Fiction and Fact

For DMR's mixed feelings about JCP's essay, I have drawn upon letters to PBW (May 6, '31); to PK (May 6, '31); to Hugh Walpole (June '31).

For the summer of '31 in London, the Morgan interview, and the Harrap quarrel, I have drawn upon letters to PBW (July 14, 20, Aug. 8, 30, Oct. 1, '31); to Bryher (July 28, Sept., Oct., Nov. 12, Dec. 22, '31); to PK (June, Aug. 24, Sept., Oct. 12, 14, Nov. 30, Dec. '31); to JA (Sept., Dec. '31); to Louise Morgan Theis (Oct. 5, 14, 17, Nov. '31); to HD (Nov. 4, '31).

I am grateful to the late Mr. J. H. Thompson for providing me with a copy of the manuscript of *Dawn's Left Hand.*

CHAPTER EIGHTEEN
Breaking Down

For the *DuBarry* reviews and Brecht, I have drawn upon letters to Bryher (Mar. 14, Apr. 11, 25, '32) and *Twentieth Century Authors.* The dust jacket of *The DuBarry* described the translator as "the well-known author of the 'Miriam' novels."

The essay on Ramuz would appear in the Summer 1936 issue of *Life and Letters To-Day.*

For the summer of '32, I have drawn upon letters to PK (June 21, July 24, 26, Aug. 22, '32); to BE (June 23, Sept. 9, '32); to PBW (July 29, [Summer], '32); to Hugh Walpole (Aug. '32); to JCP (Sept. 29, '32).

For the winter and spring of 1932–33, I have drawn upon letters to Bryher (Oct. '32; Jan. 1, [Spring], Apr. 28, May 31, June '33); to PK (Dec. '32, Mar. 2, Mar. '33); to JA (Dec. '32; Mar. '33); to PBW (Mar., May '33); to JCP (May 31, '33); JCP to DMR (Dec. 31, '32). See also "Seven Letters from Dorothy M. Richardson." I am grateful to Prof. Joseph Prescott for his generous gift to me of a copy of *Mammon.*

See *Twentieth Century Authors* and *André Gide* by Van Meter Ames for Gide's background.

DMR's essay for *Close Up* was "Almost Persuaded"; it appeared in June 1929.

For the summer and winter of 1933–34, I have used letters to PBW (June 17, July 2, Aug. 10, Aug. 28, Dec. '33); to Bryher (Nov., Dec. '33; Jan., Feb., Mar. '34); to PK (Aug. 17, 28, Sept. 12, '33; Jan. 17, '34); to Kot (Dec. 11, 29, '33; Mar. 18, '34); to JCP (Jan. '34); JCP to DMR (Dec. 1, '33; Mar. 25, '34). See also George J. Zytaruk's *The Quest for Rananim* for the fullest account of Koteliansky available, and Harry T. Moore's *The Priest of Love* and Michael Holroyd's *Lytton Strachey* for notes on Koteliansky.

For the spring and summer of 1934, I have drawn upon letters to Kot (Apr. [3], 16, June, July, Aug. 8, 30, '34); to PK (Apr. 8, June 7, 25, July 7, 12, [Late Summer], Sept. 11, Oct. 10, '34); to Bryher ([Apr.] 16, Sept. 13, '34); to PBW (June '34); to JCP (July 3, 17, 20, Sept. '34); JCP to DMR (June 22, July 18, '34).

JCP and Phyllis Playter (he was separated from his wife) spent the summer in England and came to Queen's Terrace early in July. Later in the summer, Horace Gregory and his wife, Marya Zaturenska, called, during their visit to England and Ireland.

Vasili Vasilyevich Rozanov (1856–1919) was a Russian philosopher and critic. Kot had translated his *Solitaria* (a book of essays) in 1927.

Peter Smith published eleven volumes of *Pilgrimage* (through *Clear Horizon*).

For my account of DMR's illness, I have drawn upon letters to Kot (Oct., Nov. 29, Dec. 2, Dec. 27, '34); to Bryher (Oct., Dec. '34); to JCP (Nov., Dec. 5, '34); to PK (Dec. 12, 29, '34); to PBW (Jan. '35).

CHAPTER NINETEEN
The Healer

For the continuing account of DMR's illness, and of the spring, I have drawn upon letters to JCP (Jan. 14, May 24, June '35); to Bryher (Jan. 15, n.d., Mar. 1, 6, Apr., Apr. 17, May 21, June '35); to Kot (Feb. 6, 28, '35); to PK (Feb. 11, June 3, '35).

For the summer of 1935, I have drawn upon letters to PK ([Summer], July, Aug. '35); to Kot (July 28, '35); to PBW (Sept. 11, '35).

For Macmillan (1904–55), see *The Reluctant Healer: A Remarkable Autobiography, Heaven and You,* and the *Sunday Express* (London), Aug. 24, 31, Sept. 7, 14, '52 (a four-part account of himself by Macmillan).

Agnes Maud Royden (1876–1956) was born in Liverpool, educated at Lady Margaret Hall, Oxford, was prominent in the women's suffrage movement, and published *Woman and the Sovereign State, The Church and Woman, Modern Sex Ideals.*

Macmillan and Veronica Grad appear to have met through DMR (see *The Reluctant Healer*), and he treated her. Afterward she became his "secretary, housekeeper, bookkeeper, confidante and friend."

For the fall and winter of 1935–36, I have drawn upon letters to Bryher (Oct. 12, [Nov.] 24, 27, Dec. '35; Jan. 8, 26, Feb. 4, 9, 26, Mar. 3, 8, '36); to Kot (Nov. [1], Dec. '35; Jan., Feb. 24, '36); to PBW (Nov. 15, Dec. 7, 26, '35; Feb. 3, '36); to PK (Nov. 15, Dec. 20, '35); to JCP (Dec. 19, '35; Feb. 6, '36); JCP to DMR (Nov. 12, '35).

In *Dimple Hill* DMR would have Michael Shatov seek out Amabel to find out where Miriam was, and thus begin the new phase of their relationship that would end in their marriage.

DMR's remarks about "Nook on Parnassus" occur in her letter to PBW (Nov. 15, '35).

CHAPTER TWENTY
Culminations

For the spring and summer of 1936, I have drawn upon letters to PBW (Apr. 2, May, July 12, 28, Aug. 18, Sept. 24, '36); to Bryher (Apr. 7, 9, 15, 29, May, July 4, Aug. 5, 26, Oct. 4, '36); to Kot (Apr. 14, 18, Aug. 21, '36); to Richard Church (Apr. 14, [June] 23, '36); to PK (May 31, June 9, July 3, 12, 23, Aug. 12, Oct. 6, '36).

Richard Church, poet and literary critic, died in 1972 at the age of seventy-eight.

For the winter of 1936 and the spring and summer of 1937, I have drawn upon letters to Bryher (Nov. 23, '36; Feb. 22, Mar. 12, 19, [Apr.] 15, May 5, [June 14], [Aug. 12], [Summer], Aug. 21, 28, Sept. 25, Oct. 1, 18, 25, '37); to PK (Nov. 23, Dec. 27, '36; Feb. 15, 17, Mar. 9, 19, 24, May 15, June 21, 28, July 13, 26, 29, Aug. 17, 23, Sept. [14], '37); to JCP (Oct. 26, Nov., Dec. '36; Jan. 15, Mar. 3, Mar. [18], Apr. 5, May 10, July 6, '37); to BE (Jan., Aug. 12, '37); to PBW (Jan. 14, Apr. 27, '37); to JA (Aug. 16, '37).

For the fall and winter of 1937–38, I have drawn upon letters to PK (Oct. 28, Dec. '37; Jan. '38); to BE (Nov. 10, Dec. '37); to Bryher (Dec. '37, Feb. 15, n.d., Mar. 12, 25, '38); to PBW (Jan. 27, '38); Ralph Hodgson to Richard Church (Jan. 12, '38).

I am indebted to Prof. Joseph Prescott for a copy of the brochure Church had put together, and to Mr. Church for a copy of the letter to him from Hodgson.

For the spring, summer, and fall of 1938, I have used letters to Kot (Apr. 2, 7, Aug., Oct. 28, '38); to PK (Apr. 8, Sept., Oct. [6], Nov. 15, '38); to Bryher (May 12, June 2, July 1, Sept. 23, Oct. 9, 11, 28, Nov., Dec. 7, '38); to PBW (May 19, 21, Aug., Nov. 29, Dec. 8, '38); to JCP (July 6, 8, Oct., Nov. 8, '38); to EBCJ (Nov. 11, 25, '38); Vol. 7 of the journals of Hugh Walpole (U. of Texas); Harold Nicholson's *Diaries and Letters 1930–39,* ed. Nigel Nicolson.

PART FOUR

CHAPTER TWENTY-ONE
Storms and Shadows

For the *Saturday Review* sketches, see the bibliography.

For the winter and spring of 1938–39, I have drawn upon letters to Bryher (Dec. 31, '38; Feb. 1, Apr. 13, May 11, '39); to PK (Jan. 1, Mar. 8, Apr. 4, May 24, June 19, '39); to JCP (Feb. 15, 19, Mar. 16, 31, '39); to BE (Feb. 26, Apr. 23, '39); to PBW (Mar. 16, '39); to EBCJ (Apr. 3, '39).

DMR's remarks about Woolf occur throughout her letters, in particular those to Bryher (Apr., Aug. 4, '41).

For the summer of 1939, I have used letters to PK (June 26, 28, July 7, 29, Aug. 15, Sept. 5, '39); to PBW (June 27, July 11, '39); to Bryher (July 4, Sept. 15, '39); to Kot (July 11, 13, '39); to JCP Sept. 9, '39); to Joseph H. Hone (Aug. 11, '39); and Vol. 8 of the journals of Hugh Walpole (U. of Texas). See also Nicolson's *Diaries and Letters 1939–45.*

For the fall, winter, and spring of 1939–40, I have drawn upon Nicolson, and letters to Bryher (Sept. 26, 29, Oct. 17, Nov. 4, Dec. 4, 31, '39; Jan. 15, Feb. 12, 20, Mar. 19, Apr. 17, June 3, '40); to PK (Sept. 27, Dec. '39; Jan. 9, Feb. 20, May 30, '40); to EBCJ (Oct. 24, '39); to Kot (Dec. '39); to PBW (Nov. 22, Dec. '39; Jan. 6, Feb. 21, May 2, 8, June 2, 7, 12, 21, '40); to JCP (Dec. '39; Jan. 17, 27, Apr. 24, May 10, '40); to Hugh Walpole (Feb. 26, Mar. 7, '40); Hugh Walpole to DMR (Mar. 20, '40); Hugh Walpole to Richard Church (Jan. 8, '40); DMR to Richard Church (Mar. 12, 16, '40).

I am particularly indebted to Norah Hickey and Marjorie Watts for their descriptions of the war years in Cornwall.

For the summer, fall, and winter of 1940–41, I have drawn upon letters to PK (July 4, Aug., Oct. 5, 30, Nov. 6, Dec. 8, 20, '40; Feb. 8, '41); to PBW (July 9, 26, Nov. 27, Dec. 30, '40; Jan. 27, Feb. 17, Mar. 1, '41); to Bryher (Oct. 4, 7, 31, Nov. 21, Dec. [15], 16, 22, '40; Jan. 8, 22, 31, Feb. 21, Mar. 17, 22, 30, '41).

I have also made use of Hugh Walpole's journals, Vols. 11, 12, 13, 14, 15 (Jan. '40–May 22, '41).

CHAPTER TWENTY-TWO
War and Obscurity

For my account of the war years, I have drawn upon letters to Bryher (Apr., May 2, 11, June 2, 7, July 3, 4, 14, Aug. 4, 7, Sept. 26, Oct. 17, 26, 28, Nov. 6, 12, 19, Dec. 8, '41; Jan. 5, 11, 14, 20, 27, Mar. 17, Apr. 28, May 1, 8, 17, 24, 30, June 7, 20, July 6, Aug. 11, 25, Sept. 13, 21, Nov. 4, Dec. 10, 23, '42; Jan. 4, Mar. 21, 25, Apr. 18, May 9, June 1, July 1, Aug. 22, Sept. 20, Nov. 7, 30, Dec. 6, 17, 21, 25, '43; Jan. 23, Feb. 1, 9, 18, 25, Mar. 6, 10, 30, Apr. 4, 12, 24, May 8, 12, 16, June, July 6, 10, 16, Sept. 12, '44); to PBW (May 3, 8, 19, 22, 24, 31, June 7, 10, 23, July 8, Aug. 8, 11, 18, 20, 30, Sept. 3, 16, Nov. 10, Dec. 6, '41; Jan. 3, 5, Feb. 5, 9, Mar. 7, Apr. 21, 24, May 24, June 7, 19, Aug. 10, Sept. 18, Nov. 8, [Dec.] '42; Jan. 8, Sept. 20, 27, Oct. 3, 11, Nov. 4, Dec. 18, '43; Jan. 19, Feb. 3, 5, Mar. 30, June 3, 21, Aug. 27, '44); to PK (June 14, July 21, Sept. 25, '41; June 5, July 26, Oct. 21, '42; Feb. 12, 14, [20], Mar. 6, 23, [Spring], Apr. 14, May 9, 12, 29, June 9, July 5, Aug. 6, 13, 22, 28, Oct. 19, Nov. 1, '43; Jan. 4, 15, 25, Feb. 6, 21, Mar. 14, Apr. 26, June 8, July 14, Aug. 7, '44); to JCP (July [27], Oct. 29, '41; Oct. 25, '42; June 19, July 12, Aug. 15, '43; Aug. 5, 10, '44); to BE (Aug. 24, '41; Mar. 24, '42; Mar. 11, '43); to HD (May 30, '44); to Kot (Apr. 23, 28, Aug. 11, '42; Mar. 12, '43); to JAH (May 31, Aug. 8, Dec. 29, '43; Apr. 29, Aug. 10, '44); to Claude Houghton (Feb. 18, Nov. 28, '42; Dec. 21, ['43]); Alan Odle to Claude Houghton (ten undated letters from Zansizzey).

In response to Claude Houghton's request, Alan supplied him with a bibliography of his work, describing it as "not much of a show," but going on to say that "to me, the wonder is, that anything of mine has been published at all." His list, with commentary, is as follows:

"Voltaire's Candide."

Routledge. Published 1922. 50 drawings. 12/6. Three editions.
Out of print, but second-hand copies, at slightly under published
price, were fairly plentiful before the war.

A very badly produced book, but my best,—in spirit.

"The Mimiambs of Herondas."

Fanfrolico Press, 1930. 19 drawings. Three guineas. Edition limited to 300 copies. Second-hand copies rather rare.

Contains some of my best chapter-headings but the full pages are
rather dull. Typography, and production, excellent.

"1601. A Tudor Fireside Conversation with Mark Twain."

12 drawings. Edition limited to 450 copies. Without publishers
imprint. 1936. Three guineas.

A Rabelaisian extravaganza found in Mark Twain's desk, after
his death. *Very* privately published, but an intrepid American
collector once discovered a copy in Foyles. Contains one of my
best title-pages.

"The ABC of Pen and Ink Rendering." John Austen. 1937.

Pitman. 6/⁻ probably. Presumably still in print. I contributed 4
drawings, and a short essay on my method of work.

By far the best hand-book on pen and ink drawing ever written.
But contains an absurd overestimate of myself.

"The Last Voyage." James Hanley. No. 5 of the Furnival Books.
10/⁻.

Joiner and Steele Ltd.

Frontispiece.

"Men in Darkness." James Hanley.

Bodley Head.

Wrapper design. Used as extra plate in limited edition.

Magazines

"The Golden Hind." Chapman and Hall.

Art Quarterly.

1922–3. Eight numbers.

I believe I contributed pen drawings or lithographs to every
number except the first.

Bound volumes, and odd copies, sometimes appear in Charing X
Road—rather the worse for wear. Sonnet by Dorothy in one
number.

"Vanity Fair."

Condé Nast. Published in America only.
(Now defunct)
I contributed—at intervals—from 1920 to 1930.
Scenes of social life; mildly satirical in character.
Bread and butter work at best, but "A week-end on Parnassus"—May 1924—perhaps deserves resurrection.
The Studio. 1926. Two drawings.
The Studio. Jan. 1928. Article and 6 drawings.
The Radio Times. Oct. 1931 (Date uncertain).
Drawings representing scenes from the life of François Villon.
The Argosy. Cassells. 1933–4. (Dates uncertain).
Small vignettes for stories by Poe, Sheridan le Fanu, Blackwood, etc.

Unpublished Works

"The Merrie Pranks of King Louis the eleventh."
Balzac. From the Contes Drolatiques.
Newly translated by Dorothy M. Richardson.
25 drawings. Limited edition.
Commissioned by "The Fortune Press" in 1938.
Publication held up by war.
Chapter-headings to Rabelais.
Was to have been my magnum opus. But shortly before the war—realizing the practical difficulties of the scheme—I broke up the set, and sold all the best drawings.

The local farmer whose records DMR helped to keep was Ernie Trenouth, who still lives in Trevone with his wife, Dorothy.

Early in 1942 Violet Hunt died, and DMR eventually learned, to her great surprise, that she had been left a legacy of £550 (with which she bought Savings Certificates), even though she had refused Violet Hunt's request that she agree to be one of her literary executors. Apparently DMR had gone to South Lodge, Violet's home on Campden Hill in London, several times during the summer of 1939, largely because Violet seemed so tragically lonely and felt so neglected in her slow decline. See Douglas Goldring's *South Lodge,* published in 1943. DMR read the book and thought it a "sympathetic" account.

CHAPTER TWENTY-THREE
Hillside

Until 1973, Hillside continued to be the property and home of Miss Symons, who moved into the downstairs flat when DMR left it. When she sold the house in 1973, the new owner maintained the flat for her, and she came there each summer. During the rest of the year she lived with her grandnephew Symon Kennedy, who was the infant upstairs when the Odles first moved into Hillside in 1945. Miss Symons died in July 1976 at the age of ninety-five.

My view of *March Moonlight* as unfinished is at variance with both Horace Gregory's and John Rosenberg's. See *Dorothy Richardson: An Adventure in Self-Discovery* and *Dorothy Richardson: The Genius They Forgot*.

For my account of the years until 1954, I have drawn upon letters to PBW (Oct. 25, Nov. 26, Dec. 14, 30, '44; Feb. 16, Mar. 13, June 26, Dec. 26, '45; July 14, 24, Oct. 3, '46; May 11, '47; Jan. 20, Apr. 3, 16, 30, May 15, Dec. 23, '48; Mar. 17, May 16, June 1, 16, Aug. 18, Oct. 16, 21, Nov. 12, Dec. 30, '49; Jan. 4, Apr. 21, Sept. 4, Oct. 3, 17, 20, Dec. '50; Jan. 21, Mar. 25, Apr. 17, Sept. 17, Oct. 4, Dec. 5, '51; Feb. 15, Mar. 27, May 9, July 31, Aug. 5, Sept. 3, '52); to Bryher (Oct. 28, [Nov.], Nov. 25, Dec. 5, 18, '44; [Feb.], Mar. 30, Apr. 6, 12, 19, May 15, June 25, Sept. 18, Oct. 5, Nov. 14, 28, Dec. 14, '45; Jan. 27, Feb. 2, May 2, 14, 24, 29, June, July 18, 30, Aug. 4, [24], Sept. 16, Nov. 4, Dec. 22, '46; Feb. 18, Mar. 3, Mar. 16, Apr. 2, 21, May 8, 21, 29, June 27, July 14, Sept. 4, 19, Oct. 25, Nov. 15, '47; Jan. 11, Mar. 19, Aug. 6, Nov. 10, '48; Jan. 1, Mar. 7, Apr. 20, May 24, June 20, Aug. 10, 20, Sept. 8, 28, Oct. 17, Nov. 15, 29, '49; Jan. [19], Mar. 11, May, Oct. 1, 12, 21, Nov. 11, 27, 28, Dec. '50; Jan. 25, Feb. 26, Mar. 10, May 22, June 17, July 12, Oct. 28, Dec. 22, '51; Mar. 26, May 5, June 23, July 7, 22, Sept. 16, Oct. 9, Nov. 6, 7, '52); to PK (Nov. 21, '44; Feb. 5, Mar. 12, 23, May 2, June 22, Aug. 29, Nov. 24, '45; Feb. 5, May 22, 27, June, July 3, Oct. 5, Nov. 19, '46; Jan. 11, Oct. 14, '47; Feb. 1, Feb. [15], [Mar.], Mar. 27, June 5, [Summer], Sept. 1, Nov. 12, Dec. 27, '48; Apr. 20, May 29, June 16, Sept. 8, Nov. 30, '49; Jan. 8, Mar. 4, Apr. 27, Aug. 27, Oct. 1, '50; Feb. 20, 24, Mar. 31, Apr. 29, Aug. 30, '51; Mar. 5, June 9, '52); to JCP (Dec. '44; Jan. 5, Oct. 25, Nov. 1, 15, '45; Mar. 11, Apr. 1, 5, June 24, July 10, Sept. '46; Mar. 17, Dec. 21, '47; Feb.

15, Mar. 15, June 24, 28, July 28, Dec. 2, '48; Jan. 14, Feb. 1, '51; Nov. 9, 14, '52); to JAH (Jan. 10, Apr. 29, June 7, Aug. 18, Sept. 17, 20, Nov. '45; May 6, June [1], 11, Aug. 15, Sept. 17, '46; Apr. 5, July 6, Sept. 23, Nov. 16, '47; Jan. 19, [Mar.], Apr. 28, Oct. 19, '48; Jan. 20, Feb. 17, '49); to JA (Jan. 11, Apr. 5, Oct. 6, '45; Apr. 16, Aug. 2, '46; Mar. 17, '48); to Tommy Austen (Mar. 25, Nov. 1, '48; Mar. 20, '49; Dec. 14, '50); to BE (Apr. 27, Oct. '45; Dec. 10, '46; Feb. 26, '47; Feb. 27, '48; May 2, July 1, Aug. 3, Sept. 27, '49; Mar. 31, July 2, '50; Mar. 28, Apr. 29, May 4, 10, June 13, Aug. 17, Dec. 17, '51; summer '52); to PM (Jan. 23, May 3, '45; Aug. 15, '46; Sept. 30, '47; Aug. 22, Dec. 1, '50; July 25, '52); to HD (June 16, '45; Oct. 22, ['46]; Dec. '50); to Ruth Suckow (Apr. 28, '47; Sept. 10, '49; Apr. 6, 22, '51); to Richard Church (Mar. 2, '47); to Kot (Sept. 8, '47; Dec. 30, '50); to HS ([Sept.], Nov. 26, Dec. 19, '46; Feb., Apr., May 31, July 31, Sept., Nov. 19, 26, '47; Mar. 7, Aug. 26, Oct. 24, '48; Jan. 26, Apr. 1, Aug. 5, Sept. 18, 25, Oct. 10, 29, '49; Jan. 6, Mar. 11, 18, Apr., May 8, '50; Feb. 1, 4, 15, 20, Mar. 4, May 1, 6, 18, June 3, July 26, Sept. 2, Oct. 23, '51; Feb. 1, Oct. 18, '52); to Claude Houghton (Feb. 28, '48; Jan. 8, '52); Alan Odle to Claude Houghton (five letters from Hillside); to RIO (Mar. 20, '48; Feb. 5, May 28, June 15, Aug. 26, Oct. 31, Nov. 27, Dec. 8, '49; Mar. 15, May 27, June 19, 28, Aug. 2, Sept. 9, 11, Nov. 5, [14], 22, Dec. 9, 25, '50; Feb. 13, '51; Oct. 12, '52); to Louise Morgan Theis (Mar. 26, '48; June 20, Oct. 15, '50); to Joan George (Feb. 28, '49); to Dr. Cobbledick (Dec. 10, '49; Jan. 10, May 15, [May–June], July 18, '50).

I am grateful to Joan George for her gift to me of DMR's letters to her and her father. Dr. Cobbledick and DMR shared an interest in Gide, and they were both particularly impressed by Aldous Huxley's book *The Art of Seeing*.

In 1939 Amabel Williams-Ellis and her husband had offered DMR as a home what Dorothy called their "Italianate villa" in North Wales. Mrs. Williams-Ellis was born in 1894, the eldest child of St. Loe and Henrietta Strachey.

Harry Badcock and DMR had been corresponding during the war, which he spent in Jamaica. His wife had died, and he was living with his sister. After the war, in 1946, they moved back to England, near Bury St. Edmunds. In 1949 Norah and Edward Hickey happened to meet him when he was visiting Worcester. They found him amazingly vigorous and interesting at the age of eighty-four.

Alan's death was probably due to heart failure and/or a sudden internal hemorrhage. His friend John Austen died, also quite suddenly, only a few months afterward.

DMR inscribed the set of *Pilgrimage* that is in the Padstow library: "Presented in memory of one who always wished the Padstow Library to have a copy of Pilgrimage." Signed "Dorothy M. Odle/ July 1948." Throughout the four volumes, there are a number of corrections and changes of words and phrases, clearly the result of a careful reading. For example, "lightly packed" is changed to "tightly packed," "different to" is changed to "different from," "with their separate" to "with its separate," etc.

Though the Grads lived apart for some years, they seem to have been on good enough terms to come down together to spend Christmas of 1948 with DMR. During the war Benjamin Grad had been interned in France (near Sylvia Beach, as DMR learned), and DMR corresponded with him.

Ruth Suckow, the American novelist, and her husband, Ferner Nuhn (who was also a writer), had come to see DMR in 1939, with an introduction from John Cowper Powys. DMR was especially fond of Ruth Suckow's novel *The Folks*, published in 1934. Her correspondence with them was not extensive, but was warm and friendly nonetheless.

Epilogue

I am indebted to the late Rose Odle and to Evelyn Morrison, Pauline Marrian, and P. Beaumont Wadsworth for their memories of the last years of DMR's life.

Bibliography

PART ONE

List of Writings by Dorothy M. Richardson

With a few exceptions, this list originally appeared in *English Literature in Transition* in 1965, absorbing "A Preliminary Checklist of the Periodical Publications of Dorothy M. Richardson" by Joseph Prescott, published in 1958, and including all DMR's contributions to periodicals that my research had enabled me to identify.

I. AUTOBIOGRAPHY AND LETTERS

"A few facts for you . . . ," *Sylvia Beach (1887–1962)*, pp. 127–28. [Paris]: Mercure de France, 1963.

"Beginnings: A Brief Sketch," *Ten Contemporaries: Notes Toward Their Definitive Bibliography*, 2d ser., ed. John Gawsworth (pseud. of Terence Armstrong), ppl 195–98. London: Joiner & Steele, 1933.

"Data for Spanish Publisher," ed. Joseph Prescott. *London Magazine* 6 (June 1959):14–19.

"Seven Letters from Dorothy M. Richardson," ed. Joseph Prescott. *Yale University Library Gazette* 33 (Jan. 1959):102–11.

II. BOOKS

A. Nonfiction

The Quakers Past and Present. London: Constable; New York: Dodge, 1914.

Gleanings from the Works of George Fox. London: Headley, 1914.
John Austen and the Inseparables. London: William Jackson, 1930.

B. Prefaces

Black, E. L. *Why Do They Like It?* Educational Documents I, pp.
ix–x. Paris: [?], 1927.
Dumas, F. Ribadeau. *These Moderns: Some Parisian Close-Ups,*
trans. Frederic Whyte, pp. 5–10. London: Humphrey Toulmin,
1932.

C. Novel
(First Editions)

Pointed Roofs, intro. J. D. Beresford. London: Duckworth, 1915.
Backwater. London: Duckworth, 1916.
Honeycomb. London: Duckworth, 1917.
The Tunnel. London: Duckworth, [Feb.] 1919.
Interim. London: Duckworth, [Dec.] 1919.
Deadlock. London: Duckworth, 1921.
Revolving Lights. London: Duckworth, 1923.
The Trap. London: Duckworth, 1925.
Oberland. London: Duckworth, 1927.
Dawn's Left Hand. London: Duckworth, 1931.
Clear Horizon. London: J. M. Dent & Cresset Press, 1935.

(Collected Editions)

Pilgrimage (including *Dimple Hill*). 4 vols. London: J. M. Dent &
Cresset Press; New York: Alfred A. Knopf, 1938.
Pilgrimage (including *March Moonlight*), intro. Walter Allen. 4
vols. London: J. M. Dent & Sons; New York: Alfred A. Knopf,
1967.
Pilgrimage, intro. Walter Allen. 4 vols. New York: Popular Library,
1976.

(Foreign Language Editions and Translations)

Pointed Roofs, ed. with intro. and notes by Junzaburo Nishiwaki.
Tokyo: Kenkyusha, [1934].

Toits Pointus, trans. Marcelle Sibon. Paris: Mercure de France, 1965.

III. CONTRIBUTIONS TO PERIODICALS

A. Reviews

"Days with Walt Whitman," Crank 4 (Aug. 1906):259–63.
"The Reading of *The Jungle,"* ibid. (Sept.):290–93.
"Jesus in Juteopolis," ibid. (Oct.):331–32.
"The Amazing Witness," ibid., pp. 332–34.
"In the Days of the Comet," ibid. (Nov.):372–76.
"How We Are Born," Ye Crank 5 (Jan. 1907):44–47.
"The Future in America," Ye Crank and The Open Road 5 (Feb. 1907):95–99.
"A Sheaf of Opinions: Lowes Dickinson's *A Modern Symposium,"* ibid. (Mar.):153–57.
"A French Utopia," ibid. (Apr.):209–14.
"Down with the Lords," ibid. (May):257–61.
"Notes about a Book Purporting To Be about Christianity and Socialism," ibid. (June):311–15.
"Nietzsche," *Open Road,* n.s., 1 (Nov. 1907):243–48.
"Towards the Light," ibid. (Dec.):304–8.
"Cosmic Thinking" [unsigned], *Plain Talk,* July 1913, p. 13.
"Slavery" [unsigned], ibid., pp. 13–14.
"The Reality of Feminism," *The Ploughshare,* n.s., 2 (Sept. 1917):241–46.
"A Spanish Dentist Looks at Spain," *Dental Record* 38 (Aug. 1, 1918):343–45.
Review of *Psycho-Analysis: A Brief Account of the Freudian Theory* by Barbara Low, ibid. 40 (Aug. 2, 1920):522–23.
"The Perforated Tank," *Fanfare* 1 (Oct. 15, 1921):29.
"A Sculptor of Dreams," *Adelphi* 2 (Oct. 1924):422–27.
"Portrait of an Evangelist," *New Adelphi* 1 (Mar. 1928):270–1.
"Das Ewig-Weibliche," ibid. (June):364–66.
"Mr. Clive Bell's Proust," ibid. 2 (Dec. 1928–Feb. 1929):160–62.
Review of *Experiments with Handwriting* by Robert Saudek, ibid. (June–Aug. 1929):380.
"The Return of William Wordsworth," *Adelphi* [Review Supplement], n.s., 1 (Dec. 1930):16–19.

"Man Never Is . . . ," ibid. (Mar. 1931):521–22.

Review of *Documents 33,* Apr.–Aug., *Close Up* 10 (Sept. 1933):295–96.

"Novels," *Life and Letters To-Day* 15 (Winter 1936):188–89.

"Adventure for Readers," ibid. 22 (July 1939):45–52.

B. Essays

"The Russian and His Book" [unsigned], *Outlook* 10 (Oct. 4, 1902):267–68.

"The Odd Man's Remarks on Socialism," *Ye Crank* 5 (Jan. 1907):30–33.

"Socialism and Anarchy: An Open Letter to the 'Odd Man,' " *Ye Crank and The Open Road* 5 (Feb. 1907): 89–91.

"Socialism and the Odd Man," ibid. (Mar.):147–49.

"A Last Word to the Odd Man about Socialism," ibid. (Apr.):180–82.

"Thearchy and Socialism," ibid. (May):237–39.

"The Open Road," *Open Road,* n.s., 1 (Sept. 1907):153–58.

"Women in Dentistry," *Oral Hygiene* 1 (Mar. 1911):212. Selected from *The Pittsburgh Leader.* I have been unable to locate the issue of the *Leader* in which this article first appeared.

"Diet and Teeth," *Dental Record* 32 (Aug. 1, 1912): 553–56; *Dental Practice* 13 (1912):145–49. Selected: *American Dental Journal* 11 (Apr. 1914):98–102.

"The Responsibility of Dentistry," *Dental Record* 33 (Oct. 1, 1913):633–35.

"Medical Austria in the Arena. The Encroaching Laity" [unsigned], ibid. 34 (Feb. 1, 1914):143.

"Medical Austria. A Reply From 'The Encroaching Laity' " [unsigned], ibid. (Mar. 2):217–18.

"Some Thoughts Suggested by the Austro-Hungarian Problem," ibid. (Aug. 1):519–23.

"A Plea for a Statistical Bureau," ibid. 35 (June 1, 1915):403–5.

"The Teeth of Shropshire School Children," ibid. (Sept. 2):562–64.

"Comments by a Layman" was a column that appeared, always unsigned, in the following issues of the *Dental Record:* 35 (1915):686–88, 752–54; 36 (1916):33–35, 87–89, 140–43, 190–92, 247–48, 310–12, 357–58, 427–28, 541–44, 606–7, 655–57;

37 (1917):19–20, 81–82, 119–21, 169–71, 221–22, 264–65, 320–22, 375–77, 420, 483–86, 527–29, 577–79; 38 (1918):13–15, 62–64, 110–12, 161–63, 262–64, 350–52, 391–92, 427–29, 472–73, 509–10; 39 (1919):10–11, 57–58, 99–101, 136–38, 178–80, 214–16.

"Amateur Evidence in Dietetics," *Dental Record* 36 (June 1, 1916):300–303.

"Dental Legislation at Geneva," ibid. 37 (Apr. 2, 1917):161–63.

"The Forsyth Dental Infirmary for Children," ibid. (Aug. 1): 366–69.

"The Socialization of Dentistry," ibid. 41 (Dec. 1, 1921):611–13, abstracted in *Dental Surgeon* 19 (1922):9–10.

"Science and Linguistics by Layman" [unsigned], *Dental Record* 42 (Mar. 1, 1922):149–50.

"Talent and Genius: Is Not Genius Actually Far More Common than Talent?" *Vanity Fair* 21 (Oct. 1923):118.

"Veterans in the Alps," *Sphere* 96 (Mar. 29, 1924):354.

"About Punctuation," *Adelphi* 1 (Apr. 1924):990–96. "De la Ponctuation," trans. Sylvia Beach and Adrienne Monnier, *Mesures* (Jan. 15, 1935):155–56.

"Women and the Future: A Trembling of the Veil before the Eternal Mystery of 'La Giaconda' [*sic*]," *Vanity Fair* 22 (Apr. 1924):39–40.

"Alpine Spring," *Sphere* 97 (Apr. 12, 1924):44.

"The Parting of Wordsworth and Coleridge: A Footnote," *Adelphi* 1 (May 1924):1107–9.

"A Note on George Fox," ibid. 2 (July 1924):148–50.

"Brothers Rabbit and Rat," ibid. (Aug.):247–49.

"The Role of the Background: English Visitors to the Swiss Resorts during the Winter Sports Season," *Sphere* 99 (Nov. 22, 1924):226.

"The Man from Nowhere," *Little Review* 10 (Autumn 1924–Winter 1925):32–35.

"What's in a Name?" *Adelphi* 2 (Dec. 1924):606–9.

"Women in the Arts: Some Notes on the Eternally Conflicting Demands of Humanity and Art," *Vanity Fair* 24 (May 1925):47.

"The Status of Illustrative Art," *Adelphi* 3 (June 1925):54–57.

Theobald, R. (pseud. of DMR). "Why Words?" ibid (Aug.):206–7.

"Antheil of New Jersey," *Vanity Fair* 25 (Nov. 1925):136.

Theobald, R. (pseud. of DMR). "Spengler and Goethe: A Footnote," *Adelphi* 4 (Nov. 1926):311–12.

"Continuous Performance," *Close Up* 1 (July 1927):34–37.

"Continuous Performance 2: Musical Accompaniment," ibid.
(Aug.):58–62.

"Continuous Performance 3: Captions," ibid. (Sept.):52–56.

"Continuous Performance 4: A Thousand Pities," ibid. (Oct.):60–
64.

"Continuous Performance 5: There's No Place Like Home," ibid.
(Nov.):44–47.

"The Dog and the Postman," *Animal World,* Nov. 1927, p. 125.

"Continuous Performance 6: The Increasing Congregation," *Close
Up* 1 (Dec. 1927):61–65.

"Continuous Performance 7: The Front Rows," ibid. 2 (Jan.
1928):59–64.

"A Note on Household Economy," ibid. (Feb.):58–62.

"Journey to Paradise," *Fortnightly Review,* n.s., 123 (Mar. 1,
1928):407–14.

"Continuous Performance 8," *Close Up* 2 (Mar. 1928):51–55.

"Continuous Performance 9: The Thoroughly Popular Film," ibid.
(Apr.):44–50.

"Continuous Performance 10: The Cinema in the Slums," ibid.
(May):58–62.

"The Queen of Spring," *Focus* 5 (May 1928):259–62.

"Anticipation," ibid. (June):322–25.

"Continuous Performance 11: Slow Motion," *Close Up* 2 (June
1928):54–58.

"Compensations?" *Focus* 6 (July 1928):3–7.

"Continuous Performance 12: The Cinema in Arcady," *Close Up* 3
(July 1928):52–57.

"Films for Children," ibid. (Aug.):21–27.

"Madame August," *Focus* 6 (Aug. 1928):67–71.

"Decadence," ibid. (Sept.):131–34.

"Puritanism," ibid. (Oct.):195–98.

"Where Is Miss Jameson's Suburbia?" *Evening News* (London),
Oct. 2, 1928, p. 8.

"Peace," *Focus* 6 (Nov. 1928):259–62.

"Post Early," ibid. (Dec.):327–31.

"Continuous Performance: Pictures and Films," *Close Up* 4 (Jan.
1929):51–57.

"Resolution," *Purpose* 1 (Jan.–Mar. 1929):7–9.

"Continuous Performance: Almost Persuaded," *Close Up* 4 (June 1929):51–57.

"Leadership in Marriage," *New Adelphi* 2 (June–Aug. 1929):345–48.

"Talkies, Plays and Books: Thoughts on the Approaching Battle between the Spoken Pictures, Literature and the Stage," *Vanity Fair* 32 (Aug. 1929):56.

"Continuous Performance: Dialogue in Dixie," *Close Up* 5 (Sept. 1929):211–18.

"The Censorship Petition," ibid. 6 (Jan. 1930):7–11.

"Continuous Performance: A Tear for Lycidas," ibid. 7 (Sept. 1930):196–202.

"Continuous Performance: Narcissus," ibid. 8 (Sept. 1931):182–85.

"Continuous Performance: This Spoon-Fed Generation?" ibid. (Dec.):304–8.

"Continuous Performance: The Film Gone Male," ibid. 9 (Mar. 1932):36–38.

"Continuous Performance," ibid. 10 (June 1933):130–32.

"C. F. Ramuz," *Life and Letters To-Day* 14 (Summer 1936):46–47.

"Yeats of Bloomsbury," ibid. 21 (Apr. 1939):60–66.

"A Talk about Talking," ibid. 23 (Dec. 1939):286–88.

"Needless Worry," ibid. 24 (Feb. 1940):160–63.

"Novels," *Life and Letters* 56 (Mar. 1948): 188–92.

C. Sketches

"A Sussex Auction" [unsigned], *Saturday Review* 105 (June 13, 1908):755.

"A Sussex Carrier" [unsigned], ibid. 107 (June 19, 1909):782–83.

"Hay-Time" [unsigned], ibid. 108 (July 31, 1909):132.

"A Village Competition" [unsigned], ibid. (Aug. 7):165–66.

"Haven" [unsigned], ibid. (Oct. 9):440–41.

"The Wind" [unsigned], ibid. (Dec. 4):691.

"December" [unsigned], ibid. (Dec. 25):785–86.

"The End of the Winter" [unsigned], ibid. 109 (Feb. 19, 1910):234–35.

"Lodge Night" [unsigned], ibid. 110 (Nov. 19, 1910):642–43.
"Dans la Bise" [unsigned], ibid. 111 (Jan. 14, 1911):46–47.
"Gruyères" [unsigned], ibid. (Feb. 18):208–9.
"March" [unsigned], ibid. (Mar. 4):267.
"The Holiday" [unsigned], ibid. 112 (Aug. 26, 1911):268–69.
"The Conflict" [initialed], ibid. (Nov. 25):673–74.
"Across the Year," ibid. (Dec. 23):795–96.
"Welcome," ibid. 113 (May 18, 1912):620–21.
"Strawberries," ibid. (June 22):778–79.
"August," ibid. 114 (Aug. 3):142.
"Peach Harvest," ibid. 116 (July 19, 1913):78–79.
"Dusk" [unsigned], ibid. 118 (Oct. 10, 1914):392–93.
"The Garden," *transatlantic review* 2 (Aug. 1924):141–43.

D. Short Stories

"Sunday," *Art & Letters,* n.s., 2 (Summer 1919):113–15.
"Christmas Eve," ibid. 3 (Winter 1920):32–35.
"Death," *Weekly Westminster,* n.s. 1 (Feb. 9, 1924). Reprinted in *Best British Stories of 1924,* ed. Edward J. O'Brien and John Cournos, pp. 218–20. Boston: Small, Maynard and Co., 1924.
"Ordeal," *Window* 1 (Oct. 1930):2–9. Reprinted in *Best British Short Stories of 1931,* ed. Edward J. O'Brien, pp. 183–89. Boston: Small, Maynard and Co., 1931.
"Nook on Parnassus," *Life and Letters To-Day* 13 (Dec. 1935):84–88.
"Tryst," *English Story,* 2d ser., 1941, pp. 69–73.
"Haven," *Life and Letters To-Day* 42 (Aug. 1944):97–105.
"Excursion," *English Story,* 6th ser., 1945, pp. 107–12.
"Visitor," *Life and Letters* 46 (Sept. 1945):167–72.
"Visit," ibid., pp. 173–81.
"A Stranger About," *English Story,* 9th ser., 1949, pp. 90–94.

E. Poems

'It Is Finished," *Weekly Westminster Gazette* 2 (Aug. 7, 1923):17.
'Barbara," *Sphere* 95 (Oct. 13, 1923):46. Reprinted in "Three Poems: Sussex—Discovery—Barbara," *Poetry* 27 (Nov. 1925):67–69.

"Truth," *Weekly Westminster*, n.s., 1 (Jan. 5, 1924):316. Reprinted as "Freedom" in *Modern British Poetry*, rev. ed., ed. Louis Untermeyer, p. 312. New York: Harcourt, Brace, [1925].

"Helen," *Golden Hind* 2 (Apr. 1924):31.

"Waiting," *Poetry* 24 (June 1924):142–44.

"Buns for Tea," ibid., pp. 144–45. Reprinted in *Yesterday and Today: A Comparative Anthology of Poetry*, ed. Louis Untermeyer, pp. 152–53 (New York: Harcourt, Brace, [1926]); and in *Verse of Our Day*, rev. ed., ed. Margery Gordon and M. B. King, p. 284 (New York and London: Appleton-Century, 1938).

"Discovery," *Sphere* 98 (Aug. 2, 1924):142. Reprinted in "Three Poems: Sussex—Discovery—Barbara," *Poetry* 27 (Nov. 1925):67–69.

"Disaster," *Adelphi* 2 (Sept. 1924):277.

"Spring upon the Threshold," *Sphere* 100 (Mar. 28, 1925):350.

"Three Poems: Sussex—Discovery—Barbara," *Poetry* 27 (Nov. 1925):67–69.

"Message," *Outlook* 59 (Jan. 8, 1927):28. Reprinted in *Poetry* 30 (Aug. 1927):256.

"Gift," *Outlook* 61 (June 2, 1928):678.

"Nor Dust Nor Moth," *American Mercury* 50 (May 1940):111.

"Dark Harmony," *Spectator* 164 (Dec. 18, 1942):573.

F. Novel

Interim, serialized in the *Little Review* as follows: 6 (June 1919): 3–25, (July):11–24, (Aug.):5–28, (Sept.):56–61, (Oct.):38–54, (Nov.):34–38, (Dec.):20–28; 6 (Jan. 1920):37–48, (Mar.):17–26, (Apr.):26–34; 7 (May–June):53–61.

"Work in Progress" [selection from *The Trap*], *Contact Collection of Contemporary Writers (1925)*, pp. 217–36. Paris: [Contact], 1925.

"Sleigh Ride" [selection from *Oberland*], *Outlook* 58 (Dec. 11, 1926):588.

Two Selections from *Clear Horizon*, in *Signatures: Work in Progress* 1 (Spring 1936):n.p.

"Work in Progress," *Life and Letters* 49 (Apr. 1946):20–44.

"Work in Progress," ibid. 49 (May 1946):99–114.

"Work in Progress," ibid. 51 (Nov. 1946):79–88.

G. Letters and Miscellaneous Contributions

"The Human Touch," *Saturday Review* 109 (June 4, 1910):724.

"Future of the Novel" [interview], *Pall Mall Gazette,* Jan. 20, 1921, p. 7. Reprinted in *The Future of the Novel: Famous Authors on Their Methods: A Series of Interviews with Renowned Authors,* ed. Meredith Starr, pp. 90–91. Boston: Small, Maynard & Co., [1921].

"Equilibrium," *Little Review* 8 (Spring 1922):37.

Note to the editors, ibid. 12 (May 1929):31.

"Confessions" [reply to questionnaire from the editors], ibid., pp. 70–71.

"The Artist and the World To-Day (A Symposium in which various writers define their position in relation to the life and conditions of our time)," ed. Geoffrey West, *Bookman* 86 (May 1934):94.

IV. TRANSLATIONS

Consumption Doomed by Dr. Paul Carton, Healthy Life Booklets, vol. 7, trans. pref., pp. 5–12. London: C. W. Daniel, 1913.

Some Popular Foodstuffs Exposed by Dr. Paul Carton, Healthy Life Booklets, vol. 11, trans. pref., pp. 5–9. London: C. W. Daniel, 1913.

Man's Best Food by Prof. Dr. Gustav Krüger. London: C. W. Daniel, 1914.

The DuBarry by Karl von Schumacher [*Madame DuBarry*. Zurich, 1931]. London: G. G. Harrap, [Feb.] 1932.

Mammon by Robert Neumann [*Die Macht*. Leipzig, 1931; Berlin, 1932]. London: Peter Davies, [May] 1933.

André Gide: His Life and His Works by Leon Pierre-Quint [*André Gide: Sa Vie, Son Oeuvre*. Paris, 1932]. London: Jonathan Cape; New York: Knopf, [July] 1934.

Jews in Germany by Josef Kastein (pseud. of Julius Katzenstein), pref. James Stephens, trans. forward, pp. xix–xx. London: Cresset Press, [Sept.] 1934.

Silent Hours by Robert de Traz [*Les Heures de Silence*. Paris, 1934]. London: G. Bell, [Nov.] 1934.

"Prayer," *Life and Letters To-Day* 21 (June 1939):7.

PART TWO

*Selected List of Writings
about Dorothy M. Richardson*

"According to Miriam," *Saturday Review* 124 (Nov. 24, 1917):422. Review of *Honeycomb*.

Adam International Review 31 [1967]:310–12. Issue devoted to Proust and DMR.

Aiken, Conrad. "Dorothy Richardson Pieces Out the Stream of Consciousness of Her Pilgrim, Miriam Henderson," *New York Evening Post,* May 12, 1928, p. 9. Reprinted in *A Reviewer's ABC: Collected Criticism of Conrad Aiken from 1916 to the Present,* intro. Rufus A. Blanchard, pp. 329–31. New York: Meridian, [1958]. Review of *Oberland*.

Aldrich, Earl A. "The Vista of the Stream," *Saturday Review of Literature* 4 (May 5, 1928):841. Review of *Oberland*.

Beresford, J. D. "Introduction," *Pointed Roofs,* pp. v–viii. London: Duckworth, 1915.

"The Best Fiction," *Cape Times* (Capetown), Jan. 23, 1932. Review of *Dawn's Left Hand*.

Blake, Caesar R. *Dorothy M. Richardson.* Ann Arbor: University of Michigan Press, 1960.

Bourne, Randolph. "An Imagist Novel," *Dial* 64 (May 9, 1918):451–52. Review of *Honeycomb*.

Brome, Vincent. "A Last Meeting with Dorothy Richardson," *London Magazine* 6 (June 1959):26–32.

Bryher. *The Heart to Artemis. A Writer's Memoirs.* New York: Harcourt, Brace & World, 1962.

B[ryher], W[inifred]. *"Dawn's Left Hand"* [review], *Close Up* 8 (Dec. 1931):337–38.

Byron, May. "Four New Novels," *Bookman* 60 (Apr. 1921):28–29. Review of *Deadlock*.

"Cagey Subconsciousness," *Time* 32 (Dec. 5, 1938):70. Review of *Pilgrimage*.

Chevalley, Abel. *"Les Lettres Anglaises,"* in *Vient de Paraitre* (Paris), Jan. 1928, pp. 55–56.

C[hevalley], A[bel]. *"The Trap"* [review], *Vient de Paraitre* (Paris), Aug. 1925, p. 432.

Church, Richard. "An Essay in Estimation of Dorothy Richardson's Pilgrimage," *Pilgrimage: The Life Work of Dorothy Richardson,* pp. 3-11. London: Dent & Cresset Press, [1938]. Publisher's brochure.

———. "The Poet and the Novel," *Fortnightly Review* 144 (Nov. 1938):593–604.

"Deadlock" [review], *Bookman* 60 (Apr. 1921):21.

"Deadlock" [review], *Times Literary Supplement,* Feb. 24, 1921, p. 123.

Deutsch, Babette. "Adventure in Awareness," *Nation* 148 (Feb. 18, 1939):210. Review of *Pilgrimage.*

———. "Freedom and the Grace of God," *Dial* 47 (Nov. 15, 1919):441–42. Review of *The Tunnel* and of *Mary Olivier* by May Sinclair.

———. "Imagism in Fiction," *Nation* 106 (June 1, 1918):656. Review of *Honeycomb.*

———. "A Modern Pilgrim," *Reedy's Mirror* 27 (July 5, 1918):410–11. Review of *Pointed Roofs, Backwater, Honeycomb* (American eds.).

E., B. I. "Miriam Again," *Manchester Guardian,* Nov. 20, 1931, p. 5. Review of *Dawn's Left Hand.*

Edel, Leon. *The Modern Psychological Novel 1900–1950.* New York: Lippincott, 1955; rev. ed., New York: Universal Library, 1964.

"Fiction," *Spectator,* Mar. 15, 1919, pp. 330–31. Review of *The Tunnel.*

"Fiction in Brief," *Saturday Review* 127 (Mar. 22, 1919):285. Review of *The Tunnel.*

"Fiction. Miss Richardson's New Novel," *Spectator,* Mar. 26, 1921, p. 403. Review of *Deadlock.*

"Fiction of To-Day," *Saturday Review* 122 (Aug. 5, 1916):138. Review of *Backwater.*

"A Fine New Novel," *Observer* (London), Oct. 3, 1915, p. 5. Review of *Pointed Roofs.*

Ford, Ford Madox. *The March of Literature,* p. 848. London: Allen & Unwin, 1939.

Fraser, Ronald. Review of *Dawn's Left Hand* in *Time and Tide,* Nov. 21, 1931.

Fromm, Gloria G. *See* Glikin, Gloria.

Glikin, Gloria. "Dorothy M. Richardson: The Personal 'Pilgrimage,'" *PMLA* 78 (Dec. 1963):586–600.

———"Variations on a Method," *James Joyce Quarterly* 2 (Fall 1964):42–49.

———. "Checklist of Writings by Dorothy M. Richardson," *English Literature in Transition,* 8, no. 1 (1965):1–11.

———. "Dorothy M. Richardson: An Annotated Bibliography of Writings about Her," ibid., pp. 12–35.

———. "Dorothy M. Richardson," ibid. 14, no. 1 (1971):84–88. Supplemental bibliography.

———. "Through the Novelist's Looking-Glass," *Kenyon Review* 31 (Summer 1969):297–319. Reprinted in *H. G. Wells: A Collection of Critical Essays,* ed. Bernard Bergonzi, pp. 157–77. Englewood Cliffs, N.J.: Prentice-Hall, 1976.

Gregory, Horace, "Dorothy Richardson Reviewed," *Life and Letters To-Day* 21 (Mar. 1939):36–45.

———. *Dorothy Richardson: An Adventure in Self-Discovery.* New York: Holt, Rinehart and Winston, 1967.

Hart-Davis, Rupert. *Hugh Walpole: A Biography,* pp. 90–92. London: Macmillan, 1952.

Hawkins, Ethel Wallace. "The Stream of Consciousness Novel," *Atlantic Monthly* 138 (Sept. 1926):356–60.

Herbert, Alice. "Novels of the Week," *Yorkshire Post* (Leeds), Nov. 11, 1931. Review of *Dawn's Left Hand.*

Heseltine, Olive. "Life. *The Tunnel,*" *Everyman,* Mar. 22, 1919, p. 562. Review of *The Tunnel.*

Hopkinson, Diana. *The Incense Tree,* pp. 59–60. London: Routledge & Kegan Paul, 1968.

Hyde, Lawrence. "The Work of Dorothy Richardson," *Adelphi* 2 (Nov. 1924):508–17.

Kaplan, Sydney Janet. *Feminine Consciousness in the Modern British Novel.* Urbana: University of Illinois Press, 1975.

Kumar, Shiv K. "Dorothy Richardson and Bergson 'Mémoire par excellence,'" *Notes and Queries,* n.s., 6 (Jan. 1959):14–19.

———. "Dorothy Richardson and the Dilemma of 'Being versus Becoming,'" *Modern Language Notes* 74 (June 1959):494–501.

Kunitz, Stanley J., ed., *Authors Today and Yesterday,* pp. 562–64. New York: Wilson, 1933.

———, and Howard Haycraft, eds., *Twentieth Century Authors,* pp. 1169–70. New York: Wilson, 1942.

"Latest Works of Fiction," *New York Times Book Review,* June 20, 1920, p. 320. Review of *Interim.*

"Latest Works of Fiction. *Revolving Lights,*" *New York Times Book Review,* Aug. 5, 1923, p. 24.

Lawrence, D. H. "Surgery for the Novel—or a Bomb," *Literary Digest International Book Review* 1 (Apr. 1923):5. Reprinted in *Phoenix,* ed. and intro. Edward D. McDonald, pp. 517–20. New York: Viking, 1936.

McAlmon, Robert. *Being Geniuses Together. An Autobiography,* pp. 120–22, 220–22. London: Secker & Warburg [1938]. Rev. ed. with supplementary chapters by Kay Boyle, pp. 221–23, 280–82. New York: Doubleday, 1968.

———. Letter to the editor, *Little Review* 10 (Autumn 1924–Winter 1925):48.

Mais, S. P. B. "Dorothy Richardson," *Books and Their Writers,* pp. 75–86. London: Richards, 1920.

Maisel, E. M. "Dorothy Richardson's Pilgrimage," *Canadian Forum* 19 (June 1939):89–92. Review of *Pilgrimage.*

M[ansfield], K[atherine]. "Dragonflies," *Athenaeum,* Jan. 9, 1920, p. 48. Reprinted in *Novels and Novelists,* ed. J. Middleton Murry. London: Constable, 1930. Review of *The Tunnel.*

"Miss Richardson's First Novel of a Governess's Adventures— Some Recent Works of Fiction," *New York Times Book Review,* Dec. 31, 1916, p. 577. Review of *Pointed Roofs.*

Miles, Hamish. "A Long Lane. *Revolving Lights,*" *Evening Post Literary Review,* July 28, 1923, p. 859.

"Miss Dorothy Richardson, Pioneer among Novelists," *Times* (London), June 18, 1957, p. 13.

Morgan, Louise. "How Writers Work: Dorothy Richardson," *Everyman,* Oct. 22, 1931, p. 395.

"Much Ado about Little," *New York Times Book Review,* Aug. 30, 1925, p. 9. Review of *The Trap.*

Murry, John Middleton. "The Break-up of the Novel," *Yale Review* 12 (Oct. 1922):288–304.

"New Novels. *Honeycomb,*" *Times Literary Supplement* 16 (Oct. 18, 1917):506.

"New Novels. *Interim,*" ibid. 18 (Dec. 18, 1919):766.

"New Novels. Miss Richardson's Miriam Again," *Times* (London), Oct. 22, 1935, p. 22. Review of *Clear Horizon.*

"New Novels. *Revolving Lights,*" *Times Literary Supplement,* Apr. 19, 1923, p. 266.

"Novels," *London Mercury* 1 (Feb. 1920):473–74. Review of *Interim.*

"Novels of the Week. Dorothy Richardson," *Times Literary Supplement,* Dec. 17, 1938, p. 799. Review of *Pilgrimage.*

"An Original Book," *Saturday Review Literary Supplement* 120 (Oct. 16, 1915):vi. Review of *Pointed Roofs.*

"*Oberland* Is a Novel of Quiet but Dazzling Beauty," *New York Times Book Review,* Mar. 11, 1928, p. 7.

P[hilip] L[ittell]. "Books and Things," *New Republic* 26 (Apr. 27, 1921):267. Review of *Deadlock.*

"Pilgrimage," *Nation* 109 (Dec. 6, 1919):720–21. Review of *Pointed Roofs, Backwater, Honeycomb, The Tunnel* (American eds.).

Powys, John Cowper. *Dorothy M. Richardson.* London: Joiner & Steele, 1931.

Prescott, Joseph. "Dorothy Miller Richardson," *Encyclopaedia Britannica,* vol. 19, 1958.

———. "A Preliminary Checklist of Periodical Publications of Dorothy M. Richardson," *Studies in Honor of John Wilcox,* ed. A. D. Wallace and W. O. Ross, pp. 219–25. Detroit: Wayne State University Press, 1958.

Priestley, J. B. "Fiction," *London Mercury* 8 (June 1923):208–10. Review of *Revolving Lights.*

"Proust, Joyce, and Miss Richardson," *Spectator* 130 (June 30, 1923):1084–85. Review of *Revolving Lights.*

"The Psychology of Miriam," *Punch* 181 (Dec. 2, 1931):615–16. Review of *Dawn's Left Hand.*

"Reviews. *The Tunnel,*" *Dental Record* 39 (May 1, 1919):180–81.

Rodker, John. *"The Tunnel"* [review], *Little Review* 6 (Sept. 1919):40–41.

Romilly, Giles. "Seasonal Ghosts," *Observer* (London), Dec. 30, 1951, p. 6. Notice of BBC reading of DMR's short story "Christmas Eve."

Rose, Shirley. "Dorothy Richardson's Theory of Literature: The Writer as Pilgrim," *Criticism* 12 (Winter 1970):20–37.

———. "The Unmoving Center: Consciousness in Dorothy Richardson's *Pilgrimage,*" *Contemporary Literature* 10 (Summer 1969):366–82.

————. "Dorothy Richardson's Focus on Time," *English Literature in Transition* 17 (1974):163–72.

Rosenberg, John. *Dorothy Richardson: The Genius They Forgot.* London: Duckworth, 1973.

Rosenfeld, Paul. "The Inner Life," *Saturday Review of Literature* 19 (Dec. 10, 1938):6. Review of *Pilgrimage.*

Rourke, Constance Mayfield. "Dorothy M. Richardson," *New Republic,* Nov. 26, 1919, pt. 2, pp. 14–16. Review of *Pointed Roofs, Backwater, Honeycomb, The Tunnel* (American eds.).

Savage, Henry. *The Receding Shore,* pp. 189, 221. London: Grayson & Grayson, 1933.

Scott-James, R. A. "Books to Read. The Man's Point of View and the Woman's," *Daily Chronicle* (London), Apr. 16, 1919, p. 4. Review of *The Tunnel.*

————. "New Literature. Journey without End," *London Mercury* 39 (Dec. 1938):214–15. Review of *Pilgrimage.*

————. "New Literature. Quintessential Feminism," ibid. 33 (Dec. 1935):201–3. Review of *Clear Horizon.*

Sinclair, May. "The Novels of Dorothy Richardson," *Egoist* (Apr. 1918): 57–59.

————. "The Novels of Dorothy Richardson," *Little Review* 4 (Apr. 1918):3–11.

Staley, Thomas F. *Dorothy Richardson.* Boston: Twayne, 1976.

Stern, G. B. "Saga Novels and Miss Richardson," *New York Herald Tribune Books,* Mar. 11, 1928, p. 1. Review of *Oberland.*

Trickett, Rachel. "The Living Dead—V: Dorothy Richardson," *London Magazine* 6 (June 1959):20–25.

"The Tunnel" [review], *Times Literary Supplement* 18 (Feb. 13, 1919):81.

"Varnish," *Nation and Athenaeum* 29 (July 23, 1921):621–22. Review of *Deadlock.*

Walpole, Hugh. "Realism and the New English Novel," *Vanity Fair* 20 (Mar. 1923):34.

Wells, H. G. Introduction to *Nocturne,* by Frank Swinnerton. New York: Doran, 1917.

West, Rebecca. *Dawn's Left Hand* [review], *Daily Telegraph,* Dec. 4, 1931.

Williams, William Carlos. "Four Foreigners," *Little Review* 6 (Sept. 1919):36–39.

PART THREE

Selected List of Other Related Writings

Aldington, Richard. "The Approach to M. Marcel Proust," *Dial* 69 (Oct. 1920):341–46.

Ames, Van Meter. *André Gide*. New York: New Directions, 1947.

Austen, John. *The ABC of Pen and Ink Rendering*. London: Pitman, 1937.

Beach, Sylvia. *Shakespeare and Company*. New York: Harcourt, Brace, & Co., 1956, 1959.

Bell, Quentin. *Bloomsbury*. London: Futura Publications, 1974. [Orig. publ. London: Weidenfeld & Nicolson, 1968.]

Beresford, J. D. "Experiment in the Novel," *Tradition and Experiment in Present-Day Literature*, pp. 23–25. London: Oxford University Press, 1929. [Address delivered at the City Literary Institute.]

Brome, Vincent. *H. G. Wells: A Biography*. London: Longmans, Green, 1951.

Brown, W. Sorley, *The Life and Genius of T. W. H. Crosland*. London: Cecil Palmer, 1928.

Carrington Letters & Extracts from Her Diaries, chosen and with an intro. by David Garnett. London: Jonathan Cape, 1970.

Church, Richard. *The Voyage Home*. London: William Heinemann, 1964.

Deghy, Guy, and Keith Waterhouse. *Café Royal: Ninety Years of Bohemia*. London: Hutchinson, 1955.

Devon, Cradle of Our Seamen, ed. Arthur Mee. London: Hodder & Stoughton, 1938.

Dickinson, G. Lowes. *J. McT. E. McTaggart*, with chapters by Basil Williams and S. V. Keeling. Cambridge: University Press, 1931.

Dickson, Lovat. *H. G. Wells· His Turbulent Life and Times*. New York: Athenaeum, 1969.

Edel, Leon, and Gordon N. Ray, eds. *Henry James & H. G. Wells: A Record of Their Friendship, Their Debate on the Art of Fiction, and Their Quarrel*. Urbana: University of Illinois Press, 1958.

Ellmann, Richard. *James Joyce*. New York: Oxford University Press, 1959.

Fulford, Roger. *Votes for Women: The Story of a Struggle*. London: Faber & Faber, [1957].

Garnett, David. *The Golden Echo*. London: Chatto & Windus, 1953.

Gauld, Alan. *The Founders of Psychical Research*. New York: Schocken Books, 1968.

Goldring, Douglas. *South Lodge*. London: Constable, 1943.

Gregg, Pauline. *A Social and Economic History of Britain 1760–1950*. London: Harrap, 1950.

Gregory, Horace. *The Dying Gladiator and Other Essays*. New York: Grove Press, 1961.

Guide to Abingdon. Abingdon: The Abbey Press, n.d.

Guide to Hanover. Publ. by the Society for Promoting the Interests of Foreigners in Hanover, 1905.

"The Gypsy," *Observer*, May 23, 1915, p. 3. Review of first issue.

Handbook for Travellers in Berks, Bucks, & Oxfordshire. London: John Murray, 1882.

H. G. Wells: A Comprehensive Bibliography. London: H. G. Wells Society, 1966.

Hillier, Bevis. "Café Life of the 1920s Recalled," *Times* (London), Nov. 9, 1968.

Holroyd, Michael. *Lytton Strachey: A Critical Biography*. 2 vols. London: Heinemann, 1967.

Hone, Joseph. *W. B. Yeats 1865–1939*. New York: Macmillan, 1943.

Hunt, Violet. *I Have This to Say: The Story of My Flurried Years*. New York: Boni and Liveright, 1926.

Hynes, Samuel, *The Edwardian Turn of Mind*. Princeton: Princeton University Press, 1968.

Jameson, Storm. "Bored Wives." *Evening News* (London), Oct. 1, 1928, p. 8.

Kamm, Josephine. *Rapiers and Battleaxes. The Women's Movement and Its Aftermath*. London: Allen & Unwin, 1966.

Lewis, Anthony. "Harley Street Eludes Realty Surgeons," *New York Times*, May 20, 1969, p. 12.

Liversidge, M. J. H. *The Fourteenth Century Decorated Ceiling in St. Helen's*. Abingdon: The Abbey Press, 1965.

Mackenzie, Norman and Jeanne. *The Time Traveller: The Life of H. G. Wells*. London: Weidenfeld and Nicolson, 1973.

Macmillan, William J. *Heaven and You*. London: Hodder & Stoughton, 1953.

———. *Prelude to Healing*. London: Faber & Faber, 1957.

————. *The Reluctant Healer: A Remarkable Autobiography.* New York: Crowell, 1952.

————. *This Is My Heaven: Two Treatises on Healing & Other Essential Matters,* intro. Paul Brunton. London: John M. Watkins, 1948.

Mallock, W. H. *A Human Document.* New York: Cassell, 1892.

Meyer, M. M. *H. G. Wells and His Family (As I Have Known Them),* pref. F. R. Wells. Edinburgh: International Publishing Co. [1955?].

Moore, Harry T. *The Intelligent Heart: The Story of D. H. Lawrence.* New York: Farrar, Straus & Young, 1954.

————. *The Priest of Love: A Life of D. H. Lawrence.* New York: Farrar, Straus and Giroux, 1974. [Rev. ed. of *The Intelligent Heart.*]

Nicolson, Harold. *Diaries and Letters,* ed. Nigel Nicolson. 3 vols. London: Collins, 1966, 1967, 1968.

Norman, Sylva. "Julian Grant Loses His Way," *Times Literary Supplement,* Jan. 30, 1969, p. 113.

Odle, Rose. *Salt of Our Youth.* Penzance: Wordens of Cornwall, 1972.

Patmore, Brigit. *My Friends When Young,* ed. and intro. Derek Patmore. London: Heinemann, 1968.

Pease, Edward R. *The History of the Fabian Society.* London: A. C. Fifield, 1916; rev. ed., New York: International Publishers, 1926.

Powys, John Cowper. *Autobiography.* London: Macdonald, 1967.

Ray, Gordon N. *H. G. Wells & Rebecca West.* New Haven: Yale University Press, 1974.

Robb, Janet Henderson. *The Primrose League 1883–1906.* New York: Columbia University Press, 1942.

Russell, George W. E. *Basil Wilberforce: A Memoir.* London: John Murray, 1918.

Savage, Henry. "A Cockney in Cornwall," *Book News,* 1923.

Sinclair, Frederick. "A Poet's World in Woburn Walk," *St. Pancras Journal* 2 (Dec. 1948):124–27.

Townsend, James. *A History of Abingdon.* London: Henry Froude, 1910.

Trevelyan, G. M. *English Social History: A Survey of Six Centuries, Chaucer to Queen Victoria.* London: Longmans, Green & Co., 1942.

Unwin, Sir Stanley. *The Truth about a Publisher. An Autobiographical Record.* New York: Macmillan, 1960.

Watts, Marjorie. *P.E.N.: The Early Years, 1921–1926.* London: Archive Press, 1971.

Wedgwood, C. V. *The Last of the Radicals: Josiah Wedgwood, M.P.* London: Jonathan Cape, 1951.

Wells, Amy Catherine (Robbins). *The Book of Catherine Wells, with an Introduction by Her Husband H. G. Wells.* London: Chatto & Windus, 1928.

Wells, H. G. *Experiment in Autobiography.* 2 vols. London: Gollancz & Cresset, 1934.

West, Anthony. *Heritage.* New York: Random House, 1955.

———. "H. G. Wells," *Encounter* 8 (Feb. 1957):52–59.

Woddis, M. J. "The Café Royal in War Time," *Colour* 2 (July 1915):218–20.

Woodcock, George, and Ivan Avakumovic. *The Anarchist Prince: A Biographical Study of Peter Kropotkin.* London, New York: T. V. Boardman & Co., 1950.

Woodeson, John. *Mark Gertler: Biography of a Painter, 1891–1939.* London: Sidgwick & Jackson, 1972.

Woolf, Virginia. *A Writer's Diary,* ed. Leonard Woolf. London: Hogarth, 1953.

Zytaruk, George J. *The Quest for Rananim.* Montreal and London: McGill-Queen's University Press, 1970.

Index